> NOTE: Turn to *How to Use This Book* (page xv) for further guidance in using this text. All grammar and usage lessons are based on a similar organization, and the model presented in this section walks you through a sample lesson. In addition, this section introduces you to several helpful features in the writing guide.

THIRD EDITION

A Commonsense Guide to Grammar and Usage

Larry Beason

University of South Alabama

Mark Lester

Eastern Washington University

Bedford/St. Martin's   *Boston • New York*

FOR BEDFORD/ST. MARTIN'S

Developmental Editor: Amanda Bristow
Production Editor: Bridget Leahy
Production Supervisor: Jennifer Wetzel
Marketing Manager: Brian Wheel
Editorial Assistants: Erin Durkin and Karin Halbert
Copyeditor: Alison Greene
Text Design: Claire Seng-Niemoeller
Cover Design and Art: Mark McKie
Composition: Stratford Publishing Services, Inc.
Printing and Binding: R. R. Donnelley & Sons Company

President: Joan E. Feinberg
Editorial Director: Denise B. Wydra
Editor in Chief: Karen S. Henry
Director of Marketing: Karen Melton
Director of Editing, Design, and Production: Marcia Cohen
Managing Editor: Elizabeth M. Schaaf

Library of Congress Control Number: 2002112256

Manufactured in the United States of America.

7   6   5   4

f   e   d   c

For information, write:
Bedford/St. Martin's, 75 Arlington Street, Boston, MA 02116
(617-399-4000)

ISBN: 0-312-39934-0

Preface for Instructors

A Commonsense Guide to Grammar and Usage, Third Edition, helps students write clear, error-free sentences by combining the easy access of a reference handbook with the practicality of a skills workbook. This book is intended for a range of students who need a firmer foundation in the grammar and usage of formal writing. These students might be enrolled in a beginning writing course, an ESL course, a first-year composition course, or a course in a field such as business, history, or science.

At the core of our approach is the firm belief that errors can be signs of risk taking, experimentation, and growth. Once students understand that errors are part of the learning *process* and do not necessarily reflect a lack of effort or ability, they can develop the confidence they need to recognize and correct sentence-level problems in their own writing—something they can do without an overwhelming amount of grammar terminology. We wrote this book, and agreed to revise it, because we believe students and teachers need a textbook largely devoted to commonsense ways to avoid common errors. Avoiding errors is not the most important aspect of writing effectively, but it is important enough to deserve writers' attention.

As we planned our third edition of this book, students and teachers told us to expand our audience, our models of writing, and our basic coverage. So, in improving the book, we set ourselves some challenges: meet the demands of a broader, more diverse student population and provide more models of writing and more basic coverage for students who need it. In this edition, we have added two new ESL lessons in two new ESL-focused units, provided more models of student writing and a lesson on reading in the Commonsense Writing Guide, as well as added a "Grammar Without Tears" section focused on the most basic elements of grammar and usage. Offering revised Sentence Practice exercises, basic documentation information, and a new student introduction, this guide remains primarily a grammar and usage handbook that both native and non-native speakers of English will find useful as they read, plan, draft, revise, and edit their writing.

What Does This Book Offer — and Why?

The following combination of features makes this textbook a uniquely practical resource for instructors and students.

Commonsense help for the most common errors keeps students focused on essential skills.   Using a straightforward, practice-oriented approach, *A Commonsense Guide* helps students learn to identify and correct thirty-nine common problems in written English. On the basis of research, experience, and feedback from students and teachers, we concentrate on the grammar and usage problems that occur most frequently or are most distracting in the writing of first-year college students.

Unique "commonsense tips" provide intuitive reminders. Each grammar lesson includes at least one handy tip—a commonsense way of identifying and correcting an error. Our text uses some grammatical terms, but we keep these to a minimum and provide definitions. The tips rely not on complex rules but on intuitive, practical strategies that writers actually use.

A minimum of grammatical terms means easy access to learning.   The text's explanations and tips are written in clear, everyday language, so students will be confident about (rather than intimidated by) what they are learning. We have placed special emphasis on learning how to identify and correct problems—not on learning terminology. We have even included hand-edited example errors in the table of contents so students do not have to rely on grammatical terminology to find help for a specific problem. In addition, the text includes more ways for non-native speakers of English to find helpful information: two newly organized ESL units (Units 10 and 11), two new ESL lessons (Lessons 38 and 39), an ESL index at the back of the book, and ESL icons (🌐) throughout the book.
                                                    ESL

An emphasis on the positive helps students identify, understand, and correct errors.

- First, we provide *corrected* versions of example errors. Errors are marked with an ✗, and corrections are clearly marked to help students remember what they should *do*—not just what they should avoid.

- Second, we explain *why* each error might occur—why even the most intelligent writer might be confused about formal English.

- Third, we offer *correction strategies*. This book not only helps students identify an error, it also equips them with practical strategies for revising their writing to make it error free.

A developmental sequence of activities helps students learn to fix problems.   Hands-on grammar and usage activities allow students to focus on skills that are different yet developmentally related. Brief diagnostic exercises in each unit overview and lesson allow students and teachers to decide whether or not students need to complete a given unit or lesson.

- After reading each lesson, students apply the commonsense tips by completing three *Sentence Practice* exercises. Students have the opportunity to master a basic idea or strategy before moving on to more extended writing.

- Next, students complete three *Editing Practice* exercises by applying the skills they have developed in the *Sentence Practice* exercises. In this way, they progress from examining independent sentences to combining sentences to correcting a mini-essay.

- Finally, the *Writing Practice* section of each lesson asks students to compose their own writing and correctly use the punctuation or grammatical concept covered in the lesson. In this way, students learn about errors in the context of their own writing.

A consistent framework means that students know what to expect in each lesson. All grammar lessons follow a similar format, so information is easy to locate and understand. *How to Use This Book*, an introduction with examples found on pages xv–xviii, guides students through a sample lesson.

A flexible format allows instructors to customize their courses. This text is intended to accommodate various needs and situations.

- Each grammar lesson can stand on its own. Although we have grouped lessons into units according to related errors, teachers may find that another arrangement better suits their needs and the needs of their students. The text can be used systematically or more selectively.

  When beginning a lesson, the student should complete the diagnostic exercise. If the results show a need for further study, the student should then read the information provided and do the remaining exercises. It is also useful to complete the overview for each unit for additional diagnostic work. The review at the end of each unit synthesizes and summarizes the lessons.

- The instructor can assign exercises as homework or classwork. The text can also be a *self-paced reference* students use on their own, since answers are provided for all diagnostic exercises and for four out of seven exercises in each lesson.

- The writing guide section (pages 407–52) can be integrated at any point in the grammar section. It is best that students read this entire section in the order presented in the book, but their reading can stretch out over whatever time frame works best.

User-friendly design provides easy access.   The text design is based on the ways people have actually used it. The table of contents offers an example error for each lesson so that students do not have to rely on technical terms to locate a particular topic. The Guide to Grammar Terminology presents a glossary of terms where readers need it—*before*, rather than after, the lessons. The two-color format, unit and lesson tabs, and comprehensive indexes help students locate information quickly. In the writing guide, we use tip boxes and clear, consistent headings to draw attention to places where we turn abstract concepts into practical, specific advice. The spiral binding allows the book to lie flat while users write in it or consult it in the computer lab.

Specific yet nonformulaic help on writing.   Responding to teachers' requests, we have included a nuts-and-bolts writing guide that balances two important issues. First, people often want "bottom line" advice about what to do—and what not to do—as they write. Second, many aspects of writing are too complex to be reduced to formulas and fixed rules. Beginners as well as advanced writers need to understand that writers must react to their own writing situation—not to a formula or a set of rules. Thus, we encourage students to ask critical questions to which *they* must provide answers. We also provide, however, specific concrete strategies and guidelines that can assist students in making these decisions. The following features will help make the writing process manageable.

- The planning stage of the writing process, the stage at which most beginning writers need the most help, receives special emphasis.

- Commonsense tips throughout offer accessible, practical hints for completing each stage of the writing process.

- Goal-oriented checklists and critical thinking questions guide students as they write expressive, informative, and persuasive paragraphs and essays.

- Sample student-written thesis statements, outlines, and drafts of student writing offer accessible models.

New to This Edition

More commonsense support for non-native speakers of English.   Responding to the needs of a growing number of students, we have organized specific ESL coverage into two new, easy-to-locate units (Unit Ten ESL: Choosing the Right Article and Unit Eleven ESL: Using Verbs Correctly). We have also added two new ESL lessons (Lesson 38: Information Questions and Lesson 39: Word Order in Noun Clauses) and have included improved ESL tips throughout.

More basic help for students who need it.   Following the *Commonsense* tradition of simplicity and convenience, the brief and new "Grammar without Tears" appendix features solid instruction in grammar basics and exercises for further student practice. Additionally, updated Exercise Central exercises on the Web are cross-referenced in the book for extra practice.

New documentation guide informs students how to appropriately cite sources.   This brief and to-the-point documentation coverage features the most up-to-date information on MLA citation with plenty of examples.

New lesson on reading focuses on the connections between reading and writing.   A Commonsense Writing Guide (Unit Twelve) has been updated to include a new lesson on reading that provides an overview of the connections between reading and writing and helps students understand how to respond to what they read. Student examples illustrate the critical reading and annotating process, and reading tips and checklists highlight practical strategies.

New introduction shows students why correct grammar is important.   Addressed specifically to the student, the "Why Use This Book" introduction explains the real-world implications of using correct grammar in speech and writing at school, at work, and in everyday life.

More models provide more opportunities to practice what is learned.   Extended models in the lessons on the planning and drafting stages of the writing process as well as more examples of paragraph writing on current topics provide students with further reinforcements in planning and executing what they've learned.

Practical Resources for Instructors and Students

Instructor's Resource Manual for A Commonsense Guide to Grammar and Usage contains unit- and lesson-level teaching tips, answers to all exercises and activities in the text, supplemental exercises for additional practice, an expanded section on teaching grammar and usage to non-native speakers, and suggestions for pairing the text with other Bedford/St. Martin's composition books.

A companion Web site at bedfordstmartins.com/commonsense complements the book and its features, by including hotlinks to student and instructor resources, as well as downloadable Bottom Line boxes for quick grammar reference.

Exercise Central at bedfordstmartins.com/exercisecentral, the largest such collection of interactive grammar exercises available, is thorough, simple to use, and convenient for both students and instructors. Multiple exercise sets on every topic at a variety of levels ensure that students have as much practice as they need, and at the appropriate level. Diagnostic tools can help students assess areas needing improvement, or instructors can assign specific exercises or groups of exercises. Immediate, customized feedback for all answers turns skill practice into a learning experience, and the reporting feature allows both students and instructors to monitor and assess progress.

Acknowledgments

We would like to thank the following teachers who responded to a questionnaire that allowed us to develop the third edition of this book: Mike Bellah, Amarillo College; Lisa Bernhagen, Highline Community College; Laurie B. Cox, Midlands Technical College; Sam Dragga, Texas Technical University; Barbara A. Felix, Palomar College; Lynne Henson, Palomar College; Craig Kleinman, City College of San Francisco; Melissa Knous, Angelina College; Jane Leach-Rudawski, Minneapolis Community and Technical College; Stephen Luscher, Miami-Dade Community College; Rebecca S. Mann, Guildford Technical Community College; Karen S. McKinney, Georgia Perimeter College; Julie Rodakowski, Rochester Community and Technical College; Victoria Sarkisian, Marist College; Karen L. Tomkins-Tinch, Marist College; Heidi Van Dixhorn-Nesser, Minneapolis Community and Technical College.

Furthermore, we thank the following reviewers for consulting with us on developing new sections of the third edition of *A Commonsense Guide to Grammar and Usage:* Salvatore Attardo, Youngstown State University; Wayne Berninger, Long Island University; Laurie Cox, Midlands Technical College; Barbara A. Felix, Palomar College; Randall Gwin, Minneapolis Community and Technical College; Xiaoming Li, Long Island University; Cynthia L. Vigliotti, Youngstown State University; Sharman Yoffie, Long Island University.

We extend special thanks to the people at Bedford/St. Martin's for their significant contributions to this revision: Amanda Bristow, Developmental Editor; Michelle Clark, for her work on the previous edition of *A Commonsense Guide;* Erin Durkin, Editorial Assistant; Karin Halbert, Editorial Assistant; Bridget Leahy, Production Editor; Alison Greene, Copyeditor; Chuck Christensen, former President; Joan Feinberg, President; Brian Wheel, Marketing Manager; and Claire Seng-Niemoeller, the text designer.

Finally, we wish to thank our wives, Colleen Beason and Mary Ann Lester, for their unwavering support and patience.

Larry Beason

Mark Lester

Why Use This Book—For Students

Why use this book? We believe you have a right to an answer. Not only are you paying for this book, but you will also be asked to commit time and energy to its material.

Some people enjoy the study of grammar and the formal rules that tell writers how to put words and sentences together. Most people, however, do not put such study at the top of their list of favorite things to do. So, we are not going to try to "sell" this book by claiming grammar is fun (though it can be for some people). Rather, we want readers to understand why the study of grammar and usage is worthwhile, despite the difficulties of studying language. In addition, we want you to know why this book takes a different approach than most grammar textbooks.

The most pressing reason why you should use this book is that it will help you not only in your writing courses but in many college courses and in your life beyond college. Many first-year students in college are surprised to learn how much writing is required outside the English department. Research has proven that history, business, computer science, education, and even math teachers—just to name a few—frequently ask students to write papers or documents. Furthermore, these teachers consider "how" student writers say something, not just "what" they say. A physics teacher, for example, might ask you to write a detailed lab report so that you will learn more about electricity through writing about a specific experiment. However, this teacher will not be able to tell if you have learned anything about physics unless your writing is clear. Errors such as misplaced commas or fused sentences can make a report hard to follow.

Most teachers look to general rules and conventions that indicate how words, sentences, and punctuation are supposed to be used in formal writing situations. Unless you understand these rules and conventions, numerous teachers—not just English teachers—will be confused, distracted, and even annoyed. If you have ever thought that only English teachers care about "good grammar," now is the time to realize that this assumption is dangerous—dangerous because it can harm your chances for succeeding in college.

You should be aware, however, that people in the workplace can be more strict about grammar and usage than college teachers. A study conducted by one of the authors of this textbook indicates that people in business are significantly affected by writers' errors in formal English. Professionals in the study frequently noted the importance of clear writing in jobs as diverse as banking, health care, software development, and even laboratory work for gold mining companies. These people pointed out many instances when grammatical errors, such as comma splices or misspellings, confused readers. Not only did errors confuse businesspeople about what a writer was trying to say but businesspeople also made judgments, based on those errors, about the writers' workplace skills and attitudes. That is, businesspeople sometimes assume that errors indicate negatively about the writer's ability to think logically, the writer's dedication, or even the writer's ability to work effectively with other people. Of course, some people in the study assumed that fragments and other errors were signs of a careless writer. Interestingly, though, other readers looked at the same errors and concluded that the writer was not sufficiently educated or lacked motivation in performing a great many job duties, not just writing. Such generalizations are not always valid, but it seems to be part of human nature to make large-scale judgments about people based on how well they use language in formal situations. We are not by any means saying such judgmental behavior is right, but it's what people do.

In short, we believe this book can help you enable your teachers—and other readers—to concentrate on the more important parts of your writing (namely, the content itself and not the details of your language choices).

Briefly, we also want to point out why this book can help you in ways that other grammar books might not.

First, this textbook avoids, as much as possible, technical terms and jargon. By giving commonsense explanations and understandable advice, we indicate how to avoid errors. For instance, each grammar and usage lesson focuses on a "tip" that is not really a rule but a piece of advice; this tip is easier to remember and understand than a drawn-out technical explanation. In addition, exercises in each lesson focus on applying these tips so you will remember them. Too many textbooks rely simply on asking you to find and fix errors, as if you were just a proofreader. In this book, the "Sentence Practice" exercises actually help you learn commonsense tips that draw on your intuition and what you already know about language.

Second, we think you need more than just a quick explanation and one or two examples. Thus, each lesson gives other types of guidance. We think it helps clear up confusion if you understand *why* many people make a certain type of error, so each lesson covers major misconceptions about whatever the lesson focuses on. But most information in each lesson is devoted to how to correct an error—not to rules. We avoid elaborating needlessly about these correction strategies; in fact, we believe it's best to avoid a lengthy lecture. Still, we offer more than the typical one- to two-sentence explanation found in many grammar handbooks.

Why use this book? We wrote it because we found that these strategies have helped students improve one important aspect of academic and workplace writing—grammar and usage. We believe the tools you take from this book will help you succeed in more than one classroom and in more than one stage of life.

Larry Beason

Mark Lester

How to Use This Book

A Commonsense Guide to Grammar and Usage is designed to offer you nuts-and-bolts strategies for improving your writing — especially for improving your sentences. Units One through Eleven, which focus on grammar and usage, help you to identify, understand, and correct errors in your sentences with commonsense advice and plenty of opportunities for practice. Unit Twelve, the writing guide, helps you to read, plan, draft, and revise a paragraph or an essay.

The grammar and usage lessons follow a consistent organization:

ERROR SENTENCES
Look at these examples to see whether you are making a similar error in your writing. (Note that throughout the text, un-grammatical phrases and sentences are indicated by an ✗.) Corrected versions of the example errors follow in the *Fixing This Problem* section of each lesson.

Error Sentences
CORRECTED SENTENCES APPEAR ON PAGE 20.

EXAMPLE 1: I entered my apartment and saw an unexpected guest. ✗ A cat in the middle of my living room.

EXAMPLE 2: Philip is really upset. ✗ Because someone broke a window in his car.

EXAMPLE 3: College gives you a whole new perspective. ✗ Opening your eyes to a new world.

WHAT'S THE PROBLEM?
This section explains a rule or convention of English that causes difficulty for many writers. If English is not your first language, you may want to pay special attention to material marked by this symbol:
ESL

What's the Problem?

A **fragment** is a group of words that cannot stand alone as a **complete sentence** but is punctuated as a complete sentence. If you are a non-native speaker, you should know that in English, a subject, a verb, and a complete thought are needed for a complete sentence. Many fragments lack a verb, as in Example 1, or lack a subject, as in Example 3. A fragment can also be a **dependent clause**, a clause that does not express a complete thought, as in Example 2.

WHAT CAUSES THE PROBLEM?
Understanding *why* an error occurs can help you avoid it.

What Causes the Problem?

Almost all fragments explain or expand upon an idea in the immediately preceding sentence. Fragments are not easy for writers to spot because they sound normal. In the quick give-and-take of conversation, fragments are a way of clarifying or elaborating on what we have just said without having to stop and reformulate the previous sentence. In formal written language, however, fragments are inappropriate. Readers expect formal writing to be carefully planned.

DIAGNOSTIC EXERCISE
To find out if you need help with the topic of the lesson, do this exercise. Then check your answers in the back of the book.

Diagnostic Exercise

CORRECTED SENTENCES APPEAR ON PAGE 470.

Correct all errors in the following paragraph using the first correction as a model. The number in parentheses at the end of the paragraph indicates how many errors you should find.

My roommate has an annoying habit. ~~Not putting~~ `, not putting` anything away.

He never picks up his dirty clothes. Until he has to do his laundry.

In the kitchen, there are always dirty dishes on the table. I've asked

him to at least put them in the sink. Where they are out of the way.

It is always such a mess. Cups half-full of coffee, cereal bowls with

milk in them, and cruddy silverware. The refrigerator is just as bad.

Opening the door is like taking a trip to the jungle. We really need to

do something about it. Because it is really embarrassing when

---

FIXING THIS PROBLEM IN YOUR WRITING
This section offers practical strategies for identifying and correcting the error.

Fixing This Problem in Your Writing

A fragment is almost always a continuation of the preceding sentence. To fix a fragment, we need to separate it from the previous sentence. When a fragment is by itself, isolated from preceding sentences, we are much more likely to notice that it doesn't make sense on its own. Here are three tips that will help you to isolate fragments.

COMMONSENSE TIP
Use this concrete strategy to identify or correct the error.

I REALIZE TIP: You can put *I realize* in front of most complete sentences and make a new grammatical sentence. However, when you put *I realize* in front of a fragment, the result will not make sense.

CORRECTION SEQUENCE
This sequence shows you how to apply the commonsense tip to correct the example errors. Use this same step-by-step strategy to help you identify, understand, and correct errors in your writing.

Once you identify a fragment, the easiest way to correct it is to attach it to the preceding sentence. If the fragment is a renamer or an *-ing* fragment, you will probably need to add a comma. Most adverb fragments will need no punctuation. Below, Example 1, a renamer, is attached to its preceding sentence with a comma:

EXAMPLE 1: I entered my apartment and saw an unexpected guest. ✗ A cat right in the middle of my living room.

TIP APPLIED: *I realize* I entered my apartment and saw an unexpected guest. ✗ *I realize* a cat right in the middle of my living room.

CORRECTION: I entered my apartment and saw an unexpected guest. ~~A~~ `, a` cat right in the middle of my living room.

SENTENCE PRACTICE

Do these exercises (there are three in each lesson) to practice applying the lesson's tips. You can check your answers to the first two sets against the answer key in the back of the book. A box after the first exercise set directs you to the Web for further practice.

Sentence Practice 1

CORRECTED SENTENCES APPEAR ON PAGE 470.

Find the fragments by using the *I Realize* Tip. Write *OK* above each complete sentence. Write *frag* above each fragment and identify which of the three types it is—*renamer, adverb,* or *-ing fragment.* Correct the fragment by combining it with the complete sentence next to it.

EXAMPLE: I started a poem but couldn't finish it. Because I ran out of ideas.

                            OK   frag, adverb

ANSWER: *I realize* I started a poem but couldn't finish it. *I realize* because I ran out of ideas.

                                                      because

CORRECTION: I started a poem but couldn't finish it./ ~~Because~~ I ran out of ideas.

> For more practice correcting fragments, go to Exercise Central at **bedfordstmartins.com/commonsense/1-1**.

EDITING PRACTICE

Do these exercises (there are three in each lesson) to practice identifying and correcting the error in a paragraph or mini-essay similar to one you might write. You can check your answers to the first two editing practices against the answer key in the back of the book.

Editing Practice 1

CORRECTED SENTENCES APPEAR ON PAGE 470.

Correct all fragment errors in the following paragraphs using the first correction as a model. The number in parentheses at the end of each paragraph indicates how many errors you should find.

                                                    , which

Ten percent of Americans suffer from *allergic rhinitis./* ~~Which~~ is the medical term for hay fever. The most common allergy. Hay fever is triggered by exposure to pollen. Especially grass and weed pollens. Flower pollen rarely causes allergic reactions. Because it is too heavy to float very high or far. (3)

    During the allergy season, many hay fever sufferers take a drug called an *antihistamine.* Hoping to combat sneezing, runny nose, and itchy eyes. However, there are other ways to control allergy symptoms. Such as limiting outside work when the pollen count is high, running the air conditioner in your house and car, and avoiding dust and smoke. (2)

WRITING PRACTICE

Do this activity to demonstrate your ability to avoid the error in your own writing.

Writing Practice

On your own paper, write a paragraph describing a local work of art (sculpture, photograph, painting, and so on). In a second paragraph, tell what you like or dislike about it. Use the Editing Checklist to make sure there are no fragments.

EDITING CHECKLIST
This checklist will help you identify and correct the error in your writing.

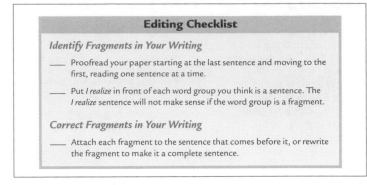

Editing Checklist

Identify Fragments in Your Writing

_____ Proofread your paper starting at the last sentence and moving to the first, reading one sentence at a time.

_____ Put *I realize* in front of each word group you think is a sentence. The *I realize* sentence will not make sense if the word group is a fragment.

Correct Fragments in Your Writing

_____ Attach each fragment to the sentence that comes before it, or rewrite the fragment to make it a complete sentence.

THE BOTTOM LINE
Here is a final reminder of the main point of the lesson. The sentence is written so that it both demonstrates and describes the concept of the lesson.

The Bottom Line

I realize you can place *I realize* in front of a complete sentence.

Using the Tabs

You may have noticed that there are tabs in the outside margins of this book. These tabs are designed to help you find your way around. If you open to a unit overview or unit review, the tab will indicate the unit number and whether you are in the **overview** or the **review**. If you flip through the book from front to back, you will notice twelve sets of tabs. These correspond to the twelve units in *A Commonsense Guide*.

Unit One

overview

If you open to an individual lesson, the tab will indicate the lesson number and a symbol for the topic of the lesson. For example, **frag** is the symbol used for Lesson 1: Fragments. You may notice that your instructor uses a similar system of symbols to indicate errors in your writing.

Lesson 1

frag

The last page of *A Commonsense Guide to Grammar and Usage* lists other common correction symbols.

Contents

Unit One	*Understanding the Basic Sentence*	14

I entered my apartment and saw an unexpected

guest,/ ~~A~~ cat in the middle of my living room.
  , *a*
      ^

I did pretty well on the last test; I got an 82.
                              ^

Unit Two	*Expanding the Basic Sentence*	36

Derek finally finished writing his book of poems,
but his publisher was not satisfied.   ^

In 1972, the Miami Dolphins won all their regular
season games,/; furthermore, they won all their
playoff games.
              ^

Unit Three   *Making Subjects and Verbs Agree*   70

Unit Four   *Using Correct Verb Tenses*   99

Unit Ten   ESL   *Choosing the Right Article*   322

Unit Eleven   ESL   *Using Verbs Correctly*   354

Guide to Grammar Terminology

This guide is an alphabetical listing of all the grammar terms used in this book. Each term is defined with an example. For some grammar terms, there are also helpful hints and suggestions. Anytime you encounter a grammar term you are unsure about, look it up in this guide.

> NOTE: Examples of the term being defined are in ***bold italic*** type.
> References to important related terms are underlined.
> Ungrammatical phrases or sentences are indicated by an ✗.

Active The term *active* or *active voice* refers to sentences in which the subject plays the role of the actor, or the "doer" of the action, as opposed to passive sentences, in which the subject is the person or thing *receiving* the action of the verb. For example, in the active sentence ***Sandy saw Pat***, the subject *Sandy* is doing the seeing, whereas in the passive sentence ***Pat was seen by Sandy***, *Pat* is the person being seen. Also see passive.

Adjective Adjectives play two different roles: (1) they modify the nouns that they precede (a ***large*** *tree*); or (2) after certain verbs like *be, seem,* and *become,* adjectives describe the subject of the sentence. For example, in the sentence *The tree is **green**,* the adjective *green* describes the subject *tree.* Also see article and proper adjective.

Adjective clause An adjective clause (also called a relative clause) always modifies the noun it follows. In the sentence *The tree **that we planted** is getting leaves,* the adjective clause *that we planted* modifies the noun *tree.* An adjective clause begins with a relative pronoun (*that* in the example sentence is a relative pronoun). There are two types of adjective clauses. Depending on the relation of the adjective clause to the noun it modifies, the clause is either an essential adjective clause or a nonessential adjective clause.

Adverb An adverb modifies a verb (*walked **briskly***), an adjective (***pretty*** *tall*), another adverb (***very*** *badly*), or a sentence (***Truthfully,*** *I do not know the answer*). Adverbs that modify verbs give *when, where, why,* and *how* information. Such adverbs normally occur at the end of a sentence but can usually be moved to the beginning; for example: *I got a ticket **yesterday**. **Yesterday**, I got a ticket.* An adverb prepositional phrase or an adverb clause also modifies a verb and may move to the beginning of the sentence.

1

Adverb clause An adverb clause modifies a verb, giving *when, where, why,* or *how* information. Adverb clauses are easily moved to the beginning of the independent clause from their normal position after the main clause; for example: *I was at the office **when you called**. **When you called**, I was at the office.*

Agreement Some words in a sentence are so closely related that the form of one determines the form of another. When such words are correctly chosen in relation to one another, they are in *agreement.* A pronoun should agree with its antecedent in terms of gender and number (*The **boy** ate **his** food*), and a subject should agree with its verb in terms of number (***He was** hungry*). Also see subject-verb agreement.

Antecedent See pronoun antecedent.

Appositive An appositive is a noun (or a noun and its modifiers) that renames (further identifies) a preceding noun. For example, in *My English teacher, **Ms. Rodriguez**, also teaches Spanish, Ms. Rodriguez* is an appositive that renames (further identifies) the noun *teacher.* Usually, two commas set off the appositive from the rest of the sentence, as in the example here.

Article Articles are a special kind of adjective that come before all other types of adjectives. For example, in the phrase ***the** tall trees,* the article *the* must come before the adjective *tall;* that is, we cannot say ✗ *tall the trees.* There are two types of articles: definite (*the*) and indefinite (*a* and *an*).

Clause A clause contains at least one subject and one verb. A clause that stands alone as a complete thought is called an independent clause or a *main clause.* All sentences must contain at least one main clause. For types of clauses that cannot stand alone, see dependent clause.

Colon The colon (:) is frequently used to introduce lists. The part of the sentence before the colon should be able to stand alone as an independent clause, for example, ***These are the three most common flavors of ice-cream: vanilla, chocolate, and strawberry.*** Do not break up an independent clause with a colon. A common error is adding a colon after the verb, for example, ✗ *The three most common flavors of ice-cream are: vanilla, chocolate, and strawberry.*

Comma splice A comma splice is the incorrect use of a comma to join two sentences or two independent clauses (✗ *Angela answered the phone, she was the only person in the office*). Also see fused sentence and run-on sentence.

Common noun A common noun refers to categories of people, places, things, and ideas, in contrast to a proper noun, which names particular individual people or places. For example, *reporter* is a common noun, but *Lois Lane* is a proper noun. Common nouns can be identified by their use of the definite article *the.* For example, *replace* and *replacement* are related words, but you can tell that *replacement* is a common noun because you can say *the replacement. Replace* is not a common noun, because you cannot say ✗ *the replace.*

Complete sentence A complete sentence is an independent clause that can be correctly punctuated with a terminal punctuation mark, such as a period, a question mark, or an exclamation point. The opposite of a complete sentence is a <u>fragment</u>, which is only part of a sentence and which cannot be punctuated correctly with a terminal punctuation mark.

Compound   A compound consists of two or more grammatical units of the same type that are joined by a <u>coordinating conjunction</u>. For example, in the sentence ***Thelma and Louise*** *went on a trip,* the phrase *Thelma and Louise* is a compound subject.

Compound sentence   When two or more sentences (<u>independent clauses</u>) are combined into one, the result is a compound sentence. A compound sentence is usually created by inserting a <u>coordinating conjunction</u> between the two "former" sentences, as in *I left the party early,* ***but*** *Angie refused to leave.*

Conjunction   The term *conjunction* means "join together." Conjunctions are words that join grammatical elements together. There are two types of conjunctions: (1) <u>coordinating conjunctions</u>—words like ***and, but,*** and ***or***; and (2) subordinating conjunctions—words like ***when, since, because,*** and ***if,*** which begin adverb clauses.

Conjunctive adverb   See <u>transitional term</u>.

Contraction   A contraction is the shortened form of a word that results from leaving out some letters or sounds. In writing, the missing letters in contractions are indicated by an apostrophe ('); for example, ***I'll*** is the contracted form of *I will.* This use of the apostrophe in contractions is different from its use to indicate possession; see <u>possessive apostrophe</u>.

Coordinating conjunction   A coordinating conjunction joins grammatical units of the same type, creating a <u>compound</u>. There are seven coordinating conjunctions, which can be remembered by the acronym *FANBOYS:* <u>*f*</u>*or,* <u>*a*</u>*nd,* <u>*n*</u>*or,* <u>*b*</u>*ut,* <u>*o*</u>*r,* <u>*y*</u>*et,* <u>*s*</u>*o*.

Count noun   A count noun is a <u>common noun</u> that can be counted: ***one cat/two cats.*** Nouns that have irregular plural forms—such as *one child/two children, one goose/two geese,* and *one deer/two deer*—are also count nouns. For nouns that cannot be counted, see <u>noncount noun</u>.

Dangling modifier   A dangling modifier is a noun modifier (usually a participial phrase) that does not actually modify the noun it is intended to modify. The modifier is said to be "dangling" because the noun it is supposed to modify is not in the sentence. For example, in the sentence ***Based on the evidence,*** *the jury acquitted the defendant,* the phrase *based on the evidence* is a dangling modifier because it does not really modify *jury.* (You cannot say that *the jury was based on the evidence.*) Also see <u>misplaced modifier</u>.

Definite article   The definite article is *the,* which can be used either with a singular or with a plural <u>common noun</u>. Use the definite article when referring to a specific object or thing that is also known to the reader or listener. For example, in the sentence *Please hand me the cup,* you can assume that the speaker is referring to a specific cup that the reader or hearer can also identify. When not referring to anything specific, or when referring to something that is *not* known to the listener, use an <u>indefinite article</u>: *a* or *an.*

Dependent clause   A dependent clause is a clause that cannot be used as a complete sentence by itself, as opposed to an <u>independent clause,</u> which can stand alone. There are three types of dependent clauses: (1) an <u>adjective clause</u> modifies a noun (*I read the book **that you recommended***); (2) an <u>adverb clause</u> modifies a verb (*I was in the shower **when the telephone rang***); and (3) a <u>noun clause</u> plays the role of subject or object (***What you see** is **what you get***). A dependent clause is also called a <u>subordinate clause.</u>

Direct quotation   A direct quotation uses quotation marks (" ") to show the reader that the words inside the marks are *exactly* what the person said or wrote; for example: *Tina said, "I know where we can buy tickets."* The opposite of a direct quotation is an <u>indirect quotation,</u> which does not use quotation marks, as in the following sentence: *Tina said that she knew where they could buy tickets.*

Elliptical adverb clause   An elliptical adverb is a reduced form of an <u>adverb clause</u> from which the subject has been deleted and the verb changed to a <u>participle</u> form. For example, in the adverb clause beginning the sentence ***When I looked for my hat,*** *I found my gloves* can be reduced to an elliptical adverb clause: ***When looking for my hat,*** *I found my gloves.*

Essential adjective clause   Every <u>adjective clause</u> (also called a *relative clause*) modifies a noun, but different types of adjective clauses are related to the nouns they modify in different ways. Essential adjective clauses (also called *restrictive* adjective clauses) narrow or limit the meaning of the nouns they modify. For example, in the sentence *All the students **who miss the test** will fail the course,* the adjective clause *who miss the test* limits or defines the meaning of the noun *students:* the students threatened with failure are only those who miss the test. Essential adjective clauses are never set off with commas. An adjective clause that does not limit or define the meaning of the noun it modifies is called a <u>nonessential adjective clause.</u>

Faulty parallelism   The term *faulty <u>parallelism</u>* refers to a series of two or more grammatical elements in which not all the elements are in the same grammatical form. For example, the sentence ✗ *Senator Blather is **loud, pompous,** a **fraud,** and **talks too much*** presents a series of four elements, but there is faulty parallelism because the first two elements (*loud* and *pompous*) are adjectives; the third element (*fraud*) is a noun; and the fourth element (*talks too much*) is a verb phrase.

Fragment   A fragment is part of a sentence that is punctuated as though it were a <u>complete sentence</u>. Typically, fragments are pieces cut off from the preceding sentence; for example: *The computer lost my paper.* ✗ ***Which I had worked on all night.*** One way to recognize a fragment is to test it with the *I Realize* Tip. You can put the words *I realize* in front of most complete sentences and make a new grammatical sentence. However, when you put *I realize* in front of a fragment, the result will not make sense.

Fused sentence A fused sentence is a type of <u>run-on sentence</u> in which two complete sentences (or independent clauses) are joined together without any mark of punctuation. ✗ *My brother caught a cold he has been out of school for a week* is an example of a fused sentence because it consists of two complete sentences (*My brother caught a cold* and *He has been out of school for a week*) that are joined without proper punctuation. A <u>comma splice</u> is a similar type of error that incorrectly joins complete sentences with a comma.

Gender Certain third-person personal pronouns are marked for gender: *she, her,* and *hers* refer to females; *he, him,* and *his* refer to males. The third-person plural pronouns *they* and *them* are not marked for gender; that is, these pronouns can refer to males, females, or both. *They* and *them* are sometimes called "gender-neutral" or "gender-exclusive" pronouns. The third-person singular pronoun *it* refers to things that do not have gender, such as concrete objects and abstractions; so do the third-person plural pronouns *they, them,* and *their.*

Gerund A gerund is the *-ing* form of a verb (the <u>present participle</u>) that is used as a noun. For example, in the sentence *I like **taking** the bus to work, taking* is the gerund. The term *gerund* can also be used to refer to the *-ing* verb together with all the words that go with it (in what is technically called a *gerund phrase*). In the example sentence, the whole phrase **taking the bus to work** is a gerund phrase.

Helping verb When two or more verbs are used together in a string, the last verb in the sequence is called the <u>main verb</u>. All the other verbs that come before the main verb are called *helping verbs.* For example, in the sentence *We **should have been** tuning our instruments,* the last verb (*tuning*) is the main verb, and all the preceding verbs (*should have been*) are the helping verbs. The first helping verb in the sequence is the only verb that agrees with the subject. The most important helping verbs are *be* and *have* (in all their different forms), plus *can, could, may, might, must, shall, should, will,* and *would.*

Indefinite article Indefinite articles appear in two forms, depending on the initial sound of the following word: *a* is used before words beginning with a consonant sound (*a yellow banana*), and *an* is used before words beginning with a vowel sound (*an old banana*). Use an indefinite article when mentioning something the reader or listener does not already know about; after that point, use the definite article *the.* For example: *I bought **an** Apple computer. The computer has **a** built-in modem. The modem is connected to my telephone line.*

Independent clause An independent clause (also called a *main clause*) can always stand alone as a <u>complete sentence</u>. Every sentence must contain at least one independent clause.

Indirect quotation An indirect quotation is a <u>paraphrase</u> of the writer or speaker's actual, verbatim words. For example, if Mr. Lopez said, "We are going to Florida tomorrow," the indirect quotation might be the following: *He said that he and his family were going to Florida the next day.* One of the distinctive features of indirect quotation is the use of *that* before the paraphrase of the writer or speaker's words. Also notice that, unlike direct quotation, an indirect quotation uses no quotation marks.

Infinitive   An infinitive is the form of a verb as it appears in the dictionary. For example, the infinitive form of *is, am, was,* and *were* is *be.* Like the *-ing* present participle form of verbs (gerunds), infinitives are often used as nouns. When serving as nouns, infinitives almost always are used with *to;* for example, *I like* **to eat** *pizza with my fingers.* As with gerunds, the term *infinitive* can also be used more broadly to include both the infinitive and the words that go with it (together called an *infinitive phrase*). In this broader sense, the infinitive in the example sentence is **to eat pizza with my fingers**.

Information question   Information questions are phrases that begin with a question word, for example: *who, what, where, why, when, how often, whose* + noun, *which* + noun or pronoun. An information question usually also contains a helping verb and a form of the verb *do.* For example, in "**Where did** *Liu go*," the verb *did* (the past tense of *do*) has been added after the question word *where.* The question word **where** seeks further specific information.

Inseparable phrasal verb   A phrasal verb is a type of compound verb. When the compound is formed from a verb and a preposition, it is called an inseparable phrasal verb because the preposition can never be moved away or "separated" from the verb. For example, in the sentence *The prince* **turned against** *the king,* the preposition *against* can never be moved away from the verb: ✗ *The prince* **turned** *the king* **against**. However, when the phrasal verb is formed with an adverb, the adverb can be moved away from the verb. A phrasal verb of this type is called a separable phrasal verb.

Introductory element   An introductory element is any kind of word, phrase, or clause that has been placed at the beginning of a sentence rather than in its expected position in the middle or at the end of the sentence. Introductory elements are usually set off from the rest of the sentence by a comma (especially if the introductory element is a phrase or a clause); for example: **Feeling a little down**, *Scrooge left the party early.*

Linking verb   Linking verbs are a class of verbs that can be followed by adjectives. For example, in the sentence *Jason* **is** *funny,* the verb *is* is a linking verb followed by the adjective *funny.* Linking verbs are not used to express action. Instead, linking verbs describe their subjects. In the example sentence, the adjective *funny* describes *Jason.*

Main clause   See independent clause.

Main verb   The main verb is the rightmost verb in a string of verbs. All the verbs that precede the main verb are helping verbs. For example, in the sentence *Cinderella must have* **eaten** *all the chilidogs,* the main verb is *eaten.* The other two verbs (*must* and *have*) are helping verbs.

Mass noun   See noncount noun.

Misplaced modifier   A misplaced modifier is any type of modifier that has been placed so far away from the word it actually modifies that it appears to modify the wrong word. For example, in the sentence *I saw the car at the station* **with the flat tire,** the modifier *with the flat tire* appears to modify *station.* When the modifier is placed next to the word it modifies, the problem disappears: *I saw the car* **with the flat tire** *at the station.* Also see <u>dangling modifier.</u>

Modifier Modifiers are words that describe or give additional information about other words in a sentence. <u>Adjectives,</u> <u>participles,</u> and <u>adjective clauses</u> modify nouns. <u>Adverbs</u> and <u>adverb clauses</u> modify verbs, adverbs, adjectives, or whole sentences.

Noncount noun A noncount noun (also called a <u>mass noun</u>) is a <u>common noun</u> that cannot be used in the plural or with number words (✗ *one homework/*✗ *two homeworks;* ✗ *one dirt/*✗ *two dirts*). A noun that can be used in the plural and with number words is called a <u>count noun.</u>

Nonessential adjective clause Every <u>adjective clause</u> (also called a *relative clause*) modifies a noun, but different types of adjective clauses have different relations with the nouns they modify. Nonessential adjective clauses (also called *nonrestrictive* adjective clauses) do not narrow or limit the meaning of the nouns they modify. Like <u>appositives,</u> nonessential clauses rename the nouns they modify, and, like appositives, they are set off with commas. For example, in the sentence *My mother,* **who was born in Tonga,** *came to the United States as a child,* the relative clause *who was born in Tonga* is nonessential because it does not narrow or define the meaning of *my mother.* My mother is still my mother no matter where she was born. A clause that defines or limits the meaning of the noun it modifies is called an <u>essential adjective clause.</u>

Nonrestrictive adjective clause See <u>nonessential adjective clause.</u>

Noun Nouns are names of people, places, things, and ideas. A noun that refers to categories (**teacher, city**) is a <u>common noun;</u> a noun that refers to actual individual persons or places (**Mr. Smith, Chicago**) is a proper noun. See also <u>count noun</u> and <u>noncount noun.</u>

Noun clause A noun clause is a group of words that work together to function as a noun, as in **Whether you go or not** *is up to you.* If you look at the noun clause by itself, you will always find a word acting like a subject and a word serving as its verb. In the example above, *you* is acting like a subject, and *go* is its verb.

Object When a noun or a pronoun follows certain verbs or any preposition, it is called an *object.* For example, in the sentence *Kermit kissed* **Miss Piggy,** the object of the verb *kissed* is *Miss Piggy.* Most pronouns have distinct object forms. Thus, to replace *Miss Piggy* with a pronoun in the example sentence, we would have to use the object form *her* rather than the subject form *she: Kermit kissed* **her.** <u>Prepositional phrases</u> consist of prepositions and their objects. For example, in the prepositional phrase *on the* **ladder,** the object of the preposition *on* is the noun *ladder.*

Parallelism The term *parallelism* refers to a series of two or more elements of the same grammatical type, usually joined by a coordinating conjunction.

For example, in the sentence *I love* **to eat, to drink,** *and* **to dance** *the polka,* there are three parallel forms—all infinitives: *to eat, to drink,* and *to dance.* Failure to express parallel elements in the same grammatical form is called <u>faulty parallelism</u>.

Paraphrase   To *paraphrase* means to rephrase something in a different grammatical form or with different wording while keeping the meaning of the original. For example, the passive sentence *I was given a present by Mary* is a paraphrase of the corresponding active sentence *Mary gave me a present.* Paraphrase is common in <u>indirect quotation</u>.

Participial phrase   A participial phrase contains either a present or a past <u>participle</u>. Participial phrases modify nouns. For example, in the sentence *The workers* **repairing the roof** *found water damage, repairing the roof* is a present participial phrase modifying the noun *workers.* In the sentence *The workers* **injured in the accident** *sued the company, injured in the accident* is a past participial phrase modifying the noun *workers.*

Participle   Participles are verb forms. There are two types of participles: (1) <u>present participles</u> (the *-ing* form of verbs such as *seeing, doing,* and *having*); and (2) <u>past participles</u> (for example, *seen, done,* and *had*). Both types of participles can be used as verbs (following certain <u>helping verbs</u>). For example, in the sentence *Michio is* **watching** *the movie,* the word *watching* is in the present participle form. In the sentence *Michio has* **watched** *the movie,* the word *watched* is in the past participle form.

   Both present participles and past participles can also be used as adjectives. For example, in the saying *A* **watched** *pot never boils,* the past participle *watched* functions as an adjective modifying the noun *pot.*

Passive   The term *passive* or *passive voice* describes sentences in which the subject is not the "doer" of the action but instead *receives* the action of the verb. For example, in the passive sentence *Sandy* **was seen** *by Pat,* the subject *Sandy* is not the person doing the seeing but instead is the person being seen. The passive voice can always be recognized by a unique sequence of verbs: the <u>helping verb</u> *be* (in some form) followed by a <u>past participle</u> verb form. In the example above, *was* is the past tense form of *be,* and *seen* is the past participle form of *see.* Sentences that are not in the passive voice are said to be in the <u>active</u> voice.

Past participle   Past participle verb forms are used in the <u>perfect tenses</u> after the <u>helping verb</u> *have* (as in *Thelma has* **seen** *that movie*) or after the helping verb *be* in <u>passive</u> sentences (*That movie was* **seen** *by Thelma*). The past participle form of most verbs ends in *-ed*—as do most past tense forms of most verbs. How, then, can we tell a past participle from a past tense? The difference is that the past participle form of a verb always follows a helping verb. For example, in the sentence *Liam has* **loved** *the movies, loved* is a past participle because it follows the helping verb *has.* In the sentence *Liam* **loved** *the movies,* however, *loved* is a past tense verb because it does *not* follow a helping verb. Past participles can also be used as adjectives (*The car* **seen** *in that commercial belongs to my uncle*).

Past tense The past tense is used to describe an action that took place at some past time; for example, *Carlos **borrowed** my car last night.* For regular verbs, the past tense form ends in *-ed.* However, there are a large number of irregular verbs that form their past tense in different ways. The most unusual past tense is found in the verb *be,* which has two past tense forms: *was* in the singular and *were* in the plural.

Perfect tenses The perfect tenses refer to action that takes place over a period of time or is frequently repeated. There are three perfect tenses: (1) present perfect (*Niles **has seen** Daphne twice this week*); (2) past perfect (*Niles **had seen** Daphne two times last week*); and (3) future perfect (*Niles **will have seen** Daphne twice by Friday*). Notice that all the perfect tenses use *have* (in some form) as a helping verb, followed by a verb in the past participle form (*seen,* in all these examples).

Personal pronoun There are three sets of personal pronouns: (1) first-person pronouns refer to the speaker (***I, me, mine; we, us, ours***); (2) second-person pronouns refer to the hearer (***you, yours***); and (3) third-person pronouns refer to another person or thing (***he, him, his, she, her, hers, it, its; they, them, theirs***). A personal pronoun can also be categorized by the role it plays in a sentence: subject (*I, we, you, he, she, it, they*) or object (*me, us, you, him, her, them*).

Phrasal verb Phrasal verbs are compounds (often with idiomatic meanings) formed from a verb plus either a preposition or an adverb. When the compound contains a preposition, the compound is called an inseparable phrasal verb because the preposition can never be separated from the verb. When the compound contains an adverb, the adverb can be moved away from the verb; these compounds are called separable phrasal verbs. Phrasal verbs are also called *two-word verbs.*

Phrase In grammatical terminology, a *phrase* is a group of related words that act as a single part of speech. The most common type is the prepositional phrase. For example, in the sentence *Kermit kissed Miss Piggy **on the balcony,*** the prepositional phrase is *on the balcony,* here acting as an adverb.

Plural Referring to more than one. Plural nouns are usually formed by adding *-s* to the singular form of the noun. Also see agreement; subject-verb agreement.

Possessive apostrophe Possessive nouns (***John's** book*) and possessive indefinite pronouns (***one's** ideas, **somebody's** book, **anybody's** guess*) are spelled with an apostrophe (') to show that the *-s* added at the end of the word is a "possessive *-s,*" as opposed to a "plural *-s.*" When an *-s* at the end of a word is both possessive *and* plural, the apostrophe goes after the *-s* (*The **girls'** dresses*). This use of the apostrophe to indicate possession is different from its use to indicate a contraction.

Preposition Prepositions are words such as *on, by, with, of, in, from, between,* and *to.* A preposition is used with a following noun or pronoun object to make a prepositional phrase.

Prepositional phrase A prepositional phrase is a phrase consisting of a preposition and its object; for example: *on the beach, at noon, by Shakespeare.* Prepositional phrases function as adverbs or adjectives. For example, in the sentence *I got a message **at my office**,* the prepositional phrase *at my office* functions as an adverb telling where I got the message. In the sentence *The chair **at my office** is not very comfortable,* the prepositional phrase *at my office* is an adjective modifying *chair.*

Present participle Present participle verb forms are used in the progressive tenses after the helping verb *be,* in some form. For example, in the sentence *Pranav and Liu were **practicing** their duets, were* is a form of the helping verb *be,* and *practicing* is in the present participle form. The present participle form is completely regular because it always ends in *-ing;* for example: *doing, being, seeing, helping.* Present participles can also be used as adjectives (*The car **turning** at the signal is a Buick*) or as nouns (***Seeing** is **believing***).

Present tense Despite its name, the most common use of the present tense is not to describe present time but, rather, to make timeless generalizations (*The earth **is** round*) or to describe habitual, repeated actions (*I always **shop** on Saturdays*).

Present tense verb forms have an added *-s* when the subject is a third-person singular pronoun (*he, she,* or *it*) or when the subject is a noun that can be replaced with a third-person pronoun. See subject-verb agreement.

Progressive tenses Progressive tenses are used to refer to actions that are ongoing at the time of the sentence — as opposed to the present tense, which is essentially timeless. The term *progressive* refers to three related verb constructions that employ *be* (in some form) as a helping verb. If *be* is in the present tense (*am, is, are*), then the construction is called the *present progressive;* for example: *The president **is visiting** Peru now.* If *be* is in the past tense (*was, were*), then the construction is called the *past progressive;* for example: *The president **was visiting** Peru last week.* If *be* is used in the future (*will be*), then the construction is called the *future progressive;* for example: *The president **will be visiting** Peru next week.*

Pronoun A pronoun can replace a noun either as a subject or as an object. Among the many different types of pronouns, the most important is the personal pronoun. Also discussed in this book is the relative pronoun, which is the kind that begins an adjective clause. Also see gender, pronoun antecedent, and vague pronoun.

Pronoun antecedent Many pronouns refer back to a person or persons or to a thing or things mentioned earlier in the sentence or even in a previous sentence. For example, in the sentences *My **aunts** live next door. **They** are my mother's sisters,* the antecedent of the pronoun *they* is *aunts.* When a pronoun might refer to more than one antecedent, it is said to exhibit "ambiguous pronoun reference." For example, in the sentence *Aunt Sadie asked Mother where* *her keys were,* the pronoun *her* is ambiguous because it might refer either to Aunt Sadie or to Mother. A pronoun that has no real antecedent is called a vague pronoun. For example, in the sentence **They** *shouldn't allow smoking in restaurants,* the pronoun *they* is vague because it does not have any actual antecedent—it does not refer to any identified individuals.

Pronoun-antecedent agreement See agreement.

Proper adjective A proper adjective is derived from a proper noun. For example, the adjective *Jamaican* in **Jamaican** *coffee* is the adjective form of the proper noun *Jamaica.* Proper adjectives are always capitalized.

Proper noun Proper nouns are the names of specific individual persons, titles, or places. Proper nouns are always capitalized; for example: **Queen Elizabeth, Michael Jordan, New York Times, Vancouver.** When a noun refers to a category rather than to a specific individual, it is called a common noun.

Quotation There are two types of quotation: (1) direct quotation, which uses quotation marks to report exactly what someone said, with word-for-word accuracy; and (2) indirect quotation, which paraphrases what a person said without using the writer or speaker's exact words. Indirect quotations are not set within quotation marks.

Relative clause See adjective clause.

Relative pronoun A relative pronoun begins an adjective clause. The relative pronouns are *who, whom, whose, which,* and *that.* Relative pronouns must refer to the noun in the independent clause that the adjective clause modifies. For example, in the sentence *I got an offer **that** I can't refuse,* the relative pronoun *that* refers to *offer.* The relative pronouns *who, whom,* and *whose* are used to refer to people. For example, in the sentence *He is a man **whom** you can rely on,* the relative pronoun *whom* refers to *man.* Using *that* to refer to people is incorrect in formal writing; for example: ✗ *He is a man **that** you can rely on.*

Restrictive adjective clause See essential adjective clause.

Run-on sentence A run-on sentence consists of two or more sentences (independent clauses) that are joined together without adequate punctuation. Joining two sentences together with only a comma is called a comma splice (✗ *My grandmother lived in Mexico when she was a girl, she moved to Texas when she was nineteen*). Joining two sentences together with no punctuation at all is called a fused sentence (✗ *Kelsey's party is this weekend I bet she's looking forward to it*).

Semicolon The semicolon (;) is used in place of a period to join two closely related independent clauses, for example **A water main in the building had burst; the floors were covered with water**.

Sentence A sentence consists of at least one independent clause (with or without an accompanying dependent clause) that is punctuated with a period, an exclamation point, or a question mark.

Separable phrasal verb A phrasal verb is a type of compound verb. When such a compound is formed from a verb and an adverb, it is called a separable phrasal verb because the adverb can be moved away or "separated" from the verb. For example, in the sentence *I **called up** my parents,* the adverb *up* can be separated from the verb by moving it after the object: *I **called** my parents **up**.* However, when the phrasal verb is formed with a preposition, the preposition can never be moved away from the verb. A phrasal verb of this type is called an inseparable phrasal verb.

Sexist language Language that stereotypes, demeans, or unfairly excludes men or women is referred to as sexist language. One of the most common forms is the sexist or gender-exclusive use of pronouns. In this example, notice how it appears that only men vote: *Everybody should vote for **his** favorite candidate for governor.*

Singular Referring to one. Also see agreement; subject-verb agreement.

Subject The subject of a sentence is the doer of the action or what the sentence is about. The term *subject* has two slightly different meanings: (1) the *simple subject* is the noun or pronoun that is the doer or the topic of the sentence, and (2) the *complete subject* is the simple subject together with all its modifiers. For example, in the sentence *The **book** on the shelf belongs to my cousin,* the simple subject is *book,* and the complete subject is *the book on the shelf.*

Subject-verb agreement This term refers to the matching of the number of a present tense verb (or a present tense helping verb if there is more than one verb) with the number of the subject of that verb. Following are three examples with different subjects: (1) *Aunt Sadie **lives** in Denver.* (2) *My aunts **live** in Denver.* (3) *Aunt Sadie and Uncle Albert **live** in Denver.*

If the subject is a third-person singular personal pronoun (*he, she, it*) or if the subject is a noun that can be replaced by a third-person singular personal pronoun (as is the case with *Aunt Sadie* in example 1), then it is necessary to add an *-s* (called the *third-person singular -s*) to the present tense verb.

If the subject *cannot* be replaced by a third-person singular pronoun (as is the case in examples 2 and 3), do *not* add the third-person singular *-s* to the present tense.

Only the verb *be* has past tense forms that change to agree with the subject: *was* is used with first-person singular and third-person singular subjects (*I **was** in Denver; Aunt Sadie **was** in Denver*); and *were* is used with all other subjects (*My aunts **were** in Denver*).

Subordinate clause See dependent clause.

Subordinating conjunction A *subordinating conjunction* (such as ***when**, **since**, **because**,* or ***if***) begins a dependent clause.

Tense The term *tense* is used in two quite different ways. (1) It can refer to the *time* in which the action of the sentence takes place: present time, past time, and future time. (2) Usually in this book, however, the term is used in a narrower, more technical sense to mean just the *form* of the verb. In this limited sense, the term refers either to the <u>present tense</u> form of a verb (*see* and *sees,* for example) or to its <u>past tense</u> form (*saw*). There is no separate future tense form in English; we can talk about future time by using the <u>helping verb</u> *will.*

Tense shifting   Tense shifting occurs in a piece of writing when the author shifts from one tense to another—usually from past tense to present tense or vice versa. For example, in the sentence *We **ate** at the restaurant that **is** on the pier,* the first verb (*ate*) is in the past tense, while the second verb (*is*) is in the present tense. In this particular sentence, the shifting from past tense to present tense is appropriate; sometimes, however, writers confuse readers by incorrectly shifting tenses when there is no reason to do so.

Transitional term   A *transitional term* shows how the meaning of a second sentence is related to the meaning of the first sentence. For example, in the pair of sentences *I had planned to leave at noon.* ***However,** my flight was delayed,* the transitional term *however* signals to the reader that the second sentence will contradict the first sentence in some way. Some other transitional terms are *nevertheless, moreover,* and *therefore.*

Vague pronoun   A pronoun must have an <u>antecedent</u> to make its meaning clear. A *vague pronoun* is one that does not seem to refer to anything or anyone in particular. For example, in the sentence ***They** should do something about these terrible roads,* the pronoun *they* is a vague pronoun because it could refer to anybody—the highway department, the police, the government.

Verb   A *verb* tells about an action in a sentence (*Alfy **sneezed***) or describes the subject of the sentence (*Alfy **seemed** angry*). Only verbs can change form to show <u>tense</u>. That is, only verbs have <u>present tense</u> and <u>past tense</u> forms. A simple test to see whether a word is a verb is to see whether you can change it into a past tense by adding *-ed* to it.

Voice   *Voice* is a technical term in grammar that refers to the relation of the subject of a sentence to the verb. If the subject is the "doer" of the action of the verb, as in the sentence ***Thelma** wrecked the car,* then the sentence is said to be in the <u>active</u> voice. However, if the subject is the recipient of the action of the verb, as in the sentence *The **car** was wrecked by Thelma,* then the sentence is said to be in the <u>passive</u> voice.

UNIT ONE
Understanding the Basic Sentence

Terms That Can Help You Understand the Basic Sentence

If you are not familiar with any of the following terms, look them up in the Guide to Grammar Terminology beginning on page 1. The numbers in parentheses indicate the lessons in which each term appears.

comma splice (2)	fragment (1)
complete sentence (1, 2)	fused sentence (2)
coordinating conjunction (2)	independent clause (2)
dependent clause (1, 2)	run-on sentence (2)

The Nuts and Bolts of Understanding the Basic Sentence

This unit will help you to understand the most basic concept in writing: the correct punctuation of complete sentences. A **complete sentence** has the following characteristics:

- It contains both a **subject** and a **verb**.

- It expresses a complete thought—a free-standing, self-contained idea.

The two lessons in this unit present the two ways that a sentence can be mispunctuated: as a **fragment** or as a **run-on**.

Lesson 1 shows you how to identify and correct fragments. In a sentence fragment, something less than a sentence has been punctuated as though it were a complete sentence. Here is an example of a fragment:

FRAGMENT: Celeste found a cat. ✗ Which she promptly took home.

CORRECTION: Celeste found a cat/ ~~Which~~ she promptly took home.
    , which

14

The fragment *which she promptly took home* contains both a subject and a verb, but it cannot stand alone as a self-contained idea. Most fragments are continuations of the preceding sentence, so the easiest way to correct fragments is to attach them to the preceding sentence.

Lesson 2 shows you how to identify and correct run-ons. In a run-on, two complete sentences have been joined together incorrectly and punctuated as though they were a single sentence. Here is an example of a run-on:

RUN-ON: ✗ The boss liked my idea, she said she would take it to the board of directors.

CORRECTION: The boss liked my idea,/; she said she would take it to the board of directors. ^

This kind of run-on is called a **comma splice** because it incorrectly uses a comma to join two complete sentences. If the two sentences had been put together without any punctuation at all, it would be another kind of run-on called a **fused sentence**. Writers sometimes create run-ons when they try to keep closely related ideas together within the same sentence. A good way to achieve the same goal is to join the related sentences together with a semicolon (;).

Can you detect problems with sentence basics?

CORRECTED SENTENCES APPEAR ON PAGE 470.

Correct fragments and run-ons in the following paragraphs using the first correction as a model. The number in parentheses at the end of each paragraph indicates how many errors you should find.

One of the highest honors that can be given in the movie industry is an Academy Award,/ , which ~~Which~~ is more commonly known as an Oscar. ^ Winning just one Oscar is a notable feat. A few movies, however, are exceptional they have won several Oscars. There are four major Oscar awards. Best actress, best actor, best director, and best picture. Only a few movies have won even three of these four awards. In 1982, *Gandhi* received Oscars for best actor, best director, and best picture, it did not win best actress. Two years later, *Amadeus* won the same three awards the best actress Oscar went to Sally Field for her role in *Places in the Heart.* In 1988, *Rain Man* captured three Oscars. Again failing to capture the best actress award. Which went to Jodie Foster for her role in *The Accused.* (6)

Some movies have done even better two movies have won all four major awards. In 1975, *One Flew over the Cuckoo's Nest* won all four of these Oscars. The first movie to win all four was *It Happened One Night.* Which won way back in 1934. (2)

LESSON 1

Fragments

Error Sentences

CORRECTED SENTENCES APPEAR ON PAGE 20.

> EXAMPLE 1: I entered my apartment and saw an unexpected guest. ✗ A cat in the middle of my living room.

> EXAMPLE 2: Philip is really upset. ✗ Because someone broke a window in his car.

> EXAMPLE 3: College gives you a whole new perspective. ✗ Opening your eyes to a new world.

What's the Problem?

A **fragment** is a group of words that cannot stand alone as a **complete sentence** but is punctuated as a complete sentence. If you are a non-native speaker, you should know that in English, a subject, a verb, and a complete thought are needed for a complete sentence. Many fragments lack a verb, as in Example 1, or lack a subject, as in Example 3. A fragment can also be a **dependent clause**, a clause that does not express a complete thought, as in Example 2.

ESL

What Causes the Problem?

Almost all fragments explain or expand upon an idea in the immediately preceding sentence. Fragments are not easy for writers to spot because they sound normal. In the quick give-and-take of conversation, fragments are a way of clarifying or elaborating on what we have just said without having to stop and reformulate the previous sentence. In formal written language, however, fragments are inappropriate. Readers expect formal writing to be carefully planned.

Diagnostic Exercise

CORRECTED SENTENCES APPEAR ON PAGE 470.

Correct all errors in the following paragraph using the first correction as a model. The number in parentheses at the end of the paragraph indicates how many errors you should find.

, not putting

My roommate has an annoying habit. ~~Not putting~~ anything away.
^

He never picks up his dirty clothes. Until he has to do his laundry.

In the kitchen, there are always dirty dishes on the table. I've asked

him to at least put them in the sink. Where they are out of the way.

It is always such a mess. Cups half-full of coffee, cereal bowls with

milk in them, and cruddy silverware. The refrigerator is just as bad.

Opening the door is like taking a trip to the jungle. We really need to

do something about it. Because it is really embarrassing when

someone visits. (4)

Fixing This Problem in Your Writing

A fragment is almost always a continuation of the preceding sentence. To fix a fragment, we need to separate it from the previous sentence. When a fragment is by itself, isolated from preceding sentences, we are much more likely to notice that it doesn't make sense on its own. Here are three tips that will help you to isolate fragments.

> LIKELY FRAGMENTS TIP: Most fragments fall into one of these three categories: *Renamers, Adverbs,* and *-ing Fragments.* If you are aware of what the most common types of fragments are, you are more likely to spot them.

Renamers. These fragments rename or explain the last noun in the preceding sentence. Example 1 illustrates this type. *I entered my apartment and saw an unexpected guest. ✗ A cat right in the middle of my living room.* The noun *cat* renames the guest. Another common example of this type begins with *which: I got mustard on my shirt. ✗ **Which** I had just gotten back from the cleaners.*

frag

Adverbs. In this category are adverb clauses that tell when, where, and especially why something happened. Example 2 illustrates this type: *Philip is really upset.* ✗ *Because someone broke a window in his car.* The fragment explains why Philip is upset.

***-ing* Fragments.** These fragments begin with a verb in the *-ing* verb form. Example 3 illustrates this kind of fragment: *College gives you a whole new perspective.* ✗ *Opening your eyes to a new world.*

> **BACKWARD PROOFREADING TIP:** Proofread your paper backward, one sentence at a time. Use one hand to cover up all but the last sentence in each paragraph. See if that sentence can stand alone. If it can, then uncover the next-to-last sentence to see if it can stand alone, and so forth.

Backward proofreading is a standard and quite effective way of identifying fragments. Try it on the three sample sentences at the beginning of this lesson. Knowing what the most likely fragments look like will help you catch them as you edit.

> ***I REALIZE* TIP:** You can put *I realize* in front of most complete sentences and make a new grammatical sentence. However, when you put *I realize* in front of a fragment, the result will not make sense.

The *I Realize* Tip is a particularly handy way to test to see if something is actually a fragment. Here is how it would be applied to each of the three sample fragments:

TIP APPLIED:　✗ *I realize* **a cat right in the middle of my living room.**

TIP APPLIED:　✗ *I realize* **because someone broke a window in his car.**

TIP APPLIED:　✗ *I realize* **opening your eyes to a new world.**

The *I Realize* Tip will help you to look at potential fragments in isolation from the preceding sentence. Note that this tip works best for sentences that are statements. It does not work for sentences that are in the form of a question (*Was my manager here?*) or a command (*Leave me alone!*).

Once you identify a fragment, the easiest way to correct it is to attach it to the preceding sentence. If the fragment is a renamer or an *-ing* fragment, you will probably need to add a comma. Most adverb fragments will need no punctuation. Below, Example 1, a renamer, is attached to its preceding sentence with a comma:

EXAMPLE 1:   I entered my apartment and saw an unexpected guest. ✗ A cat right in the middle of my living room.

TIP APPLIED: *I realize* I entered my apartment and saw an unexpected guest. ✗ *I realize* a cat right in the middle of my living room.

CORRECTION: I entered my apartment and saw an unexpected

guest/A̶ cat right in the middle of my living room.
_{, a}

Let's follow the same steps to correct Example 2.

EXAMPLE 2:   Philip is really upset. ✗ Because someone broke a window in his car.

TIP APPLIED: *I realize* Philip is really upset. ✗ *I realize* because someone broke a window in his car.

CORRECTION: Philip is really upset/ B̶e̶c̶a̶u̶s̶e̶ someone broke a window in his car.
because

Another way to correct a fragment is to expand the fragment to a complete sentence. When you find a fragment, decide if the material in the fragment is worth emphasizing. If it is, expand the fragment to a full sentence rather than tuck it away as a part of the preceding sentence. For example, here is how you might rewrite Example 3 to make the fragment a full sentence:

EXAMPLE 3:   College gives you a whole new perspective. ✗ Opening your eyes to a new world.

TIP APPLIED: *I realize* college gives you a whole new perspective. ✗ *I realize* opening your eyes to a new world.

CORRECTION: College gives you a whole new perspective. O̶p̶e̶n̶i̶n̶g̶ your eyes to a new world.
It opens

Sentence Practice 1

CORRECTED SENTENCES APPEAR ON PAGE 470.

Find the fragments by using the *I Realize* Tip. Write *OK* above each complete sentence. Write *frag* above each fragment and identify which of the three types it is—*renamer, adverb,* or *-ing fragment.* Correct the fragment by combining it with the complete sentence next to it.

EXAMPLE: I started a poem but couldn't finish it. Because I ran out of ideas.

OK   frag, adverb

ANSWER: *I realize* I started a poem but couldn't finish it. *I realize* because I ran out of ideas.

because

CORRECTION: I started a poem but couldn't finish it./ ~~Because~~ I ran out of ideas.

1. Jeff ran into the house. Carrying three bags of groceries.

2. He fell down. Because he was careless.

3. My history teacher gave us our final exam. Which I think I managed to pass.

4. The Tuskegee Airmen won over 850 medals in World War I. They were African Americans who graduated from a segregated training program for pilots.

5. They flew over 15,233 sorties. Between 1943 and 1945.

 For more practice correcting fragments, go to **Exercise Central** at **bedfordstmartins.com/commonsense/1-1**.

Sentence Practice 2

CORRECTED SENTENCES APPEAR ON PAGE 470.

Find the fragments by using the *I Realize* Tip. Write *OK* above each complete sentence. Write *frag* above each fragment, and identify which of the three types it is—*renamer, adverb,* or *-ing fragment.* Correct the fragment by combining it with the complete sentence next to it.

EXAMPLE: We gave up. Having lost all confidence.

OK   frag, -ing fragment

ANSWER: *I realize* we gave up. *I realize* having lost all confidence.

, having

CORRECTION: We gave up./ ~~Having~~ lost all confidence.

1. A capital offense is a crime punishable by death. A penalty for only the most serious of crimes.

2. This magazine article is about the Valley of Ten Thousand Smokes. Which is a valley in Alaska having a number of volcanic fissures.

3. I vividly recall January 12, 2002. The day my parents made a surprise visit while I was in the middle of hosting a wild party.

4. Our astronomy class took a field trip to Mount Palomar, California. Where one of the world's largest telescopes is located.

5. Russell bought a new pet. It's a green-cheeked conure.

Sentence Practice 3

The first line in each of the following pairs is a complete sentence. The second line is a fragment. For each pair, write a new sentence by correctly attaching the fragment to the complete sentence. Use a comma if necessary.

> EXAMPLE: **We played softball.**
> **Even though it was raining.**

> ANSWER: **We played softball./ ~~Even~~ *, even* though it was raining.**
> ^

1. Fluoride is added to most drinking water in the United States. Even though some people believe fluoride is a harmful additive.

2. Great Britain dominated most of the Persian Gulf until the late 1960's. When it agreed to relinquish its power there.

3. I have several difficult classes. Such as Physics 220.

4. Joan of Arc was burned at the stake. When she was nineteen years old.

5. My neck hurts. Because I slept in an awkward position.

Editing Practice 1

CORRECTED SENTENCES APPEAR ON PAGE 470.

Correct all fragment errors in the following paragraphs using the first correction as a model. The number in parentheses at the end of each paragraph indicates how many errors you should find.

Ten percent of Americans suffer from *allergic rhinitis*./ ~~Which~~ *, which*
is the medical term for hay fever. The most common allergy.
Hay fever is triggered by exposure to pollen. Especially grass and
weed pollens. Flower pollen rarely causes allergic reactions.
Because it is too heavy to float very high or far. (3)

During the allergy season, many hay fever sufferers take a
drug called an *antihistamine*. Hoping to combat sneezing,
runny nose, and itchy eyes. However, there are other ways to
control allergy symptoms. Such as limiting outside work when
the pollen count is high, running the air conditioner in your house
and car, and avoiding dust and smoke. (2)

Editing Practice 2

CORRECTED SENTENCES APPEAR ON PAGE 471.

Correct all fragment errors in the following paragraphs using the first correction as a model. The number in parentheses at the end of each paragraph
indicates how many errors you should find.

Several players have now broken Babe Ruth's long-standing
records./ ~~Most~~ *, most* home runs in a season and most career home
runs. However, Babe may well be the most famous baseball player
of all time. Largely because of his personality as much as his
baseball playing. He played with an enthusiasm that excited the
fans. (1)

Babe's personality frequently made news. Even when his
character got him into trouble. In 1922, his behavior resulted in
five suspensions, and in 1925 his drinking and quarreling with

frag

management resulted in a $5,000 fine. A huge amount at the time for even well-paid players. He gained even more fame, though, when he turned himself around. Hitting a record sixty home runs in 1927. He had a comeback again in the World Series of 1932. After a September attack of what was thought to be appendicitis, he fought back and played all games in the World Series. In which he batted .333. Even in his retirement, he remained a popular favorite and a spokesperson for the game he loved. (4)

Editing Practice 3

Correct all fragment errors in the following paragraph using the first correction as a model. The number in parentheses at the end of the paragraph indicates how many errors you should find.

     Our college installed a new piece of artwork/ ‚ᵃ A statue in front of the library. It is a tribute to the men and women. Serving in the armed forces. It is a special tribute to veterans of the Vietnam War. A war that greatly divided our country. Part of the cost was paid by donations from alumni. Mostly veterans themselves. The remainder of the cost was paid by a local company. Which has close connections with our school. (4)

Writing Practice

On your own paper, write a paragraph describing a local work of art (sculpture, photograph, painting, and so on). In a second paragraph, tell what you like or dislike about it. Use the Editing Checklist to make sure there are no fragments.

Editing Checklist

Identify Fragments in Your Writing

_____ Proofread your paper starting at the last sentence and moving to the first, reading one sentence at a time.

_____ Put *I realize* in front of each word group you think is a sentence. The *I realize* sentence will not make sense if the word group is a fragment.

Correct Fragments in Your Writing

_____ Attach each fragment to the sentence that comes before it, or rewrite the fragment to make it a complete sentence.

The Bottom Line

I realize you can place *I realize* in front of a complete sentence.

LESSON 2
Run-ons: Fused Sentences and Comma Splices

Error Sentences

CORRECTED SENTENCES APPEAR ON PAGE 28.

EXAMPLE 1: ✗ I did pretty well on the last test I got an 82.

EXAMPLE 2: ✗ The next test will be tougher, we're right to be worried about it.

What's the Problem?

A **run-on sentence** contains two **independent clauses** that have been joined together without correct punctuation. (An independent clause can be punctuated with a period as a complete sentence.) Run-on sentences fail to show the reader where one idea ends and the next idea begins.

There are two types of run-on sentence errors. When two independent clauses have been joined with no punctuation at all, the error is called a **fused sentence**. Example 1 illustrates this type of error. When two independent clauses have been joined by a comma (without a coordinating conjunction like *and, but, or*), the error is called a **comma splice**. Example 2 illustrates this type of error. Since fused sentence errors and comma splice errors have similar causes and correction strategies, we will treat them together as run-on sentences.

What Causes the Problem?

In most run-on sentences, the complete ideas expressed by two independent clauses are very closely related — so closely related, in fact, that the writer does not want to separate the ideas into two different sentences. Most often, the idea in the first independent clause is a statement or assertion, and the idea in the second independent clause comments on or reacts to the idea in the first. In a run-on sentence, the writer confuses the reader by failing to correctly signal where the first complete idea ends and the second complete idea begins.

Diagnostic Exercise

CORRECTED SENTENCES APPEAR ON PAGE 471.

Correct all run-on errors in the following paragraph using the first correction as a model. The number in parentheses at the end of the paragraph indicates how many errors you should find.

My friend Miranda is a junior majoring in criminal justice ~~she~~ .She plans to go to law school. Most law schools accept applicants from all majors, she thinks that majoring in criminal justice would help her prepare for law. All law schools do require good grades and a high score on the LSAT. Her grades are high she has about a 3.8 GPA currently. She works very hard, she studies more than any person I know. She plans to take the LSAT this fall she will be studying for it on top of everything else. I admire her energy, I'm sure she has what it takes to be a good law student. (5)

Fixing This Problem in Your Writing

Run-ons are easy to correct once you have identified them. The problem is finding them to begin with. Here are two techniques for spotting run-on sentences in your writing.

> **IMAGINARY PERIOD TIP:** If a sentence contains two separate ideas, put an imaginary period between them. Now ask: Can BOTH parts that are divided by this imaginary period stand alone as complete sentences? If both new sentences can stand alone, then the sentence is a run-on.

Here is the Imaginary Period Tip applied to the two sample sentences:

EXAMPLE 1: ✗ I did pretty well on the last test I got an 82.

TIP APPLIED: I did pretty well on the last test. I got an 82.

EXAMPLE 2:   ✗ The next test will be tougher, we're right to be worried about it.

                                                          . We're
TIP APPLIED: The next test will be tougher ~~, we're~~ right to be
                                                          ^
               worried about it.

In both cases, the two new sentences created by the imaginary period can stand alone as independent clauses. The Imaginary Period Tip shows us that both example sentences are run-ons.

You might try combining the Imaginary Period Tip with the *I Realize* Tip from Lesson 1 (see page 19). The *I Realize* Tip helps confirm that the two new sentences actually are independent clauses:

TIP APPLIED: *I realize* I did pretty well on the last test.
                I realize I got an 82.

TIP APPLIED: *I realize* the next test will be tougher.
                I realize we're right to be worried about it.

The easiest way to correct run-ons is to punctuate the two independent clauses as complete sentences by using periods. Another way is to combine them with a comma and a **coordinating conjunction** (*for, and, nor, but, or, yet, so*). A third way is to separate the two independent clauses with a semicolon (;). (Semicolons are followed by a single space and no capital letter.) A semicolon combines two independent clauses within the boundary of a single sentence. In other words, semicolons correctly accomplish the same goal that run-ons do incorrectly—they keep closely related ideas together within the same sentence. Here are the two example sentences correctly punctuated with semicolons. We have used the Imaginary Period Tip to make certain each clause is independent.

EXAMPLE 1:   ✗ I did pretty well on the last test I got an 82.

TIP APPLIED: I did pretty well on the last test. I got an 82.

CORRECTION: I did pretty well on the last test; I got an 82.
                                                   ^

EXAMPLE 2:   ✗ The next test will be tougher, we're right to be worried about it.

TIP APPLIED: The next test will be tougher. We're right to be worried about it.

CORRECTION: The next test will be tougher ~~,~~/; we're right to be
                                                      ^
               worried about it.

Sentence Practice 1

CORRECTED SENTENCES APPEAR ON PAGE 471.

Find the independent clauses in the following run-on sentences by using either the Imaginary Period Tip or the *I Realize* Tip. Correct each run-on by inserting a semicolon between the two independent clauses or by adding a comma and a coordinating conjunction. If a sentence does not contain a run-on, write *OK* above it.

EXAMPLE: My friend owns two pigs he keeps them as house pets.

IMAGINARY PERIOD TIP: My friend owns two pigs. He keeps them as house pets.

I REALIZE TIP: *I realize* my friend owns two pigs. *I realize* he keeps them as house pets.

CORRECTION: My friend owns two pigs; he keeps them as house pets.

1. Colleen called me today, she wants to know if I can help her with her homework.

2. London was the first city to have a population of over one million, it reached that milestone in 1811.

3. My son wants to buy a snake, his mother is not happy about the idea.

4. The mascot for Yale is now a bulldog, its mascot over a hundred years ago was a cat.

5. Columbia was once considered part of South America, its government decided in 1903 to proclaim Columbia was part of North America.

For more practice correcting run-ons, go to **Exercise Central** at **bedfordstmartins.com/commonsense/1-2**.

Sentence Practice 2

CORRECTED SENTENCES APPEAR ON PAGE 471.

Find the independent clauses in the following run-on sentences by using either the Imaginary Period Tip or the *I Realize* Tip. Correct each run-on by inserting a semicolon between the two independent clauses or by adding a comma and a coordinating conjunction. If a sentence does not contain a run-on, write *OK* above it.

EXAMPLE: Susan has a portrait above her desk, it is her
daughter.

IMAGINARY
PERIOD TIP: Susan has a portrait above her desk. It is her
daughter.

I REALIZE TIP: *I realize* Susan has a portrait above her desk. *I realize*
it is her daughter.

CORRECTION: Susan has a portrait above her desk; it is her
daughter.

1. When Benita first decided to go to college, her parents insisted that
she go to SUNY Potsdam.

2. The first home TV set was demonstrated in 1928, it measured only
three inches by four inches.

3. The street lights in the city of Hershey look strange, they resemble
Hershey's chocolate kisses.

4. I read *Naked Lunch,* which is a controversial book by William
Burroughs.

5. The book was originally titled *Naked Lust,* the name changed because
a friend could not read Burroughs's handwriting.

Sentence Practice 3

Combine each pair of sentences by attaching the second sentence to the first
with a comma and an appropriate coordinating conjunction (*for, and, nor,
but, or, yet, so*).

EXAMPLE: My sister plans to go to college next year.
She is sending out dozens of applications now.

ANSWER: My sister plans to go to college next year. ~~She~~ *, so she* is
sending out dozens of applications now.

1. A fire alarm went off today. This blessed event postponed my geology
test.

2. There was not a fire. It was just a prank.

3. My radio seems broken. Perhaps it just needs new batteries.

4. Ernest Hemingway frequently revised his writing. He supposedly rewrote the last page of *A Farewell to Arms* thirty-nine times.

5. The first American novel to sell over a million copies was *Uncle Tom's Cabin*. It was published in 1852.

Editing Practice 1

CORRECTED SENTENCES APPEAR ON PAGE 471.

Correct all run-on errors in the following paragraph using the first correction as a model. The number in parentheses at the end of the paragraph indicates how many errors you should find.

Sausage is a popular food around the globe; it has been around for
                                                    ^
centuries. Nobody knows for sure who first thought of stuffing ground

meat into a casing to form what we now call "sausage." Over 3,500

years ago, the Babylonians made sausage, the ancient poet Homer

referred to sausage in his classic work *The Odyssey*. Romans were par-

ticularly fond of sausages they made them from ground pork and pine

nuts. In fact, the word *sausage* comes from the Latin word *salsus* it is

roughly translated as "salty." One Roman ruler thought sausages were

divine, he would not permit the lower classes to eat them. (4)

Editing Practice 2

CORRECTED SENTENCES APPEAR ON PAGE 472.

Correct all run-on errors in the following paragraphs using the first correction as a model. The number in parentheses at the end of each paragraph indicates how many errors you should find.

                                                  , but
My cousin has never been the overly romantic type recently he
                                                        ^
put on quite a presentation when he proposed to his girlfriend. He did

so on her birthday he put the ring inside a toy packet that he placed in a Cap'n Crunch box. It took a bit of effort to get her to open the cereal box and wade through the cereal to the "toy surprise" inside. He carefully timed the proceedings, he wanted to be sure that she found the ring during halftime of the Dallas Cowboys game on TV he was also sure to be reclining in his armchair. (3)

When she found the ring, he gallantly hit the mute button for the TV, he said that he would like for her to be his wife. The ring, by the way, was not a real wedding ring it was a plastic ring with a tiny boot jingling from it. She took it all in stride she knew he was just trying to make the event memorable by adding some humor. I suppose she appreciated his humor, she never did give him an answer. (4)

Editing Practice 3

Correct all run-on errors in the following paragraphs using the first correction as a model. The number in parentheses at the end of each paragraph indicates how many errors you should find.

Politeness is not as simple as it may seem; it certainly goes beyond table manners. Some language researchers argue that politeness is a way to show people that we approve of them or that we are not trying to tell them what to do or think. These researchers have studied diverse cultures and found that such politeness is a worldwide phenomenon, it is central to the human experience. (1)

Politeness is often subtle it does not have to be an explicit "thank you" or "please." For instance, consider how you ask somebody to close a door you might say, "Will you close the door?" The question is not a demand, it is simply a request for information. The listener knows your real point but does not have to feel that he or she is being ordered around. (3)

Writing Practice

On your own paper, write a paragraph or two describing someone's politeness (or rudeness). Try to use several sentences containing two complete ideas. Use the Editing Checklist to see whether each sentence you wrote is punctuated correctly.

Editing Checklist

Identify Run-ons in Your Writing

____ If a sentence contains two ideas, insert an imaginary period between them. The sentence is a run-on if the two ideas can stand alone as independent clauses.

____ After inserting an imaginary period, put *I realize* in front of each sentence to confirm that each is an independent clause.

Correct Run-ons in Your Writing

____ Join two independent clauses with a semicolon or with a comma and a coordinating conjunction.

____ Or, separate two independent clauses by using a period and making each into a separate sentence.

The Bottom Line

If you combine two sentences, use the appropriate punctuation to separate the two ideas; a semicolon is one way to do so.

UNIT ONE: Understanding the Basic Sentence

To write effectively, you must be able to recognize and correctly punctuate basic sentences. Every basic sentence has these components:

- a subject and verb

- a self-contained, complete idea

Another term for a basic sentence is an independent clause. This unit presented two ways in which writers mispunctuate basic sentences.

Fragments

Fragment errors rarely occur in isolation. A fragment is usually a continuation of the preceding sentence. Fragments, especially in your own writing, are hard to spot unless you can see them in isolation from the preceding sentence. Use these tips to help you identify fragments in your writing:

LIKELY FRAGMENTS TIP: Most fragments fall into one of these three categories: *Renamers, Adverbs,* and *-ing Fragments.* If you are aware of what the most common types of fragments are, you are more likely to spot them when you are proofreading.

BACKWARD PROOFREADING TIP: Proofread your paper backward, one sentence at a time. Use one hand to cover up all but the last sentence in each paragraph. See if that sentence can stand alone. If it can, then uncover the next-to-last sentence to see if it can stand alone, and so forth.

The final tip is probably the best way to actually test a sentence to see if it is really an independent clause or a fragment:

I REALIZE **TIP:** You can put *I realize* in front of most complete sentences and make a new grammatical sentence. However, when you put *I realize* in front of a fragment, the result will not make sense.

There are two ways to correct a fragment. The simplest way is to attach the fragment to the preceding sentence. Another way, if the idea within the fragment deserves emphasis, is to make it into an independent clause and punctuate it as a sentence.

Run-ons

Run-ons result from joining two independent clauses into one sentence without correct punctuation. Here is a tip to help you to spot run-ons:

> **IMAGINARY PERIOD TIP:** If a sentence contains two separate ideas, put an imaginary period between them. Now ask: Can BOTH parts that are divided by this imaginary period stand alone as complete sentences? If both new sentences can stand alone, then the sentence is a run-on.

To confirm that there really are two independent clauses in a sentence, apply the *I Realize* Tip from Lesson 1.

Once you have identified a run-on, you can correct it by separating the two independent clauses with a period, a semicolon, or a comma and a coordinating conjunction.

Review Test

Correct fragment and run-on errors in the following paragraphs using the first correction as a model. The number in parentheses at the end of each paragraph indicates how many errors you should find.

I read an article on washing clothes. ~~After~~ *after* I shrank an expensive sweater. I thought I could just toss everything in the washer. Without checking the color or type of fabric. I learned a valuable lesson I just wish it hadn't been such an expensive lesson, though. (2)

Most items made of heavy cotton can be washed in very hot water, they won't shrink. It is best if white cotton items are washed by themselves. Because they can pick up colors from other things being washed. Lightweight cottons do best in warm water. Unless they are dark colors. Which always require cold water. (4)

Badly soiled laundry needs to be washed in very hot water. Unless the garment label says otherwise. That is how I ruined my sweater, I simply didn't know to look at its label. (2)

UNIT TWO
Expanding the Basic Sentence

Terms That Can Help You Expand the Basic Sentence

If you are not familiar with any of the following terms, look them up in the Guide to Grammar Terminology beginning on page 1. The numbers in parentheses indicate the lessons in which each term appears.

adverb clause (5)   run-on (3)
conjunctive adverb (3)   subordinate clause (5)
coordinating conjunction (3, 4)   subordinating conjunction (5)
independent clause (3)

The Nuts and Bolts of Expanding the Basic Sentence

This unit will help you expand the basic sentence with multiple clauses and correctly punctuate multiple-clause sentences. A basic sentence contains only a single independent clause—a clause that expresses a single, complete idea and can stand alone. This unit presents three different ways of combining clauses to produce more sophisticated sentences—sentences that connect or relate two ideas. Each way has its own punctuation rules.

Lesson 3 shows you how to combine two independent clauses with a comma and a coordinating conjunction. This is the simplest and most common way to link two ideas together. Here is an example:

BASIC SENTENCE 1:   Thelma drove the car.

BASIC SENTENCE 2:   Louise read the road map.

COMBINED   Thelma drove the car, **and** Louise read the
SENTENCES: road map.

Lesson 4 shows you how to punctuate transitional terms. A transitional term (often called a conjunctive adverb) clarifies the relationship between two ideas. Below is an example involving two ideas that are separated by a semicolon. The transitional term (*therefore*) helps readers understand just how closely connected these two ideas are.

BASIC SENTENCE 1:	Thelma drove the car.
BASIC SENTENCE 2:	She decided where they went.
COMBINED SENTENCES:	Thelma drove the car; **therefore,** she decided where they went.

Lesson 5 shows you how to combine two clauses when one clause begins with a subordinating conjunction. Here is an example:

BASIC SENTENCE 1:	Thelma was the only one who knew how to shift.
BASIC SENTENCE 2:	She drove the car.
COMBINED SENTENCES:	**Because** Thelma was the only one who knew how to shift, she drove the car.

Can you detect problems with multiple-clause sentences?

CORRECTED SENTENCES APPEAR ON PAGE 472.

Correct punctuation problems in the following paragraphs using the first correction as a model. The number in parentheses at the end of each paragraph indicates how many errors you should find.

Linguists have long noted that children learn their native language at about the same age,/ and in quite similar ways. Although linguists do not fully understand the reason they do know that children go through distinct stages. The early laughing and babbling stages seem like imitations of adult language yet they are largely innate. Because even profoundly deaf children laugh and babble just like hearing children researchers conclude that the early language stages are at least partially genetic. (3)

When children are around eighteen months they produce their first truly meaningful words. Around two years many children combine pairs of words to form what are called "two-word" sentences. Although the grammar of "two-word" sentences differs substantially from adult grammar the grammar of children's "two-word" sentences is quite stable and regular. Some children stay at the "two-word" stage for months, and are able to express quite complex ideas, however there is no such thing as a "three-word" or "four-word" grammar stage. When children break out of the "two-word" stage they jump directly to a simplified form of the adult language. (6)

LESSON 3

Commas with *And, But, Or,* and Other Coordinating Conjunctions

Error Sentences

CORRECTED SENTENCES APPEAR ON PAGE 41.

EXAMPLE 1: ✗ Derek finally finished writing his book of poems but his publisher was not satisfied.

EXAMPLE 2: ✗ A moose wandered into town, and scared several kids.

What's the Problem?

Coordinating conjunctions are the most common way of joining two **independent clauses** (see Lesson 1 for tips on identifying independent clauses). There are seven coordinating conjunctions. The easiest way to remember them is by the acronym FANBOYS: *for, and, nor, but, or, yet, so.*

Coordinating conjunctions, or FANBOYS, are punctuated in two different ways depending on what the conjunctions join. When one of the FANBOYS joins two complete independent clauses, put a comma in front of it. In Example 1, *but* joins two independent clauses, but the comma has been left out. When one of the FANBOYS joins just parts of sentences, do not use a comma. This is the problem in Example 2, where a comma is mistakenly used with *and* when what follows — *scared several kids* — is only part of a complete sentence and cannot stand alone.

What Causes the Problem?

Writers use commas with coordinating conjunctions depending on whether the FANBOYS join complete sentences or just parts of sentences. The problem, of course, is that first you have to figure out what the FANBOYS join together — complete sentences or just parts of sentences — before you know whether or not to use a comma.

Diagnostic Exercise

CORRECTED SENTENCES APPEAR ON PAGE 472.

Correct all comma errors in the following paragraph using the first correction as a model. The number in parentheses at the end of the paragraph indicates how many errors you should find.

When he reached the Americas, Christopher Columbus believed he had reached the East Indies, so he called the people that he found *Indians.* That term is still used but many indigenous people prefer the term *Native Americans.* We tend to think of Native Americans as a group yet that is really a mistake because there are vast differences in their cultures and languages. We tend to think of the tribes from the plains as being the typical Native Americans for those are the tribes we see represented in movies, and on TV. The plains tribes hunted buffalo, and lived in tepees but northwest coastal tribes never saw a buffalo or a tepee in their lives. Instead, hunted whales, and lived in wooden houses. (7)

Fixing This Problem in Your Writing

The following tip helps determine whether you can correctly use a comma with the FANBOYS:

IMAGINARY PERIOD TIP: Test each use of FANBOYS by putting an imaginary period right before it. Can BOTH parts that are divided by this imaginary period now stand alone as complete sentences? If both new sentences can stand alone, use a comma with the FANBOYS. If either one of the parts is not a complete sentence, then do not use a comma with the FANBOYS.

You may have heard that it is ungrammatical to begin a sentence with a coordinating conjunction (for example, *And she landed a great job after college*), but that is not always true. Many skillful writers use periods with coordinating conjunctions for emphasis, especially with *but* and *yet*. However, as with any technique for adding extra emphasis, use it sparingly. The normal and expected punctuation for two independent clauses joined by a coordinating conjunction is a comma.

Here is how the Imaginary Period Tip can be applied to the two example sentences:

EXAMPLE 1:   ✗ Derek finally finished writing his book of poems but his publisher was not satisfied.

TIP APPLIED: Derek finally finished writing his book of poems. But his publisher was not satisfied.

CORRECTION: Derek finally finished writing his book of poems, but his publisher was not satisfied.

The Imaginary Period Tip confirms that *but* is used with two independent clauses. Correct the sentence to show their relationship by joining the clauses with a comma.

Now turn to the second example sentence:

EXAMPLE 2:   ✗ A moose wandered into town, and scared several kids.

TIP APPLIED: A moose wandered into town. ✗ And scared several kids.

CORRECTION: A moose wandered into town, and scared several kids.

The Imaginary Period Tip shows that *and* is not used with two independent clauses. Therefore, do not use a comma with *and*.

Sentence Practice 1

CORRECTED SENTENCES APPEAR ON PAGE 472.

Correct the comma errors in the following sentences. If there is no error, write *OK* above the sentence. Confirm your corrections by applying the Imaginary Period Tip.

EXAMPLE: *This paper is torn. But can still be used for scratch paper.*
     This paper is torn, but can still be used for scratch paper.

coord

1. Pig iron is refined in a blast furnace, and contains iron along with small amounts of manganese and other minerals.

2. Mata Hari was a famous spy for Germany in World War I, but she was born in Holland.

3. Tom decided he would walk to class, but changed his mind when it started raining.

4. You should return this book to the library, or you can renew it by phone.

5. John Glenn was the first American astronaut to orbit the planet and Scott Carpenter was the second.

For more practice using commas, go to **Exercise Central** at **bedfordstmartins.com/commonsense/2-3**.

Sentence Practice 2

CORRECTED SENTENCES APPEAR ON PAGE 473.

Correct the comma errors in the following sentences. If there is no error, write *OK* above the sentence. Confirm your corrections by applying the Imaginary Period Tip.

My friend Al didn't need a car. Nor could he afford one.
EXAMPLE: My friend Al didn't need a car, nor could he afford one.
                                                         ^

ESL

[Non-native speakers of English will notice the odd fact that after the coordinating conjunction *nor* the subject and verb are reversed—*could he* rather than *he could*. This is grammatically correct. Be sure, however, to use a comma before *nor* when *nor* joins two independent clauses.]

1. Jeremy did not arrive on time today, nor did he arrive on time yesterday.

2. This paper is torn, yet I can still use it for scratch paper.

3. My father bought an old sword in England but he paid too much.

4. Jan asked me if I would loan her my notes, and I was more than happy to help.

5.   Tony is dropping by my place to deliver a message and I suppose I should clean up a bit.

Sentence Practice 3

Combine each pair of sentences using a coordinating conjunction of your choice. If you want to keep both as independent clauses, you must use a comma with the coordinating conjunction. If you reduce one of the sentences to less than an independent clause, do not use a comma with the coordinating conjunction. See if you can combine them both ways.

EXAMPLE: My hat doesn't fit very well.
It keeps falling off when I ride my bike.

ANSWER: My hat doesn't fit very well, **so** it keeps falling off when I ride my bike.
My hat doesn't fit very well **and** keeps falling off when I ride my bike.

1.   Jack brought his cell phone. He does not have it turned on.

2.   Florida is the flattest state. It's highest and lowest points differ by only 345 feet.

3.   This desk is too big. That one is too small.

4.   My sociology teacher told us never to be late. He comes in late every day.

5.   Texas leads the nation in averaging over 120 tornadoes a year. Oklahoma averages about 56 a year.

Editing Practice 1

CORRECTED SENTENCES APPEAR ON PAGE 473.

Correct all errors involving commas and coordinating conjunctions in the following paragraph using the first correction as a model. The number in parentheses at the end of the paragraph indicates how many errors you should find.

Writing is a form of visible language, but there is a form of
                                                       ^
writing that is not meant to be seen. Braille is written as a series of dots

or bumps so visually impaired people can "read" it with their fingers. It is written as a series of cells and each cell contains dots that can be variously arranged. Each particular arrangement of dots has its own meaning but what the dots represent depends on the style of Braille. There are two forms of Braille: Grade 1, and Grade 2. Grade 1 Braille is a system in which the dots represent letters, and some very short words. Grade 2 Braille is not a completely different system but it is a shorthand version of Grade 1 that is much harder to read. (6)

Editing Practice 2

CORRECTED SENTENCES APPEAR ON PAGE 473.

Correct all errors involving commas and coordinating conjunctions in the following paragraph using the first correction as a model. The number in parentheses at the end of the paragraph indicates how many errors you should find.

Humans appear to be the only animals to use language naturally, but there is much about language we may never know. People have come up with various theories. There is no way to prove or disprove these theories so they are more a curiosity than a scientific hypothesis, and have acquired nicknames befitting their status. According to the "bow-wow" theory, speech began as imitation of animal sounds, or cries. All languages have sounds that imitate animal sounds yet these words are so isolated from the rest of vocabulary that it is hard to attach much significance to them. The "pooh-pooh" theory is the name for the theory that speech arose from instinctive noises resulting from pain, or fear. For instance, a gasp or cry of fear may have been the primitive beginnings of words used to express those emotions but again these words are too marginal to be the basis of our language system. (6)

Editing Practice 3

Correct all errors involving commas and coordinating conjunctions in the following paragraph using the first correction as a model. The number in parentheses at the end of the paragraph indicates how many errors you should find.

I still have much to learn about using a computer‚ but my computer skills have improved over the last couple of years. I once used the computer as a glorified typewriter, and knew very little about spreadsheets and graphics programs. Most of the time, all I did was word processing so I became pretty good at it. At first, I did not even know how to use the spell-checking function but now I can't imagine writing without it. It took a long time for me to get good at word processing for I didn't have anybody around who could show me. As a result, I am very happy to teach others, and have even gotten paid for it occasionally. I do all my work on computers now and I honestly believe that my writing is better because I can revise, and edit so much more efficiently. (7)

Writing Practice

On your own paper, write a paragraph or two describing your experiences with or attitudes toward computers. Try to include five sentences that join independent clauses with coordinating conjunctions and commas. Use the Editing Checklist to see whether each sentence is punctuated correctly.

Editing Checklist

Identify Errors in Using Coordinating Conjunctions in Your Writing

_____ Put an imaginary period before each coordinating conjunction (the FANBOYS) to create possible new sentences.

_____ Check to see if both newly created sentences can stand alone.

Correct Errors in Using Coordinating Conjunctions in Your Writing

_____ If both can stand alone, then use a comma in front of the coordinating conjunction.

_____ If neither one can stand alone, then do not use a comma.

The Bottom Line

See whether what comes before *and, but,* or *or* can stand alone, **and** do the same with what comes after *and, but,* or *or.*

LESSON 4
Punctuating Transitional Terms

Error Sentences

CORRECTED SENTENCES APPEAR ON PAGE 50.

EXAMPLE 1: ✗ The Hope diamond may be the best-known large diamond, however, the Culliman diamond was even larger.

EXAMPLE 2: ✗ In 1972, the Miami Dolphins won all their football games in their regular season. ✗ <u>Furthermore</u> they won all their playoff games.

What's the Problem?

Transitional terms (sometimes called **conjunctive adverbs**) are words such as *furthermore* and *however*. Transitional terms usually consist of one word, although they can also consist of more than one (as with *in fact* and *for instance*). These terms have little meaning by themselves, but they are important "signpost" words that allow readers to see a connection between two ideas. At times, these two ideas are in separate sentences. At other times, the two ideas are in one sentence that uses a semicolon to separate the ideas. Either way, transitional terms make it clear how one idea relates to a preceding one.

Transitional terms can lead to two types of punctuation problems. Example 1 illustrates the most significant problem: a comma splice (see Lesson 2). As seen in Example 1, a transitional term—even if it has commas around it—*cannot* be used to separate what could be two separate sentences. A semicolon (or even a period) could be used in place of the comma before *however* to avoid the error, but a transitional term does not take the place of the appropriate punctuation. In fact, you could eliminate *however* altogether and still use the semicolon to avoid the comma splice.

The second type of problem is far less severe: the omission of commas around transitional terms that do not separate independent clauses. In formal writing, transitional terms are usually set off by commas unless doing so would create an error such as seen in Example 1. Normally, you should place a comma at least after the transitional term. In Example 2 *furthermore* lacks a comma after it. If *furthermore* appeared in the middle of the sentence, this term would require a comma before and after it.

What Causes the Problem?

Writers make mistakes in punctuating transitional terms for several reasons. First, some of these terms seem to have the same meaning as **coordinating conjunctions**. For instance, the transitional term *however* means about the same thing as the coordinating conjunction *but*. The problem is that *but* and other coordinating conjunctions (such as *and*) can be used with just a comma to separate what could be two sentences. Transitional terms such as *however* cannot be used with a comma to separate sentences. People who confuse coordinating conjunctions with transitional terms create errors such as Example 1. Some writers also create errors when they mistakenly assume that all transitional terms must have a comma before them. It is extremely important to remember that a comma should *not* be placed before these terms if doing so would create a comma splice.

In terms of errors such as Example 2 that omit commas, handbooks and teachers do not always agree on whether it is necessary to set off all transitional terms with commas. Although hardly any teacher would approve of Example 1, some do not consider Example 2 a problem because *furthermore* seems to "flow" into the rest of the sentence. Writers can, as a result, easily be confused by this lack of consistency.

We suggest using commas because they draw attention to the transitional words, thus helping readers make connections between two ideas. Most teachers, in addition, seem to prefer the more formal guideline of using commas whenever possible with transitional terms.

Diagnostic Exercise

CORRECTED SENTENCES APPEAR ON PAGE 473.

Correct all errors involving transitional terms in the following paragraph using the first correction as a model. The number in parentheses at the end of the paragraph indicates how many errors you should find. (Only one error per transitional term—semicolon and comma errors are not counted separately.)

Many places around the globe have universal appeal. They

are, however, not necessarily accessible to the general public. An
     ^   ^

international committee has designated some sites as World Heritage

Sites that have international value and responsibility. In the United States for example the committee chose Yosemite Park and the Statue of Liberty. Both of these sites are part of our national parks system. We tend to take our national parks system for granted, however, it is really quite unusual. Very few developed countries have extensive public land, consequently their important public sites are little more than individual buildings. The vast size of some national parks in the American West make them unique, therefore they have attracted visitors from every country. (4)

Lesson 4

trans

Fixing This Problem in Your Writing

As noted, the safest approach is to use commas to set off transitional words. However, you first must be able to recognize them. Here is a chart that lists the more common ones grouped into four categories according to their meaning.

TRANSITIONAL TERMS

In addition	**Example**	**On the other hand**	**As a result**
again	for example	however	accordingly
also	for instance	nevertheless	consequently
besides	in fact	nonetheless	subsequently
further(more)		otherwise	thus
likewise		still	therefore
moreover		instead	
similarly			

Look for such words that establish a relationship between two ideas (such as two sentences or two **independent clauses**). Then, use this next tip to determine if indeed it is a transitional term.

MOVEMENT TIP FOR TRANSITIONAL TERMS: A transitional term can always be moved around (or even deleted). The term can begin a clause or be moved to the end. Sometimes, the term can be placed in the middle of the sentence or independent clause in which it appears.

Lesson 4

trans

ESL

If a word establishing a relationship between ideas can be moved around, it is probably a transitional word. Coordinating conjunctions such as *but* and *or cannot* be moved. Words such as *because* and *while* also cannot be moved around, despite seeming similar in some ways to transitional terms. Thus, the Movement Tip helps determine what is a transitional term.

How do you know *where* a transitional term can be moved in a sentence? Unfortunately, it is difficult to find a rule on this matter. A native speaker of English can usually rely on intuition about what "sounds right," but a non-native speaker may have to consult with a native speaker to see where a transitional term can be moved.

Once you have determined a word is a transitional term, make sure you do not create a comma splice in using it. In other words, use a semicolon before the term if it separates what could be one sentence from what could be another sentence. However, avoid leaving out commas completely. Normally, a comma goes after the transitional term. If the term is in the middle of an independent clause, put a comma before and after the term.

Here is how the Movement Tip can be applied to the example sentences:

EXAMPLE 1:   ✗ The Hope diamond may be the best-known large diamond, however, the Culliman diamond was even larger.

TIP APPLIED: ✗ The Hope diamond may be the best-known large diamond**; however,** the Culliman diamond was even larger.
...; the Culliman diamond, **however,** was even larger.
...; the Culliman diamond was even larger, **however.**
(All three versions are correct as long as a semicolon is used.)

EXAMPLE 2:   In 1972, the Miami Dolphins won all their football games in their regular season. ✗ Furthermore they won all their playoff games.

TIP APPLIED: **Furthermore,** they won all their playoff games.
They won, **furthermore,** all their playoff games.
They won all their playoff games, **furthermore.**
(Each version is technically correct, although the last one might seem too formal or even awkward.)

Because the boldfaced terms can be proven to be transitional terms, they cannot be used to combine sentences, as was done in Example 1. However, the transitional terms in both examples should be set off with at least one comma.

Sentence Practice 1

CORRECTED SENTENCES APPEAR ON PAGE 473.

Underline the transitional terms in the following sentences, and punctuate each sentence correctly. Confirm your answer by moving the transitional term to another position in its clause. If the sentence contains no transitional terms, write *none* above the sentence.

	none
EXAMPLE:	In the early 1800's, Tecumseh roused most tribes east of the Mississippi in an attempt to drive out the whites.
	His forces, however, were defeated by General Harrison.
CONFIRMATION:	However, his forces were defeated by General Harrison.

1. Bill said he might be late. Indeed he was four hours late.

2. Little is known about the Pilgrim ship *Mayflower;* we do know however that it weighed about 180 tons.

3. English is the predominate language in the United States, nevertheless, over 300 languages are spoken within its borders.

4. The oldest known weapon is a broken spear found in Great Britain; it is estimated to have been made around 200,000 B.C.

5. A serious accident has caused major delays. In fact some commuters have decided to stay home.

 For more practice using transitional terms, go to **Exercise Central** at **bedfordstmartins.com/commonsense/2-4**.

Sentence Practice 2

CORRECTED SENTENCES APPEAR ON PAGE 474.

trans

Underline the transitional terms in the following sentences, and punctuate each sentence correctly. Confirm your answer by moving the transitional term to another position in its clause. If the sentence contains no transitional terms, write *none* above the sentence.

EXAMPLE: Most fans believe a football team must have a coach,/; nonetheless, the Chicago Bears won the 1943 championship without a head coach.

CONFIRMATION: Most fans believe a football team must have a coach; the Chicago Bears, nonetheless, won the 1943 championship without a head coach.

1.   Sean Connery is remembered most for his James Bond movies. However he won an Oscar for a different role in *The Untouchables.*

2.   Scott Joplin wrote over sixty musical compositions. He wrote for instance an opera entitled *Treemonisha.*

3.   Some people consider Scotland part of England, but both are part of the United Kingdom.

4.   The top position in the British army is field marshal. The top position in its navy in contrast is admiral of the fleet.

5.   The singer Prince has gone by more than one name, for example, his birth name is Prince Rogers Nelson.

Sentence Practice 3

Combine the two short sentences with a semicolon and an appropriate transitional term (see the list on page 49). Underline the transitional term.

EXAMPLE: My parents want me to major in accounting.
I want to major in drama.

ANSWER: My parents want me to major in accounting; however, I want to major in drama.

1. The doctors diagnosed the problem.
   They were able to recommend a treatment.

2. There has been a 20 percent increase in fertilizer use.
   Food production has increased substantially.

3. The legislature has set new limits on enrollments.
   Each school must reassess its admission policies.

4. The experiment had failed.
   It had damaged the equipment badly.

5. The witch had frightened Dorothy and her friends.
   They decided to continue their trip.

Editing Practice 1

CORRECTED SENTENCES APPEAR ON PAGE 474.

Correctly punctuate all transitional terms in the following paragraphs using
the first correction as a model. The number in parentheses at the end of each
paragraph indicates how many errors you should find.

  My friend Collette is moving to Oakland, California, *consequently* ~~consequently~~

she wants to fix up her house and sell it. My wife said that we should

help her because we owed her a favor. Her realtor advised her to

repaint the living room, moreover, she needed to have the carpets

cleaned professionally. She also said that the kitchen was the

room that made the biggest impression on potential buyers,

therefore we need to spend most of our time making it more

attractive. (2)

  The biggest task was working on the cabinets, therefore we began

by taking them apart. The shelves were in good shape, however they

needed to be stripped and cleaned. We replaced all the cabinet knobs with ceramic ones, then we had to get matching handles for the drawers. The biggest job was cleaning the appliances, for example we had to completely disassemble the range and clean every single part. We really got tired of the whole project, nevertheless we knew that all our hard work would really make a difference in selling the house. (5)

Editing Practice 2

CORRECTED SENTENCES APPEAR ON PAGE 474.

Correctly punctuate all transitional terms in the following paragraphs using the first correction as a model. The number in parentheses at the end of each paragraph indicates how many errors you should find.

Americans are proud of their political history,/; nonetheless, there are some unpleasant episodes. One particularly troubling aspect is the many attempts to kill presidents, for example we all know about the assassinations of Presidents Lincoln and Kennedy. These are the only two assassinations that most Americans know about, in fact there were two other assassinations of sitting presidents: Presidents Garfield in 1881 and McKinley in 1901. More recently, two men tried to shoot their way into a house where President Truman was staying, however their plot failed when one was killed by a guard. (3)

One might think that assassinations of political leaders are political acts, in fact most assassinations of American presidents were apparently individually motivated. Lee Harvey Oswald, who assassinated President Kennedy, was deeply disturbed, likewise

John Hinkley, who attempted to assassinate President Reagan, was mentally ill. The most extreme example is John Schrank, who attempted to assassinate President Theodore Roosevelt. Schrank appeared to be delusional, moreover he said that McKinley's ghost had told him to kill Roosevelt. (3)

Editing Practice 3

Correctly punctuate all transitional terms in the following paragraphs using the first correction as a model. The number in parentheses at the end of each paragraph indicates how many errors you should find.

Empanadas are a South American meat pie**/;** however some historians argue that empanadas originated in the Middle East centuries ago. From there, they spread to southern Europe, then they were introduced into the Western Hemisphere by the conquistadors in the fifteenth century. Empanadas may have a single origin, nevertheless they take quite different forms in different countries. They tend to make use of local ingredients, for example in Central America corn is used, but in Spain and Portugal wheat is used. (3)

Empanadas are usually filled with meat or fish, however some people prefer vegetable filling. There are great differences in seasonings, consequently empanadas vary quite a bit from place to place. All empanadas tend to be rather highly spiced, for example many people season them with paprika, chili powder, and black pepper. No matter how they are filled, empanadas are all baked or fried, moreover they are all delicious. (4)

Writing Practice

On your own paper, write a paragraph or two describing one of your favorite foods or meals. Try to use at least four transitional terms. Use the Editing Checklist to make sure that the transitional terms are properly punctuated.

Editing Checklist

Identify Transitional Terms in Your Writing

____ Look for words that establish a clear connection between two ideas.

____ Check to see if you can move the word (or words) around in the sentence. If so, they are probably transitional terms.

Correct Errors in Punctuating Transitional Terms in Your Writing

____ Use a semicolon before a transitional term *if* (and only if) what comes *before* and what comes *after* could each be separate sentences. Also, place a comma right after the transitional term.

____ In other instances, set off a transitional term with at least one comma.

The Bottom Line

A transitional term helps readers understand the relationship between independent clauses, however, you should use at least one comma and sometimes a semicolon along with the transitional term.

LESSON 5

Punctuating Adverb Clauses

Error Sentences

CORRECTED SENTENCES APPEAR ON PAGE 59.

EXAMPLE 1: ✗ Whenever I need to go shopping I take the car to work.

EXAMPLE 2: ✗ You can't get onto the Internet, until the network is repaired.

What's the Problem?

An adverb clause is a **dependent clause** that answers the question *when, where, why,* or *to what degree* about the verb in a sentence. Dependent clauses can never stand alone; they must always be attached to an independent clause. Adverb clauses have one unique feature that sets them apart from all other clauses, independent or dependent: Adverb clauses can be inverted. That is, they can be moved from their normal position following the independent clause to a position preceding the independent clause. When this happens, they are called "introductory" or "inverted" clauses and must be set off from the rest of the sentence with a comma. This explains the problem in Example 1. *Whenever I need to go shopping* should be followed by a comma and then the independent clause *I take the car to work.* When an adverb clause follows the independent clause, it should not be set off with a comma. In Example 2, the writer has incorrectly placed a comma after the independent clause.

What Causes the Problem?

Some writers get confused because there is no rule requiring that writers should *always* use commas or *never* use commas with adverb clauses. What's important is the position of the adverb clause in the sentence. In a sentence that begins with an introductory adverb clause, the comma signals the reader where the introductory adverb clause ends and the main clause begins. When the adverb clause follows the main clause, no comma is needed because the adverb clause appears in the normal adverb position at the end of the sentence. In other words, adverb clauses require commas only when they are not in their normal position in a sentence.

Diagnostic Exercise

CORRECTED SENTENCES APPEAR ON PAGE 474.

Correct all errors involving adverb clauses in the following paragraph using the first correction as a model. The number in parentheses at the end of the paragraph indicates how many errors you should find.

After everybody was asleep Monday night‚ there was a fire in the
                                                   ^
dorm next door. Fortunately, a smoke-detector went off, when smoke

got into the staircase. While the fire department was fighting the fire

six rooms were totally destroyed. A friend of mine in another part of

the building lost all her clothing, because of the smoke and water

damage. If school officials close down the dorm she will have to find a

new place to live. I heard they will make a decision tomorrow, as soon

as they get a report from the fire inspectors. (5)

Fixing This Problem in Your Writing

The first step in correcting problems with adverb clauses is to identify them in your writing. Adverb clauses begin with **subordinating conjunctions**. Here is a list of the most common ones grouped according to meaning:

SUBORDINATING CONJUNCTIONS

Cause	**Condition**	**Contrast**	**Place**	**Time**
as	as if	although	where	after
because	assuming that	even though	wherever	as soon as
since	if	though		before
so that	in case			since
	unless			until
	when			when
	whether			whenever

Here is a reliable tip for identifying adverb clauses:

> **ADVERB CLAUSE MOVEMENT TIP:** If it is a clause and if you can move it, then it has to be an adverb clause. Adverb clauses are the only type of clause that can be moved from one part of the sentence to another.

Keep in mind that the use of commas depends on where the adverb clause is. If the adverb clause is in its normal position at the end of the sentence, do not use a comma. However, if the adverb clause has been inverted and placed at the beginning of the sentence, then be sure to set it off with a comma to show the reader where the independent clause begins.

EXAMPLE 1: ✗ Whenever I need to go shopping I take the car to work.

TIP APPLIED: I take the car to work whenever I need to go shopping.

We know that *Whenever I need to go shopping* is an adverb clause because it can be moved. Now, look at the position. If the adverb clause begins the sentence, set it off with a comma.

CORRECTION: Whenever I need to go shopping, I take the car to work.

EXAMPLE 2: ✗ You can't get onto the Internet, until the network is repaired.

TIP APPLIED: Until the network is repaired, you can't get onto the Internet.

If an adverb clause follows the independent clause, do not set it off with a comma.

CORRECTION: You can't get onto the Internet,/ until the network is repaired.

Sometimes rules have exceptions. There is one type of adverb clause that should *always* be set off with a comma no matter where it appears in a sentence.

> **CONTRAST TIP:** If an adverb clause conveys a sense of contrast by using the subordinating conjunctions *although, even though,* or *though,* the adverb clause must always be set off with a comma even if it is at the end of the sentence.

Here are examples of sentences containing these three subordinating conjunctions:

> EXAMPLE: We decided to stop for the night, **although** it was still pretty early.

> EXAMPLE: I didn't like the movie, **even though** everybody else thought it was terrific.

> EXAMPLE: I stayed up watching *The Late Show,* **though** I had a test in the morning.

As you can tell from the examples, *although, even though,* and *though* signal that the meaning of the adverb clause is contrary to what we would expect from the first part of the sentence.

Sentence Practice 1

CORRECTED SENTENCES APPEAR ON PAGE 474.

In each of the following sentences, underline the adverb clause and correct the comma error. Confirm your answer by moving the adverb clause to another position in the sentence.

> EXAMPLE: <u>When we got the tests back</u>, we all went out for coffee.

> CONFIRMATION: We all went out for coffee <u>when we got the tests back.</u>

1. When I visit my parents in New Mexico I always bring them something from my part of the country.

2. I will go with you, after I finish eating.

3. After Omar competed in the third basketball tournament of the season he was not eager to travel again.

4. Because the test included over a hundred questions I could not finish it in just fifteen minutes.

5. Stephanie wants to leave, because she smelled a strange odor in the room.

For more practice punctuating adverb clauses, go to **Exercise Central** at
bedfordstmartins.com/commonsense/2-5.

Sentence Practice 2

CORRECTED SENTENCES APPEAR ON PAGE 475.

In each of the following sentences, underline the adverb clause and correct the comma error. Confirm your answer by moving the adverb clause to another position in the sentence.

EXAMPLE: I was upset,/ because I should have known better.

CONFIRMATION: Because I should have known better, I was upset.

1. While we were watching some children playing in the park Bill and I talked about our own childhood.

2. Although sharks are normally found in salt water some freshwater sharks exist in Nicaragua.

3. We need to stop at the next gas station even though we stopped at one just an hour ago.

4. Because I tend to work forty hours each week I have to spend most of my weekends studying.

5. Whenever you are ready to leave I will be happy to go.

Sentence Practice 3

Combine each pair of sentences by turning the second sentence into an adverb clause. Pick an appropriate subordinating conjunction from the list on page 58. Underline the adverb clause, and show that it can be used both before and after the independent clause. Punctuate each version correctly.

EXAMPLE: I need to hang up.
             I have to go to class now.

ANSWER: I need to hang up because I have to go to class now.
           Because I have to go to class now, I need to hang up.

1. I cannot study.
   You are beating those drums.

2. Our party was cancelled with little notice.
   The person hosting it had to leave town.

3. You made a strange comment about Ray.
    Everyone was offended.

4. The test will be in two weeks.
    The teacher decides to postpone it.

5. Ellen should not come to class.
    She gets better.

Editing Practice 1

CORRECTED SENTENCES APPEAR ON PAGE 475.

In the following paragraphs, correctly punctuate each sentence that contains an adverb clause. The number in parentheses at the end of each paragraph indicates how many errors you should find.

Since I wanted to get into shape, I decided to buy a weight machine that I could use in my basement. I picked the machine I wanted, after I had looked at about a dozen different kinds. Surprisingly, it had many features the other machines didn't have even though it was one of the cheaper ones. (2)

Unfortunately, I forgot to compare two things: the height of the weight machine and the height of my basement. When I finally assembled the metal monster I discovered that it was four inches higher than my basement ceiling. I was furious at myself, because I had made such a dumb mistake. As the thing was such a hassle to move I didn't want to haul it back to the store. As a last resort, I punched a hole through the sheet-rock ceiling. Whenever I go into the basement now I see this really ugly hole in my ceiling. Next time, I'll need to plan ahead. (4)

Editing Practice 2

CORRECTED SENTENCES APPEAR ON PAGE 475.

In the following paragraphs, correctly punctuate each sentence that contains an adverb clause. The number in parentheses at the end of each paragraph indicates how many errors you should find.

Although many people may not be aware of it, Pearl Buck was the first American woman to win a Nobel Prize in literature. After they had spent years as missionaries in China her parents returned to the United States for a short time in the early 1890's, during which time Pearl was born. When she was just three months old Pearl returned to China with her parents. She grew up speaking Chinese, because her family lived among the Chinese rather than in a Western compound. (3)

While they were living in China there were many protests against the Western governments that had controlled China's economy for years. Since she had lived among ordinary people Pearl was very aware of their daily struggles for bare survival. Because she had such a depth of personal experience in China her most famous novel, *The Good Earth,* reflected her compassion for the Chinese and their culture. When Pearl Buck died President Nixon said that she served as a "human bridge between the civilizations of the East and West." (4)

Editing Practice 3

In the following paragraphs, correctly punctuate each sentence that contains an adverb clause. The number in parentheses at the end of each paragraph indicates how many errors you should find.

Lesson 5

adv cl

When I entered school last year, I had no idea what my
      ^
major would be. Because I had many interests I couldn't decide
whether I should major in accounting, computer programming,
health administration, or business management. In my first year,
it didn't make too much difference, because I had to get the core
requirements out of the way. Now in my second year, I need to
get ready to declare a major. Even after I had met with an
academic advisor I could not make up my mind. I was undecided
and stressed out for weeks. (3)

After I had whined about making up my mind all semester
a friend had a long talk with me. Our discussion really helped
me; because she told me to think about what I wanted to be
doing ten years from now. Before we had this talk I had tended
to think just about the subject I liked right now — not the sort
of jobs I wanted to do after graduation. Admittedly it was a
simple idea, but it never hit home, until I talked to someone
else in the same situation. I finally decided that health
administration would combine my interest in caregiving with
my interests in finance, management, and technology. (4)

Writing Practice

On your own paper, write a paragraph describing the field you are concentrating in and why it interests you now. In a second paragraph, imagine what
you might be doing in that field ten years from now. Try to use as many
adverb clauses as possible. Use the Editing Checklist to ensure that they are
punctuated correctly.

Editing Checklist

Identify Errors in Punctuating Adverb Clauses in Your Writing

____ Identify adverb clauses by seeing if you can move the clause to either end of the sentence.

Correct Errors in Punctuating Adverb Clauses in Your Writing

____ If the adverb clause is at the beginning of the sentence, be sure to separate it from the independent clause by a comma.

____ If the adverb clause is at the end of the sentence, don't use a comma unless the adverb clause begins with *although, even though,* or *though.*

The Bottom Line	If you use an introductory adverb clause, be sure to set if off with a comma.

UNIT TWO: Expanding the Basic Sentence

REVIEW

Expanding a basic sentence to include multiple clauses allows a writer to connect related ideas in more precise ways within a single sentence. This unit presented three ways of connecting ideas: coordinating conjunctions, transitional terms, and adverb clauses.

Commas with *And, But, Or,* and Other Coordinating Conjunctions

The seven coordinating conjunctions are known by the acronym FAN-BOYS: *for, and, nor, but, or, yet, so.* When a coordinating conjunction joins two independent clauses, it should be preceded by a comma. When a coordinating conjunction joins pieces of a single clause, it does not require a comma. Here is the tip for telling the two situations apart:

> IMAGINARY PERIOD TIP: Test each use of FANBOYS by putting an imaginary period right before it. Can BOTH parts that are divided by this imaginary period now stand alone as complete sentences? If both can stand alone, use a comma with the FANBOYS. If either one is not a complete sentence, then do not use a comma with the FANBOYS.

Punctuating Transitional Terms

Here is a list of the most common transitional terms grouped by meaning:

In addition: *again, also, besides, further(more), likewise, moreover, similarly*

As a result/example: *accordingly, consequently, for example, in fact, then, therefore, thus*

On the other hand/or else: *however, nevertheless, otherwise, still*

Transitional terms indicate how one idea relates to a previous idea. Transitional terms by themselves cannot be used to separate two clauses. The *only* function of such terms is to help readers connect one idea to another, so transitional terms are not absolutely necessary. When you use transitional terms in formal writing, set them off with one comma if they come at the beginning or end of independent clauses. Use two commas if they appear in the middle.

> **TRANSITIONAL TERM MOVEMENT TIP:** Transitional terms can always be moved around inside their own independent clause. They can begin the clause or be moved to the end. They can often (but not always) be placed in the middle of the clause near the verb. Coordinating conjunctions, on the other hand, are immobile; they are always locked into place at the beginning of the second clause.

Punctuating Adverb Clauses

Adverb clauses begin with subordinating conjunctions. Here is a list of the most common ones grouped by meaning:

Cause: *as, because, since, so that*

Condition: *as if, assuming that, if, in case, unless, when, whether*

Contrast: *although, even though, though*

Place: *where, wherever*

Time: *after, as soon as, before, since, until, when, whenever*

Here is a tip for identifying adverb clauses:

> **ADVERB CLAUSE MOVEMENT TIP:** If it is a clause, and if you can move it, then it has to be an adverb clause. Adverb clauses are the only type of clause that can be moved from one part of the sentence to another.

An introductory adverb clause is always set off with commas to show the reader where the introductory clause ends and the independent clause begins. When adverb clauses follow the independent clause, no comma is required. There is, however, one exception to this rule. Here is a tip for remembering how to punctuate adverb clauses that begin with *although, even though,* or *though.*

> **CONTRAST TIP:** If an adverb clause shows contrast by using the subordinating conjunctions *although, even though,* or *though,* the adverb clause must always be set off with a comma, even if it is at the end of the sentence.

Review Test

Combine the following pairs of sentences with an appropriate coordinating conjunction, transitional term, or subordinating conjunction. Punctuate each combined sentence correctly. An example of each type is given below:

EXAMPLE:
My answering machine was broken.
I missed a number of messages.

COORDINATING
CONJUNCTION:
My answering machine was broken, *and*
I missed a number of messages.

TRANSITIONAL TERM:
My answering machine was broken; *consequently,*
I missed a number of messages.

SUBORDINATING
CONJUNCTION:
Because my answering machine was broken,
I missed a number of messages.

1. It was getting dark.
   We turned on the lights.

2. Many are nominated for an Academy Award.
   A select few win one.

3. The campaign was drawing to a close.
   Senator Fogg was exhausted.

4. I thought I had the right combination.
   My lock still wouldn't open.

5. We wanted to go to London.
   We needed a lot of money.

6. The economy was strong.
   Politicians were talking about a tax cut.

7. I had a previous commitment.
   I couldn't go home for the weekend.

8. We worked on the proposal all night.
   We thought we had a good chance of getting the job.

9. August was growing to a close.
    It was as hot as ever.

10. The book made a big impression on me.
    I recommended it to all my friends.

11. I can't read a note.
    I love music.

12. The cost was completely out of line.
    We will have to resubmit our bid.

UNIT THREE
Making Subjects and Verbs Agree

OVERVIEW

Terms That Can Help You Understand Subject-Verb Agreement

If you are not familiar with any of the following terms, look them up in the Guide to Grammar Terminology beginning on page 1. The numbers in parentheses indicate the lessons in which each term appears.

compound subject (8)	subject (6, 7, 8)
plural (6, 7)	subject-verb agreement (6, 7, 8)
singular (6, 7)	verb (6, 7, 8)

The Nuts and Bolts of Subject-Verb Agreement

This unit will help you to make your subjects and verbs agree in your writing. By "agree," we mean that the **subject** of any sentence must match the **verb** in number. For example, a singular subject (one person, place, or object) should be paired with the singular form of a verb. A plural subject (more than one person, place, or object) should be paired with the plural form of a verb.

SINGULAR: The <u>student</u> <u>uses</u> the Internet for research.

PLURAL: The <u>students</u> <u>use</u> the Internet for research.

One basic rule to follow in making subjects and verbs agree is to add an -*s* to the **present tense** form of the verb if the subject is *he, she,* or *it* or if the subject can be replaced by one of these **personal pronouns**. The lessons in this unit deal with three common errors writers make in subject-verb agreement.

70

Lesson 6 shows you how to make the subject and verb agree when the subject phrase is so long or complicated that the actual subject gets lost. Here is an example of an error involving a lost subject.

> EXAMPLE: ✗ The cost of all the repairs we needed to make were more than we could afford.

>   *was*
> CORRECTION: The cost of all the repairs we needed to make ~~were~~ more than we could afford.

The verb in this sentence must agree with the subject *cost*, not the nearby noun *repairs*.

Lesson 7 shows you how to make the subject and verb agree when the subject follows the verb, as in sentences that begin with *there is* or *there was*. Here is an example of this type of error.

> EXAMPLE: ✗ There is usually some leftovers in the refrigerator.

>   *are*
> CORRECTION: There ~~is~~ usually some leftovers in the refrigerator.

The verb in this sentence must agree with the subject *leftovers*.

Lesson 8 shows you how to make the subject and verb agree when the sentence includes a **compound subject** (two or more subjects joined by *and*). Here is an example of an error involving a compound subject.

> EXAMPLE: ✗ Good planning and careful follow-through is necessary for success in any field.

>   *are*
> CORRECTION: Good planning and careful follow-through ~~is~~ necessary for success in any field.

The verb in this sentence must agree with the compound subject *planning and follow-through*.

Can you detect problems with subject-verb agreement?

CORRECTED SENTENCES APPEAR ON PAGE 475.

Correct all subject-verb agreement errors in the following paragraphs using the first correction as a model. The number in parentheses at the end of each paragraph indicates how many errors you should find.

When I was in high school, my family enjoyed camping, so nearly every school vacation, we would go camping. We soon realized that there ~~is~~ ^{are} two completely different kinds of campers. We called them the "nature lovers" and the "homeboys." The people whom we called "nature lovers" enjoy setting up camp in small, isolated sites where there is often no toilet facilities. Of course, the food and water is a constant concern, especially when all supplies have to be carried in. "Nature lovers" always try to have a minimal impact on the area that they have camped in. For example, their trash and garbage is always taken out. (3)

The "homeboys," on the other hand, are people who want to go to the mountains, beach, or desert without ever actually leaving home. They buy a mobile home—an entire apartment complete with living room, kitchen, and bathroom—that have been mounted on wheels. There is some mobile homes that even come equipped with satellite dishes so that the "homeboys" will not miss any TV programs while they are in the wilderness. (2)

LESSON 6
Agreement with Lost Subjects

Error Sentences

CORRECTED SENTENCES APPEAR ON PAGE 74.

EXAMPLE 1: ✗ Matt's beach house, one of the cottages on Ocean Street near the boardwalk, were not damaged by the hurricane.

EXAMPLE 2: ✗ The advantages of this entertainment system is that it is compact and that it is less expensive than what you would pay if you bought the cassette recorder, CD player, and radio separately.

What's the Problem?

The problem in a lost-subject error is that the verb agrees with a word that is not the actual subject—usually with a noun that is closer to the verb than the actual subject is. In Example 1, *were* is **plural** to agree with *cottages,* but the real subject is *house,* which is **singular** and should have a singular verb. Example 2 has the opposite error. The singular verb *is* agrees with *system* but should be plural to agree with *advantages.*

What Causes the Problem?

When the subject phrase is long or complicated, writers tend to lose track of the actual subject. Instead, they make the verb agree with the noun or pronoun nearest to it rather than with the actual subject back at the beginning of the sentence.

Diagnostic Exercise

CORRECTED SENTENCES APPEAR ON PAGE 476.

Correct all errors involving lost-subject agreement in the following paragraph using the first correction as a model. The number in parentheses at the end of the paragraph indicates how many errors you should find.

The beginning of the first public schools in the United States ~~date~~ *dates* from the early 1800's. The pressure to create public schools open to children of working-class parents were a direct result of the union movements in large cities. In response, state legislatures gave communities the legal right to levy local property taxes to pay for free schools open to the public. By the middle of the nineteenth century, control of school policies and curriculum were in the hands of the state government. As school populations outgrew one-room schoolhouses, the design of school buildings on the East Coast were completely changed to accommodate separate rooms for children of different ages. Before this time, all children in a schoolhouse, regardless of age, was taught together in the same room by the same teacher. (4)

Fixing This Problem in Your Writing

ESL

If you are a non-native speaker, you should know that in English, the subject of a sentence is usually the *first noun* or *pronoun* in the sentence (excluding introductory elements). The following tip will help you find the subject.

> **FIRST-WORD TIP:** When you check verbs for subject-verb agreement, jump back to the beginning of the sentence and find the *first* word that makes sense as the subject. In nearly all cases, that first word will be the subject.

Here is how jumping to the beginning of the sentence and taking the first word that makes sense would have correctly identified the subject in the first sample sentence:

EXAMPLE 1: **✗** Matt's beach house, one of the cottages on Ocean Street near the boardwalk, were not damaged by the hurricane.

TIP APPLIED: *subject*
Matt's beach house, one of the cottages . . .

CORRECTION: Matt's beach house, one of the cottages on Ocean

Street near the boardwalk, ~~were~~ *was* not damaged by
the hurricane.

The first possible word that makes sense as the subject of the sentence is
house (not *cottages*). The subject is singular, so the verb should also be singular.

EXAMPLE 2: ✗ The advantages of this entertainment system is that
it is compact and that it is less expensive than what
you would pay if you bought the cassette recorder,
CD player, and radio separately.

TIP APPLIED: The advantages of this entertainment *subject* system...

CORRECTION: The advantages of this entertainment system ~~is~~ *are* that
it is compact and that it is less expensive than what
you would pay if you bought the cassette recorder,
CD player, and radio separately.

The first word that makes sense as the subject of the sentence is *advantages*
(not *system*). The subject is plural, so the verb should also be plural.

Sentence Practice 1

CORRECTED SENTENCES APPEAR ON PAGE 476.

In the following sentences, the dictionary form of the verb is in **boldface**
type. Jump to the beginning of the sentence and find the first word that
makes sense as the subject. Underline this subject and then make the verb
agree with it.

EXAMPLE: Uncle Buck's <u>investment</u> in a scheme to make robot

vacuum cleaners ~~seem~~ *seems* to have failed.

1. The newest schedule for fall classes **are** ready.

2. The federal government's proposal for the pricing of prescription
   drugs **were** just published in the Federal Register.

3. The problems with his idea about the contest **is** what we would have expected.

4. In the first place, access to the computers in all campus buildings **require** a student ID.

5. I understand that the problems with the heating system **has** been fixed.

 For more practice in agreement with lost subjects, go to **Exercise Central** at **bedfordstmartins.com/commonsense/3-6**.

Sentence Practice 2

CORRECTED SENTENCES APPEAR ON PAGE 476.

In the following sentences, the dictionary form of the verb is in **boldface** type. Jump to the beginning of the sentence and find the first word that makes sense as the subject. Underline this subject and then make the verb agree with it. If the form of the verb is correct, write *OK* above it.

> *OK*
> EXAMPLE: The carpets we got for the new house **need** to be professionally cleaned.

1. The characteristics of the early hominid found in Java **be** still in debate.

2. Uncertainty about the terms of the agreements **have** thrown the issue into the courts.

3. As a result of the election, the public awareness of the issues **have** been heightened.

4. Senator Blather's motion to adjourn until after the holidays **be** rejected.

5. The painting, a Dutch still life in the manner of Rembrandt, **be** sold at auction after the war.

Sentence Practice 3

Combine the following sentences by adding the information in the second sentence to the subject in the first sentence and choosing the correct verb form. In the new sentence, underline the subject once and the verb twice.

EXAMPLE: **Most programs (is/are) quite informative.**
The programs are on the History Channel.

ANSWER: **Most programs on the History Channel are quite informative.**

Lesson 6

s-v
agr

1. The reporter (has/have) filed her story.
    The reporter is covering the trials.

2. Most movies (turns out/turn out) to be a disappointment.
    Most movies are based on best-selling novels.

3. The hearings (was/were) a complete waste of time.
    The hearings were chaired by Senator Blather.

4. The files (is/are) not to leave the office.
    The files are kept in the locked cabinet.

5. The families (deserve/deserves) some privacy.
    The families were involved in the accident.

Editing Practice 1

CORRECTED SENTENCES APPEAR ON PAGE 476.

Correct all errors in the following paragraphs using the first correction as a model. The number in parentheses at the end of each paragraph indicates how many errors you should find.

The house cat is one of the oldest domesticated animals.

believe
Researhers who study the history of the cat ~~believes~~ that the
              ^

ancestor of all of today's domestic cats were a species of small wildcats found in Africa and Europe. The first group of people to bring cats into human habitations were in Africa. (2)

However, the first actual domestication of cats as residents with humans was carried out by the Egyptians, who tamed cats to hunt rats and mice in grain storehouses. The pet cats of an important official or government officer was sacred. When one of these sacred cats were killed by a servant, even accidentally, the servant would be severely punished, possibly even put to death. (2)

Editing Practice 2

CORRECTED SENTENCES APPEAR ON PAGE 476.

Correct all errors in the following paragraph using the first correction as a model. The number in parentheses at the end of the paragraph indicates how many errors you should find.

One of the largest families of vertebrate animals ~~are~~ *is* the family of reptiles. Reptiles include alligators, crocodiles, lizards, snakes, and turtles. They share the feature of being cold-blooded. Reptiles are among the oldest families of animals on earth. Reptiles played a key role in bringing animal life out of the oceans and onto land through the evolution of eggs. Reptiles evolved from amphibians, the first creatures to come onto land. The great evolutionary advantage of reptiles were their eggs. Reptile eggs, with their leathery membrane or hard shell, has a great advantage: the embryo is encased in its own self-contained sack of fluid. The ability of reptiles to reproduce away from bodies of water give reptiles an enormous advantage over amphibians and explain

why reptiles were able to expand into all the dry areas of the

world. (4)

Editing Practice 3

Correct all errors in the following paragraph using the first correction as a model. The number in parentheses at the end of the paragraph indicates how many errors you should find.

Many infants, despite going to sleep peacefully at the beginning

of the night, ~~wakes~~ *wake* once or twice before morning. Parents often

suspects hunger is the cause of the nighttime waking. This may

be true for a younger baby. However, an infant who is over six

months old and weighs at least fifteen pounds usually sleep from

8:00 P.M. until 5:00 or 6:00 A.M. without needing to eat. Some

babies who are put into bed asleep at the beginning of the night

has not learned to fall asleep on their own. These little ones

call for a parent to come and soothe them back to sleep.

Separation anxiety, especially in a nine- to twelve-month-old,

cause other babies to need the comfort of a parent in the middle

of the night. Unfortunately, parents of a night waker gets used

to surviving on less sleep. (5)

Writing Practice

On your own paper, write a paragraph or two about what causes you to wake during the night. How do you get back to sleep? Use the Editing Checklist to guide you in identifying the real subject of each sentence. Then, check each sentence for subject-verb agreement.

Lesson 6

s-v
agr

Editing Checklist

Identify Lost-Subject Errors in Your Writing

_____ Jump back to the beginning of each sentence and find the first word that makes sense as the subject.

_____ Cross out all words between the subject and the verb.

Correct Lost-Subject Errors in Your Writing

_____ If the subject and verb do not agree in number, change the form of the verb to match the subject. Use a singular verb form for a singular subject. Use a plural verb form for a plural subject.

The Bottom Line	**Subjects** that are not next to their verb still **determine** whether the verb is singular or plural. Jump back to the beginning of the sentence to find the subject.

LESSON 7
Agreement with
There is and *There was*

Error Sentences

CORRECTED SENTENCES APPEAR ON PAGE 83.

> EXAMPLE 1: ✗ There is a million stories in every big city.
>
> EXAMPLE 2: ✗ There was dozens of books piled on the couch.

What's the Problem?

Non-native speakers should note that English, like most languages, has a special construction to point out the existence of something. In English, we use *there* plus some form of the verb *be* (or a similar verb like *seem* or *appear*) for this purpose. For example, you might want to call a waiter's attention to a dead fly floating in your soup by saying, "Waiter! *There is* a fly in my soup!" In this construction, the subject (*fly*) *follows* the verb (*is*). A problem occurs when the **subject** is **plural** but the verb is **singular** as in example sentences 1 and 2.

ESL

What Causes the Problem?

This type of construction creates a problem with **subject-verb agreement** because the subject is not in its normal position. We create sentences of this type by moving the subject to *follow* the verb and filling the vacant subject position with *there*. In conversation, we tend to use the singular form of the verb *be,* as though the verb were agreeing with the empty word *there.*

Diagnostic Exercise

CORRECTED SENTENCES APPEAR ON PAGE 477.

Correct all errors in the following paragraph using the first correction as a model. The number in parentheses at the end of the paragraph indicates how many errors you should find.

are
Each year there ~~is~~ many new movies coming out of Hollywood.
^

Each is designed for a certain segment of the moviegoing audience.

There is car-crash films aimed at males under thirty. There is

heart-warming romantic comedies for women over twenty. There

is even the dreadful "slasher" movies for an audience that it is

better not to think about. (3)

Fixing This Problem in Your Writing

The following tip shows that the *there* in a "there exists" sentence is an empty word used as a placeholder for the real subject.

> *THERE* DELETION TIP: Rearrange the word order of the sentence to elimi-
> nate *there*. If this paraphrase is grammatical, then the original sentence
> contains an "existential there" construction.

This paraphrase has the additional advantage of helping identify the real subject of the sentence. You may even decide that the paraphrase results in a livelier sentence than the *there is/there was* construction of the original version.
    Once you know that a sentence contains a *there is/there was* construction, you have to make sure that the verb agrees with the actual subject, not with the placeholder word *there*.

> BEHIND-THE-VERB TIP: In *there is/there was* sentences, the subject is the
> first word after the verb that makes sense as a subject.

Here is how you can use the *There* Deletion Tip to identify whether the sample sentences contain the *there is/there was* construction:

EXAMPLE 1:   ✗ There is a million stories in every big city.

TIP APPLIED: A million stories are in every big city.

EXAMPLE 2:   ✗ There was dozens of books piled on the couch.

TIP APPLIED: Dozens of books were piled on the couch.

Now you can use the Behind-the-Verb Tip to find the real subject and make the verb agree with it.

EXAMPLE: ✗ There is a million stories in every big city.

                       subject

TIP APPLIED: There is a million stories . . .

                 are

CORRECTION: There ~~is~~ a million stories in every big city.
                 ^

EXAMPLE: ✗ There was dozens of books piled on the couch.

                   subject

TIP APPLIED: There was dozens . . .

                 were

CORRECTION: There ~~was~~ dozens of books piled on the couch.
                 ^

Lesson 7

s-v
agr

Sentence Practice 1

CORRECTED SENTENCES APPEAR ON PAGE 477.

Using the Behind-the-Verb Tip, underline the first word or words following the verb that make sense as a subject. If there is an error in subject-verb agreement, write the correct form of the verb above the incorrect verb.

               are

EXAMPLE: There ~~is~~ never enough <u>hours</u> in the day to get
             ^
           everything done.

1. There was still dozens of presents to wrap.

2. Recently, there has been complaints about the noise in the dorms.

3. In the past, there was many more independently operated grocery stores.

4. There is still five shopping days until Christmas.

5. I didn't like the ending because there was too many loose ends that were not tied up.

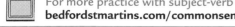 For more practice with subject-verb agreement, go to **Exercise Central** at **bedfordstmartins.com/commonsense/3-7**.

Sentence Practice 2

CORRECTED SENTENCES APPEAR ON PAGE 477.

Underline the first word or words following the verb that make sense as a subject. If there is an error in subject-verb agreement, write the correct form of the verb above the incorrect verb.

EXAMPLE: There <ins>*are*</ins> ~~is~~ a <u>book store</u> and a <u>coffee shop</u> in the building.

1. There was an old woman who lived in a shoe.

2. Since it had snowed all night, there was only some trucks and buses on the road.

3. There is some cookies and pastries to go with the coffee.

4. Fortunately, there was a flashlight and some candles in the closet.

5. There is lots of things for the kids to do there.

Sentence Practice 3

Rewrite the following sentences as *there is/there are* sentences.

EXAMPLE: **An opener is in the drawer.**

ANSWER: **There is an opener in the drawer.**

1. A tavern is in the town.

2. A really nasty flu is going around.

3. A light golden haze is on the meadow.

4. Some good movies are playing this weekend.

5. Lots of fish are in the ocean.

Editing Practice 1

CORRECTED SENTENCES APPEAR ON PAGE 477.

Correct all errors in the following paragraphs using the first correction as a model. The number in parentheses at the end of each paragraph indicates how many errors you should find.

Lesson 7

s-v
agr

There ~~is~~ *are* two countries in the Iberian Peninsula: Spain and

Portugal. Portugal occupies most of the western coast, while Spain

covers the rest of the peninsula. There is three basic regions in the

peninsula: coastal plains on the west, south, and east; a long strip of

mountains across the northern part; and a huge, dry plateau that

covers most of the central area. (1)

Although the coastal plains account for only a tiny portion of the land

mass of the peninsula, there is a high percentage of the population in that

region. Along the coast, there is both a mild climate and fertile soil. In

addition, there is many rivers that flow into the plains from the mountains

in the interior of the country. These rivers provide irrigation water for the

fields and orchards in the coastal plains. Especially along the southern

coast, there is thousands of acres of orange and lemon orchards. (3)

Editing Practice 2

CORRECTED SENTENCES APPEAR ON PAGE 477.

Correct all errors in the following paragraphs using the first correction as a model. The number in parentheses at the end of each paragraph indicates how many errors you should find.

The largest distinctive geographical feature in the United States

and Canada is the Rocky Mountains. In the lower forty-eight states, *are*

there ~~is~~ eight states that contain a portion of the Rockies: Idaho,
          ^

Montana, Wyoming, Nevada, Utah, Colorado, New Mexico, and

Arizona. There is even branches of the mountains that extend north

through two Canadian provinces and into Alaska. There is rich veins

of minerals, especially gold, silver, copper, lead, and zinc, in the region.

Nowadays, however, there is greater riches in liquid mining: petroleum

and natural gas. (3)

The great natural beauty of the Rocky Mountains has made them

very popular. There is many National Parks throughout the region; two

of the best known are Yellowstone and Glacier National Parks. There is

many winter sports, especially downhill and cross-country skiing, that

have made the Rocky Mountains as important as the Alps as a winter

tourist destination. (2)

Editing Practice 3

Correct all errors in the following paragraphs using the first correction as a
model. The number in parentheses at the end of each paragraph indicates
how many errors you should find.

are

There ~~is~~ many reasons to visit the quaint coastal town of
        ^

Kennebunkport, Maine. Though the town gained national attention as

the summer home of former president George and Barbara Bush, there

is several natives of Kennebunkport who will argue that the publicity

hasn't changed this historic seaside town a bit. (1)

The Kennebunkport community boasts several attractions for

visitors and residents. There is museums, beaches, and even a wildlife

refuge. Children and adults will enjoy the Seashore Trolley Museum, founded over sixty years ago when there was plans to destroy several

Biddeford and Saco Railroad open trolleys. For those who eat seafood,

there is a delicious variety offered in several local restaurants, but of

course most visitors arrive wanting Maine lobster. If you happen to find

yourself in Kennebunkport in early December, there is several events

included in the town's annual Christmas Prelude: caroling, art shows,

and a Christmas parade. (3)

Lesson 7

s-v
agr

Writing Practice

Using the Editing Practice essays in this lesson as your model, write a paragraph or two that describe the geography, climate, or attractions of a place
that you are familiar with. Try to use as many examples of the *there is/there
was* construction as you can. Then, use the Editing Checklist to show that all
uses of *there is/there was* are correct.

Editing Checklist

Identify There is/There was *Errors in Your Writing*

____ Whenever you use *there,* check to see whether the sentence contains a
there is or *there was* construction by rearranging the order of words in
the sentence and eliminating *there.* This will help you to find the real
subject of the sentence.

Correct There is/There was *Errors in Your Writing*

____ If the subject and verb do not agree in number, change the form of
the verb to match the subject. Use a singular verb form for a singular
subject. Use a plural verb form for a plural subject.

The Bottom Line	There **is** often a **subject** after the verb in a *there is* or *there was* construction.

LESSON 8

Agreement with Compound Subjects

Error Sentences

CORRECTED SENTENCES APPEAR ON PAGE 90.

EXAMPLE 1: ✗ The pencils and some paper is on the desk.

EXAMPLE 2: ✗ Our genetic make-up and our personal experience makes us who we are.

What's the Problem?

When two (or more) subjects are joined by *and,* they are called a **compound subject.** When using compound subjects, writers have a tendency to use a singular verb, even though compound subjects are normally plural. This is the problem in Examples 1 and 2.

What Causes the Problem?

Compound subjects create a problem for some writers because writers may incorrectly think of them as a single collective unit. Although this argument has a certain logic to it, the usual grammatical convention is that compound subjects are plural and must have plural verbs.

Sometimes writers are aware that the verb must agree with the subject of the sentence, but they incorrectly consider only the noun closest to the verb and not the entire subject.

Diagnostic Exercise

CORRECTED SENTENCES APPEAR ON PAGE 477.

Correct all errors in the following paragraph using the first correction as a model. The number in parentheses at the end of the paragraph indicates how many errors you should find.

I work in a busy law office. Even though we now have voice mail,

take

answering the phone and writing down messages ~~takes~~ up a lot of my

^

time. I am also responsible for maintaining the law library, although

most of the time I do nothing more glamorous than shelving. The law

books and reference material is always left scattered around the library,

and some of the lawyers even leave their dirty coffee cups on the tables.

I used to have a relatively comfortable working area, but the new

computer terminal and modem has now taken up most of my personal

space; that's progress, I guess. Despite all the stress, meeting the needs

of clients and keeping track of all the information required in a modern

law office makes it a fascinating job. (3)

Lesson 8

s-v agr

Fixing This Problem in Your Writing

Whenever your sentence contains *and,* check to see whether the *and* has joined two subjects together to create a compound subject. If so, then the subject is plural, and you must also use a plural verb.

Following is a tip to help you identify compound subjects.

> *THEY* **TIP:** Whenever *and* is used in the subject part of a sentence, see whether you can replace the entire subject portion with the pronoun *they.* If you can, then the subject is a compound, and the verb must be made plural to agree with *they.*

This rule applies *only* to *and.* It does not apply when the subjects are joined by *or.* When subjects are joined by *or,* the rules are completely different: the verb agrees only with the *nearest* subject, which may be either singular or plural.

Here is how replacing the compound subject with *they* identifies the right form of the verb in the two example sentences.

EXAMPLE 1:   ✗ The pencils and some paper is on the desk.

They

TIP APPLIED: ✗ ~~The pencils and some paper~~ is on the desk.

Since we know that the substitution of *they* for *the pencils and some paper* makes sense, we know that the sentence contains a compound subject. When *they* is the subject, it is easy to tell that the verb must be plural: *They are on the desk.* Thus, the verb with the compound must also be plural:

>   *are*
> CORRECTION: The pencils and some paper ~~is~~ on the desk.

> EXAMPLE: ✗ Our genetic make-up and our personal experience makes us who we are.

>   *They*
> TIP APPLIED: ✗ ~~Our genetic make-up and our personal experience~~ makes us who we are.

Since we know that the substitution of *they* for *our genetic make-up and our personal experience* makes sense, we know that the sentence contains a compound subject. When *they* is the subject, it is easy to tell that the verb must be plural: *They make us who we are.* Thus, the sentence with the compound must also be plural:

> CORRECTION: Our genetic make-up and our personal experience
>   *make*
>   ~~makes~~ us who we are.

Sentence Practice 1

CORRECTED SENTENCES APPEAR ON PAGE 478.

Underline the compound subjects in the following sentences. If there is an error in subject-verb agreement, make the necessary correction.

>   *were*
> EXAMPLE: Two <u>dollars</u> and some <u>loose change</u> ~~was~~ not going to be enough.

1. The milk and the eggs was still in the car.

2. The causes and treatments of chronic disease is becoming much better understood.

3. You don't have to be a health nut to believe that vegetables and fruit is the basis of a good diet.

4. Weekends and holidays lasts forever when you're not busy.

5. The advantages and disadvantages always seems to balance out somehow.

 For more practice with subject-verb agreement, go to **Exercise Central** at **bedfordstmartins.com/commonsense/3-8**.

Sentence Practice 2

CORRECTED SENTENCES APPEAR ON PAGE 478.

Underline the compound subjects in the following sentences. If there is an error in subject-verb agreement, make the necessary correction.

> EXAMPLE: <u>Thunder</u> and <u>lightning</u> always ~~scares~~ *scare* my dog.

1. A rifle and a shotgun is used for very different kinds of hunting.

2. French, Latin, and German is the main source of English vocabulary.

3. The heat and humidity makes it very uncomfortable in the summer.

4. A cup of coffee and a cigarette doesn't make a complete meal.

5. What we see and what we get is not always the same thing.

Sentence Practice 3

Combine the following sentences by making a compound subject. Make the verb agree with the new subject. Underline the subject once and the verb twice in your new sentence.

> EXAMPLE: The dishpan is under the sink.
> The soap is under the sink.

> ANSWER: <u>The dishpan and the soap</u> <u><u>are</u></u> under the sink.

1. Time waits for no man.
    Tide waits for no man.

2. Communism was a powerful force in the middle of the century.
    Fascism was a powerful force in the middle of the century.

3. The captain was reviewing the troops.
    The major was reviewing the troops.

4. What we say is important.
    What we do is important.

5. The advancing storm was enough to make us turn back.
    The gathering darkness was enough to make us turn back.

Editing Practice 1

CORRECTED SENTENCES APPEAR ON PAGE 478.

Correct all errors in the following paragraphs using the first correction as a model. The number in parentheses at the end of each paragraph indicates how many errors you should find.

>   In Mozart's opera, *Don Giovanni,* comedy and melodrama ~~is~~ *are* mixed together in an unusual way. For example, the character and personality of Don Giovanni is surprisingly complex. His charm and bravery makes him almost a hero at times. Yet at other times, his aristocratic arrogance and deliberate cruelty to women makes him a complete villain. The seduction of a willing woman and a rape is the same to him. (4)

>   The role and character of his servant Leporello is also unusual. At first, his constant complaining and caustic asides to the audience makes Leporello seem to be just a conventional comic sidekick. Yet in some ways, his observations and reactions to his master's behavior becomes the center of attention. Leporello's admiration for the Don's charm and his repulsion at the Don's treatment of women reflects the audience's equally mixed feelings. (4)

Editing Practice 2

CORRECTED SENTENCES APPEAR ON PAGE 478.

Correct all errors in the following paragraph using the first correction as a model. The number in parentheses at the end of the paragraph indicates how many errors you should find.

Barbara Kingsolver is the author of six books and a number of

short stories. Her books and stories ~~has~~ *have* attracted a wide following.

One of her most recent novels is *Animal Dreams.* Codi, her sister,

and their father is the focus of our attention. The story deals with

Codi's reluctant return home to a small town in Arizona to take

care of her father, who is dying. The events that take place in

the story are seen either from Codi's perspective or from her

father's point of view. The past and the present constantly runs

together in their minds. One of the main themes in the book is

Codi's discovery of how deeply her present life and actions has

been affected by dimly remembered events in her childhood.

At first, it seems that Codi's father is totally out of touch with reality

because he seems hopelessly stuck in the past. However, as Codi

begins to reconstruct a clearer picture of her own childhood,

it is her father's vivid memories that actually provide the key

to her adult understanding of her past. (3)

Editing Practice 3

Correct all errors in the following paragraph using the first correction as a model. The number in parentheses at the end of the paragraph indicates how many errors you should find.

                                              take
    The town and its inhabitants gradually ~~takes~~ on greater and
                                              ^

greater importance. Codi gradually begins to see how important

the little town and its inhabitants is to her past and present life.

The town, because of its unbroken connection from the past to the

present, gradually becomes more and more important to Codi.

In fact, the town and its people evolves to become one of the central

characters in the book. Finally, it is the town and its people, living

and dead, that brings Codi back to life as a complete person who can

connect her past to her present. In addition to its serious themes, the

book is very funny. Kingsolver's sharp eye and wit makes every scene

and conversation vivid and convincing. (4)

Writing Practice

Using the Editing Practice essays in this lesson as a model, write a paragraph or two about a fictional character from a movie, play, or book. What are the personality features that make this person interesting? Try to use as many examples of compound subjects as you can. Then, use the Editing Checklist to show that the verbs you have used with compound subjects are correct.

Editing Checklist

Identify Compound-Subject Errors in Your Writing

____ When you see *and* in the subject part of your sentence, use the *They* Tip to see if you have a compound subject.

____ If *they* makes sense when it replaces the subject, the subject is compound and requires a plural verb.

Correct Compound-Subject Errors in Your Writing

____ If the subject and verb do not agree in number, change the form of the verb to match the subject. Use a plural verb form for a compound subject.

Lesson 8

*s-v
agr*

The Bottom Line	A noun or pronoun and another noun or pronoun joined by *and* make a compound subject.

UNIT THREE: Making Subjects and Verbs Agree

REVIEW

Writers make errors in subject-verb agreement when they make the verb agree with a word that is not the actual subject of the sentence. Unit Three introduced three types of errors writers make in trying to make subjects and verbs agree: lost-subject errors, *there is/there was* errors, and compound-subject errors.

Agreement with Lost Subjects

When many words separate the subject of a sentence from the verb, writers tend to overlook the actual subject and make the verb agree with a word that is near to it. Here is a tip that will help you find the real subject of a sentence:

> **FIRST-WORD TIP:** When you check verbs for subject-verb agreement, go back to the beginning of the sentence and find the *first* word that makes sense as the subject. In nearly all cases, that first word will be the subject.

Agreement with *There is* and *There was*

When a sentence points out the existence of something using a *there is/there was* construction, writers tend to make the verb singular even when the actual subject is plural. The following tip shows that the *there* in a "there exists" sentence is an empty word used as a placeholder for the real subject:

> ***THERE* DELETION TIP:** Rearrange the word order of the sentence to eliminate *there*. If this paraphrase is grammatical, then the original sentence contains an "existential there" construction.

Check for errors in subject-verb agreement every time you use *there is/there was* to mean "there exists"; make the verb agree with the first word *after* the verb that makes sense as the subject. Here is a tip that will help you find the real subject of the sentence:

> **BEHIND-THE-VERB TIP:** In *there is/there was* sentences, the subject is the first word after the verb that makes sense as a subject.

96

Agreement with Compound Subjects

When there is a compound subject, writers sometimes think of the compound as a single unit and mistakenly use a singular verb. Subjects that include *and* are generally compound subjects and are grammatically plural when it comes to subject-verb agreement. Check for a compound subject and for an error in subject-verb agreement any time there is an *and* in the subject part of the sentence. To be sure that you have used the correct verb form with a compound subject, use the following tip:

Unit Three

review

> *THEY* TIP: Whenever *and* is used in the subject part of a sentence, see whether you can replace the entire subject portion with the pronoun *they*. If you can, then the subject is a compound and the verb must be made plural to agree with *they*.

Review Test

Underline the subjects in every sentence. Then, correct all errors using the first correction as a model. The number in parentheses at the end of each paragraph indicates how many errors you should find.

Although European explorers came to the New World in search

of gold, the new <u>fruits</u> and <u>vegetables</u> of the New World ~~was~~ much
were

more important to the Old World than all the gold they ever found.

Before contact with the New World, there was no tomatoes, corn,

or potatoes in the Old World. However, for many of us, the greatest

gift of all the New World's many agricultural products were the food

and beverage that we call *chocolate.* All products containing chocolate

in any form comes from the seeds of the cacao tree. The Mayas in

Central America was the first to discover how to produce chocolate

from cacao seeds. (4)

A number of large, melon-shaped pods grow directly on the trunk

and larger branches of the cacao tree. Each of these pods contain up to forty almond-shaped seeds. The seeds, after being removed from the pod, fermented, and dried, is transformed into the commercial cocoa bean. (2)

The first step in producing chocolate from the cacao beans are to remove the outer shells. What remains after the shells have been removed are called *nibs.* Nibs contain a high percentage of a natural fat called *cocoa butter.* When nibs are heated and ground, the cocoa butter is released. The mixture of cocoa butter and finely ground nibs form a liquid called *chocolate liquor.* The chocolate liquor, after being cooled and molded into little cakes, are what we know as baking chocolate. Baking chocolate and sugar is at the heart of all those wonderful chocolate goodies that we would all die for. (5)

UNIT FOUR
Using Correct Verb Tenses

Terms That Can Help You Understand Verb Tenses

If you are not familiar with any of the following terms, look them up in the Guide to Grammar Terminology beginning on page 1. The numbers in parentheses indicate the lessons in which each term appears.

helping verb (10)	**perfect tense (10)**
participle (10)	**present tense (9)**
past participle (10)	**tense (9, 10)**
past tense (9, 10)	**verb (9, 10)**

The Nuts and Bolts of Verb Tenses

Verb *tense* indicates when the action in a sentence occurred. The lessons in Unit Four show you how to use the past tense, the present tense, and the perfect tense correctly.

Lesson 9 shows you how to avoid improper *tense shifting* between the present and past tenses. Knowing when to shift from one to the other requires an understanding of the fundamentally different roles of the two tenses. The **present tense** is used to state facts or make generalizations. The **past tense** is used to narrate events completed in the past.

EXAMPLE: ✗ Michelle took the baby to day care whenever she has to work.

CORRECTION: Michelle ~~took~~ *takes* the baby to day care whenever she has to work.

Lesson 10 shows you how to use the **perfect tenses**, which are made with the **helping verb** *have* (in some form) followed by a verb in the **past participle** form. If you use a present tense form of *have*, you create a *present perfect* verb (*Jesse has seen that movie dozens of times*). If you use the past tense *had*, you create a *past perfect* verb (*Akshitha had seen the movie before she read*

99

the book). Sometimes writers mistakenly use the past tense when they should use either the present perfect or the past perfect.

> EXAMPLE: ✗ I felt much more secure ever since we installed a home alarm system.

> CORRECTION: *have*
> ✗ I felt much more secure ever since we installed a home alarm system.
> ⌃

Unit Four

overview

Can you detect problems with verbs?

CORRECTED SENTENCES APPEAR ON PAGE 478.

Correct all verb errors in the following paragraph using the first correction as a model. The number in parentheses at the end of the paragraph indicates how many errors you should find.

My wife and I really disagree about old movies. I always ~~loved~~ *love* to watch them, but my wife is bored by them. She would just as soon watch paint dry as sit through an old film. Last night, for example, we have watched Hitchcock's 1938 mystery *The Lady Vanishes*. She fell asleep in the middle of it. After the movie finished, I woke her up and started talking about what a great movie it was. She was not impressed. To her, the poor quality of the print makes watching it a chore rather than a pleasure. Whenever I watch an old movie, I noticed the quality problems for the first few minutes, but they never seem to bothered me after that. (6)

LESSON 9

Present, Past, and Tense Shifting

Error Sentences

CORRECTED SENTENCES APPEAR ON PAGE 103.

EXAMPLE 1: ✗ Whenever we went to a restaurant, my father always makes a fuss about ordering exactly the right wine.

EXAMPLE 2: ✗ She went to Trident Technical College, which was in South Carolina.

What's the Problem?

Readers usually expect a piece of writing to maintain a consistent use of **tense** from beginning to end. For instance, in Example 1, the writer starts in the **past tense** (*we went*) and then, for no apparent reason, shifts to the **present tense** (*my father always makes a fuss*).

However, sometimes the opposite is true: the sentence is wrong if we don't shift. For instance, in Example 2, the writer needs to shift the past tense *was* to the present tense *is* because, as the sentence is written, it implies something that the writer does not mean: that Trident Technical College is no longer in South Carolina.

What Causes the Problem?

Once writers commit themselves to a tense (either present or past), they must stick with it *unless* there is a reason to shift tenses. Readers find inappropriate *tense shifting* distracting at best and often misleading. Sometimes, though, as we saw in Example 2, there are good reasons to shift from one tense to another. The trick, of course, is knowing what these reasons are.

The differences between the past tense and the present tense go beyond just their difference in time. The two tenses have different functions, and we shift between them as we have need of those functions. The past

101

tense is used to describe an event that happened in the past (*The phone rang during dinner last night*), while the present tense is used to make a statement or generalization that is not tied to a past event (*The phone always rings during dinner*).

Diagnostic Exercise

CORRECTED SENTENCES APPEAR ON PAGE 479.

Lesson 9

shift

Correct all errors in the following paragraph using the first correction as a model. The number in parentheses at the end of the paragraph indicates how many errors you should find.

Last summer we took a trip to Provence, a region in the southeast

borders

corner of France, which ~~bordered~~ on Italy. The name *Provence*

referred to the fact that it was the first province created by the

ancient Romans outside the Italian peninsula. Today, Provence still

contained an amazing number of well-preserved Roman ruins.

While there were a few big towns on the coast, Provence was famous

for its wild country and beautiful scenery. Provence was especially

known for its abundance of wildflowers in the spring. These flowers

were used to make some of the world's most expensive perfumes. (6)

Fixing This Problem in Your Writing

Your writing needs to show whether you are telling about events that happened and were completed in the past (in which case you would use the *past tense*) or whether you are making a statement of fact or a generalization whose validity is not limited to the past (in which case you would use the *present tense*).

People use the past tense to tell stories. For example, most novels are written in the past tense. The present tense is used for "timeless" statements and generalizations. For example, most nonfiction writing that deals with description or analysis is written in the present tense. (Notice that this paragraph uses the present tense to make a "timeless" generalization.) Writing contains a great deal of tense shifting because the past and present tenses have complementary functions. For example, generalizations (in the present tense) often need the support of concrete examples, which are often descriptions of events (past tense). Stories (past tense) often include generalizations about what happened that are not only true for the time of the story but will continue to be true indefinitely (present tense). Here are two tips that will help you in deciding which tense to use.

> **PAST TENSE TIP:** Use the past tense when describing or discussing events that were completed in the past.

Here is the Past Tense Tip applied to Example 1.

> EXAMPLE 1:   ✗ Whenever we went to a restaurant, my father always makes a fuss about ordering exactly the right wine.

> TIP APPLIED: Whenever we went to a restaurant, my father always
> *made*
> ~~makes~~ a fuss about ordering exactly the right wine.
> ^

In this sentence, both actions (going to the restaurant and making a fuss about ordering) happened in the past. The entire sentence, then, must be written in the past tense.

> **PRESENT TENSE TIP:** Use the present tense to make statements of fact or generalizations that are true now and will continue to be true indefinitely unless something happens to change the situation.

Here are the Past Tense and Present Tense Tips applied to Example 2.

> EXAMPLE 2:   ✗ She went to Trident Technical College, which was in South Carolina.

> TIP APPLIED: She went to Trident Technical College, which ~~was~~ in
> *is*
> South Carolina.
> ^

In this sentence, a shift in tense is necessary. *She* has finished attending Trident Technical College, so the use of the past tense in this part of the sentence is correct. However, the college is still, and probably will always be, in South Carolina. In the second part of the sentence, the writer must shift to present tense.

Here is another tip to help you remember when to use the present tense.

> HABITUAL-ACTIONS TIP: Use the present tense to describe habitual or repeated actions.

EXAMPLE: **Sam is always late for meetings.**

This sentence is a generalization about Sam's habitual behavior. It would still be a valid statement even if Sam showed up early for his next meeting.

Here is an example of how to shift from tense to tense according to the meaning you need to express:

EXAMPLE: **Shakespeare wrote *Hamlet* around 1600. The action of the play is set in Elsinore Castle in Denmark. Critics have always considered this one of Shakespeare's most complex plays.**

The first sentence is in the past tense because it describes an event (Shakespeare's writing of *Hamlet*) that was completed in the past (Past Tense Tip). The second sentence is in the present tense because it is a "timeless" statement of fact about the setting of the play (Present Tense Tip). The third sentence is in the present tense because it describes the habitual behavior of critics (Habitual-Actions Tip).

Sentence Practice 1

CORRECTED SENTENCES APPEAR ON PAGE 479.

Correct the present and past tense errors in the following sentences by drawing a line through each error and writing the correct tense above it. If the sentence is correct, write *OK* above it.

seem
EXAMPLE: **I always ~~seemed~~ to be running late on Mondays.**
             ^

1. Key West was the southernmost point in the continental United States.

2. Whenever the weather changes, my joints started to ache.

3. We visited one ancient monument after another until they all run together.

4. Shakespeare is idolized in the nineteenth century.

5. I-405 went around downtown Seattle.

Lesson 9

shift

For more practice with past and present tense shifting, go to **Exercise Central** at **bedfordstmartins.com/commonsense/4-9**.

Sentence Practice 2

CORRECTED SENTENCES APPEAR ON PAGE 479.

Correct the present and past tense errors in the following sentences by drawing a line through each error and writing the correct tense above it. If the sentence is correct, write *OK* above it.

EXAMPLE: It always seems to rain whenever we ~~went~~ to the beach.
                                                                                go
                                                                                 ^

Lesson 9

shift

1.   Telephone marketers always call when we were eating.

2.   According to the style sheet, scientific papers were rarely written in the first person.

3.   I always try to return messages before I left the office.

4.   She broke her ankle skiing down the trail that led to the ranger cabin.

5.   When it rains, it poured.

Sentence Practice 3

Combine the following sentences by replacing the IT in the first sentence with the entire second sentence. The verb in the second sentence is in bold. Change the verb to the correct form according to the meaning of the new, combined sentence.

EXAMPLE: We all know that IT.
                      Boxing Day **be** the day after Christmas.

ANSWER: We all knew that Boxing Day **is** the day after Christmas.

1.   I think that IT.
      A matinee performance typically **start** at two.

2.   I got a shock when IT.
      I **plug** that old lamp in.

3. She always call her kids when IT.
   She **be** going to be late.

4. Artists today are still influenced by IT.
   The art styles that **originate** in prewar Germany.

5. After all our work, we discoverd that IT.
   The answer **be** in the back of the book.

Lesson 9

shift

Editing Practice 1

CORRECTED SENTENCES APPEAR ON PAGE 479.

Correct all errors in the following paragraph using the first correction as a model. The number in parentheses at the end of the paragraph indicates how many errors you should find.

> *discovered*
> Last night I ~~discover~~ how to use the Internet to keep track
> of my 401k plan. I visited the financial company's Web site, which
> included a range of resources to help even the most intimidated
> investor. The first thing I had to do is establish a personal
> identification number (or PIN), just like I did when I get a new
> bank card last year. When I gained access to my account, I am
> able to check my balance, see how much I contribute each month,
> and shift my money into different funds. The best feature was
> that I can use these resources twenty-four hours a day. This beats
> trying to reach the customer service staff between 9:00 A.M. and
> 5:00 P.M., especially since I worked until 5:30. (6)

Editing Practice 2

CORRECTED SENTENCES APPEAR ON PAGE 479.

Correct all errors in the following paragraphs using the first correction as a model. The number in parentheses at the end of each paragraph indicates how many errors you should find.

Although William Shakespeare died in 1616, performances

of his plays ~~were~~ *are* alive and well today. A number of theaters and

summer festivals were devoted to performing his plays. In England,

the Royal Shakespeare Company performed in London and Stratford-

upon-Avon (the small town where Shakespeare was born). In Canada,

there was a highly successful Shakespeare festival every summer in

Stratford, Ontario. In the United States, there were theatrical organi-

zations devoted to performing Shakespeare's plays in Washington,

D.C., New York, San Diego, and the small college town of Ashland,

Oregon. (4)

Ashland's Shakespeare Festival begins almost by accident as

an outgrowth of the old Chautauqua circuit that provides entertain-

ment to rural America before the days of radio and movies. After the

collapse of Chautauqua, Ashland finds itself with a good-sized summer

theater facility, and faculty from the college decide to stage a few

Shakespearean plays. (4)

Lesson 9

shift

Editing Practice 3

Correct all errors in the following paragraphs using the first correction as a
model. The number in parentheses at the end of each paragraph indicates
how many errors you should find.

A few years ago, I was a juror in a murder trial. The defendant

was a member of the local mob who ~~is~~ *was* accused of conspiring to

kill the head of another gang. The prosecution's entire case rested

on the testimony of a police informant who had been a friend

of the accused. According to the judge, the rules of evidence in a

conspiracy case were quite different from the rules governing evidence when the defendant was accused of actually committing

a criminal act. (2)

The process of jury deliberation was very interesting. As we

discussed the evidence, we had amazingly different recollections about

what we had heard. We even have different memories of basic factual

information. What was remarkable was that we eventually reached a

consensus and delivered a verdict that we all feel was fair. (2)

Writing Practice

On a separate sheet of paper, write about some event you experienced in the past using one of the Editing Practice essays as a model. Then, step back from that experience and make some generalizations about it. Use the Editing Checklist to show that every use of the present tense and the past tense in your essay is correct.

Editing Checklist

Identify Problems with Verb Tenses and Tense Shifting

_____ Identify the verb in your sentence.

_____ Ask yourself whether you are telling about an event that happened and was completed in the past or whether you are making a statement of fact or a generalization.

Correct Problems with Verb Tenses and Tense Shifting

_____ Use the past tense when describing or discussing events that happened and were completed in the past.

_____ Use the present tense to make statements of fact or generalizations that are true now and will continue to be true in the future.

_____ If your sentence combines a description of a past event with a generalization, you need to shift from the past tense to the present tense within the sentence.

| **The Bottom Line** | **Keep** the verbs in a sentence in the same tense unless you **have** a reason for shifting tenses. |

shift

LESSON 10
The Past and the Perfect Tenses

Error Sentences

CORRECTED SENTENCES APPEAR ON PAGES 112–13.

vt

EXAMPLE 1: ✗ We regretted our choice ever since we bought that car.

EXAMPLE 2: ✗ When we bought the house last year, it was empty for ten years.

What's the Problem?

The **perfect tenses** are formed with the helping verb *have* in some form followed by the **past participle** form of a second verb. When the present tense forms of *have* (*have, has*) are used, the resulting construction is called the *present perfect* tense; for example: *We have seen that movie; Raoul has answered that question before.*

The past tense of *have* (*had*) is used to form the *past perfect* tense; for example: *Marta had reported the accident before the police arrived.*

The most common mistake is that writers use the past tense when they should use either the present perfect tense (Example 1) or the past perfect tense (Example 2).

You should use the present perfect tense to indicate an action that began in the past and continues to the present (*Senator Longterm has served for 18 years*) or an action that began and ended at an unspecified time in the past (*Senator Longterm has won three elections*).

The past perfect tense indicates an action that took place in the past before another past action (*I had admired Senator Longterm before the newspaper revealed the scandal*) or a past action that ended at a specific time (*I had met the senator in 1989*).

What Causes the Problem?

The present perfect and the past perfect tenses allow us to show rather subtle differences in past time relationships. In conversation, speakers often fail to use the perfect tenses, especially the past perfect, because they do not usually plan out their sentences before they speak. Writers also tend to use the past tense incorrectly for all time relationships in the past.

Diagnostic Exercise

CORRECTED SENTENCES APPEAR ON PAGE 479.

Correct all errors in the following paragraph using the first correction as a model. The number in parentheses at the end of the paragraph indicates how many errors you should find.

Lesson 10

vt

                                        have been

Unfortunately, most people ~~were~~ involved in an automobile

^

accident at some time. I was involved in several, but my luckiest

accident was one that never happened. Just after I got my driver's

license, I borrowed the family car to go to a party. Although it was

a very tame party, I left feeling a little hyper and silly. It was night,

and there were no street lights nearby. I parked a little distance

from the house, so my car was by itself. I got into the car and

decided to show off a little bit by throwing the car into reverse and

flooring it. I went about 20 yards backward before I thought to

myself that I was doing something pretty dangerous. I slammed

on the brakes in a panic. I got out of the car and found that my

back bumper was about 4 inches from a parked car that I never saw.

Whenever I feel an urge to push my luck driving, I remind myself

of the accident that almost happened. (6)

Fixing This Problem in Your Writing

This tip shows you when to use the present perfect tense:

> **PRESENT PERFECT TIP:** Use the present perfect when a past action con-
> tinues up to the present moment.

The difference between the past and the present perfect is that the past tense refers to a *completed* past event, but the present perfect refers to something that started in the past and continues to the present. Compare the following sentences:

PAST: **Louise <u>lived</u> in Chicago for ten years.**

PRESENT PERFECT: **Louise <u>has lived</u> in Chicago for ten years.**

In the first sentence, we know that Louise does not live in Chicago anymore; the period of her residence ended some time in the past. In the second sentence, the present perfect means that the ten-year period continues and that Louise *still* lives in Chicago.

Let's apply the Present Perfect Tip to the first sample sentence:

EXAMPLE 1:   **✗ We regretted our choice ever since we bought that car.**

The problem is the incompatibility between the over-and-done-with meaning of the past tense and the fact that the writer still regrets the choice of car today.

TIP APPLIED: **We _have_ regretted our choice ever since we bought that car.**

This tip shows you when to use the past perfect tense.

> **PAST PERFECT TIP:** Use the past perfect to show that one event in the past was completed *before* a more recent past event took place.

The past perfect tense enables us to describe the time sequence between two different past events, one of which happened before the other. Let's look at Example 2:

EXAMPLE 2:   **✗ When we bought the house last year, it was empty for ten years.**

There are two past events here: (1) a ten-year period before last year during which time the house had stood empty and (2) the moment last year when the writer bought the house.

had been
TIP APPLIED: **When we bought the house last year, it ~~was~~ empty for ten years.**
                                                                      ^

Writers often use the past perfect tense to imply that one past event *caused* a later past event. For example, the sentence *They <u>had gotten</u> into a big fight just before they <u>broke</u> up* implies that they broke up *because* of their big fight.

Sentence Practice 1

CORRECTED SENTENCES APPEAR ON PAGE 480.

The following sentences contain mistakes involving the use of the past, the present perfect, and the past perfect tenses. Correct each error as shown in the following example.

had closed
EXAMPLE: **The storm ~~closed~~ the runways before we got clearance to take off.**
                            ^

1. We had a test every week this semester.

2. It has rained last week during the parade.

3. When we returned from vacation, we found that our house was broken into.

4. I was interested in Egyptology for years.

5. After Holmes solved a case, Watson wrote it up for posterity.

 For more practice using the past and perfect tenses, go to **Exercise Central** at **bedfordstmartins.com/commonsense/4-10**.

Sentence Practice 2

CORRECTED SENTENCES APPEAR ON PAGE 480.

The following sentences contain mistakes involving the use of the past, the present perfect, and the past perfect tenses. Correct each error as shown in the following example.

have seen
EXAMPLE: Ever since I got my DVD player, I ~~saw~~ dozens of movies.
                                                ^

1.   He has wrecked his knee making a tackle on the first play of the game.

2.   I already noticed the problem before you told me about it.

3.   He worked overtime for the past six months.

Lesson 10

4.   We had to forfeit the game after we used an ineligible player.

vt

5.   It snowed every day since Christmas.

Sentence Practice 3

Combine the following sentences by adding the underlined information in the second sentence to the first sentence. Change the past tense of the first sentence to the present perfect or past perfect tense as appropriate.

EXAMPLE: The board met.
They met every Monday this past year.

has met
ANSWER: The board ~~met~~ every Monday this past year.
                             ^

1.   The whistle already sounded.
This was before the ball went into the net.

2.   We worked on our car.
We worked since early this morning.

3.   I just stepped into the shower.
I did that when the phone rang.

4.   Our team played together.
They did that for three seasons now.

5.   Fortunately, Elvis already left the building.
He left before the reporters arrived.

Editing Practice 1

CORRECTED SENTENCES APPEAR ON PAGE 480.

Correct all errors in the following paragraph using the first correction as a model. The number in parentheses at the end of the paragraph indicates how many errors you should find.

has

America had a love affair with the automobile ever since its

^

invention. However, our attitudes about automobile safety were always

ambivalent, even contradictory. Over the years, we were willing to pay

a lot of money for automobiles that go faster and faster, but we always

seemed to be unwilling to deal with the safety consequences of this

increased speed. An interesting case in point is the recent decision by

the federal government to eliminate the 55-mile-per-hour speed limit

on interstate highways. We had this speed limit since the 1970's.

Interestingly, the speed limit was put into effect not as a safety measure

but as a way to save gasoline during the oil embargo at the time. (4)

Lesson 10

vt

Editing Practice 2

CORRECTED SENTENCES APPEAR ON PAGE 480.

Correct all errors in the following paragraph using the first correction as a model. The number in parentheses at the end of the paragraph indicates how many errors you should find.

had been

My friend Dale ~~was~~ living on his parents' farm his whole life

^

when he made himself unwelcome at home. Just before Dale got his

license, his father bought a new car that was his pride and joy. One day,

after Dale and his best friend were out someplace fooling around, Dale

got home late for one of his chores: rounding up the cows for milking.

Dale drove his dad's new car into the pasture to get the cows, something his father expressly prohibited. When he was out in the pasture, the horn got stuck, so Dale pulled out various wires until the horn stopped. That night, after his father went to bed, Dale sneaked into the barn and rewired the horn in the dark. The next morning, when his father started the car, it burst into flames. (4)

Lesson 10

vt

Editing Practice 3

Correct all errors in the following paragraphs using the first correction as a model. The number in parentheses at the end of each paragraph indicates how many errors you should find.

have had
Among all the bad news we ~~had~~ recently, there is one piece of encouraging information. The number of deaths resulting from traffic accidents steadily declined over the past few years. Researchers cited a number of reasons: improved safety of vehicles, increased use of seat belts and air bags, and fewer drunk drivers. Automobile manufacturers were always very reluctant to mention safety, because their entire marketing strategy was based on selling the glamour of cars and driving. Fortunately, this situation changed since the federal government mandated national safety standards. Now, companies compete over who achieved the highest levels of safety. (5)

Perhaps the biggest single factor in declining death rates in this decade was the increased use of seat belts. Now, most of us would never start the car until we fastened our seat belt first. Another big change affecting the accident rate was the general decline in the use of alcohol throughout society in recent years. Americans just do not drink and drive as much as we used to. (3)

Writing Practice

On your own paper, write a short essay about an automobile accident or some aspect of automobile safety. Try to use a mixture of the past tense and the two perfect tenses. Use the Editing Checklist to show that the tenses in your essay are correct.

Editing Checklist

Lesson 10

vt

Identify Errors in Using the Past and the Perfect Tenses

_____ Identify the past tense verb in your sentence.

_____ Ask yourself whether you are describing an event that began and ended entirely in the past or one that began in the past and continues into the present.

_____ Check to see whether you are connecting two past events in a single sentence.

Correct Errors in Using the Past and the Perfect Tenses

_____ If you are describing an event that began and ended entirely in the past, use the past tense (usually the *-ed* form of the verb).

_____ If you are describing an event that began in the past and continues into the present, use the present perfect tense (present tense form of *have* + past participle).

_____ If you are connecting two past events in a single sentence, use the past perfect tense (past tense form of *have* + past participle).

The Bottom Line

Use the present perfect for actions that began in the past and continue up to the present. Use the past perfect for showing that an earlier event had ended before a later event started.

UNIT FOUR: Using Correct Verb Tenses

The lessons in Unit Four discussed how to use verb tenses correctly.

Present, Past, and Tense Shifting

The present tense and the past tense have completely different functions. The present tense is used to express statements of fact or generalizations or to describe habitual actions. The past tense is used to describe an event that began and was completed in the past. Unless you have a reason to shift tenses, you must use one tense consistently. Use this tip to help you decide if the past tense is appropriate:

> **PAST TENSE TIP:** Use the past tense when describing or discussing events that were completed in the past.

There are two closely related uses of the present tense.

> **PRESENT TENSE TIP:** Use the present tense to make statements of fact or generalizations that are true now and will continue to be true indefinitely unless something happens to change the situation.

> **HABITUAL-ACTIONS TIP:** Use the present tense to describe habitual or repeated actions.

The Past and the Perfect Tenses

The past tense is used for describing an event that was completed in the past. The perfect tenses allow writers to show subtle differences in past time relationships by describing action that is completed with respect to a second moment in time. The present perfect refers to a past event that continues up to the present moment. Use this tip to help you remember when to use the present perfect tense:

> **PRESENT PERFECT TIP:** Use the present perfect when a past action continues up to the present moment.

The past perfect shows the relationship between two past events. Use this tip to help you remember when to use the past perfect tense:

> **PAST PERFECT TIP:** Use the past perfect to show that one event in the past was completed before a more recent past event took place.

Review Test

Correct the verb errors in the following paragraphs using the first correction as a model. The number in parentheses at the end of each paragraph indicates how many errors you should find.

Unit Four

review

  Thanks to federal regulations, industrial pollution ~~was~~
has been ^
significantly reduced over the past several decades. However,

we begin to realize that there is another form of water pollution

that was completely outside state and federal regulation:

"nonpoint-source" pollution. Existing regulations dealt with

pollution that has a distinct point of origin—a particular factory

or plant, for example, whose unregulated discharge can be directly

measured. "Point-of-origin" pollution consists of relatively

high levels of pollutants in a small area. The effects that a particular

point-of-origin had on the immediate area are easy to identify,

and we can cost them out. (4)

  Nonpoint-source pollution is a different matter altogether.

Every time we get into our car and start it up, we release a relatively

small amount of various pollutants into the atmosphere. These

pollutants are dispersed over such a wide area that nobody

can tell where they came from or even when they are put into the air.

The problem that defeated environmental agencies for years is

how to deal with such overwhelming numbers of little polluters.
A similar problem existed for years with runoff. Every time it rains,
water dissolves the grease and oil on our driveways and washes
it off into nearby streams. The amount of pollution per square foot
of paved surface is not very great, but the cumulative effect from
millions of square feet of pavement can be devastating. (3)

Unit Four

review

UNIT FIVE
Understanding Pronouns

Terms That Can Help You Understand Pronouns

If you are not familiar with any of the following terms, look them up in the Guide to Grammar Terminology beginning on page 1. The numbers in parentheses indicate the lessons in which each term appears.

agreement (11)
noun (12, 13, 14, 15)
object (13)
personal pronoun (11, 13, 15)
preposition (13)
pronoun (12, 13, 14)

pronoun antecedent (11, 12)
relative pronoun (14)
sexist language (15)
subject (13, 14)
verb (13, 14)

Unit Five

overview

The Nuts and Bolts of Understanding Pronouns

Pronouns are an important part of many languages. As noun replacers, they help us avoid having to use the same words over and over (as in *Ms. Ramone stopped by yesterday, and Ms. Ramone took us for a ride in Ms. Ramone's new car*). Pronouns are useful because they can fit into almost any sentence.

But the adaptability of pronouns also creates problems. Because they can refer to so many things, writers must take care to make the reference of each pronoun clear. The lessons in this unit address some common difficulties involving pronouns:

Lesson 11 shows you how to make a pronoun and the word it refers to either both singular *or* both plural.

EXAMPLE: ✗ The person who called didn't leave their phone number.

CORRECTION: The person who called didn't leave ~~their~~ *her* phone number.

Lesson 12 shows you how to make clear what a pronoun refers to.

EXAMPLE: ✗ Our dog gets so mad at the cat that it chases its tail.

CORRECTION: Our cat gets the dog so mad it chases its own tail.

121

Lessons 13 and 14 help you to choose between similar pronouns: *I* or *me*? *she* or *her*? *he* or *him*? (see Lesson 13); *who, whom,* or *that*? (see Lesson 14).

> EXAMPLE: ✗ Dolly and me went skiing.
>
>   *I*
>
> CORRECTION: Dolly and ~~me~~ went skiing.
>
> EXAMPLE: ✗ Our group decided whom would type our paper.
>
>   *who*
>
> CORRECTION: Our group decided ~~whom~~ would type our paper.

Lesson 15 helps you to use nonsexist language to ensure that nouns and pronouns refer, as appropriate, to both males and females.

> EXAMPLE: ✗ Everyone should have completed his assignment.
>
>   *the*
>
> CORRECTION: Everyone should have completed ~~his~~ assignment.

Unit Five

overview

Can you detect pronoun problems?

CORRECTED SENTENCES APPEAR ON PAGE 480.

Correct all errors in the following paragraphs using the first correction as a model. The number in parentheses at the end of each paragraph indicates how many errors you should find.

>   *who*
>
> My friend Richard told me that Clyde, the guy ~~whom~~ sits
>
> next to him in his English class, decided to quit school because
>
> he'd rather be a rock singer. Richard and me both laughed at this
>
> at first, but maybe it is a smart decision. Clyde has changed his
>
> major at least four times this year; that is what Richard told me.
>
> Although a person might change their major a few times, changing
>
> it too often indicates a good deal of uncertainty and can put him
>
> back several years. (5)

Clyde usually managed to bring up rock music in discussions with Richard, our classmates, and I. Often, Clyde's comments would seem completely irrelevant, but everybody bit their tongue and let him go on and on about Radiohead, System of a Down, or another rock group that somehow Clyde managed to fit into the discussion. Of course, a student has a right to speak up. However, they shouldn't bring up their role models at every opportunity. (4)

Unit Five

overview

LESSON 11
Pronoun Agreement

Error Sentences

CORRECTED SENTENCES APPEAR ON PAGE 126.

EXAMPLE 1: ✗ A teacher should explain their assignments carefully.

EXAMPLE 2: ✗ Did everybody cast their vote in the last election?

What's the Problem?

Personal pronouns include *I, he, she, it, they, we,* and all their varied forms, such as *me, him, his, her, its, their,* and *them.* A personal pronoun often refers back to a person, place, or thing (called a **pronoun antecedent**). This pronoun and antecedent should be in **agreement**; that is, they should match in terms of number, person, and gender (see Lesson 15 for information about agreement involving gender).

This lesson focuses on the most common problem: making sure the personal pronoun agrees in number with its antecedent. In Example 1, the antecedent of *their* is *teacher.* An error occurs because *their* is plural (more than one person) while *teacher* is singular (one person). In Example 2, *everybody* is singular, while *their* is again (and always) plural.

What Causes the Problem?

ESL

Non-native speakers should note that some writers make errors in pronoun agreement when an antecedent seems to refer to many people when technically it includes only one person (even if that one person can be anybody). In Examples 1 and 2, *teacher* and *everybody* are generalizations about any teacher or person, thus giving the feeling that they are about *all* teachers and people — that they are plural. Nonetheless, grammatically they are singular.

Another reason this error occurs is that writers do not want to be sexist. If Examples 1 and 2 used *his* instead of *their,* the writer would avoid an agreement error but might be considered sexist for excluding females (see Lesson 15). Writers should avoid both kinds of problems — agreement errors and sexist use of pronouns.

124

Diagnostic Exercise

CORRECTED SENTENCES APPEAR ON PAGE 481.

Correct all errors in the following paragraph using the first correction as a model. The number in parentheses at the end of the paragraph indicates how many errors you should find.

> *Soldiers commit*
> ~~A soldier commits~~ a war crime when they violate the norms
> of acceptable behavior in times of war. Few people want war,
> but most want their rights and those of others to be respected
> as much as possible when war occurs. For instance, almost
> everybody agrees that a prisoner should have their physical needs
> attended to and should not be physically or mentally tortured.
> An officer who orders their troops to massacre civilians is also
> considered to be committing a war crime; the My Lai massacre
> during the Vietnam War is an example. (2)

Fixing This Problem in Your Writing

As seen in the sample sentences, many agreement errors involve one particular pronoun (*they*) and its various forms (*their, them*). Here is a tip to help you decide if the antecedent is singular or plural:

> *ARE* TIP: When using *they, their,* or *them,* make sure the antecedent is also *plural.* One way to do so is to see whether this antecedent would take the plural verb *are* after it. If this plural verb does not seem to fit, the antecedent is probably *singular* and thus not in agreement with *they, their,* or *them.*

In Example 1, *their* must be referring to *teacher,* but *teacher* is singular.

EXAMPLE 1:   ✗ A teacher should explain their assignments carefully.

TIP APPLIED: ✗ A teacher are...

Example 2 is trickier because *everybody* has a plural "feel" to it. But would you say *Everybody are?*

EXAMPLE 2:   ✗ Did everybody cast their vote in the last election?

TIP APPLIED: ✗ Everybody are...

Everybody cannot take *are* as a verb, so it cannot be plural. The tip shows that Example 2 incorrectly uses the plural *their* to refer to the singular *everybody*.

There are three ways to correct pronoun agreement errors. The first way is to use a plural antecedent.

EXAMPLE 1:   ✗ A teacher should explain their assignments carefully.

TIP APPLIED: ✗ A teacher are...

CORRECTION: Teachers
               A teacher should explain their assignments carefully.

The second way is to revise so you don't need a personal pronoun. In Example 2, for example, the writer could easily use *a* instead of *their*.

EXAMPLE 2:   ✗ Did everybody cast their vote in the last election?

TIP APPLIED: ✗ Everybody are...

CORRECTION: Did everybody cast their vote in the last election?
                                     a

The third way is to use *his or her* instead of *their* with a singular subject.

EXAMPLE 3:   ✗ Did everybody cast their vote in the last election?

TIP APPLIED: ✗ Everybody are...

CORRECTION: Did everybody cast their vote in the last election?
                                  his or her

Sentence Practice 1

CORRECTED SENTENCES APPEAR ON PAGE 481.

In each sentence underline the pronoun once and the antecedent twice, connecting them with a line to show their relationship. Write *plural* or *singular* above the pronoun and its antecedent. Correct any agreement problems. If a sentence has no agreement problem, write *OK* above it.

                    singular   plural
                                                        his or her
EXAMPLE: Everybody in my composition class had their

             first essay returned.

Lesson 11

pron agr

1. A doctor must have insurance covering them against malpractice.

2. Everyone must bring their part of the report tomorrow.

3. A college student has to pick a field that interests them, but they also have to keep an eye on the job market. [*Hint:* A sentence can have more than one agreement error.]

4. I asked my roommates whether they wanted to go out to eat, but they had already eaten.

5. Anybody who hasn't turned in their test should do so now.

 For more practice with pronoun agreement, go to **Exercise Central** at **bedfordstmartins.com/commonsense/5-11**.

Sentence Practice 2

CORRECTED SENTENCES APPEAR ON PAGE 481.

In each sentence underline the pronoun once and the antecedent twice, connecting them with a line to show their relationship. Write *plural* or *singular* above the pronoun and antecedent. Correct any agreement problems. If a sentence has no agreement problem, write *OK* above it.

> *singular*   *plural*
>
>   *All the teachers*   *are*
> EXAMPLE: ~~Every teacher I have~~ this quarter ~~is~~ giving their
>   ^   ^
> final exam on the same day!

1. Someone parked their car in a place where it will surely be towed.

2. Almost everyone brought his or her book to class today.

3. Most people who can recall the assassination of John F. Kennedy seem able to remember exactly what they were doing when they heard the news.

4. Did somebody take my book instead of theirs?

5. Out of thirty people in my dorm, nobody wants to room with me.

Sentence Practice 3

Combine the following sentences with *and* or *but*. Make whatever changes are necessary in the first sentence to eliminate errors in pronoun agreement.

EXAMPLE: A teacher has to act like a drill sergeant.
            They also need the patience of a saint.

ANSWER: <u>Teachers</u> have to act like drill sergeants, but they
            also need the patience of a saint.

1. A humanitarian aid worker works very hard.
    They don't get paid very much.

2. Everyone here needs to be quiet for a moment.
    They can continue talking after I finish adding these numbers.

3. A mall is a convenient place to shop.
    These all seem the same.

4. Someone ate at this table before us.
    They were sloppy.

5. Each book in this room is old.
    These are part of a valuable collection.

Lesson 11

pron
agr

Editing Practice 1

CORRECTED SENTENCES APPEAR ON PAGE 481.

Correct all errors in the following paragraphs using the first correction as a model. The number in parentheses at the end of each paragraph indicates how many errors you should find.

                                                        its

No other European country has ever spread ~~their~~ people and

culture around the globe more than England. Each country, of

course, has had their effects on the world. However, by the end

of the nineteenth century, England had its culture firmly planted

around the world in such diverse places as Canada, the Caribbean,

India, Australia, and South Africa. (1)

Not everyone in England approved of their country's attempt to colonize the world, but most Britons supported colonization because of the economic benefits of commerce with the colonies. A British citizen had much to gain from their country's colonization, but the people within the colonies suffered a loss of freedom and dignity by being controlled by a far-away government. (2)

Editing Practice 2

CORRECTED SENTENCES APPEAR ON PAGE 481.

Correct all errors in the following paragraphs using the first correction as a model. The number in parentheses at the end of each paragraph indicates how many errors you should find.

Lesson 11

*pron
agr*

Almost everybody who has taken an English class has written a book report about something ~~they have~~ *he or she has* read for the class. For one assignment, my English instructor, Ms. Kaplan, asked everyone to read two books that they wanted to read. In high school, almost every English teacher I had made a similar assignment, but they usually asked us to write a summary to prove we had read the book. (2)

Ms. Kaplan, though, said that she didn't want to "test" us about the books we read or make us feel that we had to scrutinize each page for their "hidden" meaning. She simply asked us to announce the books we read and then be ready to recommend or not recommend them to the rest of the class. Almost everybody seems to have read their first selection and truly enjoyed it. One classmate was so enthusiastic about *The Catcher in the Rye,* the novel they read for the assignment, that I decided to read it next. (3)

Editing Practice 3

Correct all errors in the following paragraphs using the first correction as a model. The number in parentheses at the end of each paragraph indicates how many errors you should find.

My literature class read Mary Shelley's *Frankenstein,* published

in 1818. ~~Almost everyone has~~ *Most people have* seen a Frankenstein movie, but they

probably haven't read the novel and noticed how much liberty a

Hollywood director takes when they translate a classic novel to

the big screen. (1)

A typical moviegoer might be surprised when they discover

that in the original novel the monster learned to speak in complete

sentences. Movie directors like to put metal bolts in the necks of

their Frankenstein monsters, but Shelley's monster had none.

Also, a person might be amused or frightened by a Frankenstein

movie, but on reading the novel they would probably think

more about the relationships among science, society, and

nature. (2)

Lesson 11

pron
agr

Writing Practice

Write a paragraph or two describing the positive and negative effects a horror film might have on a moviegoer. Try to use *they, their,* or *them* at least five times. Use the Editing Checklist to correct any errors in pronoun-antecedent agreement in your sentences.

Editing Checklist

Identify Pronoun Agreement Errors

_____ Locate each use of *they, their,* or *them* along with their antecedents (the person, place, or thing that these pronouns refer to).

_____ If the antecedent is *singular,* there is an agreement error. If you're not sure whether the antecedent is singular or plural, use the *Are* Tip.

Correct Pronoun Agreement Errors

_____ You can usually correct the error by rewording the antecedent so that it is plural or by rewording the sentence so that you do not need a pronoun at all.

_____ Another correction strategy is to use *his or her* instead of *their* with a singular subject.

Lesson 11

*pron
agr*

The Bottom Line

Pronouns should agree with **their** antecedents.

LESSON 12

Vague Pronouns:
This, That, and *It*

Error Sentences

CORRECTED SENTENCES APPEAR ON PAGE 134.

EXAMPLE 1: Contrary to her campaign promises, the governor announced cutbacks in welfare and an increase in education spending. ✗ That is sure to anger voters.

EXAMPLE 2: Two of our favorite hobbies are fishing and skiing. ✗ It requires a lot of money for good equipment.

What's the Problem?

Native and non-native speakers of English should note that many pronouns refer back to a previous **noun** or **pronoun**, which is called the **pronoun antecedent**. A problem occurs when this antecedent is missing or unclear. This is the case in Examples 1 and 2. This lesson focuses on three pronouns that are often used vaguely: *this, that,* and *it.* Keep in mind, though, that *this, that,* and *it* can serve other functions in English in addition to taking the place of an antecedent.

What Causes the Problem?

A speaker can use *this, that,* and *it* without creating much confusion because physical gestures (such as pointing) can clarify what *this* or *that* is. Readers also have ways of figuring out what a vague pronoun refers to, but if figuring it out is too much work, a reader is likely to lose interest or miss the meaning entirely. It is the writer's responsibility to make the relationships between pronouns and their antecedents clear to readers. A writer who uses pronouns precisely has a much greater chance of being understood than one who forces readers to work to figure out which pronoun goes with which antecedent.

CORRECTED SENTENCES APPEAR ON PAGE 481.

Using the first correction as a model, correct all vague uses of *this*, *that*, and *it* in the following paragraphs. The number in parentheses at the end of each paragraph indicates how many changes you should make.

"Star Wars" was the name of a military program as well as a
movie. ~~It~~ *The program* was a large research-and-development program calling for military defense in outer space. This was initiated by President Reagan in the 1980's, and it had the official title of "Strategic Defense Initiative." The public never embraced that as much as the catchier title "Star Wars," however. (2)

Star Wars, George Lucas's 1977 film about a space-age military battle, was fresh in the minds of the American people. It was what people could visualize when President Reagan introduced his new program. This illustrates the point that many people want to connect new information with something they already know. It helps us to understand and make sense of new things. (3)

Lesson 12

pron
ref

Fixing This Problem in Your Writing

To avoid vague use of *this*, *that*, and *it*, check to see if you can easily locate the pronoun antecedent.

ANTECEDENT TIP: Locate what you think the pronoun refers to (the antecedent). Make sure this antecedent is a person, place, or thing— not another part of speech or an entire sentence. Make sure there is no "want-to-be antecedent"—another person, place, or thing that the pronoun could possibly be referring to.

In Example 1, *That* seems to be referring to the entire idea of the first sentence. One way to correct the problem is to add a noun after *That*, changing *That* into an adjective, which doesn't require an antecedent.

> EXAMPLE 1:   Contrary to her campaign promises, the governor announced cutbacks in welfare and an increase in education spending. ✗ That is sure to anger voters.

> CORRECTION: Contrary to her campaign promises, the governor announced cutbacks in welfare and an increase in education spending. That <u>inconsistency</u> is sure to anger voters.

In the following revision, the writer has revised the sentence before the pronoun to provide an antecedent, *reversal.*

> CORRECTION: The governor announced cutbacks in welfare and an increase in education spending, a <u>reversal</u> of her campaign promises. <u>That</u> is sure to anger voters.

In Example 2, *It* could refer to *fishing, skiing,* or *fishing and skiing,* but if the last of these possibilities is intended, the correct pronoun is the plural form *They.* Another likely possibility is that the writer really wants *It* to refer to *good equipment* even though the sentence is not constructed to make such a reference. Here are two corrections that eliminate the pronoun:

> EXAMPLE 2:   Two of our favorite hobbies are fishing and skiing. ✗ It requires a lot of money for good equipment.

> CORRECTION: Two of our favorite hobbies, fishing and skiing, require a lot of money for good equipment.

> CORRECTION: Two of our favorite hobbies are fishing and skiing. <u>Good equipment</u> requires a lot of money.

Lesson 12

pron ref

Sentence Practice 1

CORRECTED SENTENCES APPEAR ON PAGE 482.

If the underlined pronoun is vague, correct the sentence using one of the methods described in this lesson. If the pronoun is not vague, write *OK* above it and underline the antecedent.

EXAMPLE: I hurried to answer the phone, and <u>this</u> caused me to
            mad rush
            fall and sprain my ankle.
                                      ^

1. In 1920, the largest known meteorite was found. <u>It</u> weighed some
    65 tons.

2. The printer for the computer is not working, and I have a paper that is
    due in an hour. I knew <u>this</u> was going to happen!

3. There are approximately 320,000 icebergs in the world. <u>This</u> could
    change, however.

4. So far, the election results indicate that the governor will be reelected.
    <u>That</u> is a surprise.

5. I found a shorter way to get from school to my apartment so that I can
    avoid all the traffic. <u>It</u> is nice.

 For more practice with vague pronouns, go to **Exercise Central** at
bedfordstmartins.com/commonsense/5-12.

Lesson 12

pron
ref

Sentence Practice 2

CORRECTED SENTENCES APPEAR ON PAGE 482.

If the underlined pronoun is vague, correct the sentence using one of the
methods described in this lesson. If the pronoun is not vague, write *OK*
above it and underline the antecedent.

EXAMPLE: My roommate told me her teacher gave a lecture
                              The lecture
            on the Industrial Revolution. <s>It</s> lasted almost
                                           ^
            two hours.

1. Alena called again to complain about how nobody remembers her
    birthday. <u>It</u> took over an hour of my time.

2. We need a new air conditioner at our house, but <u>that</u> will not happen
    soon.

3. Cincinnati was a boomtown because of its strategic location. In the early 1800's, <u>it</u> was built on the increasingly busy Ohio River.

4. "The Battle Hymn of the Republic" first appeared as a poem, not a song. Most Americans do not know <u>that</u>.

5. World War I was ended by the Versailles Treaty; <u>this</u> also led to the formation of the League of Nations.

Sentence Practice 3

Lesson 12

pron
ref

The second sentence in each pair contains a vague pronoun in capital letters. Rewrite the second sentence so that it makes a clear reference.

EXAMPLE: **My roommate met an old friend recently.**
SHE is going to graduate school now.

ANSWER: **Her friend is going to graduate school now.**

1. A bird appeared yesterday outside the window of my bathroom.
   IT is not pretty.

2. My English teacher kept us fifteen minutes after we were supposed to leave.
   THIS made me unhappy.

3. The crack in my car window is getting bigger and bigger.
   I knew THAT would happen.

4. Besides bringing a shovel, my friend also brought food for us to eat while camping.
   We might not need IT, but the food will come in handy.

5. Louis Farrakhan organized the Million Man March to promote responsibility and protest violence.
   THAT occurred in 1995.

Editing Practice 1

CORRECTED SENTENCES APPEAR ON PAGE 482.

Correct all errors in the following paragraphs using the first correction as a model. The number in parentheses at the end of each paragraph indicates how many errors you should find.

Some great books do not become great until long after they
situation
are written. This is particularly evident with a book written by
⌃

William Bradford. He wrote *Of Plimouth Plantation,* one of the oldest

books written by Europeans exploring and colonizing the Western

Hemisphere. This was not widely known until 1856, when it was

published, but it was written some two hundred years earlier. (1)

This book, written by the governor of Plymouth Colony,

chronicles the story of the Pilgrims until 1646. Bradford's book offers

considerable detail on the day-to-day lives of the colonists. It contains

the oldest-known copy of the Mayflower Compact, which was an

agreement among the Pilgrims for a democratic-style government.

It disappeared about the time of the American Revolution but was

discovered many years later and finally published. (1)

Lesson 12

*pron
ref*

Editing Practice 2

CORRECTED SENTENCES APPEAR ON PAGE 482.

Correct all errors in the following paragraphs using the first correction as a model. The number in parentheses at the end of each paragraph indicates how many errors you should find.

Slavery
Slavery has been a sore spot in the history of the United States. It
⌃

is especially troubling considering the role of African Americans in the founding of the country. In 1774, a group of slaves in the American colonies made a famous appeal to Thomas Gage, who was the royal governor of Massachusetts Colony. It proclaimed that they as slaves had a right to the freedoms that the colonists sought from Britain. This was shared by Benjamin Franklin, Alexander Hamilton, and other colonists opposing slavery. (2)

When the Revolution began, African Americans were excluded from the American army. That changed, however, when the British encouraged the slaves to join their army. Approximately five thousand African Americans would eventually join the American army. This allowed many to win freedom as a result of their service, but America as a whole would still allow slavery until the Civil War. (2)

Lesson 12

pron
ref

Editing Practice 3

Correct all errors in the following paragraph using the first correction as a model. The number in parentheses at the end of the paragraph indicates how many errors you should find.

I'm trying to make the transition from playing "jungle ball"
                                          transition
volleyball to regulation volleyball. This isn't easy. One major

difference is it requires more teamwork, and that means paying more
              ^
attention to how I set the ball to my teammates. In jungle ball, each player tends to play almost any ball within reach (or at least this is what my team does). That sort of play is fun and gives us a good workout, but too often we have collisions when each person tries to spike every ball over the net. Still, jungle ball has given me some practice in serving, hitting, and occasionally even setting the ball. (3)

Writing Practice

Write a paragraph or two explaining your first efforts to learn a new sport or hobby. Try to include *this, that,* and *it* (any combination) at least five times. Use the Editing Checklist to correct any pronoun errors in your sentences.

Editing Checklist

Identify Vague Pronouns in Your Writing

____ When using *this, that,* and *it* to refer to something you have just written, look for the antecedent — the person, place, or thing the pronoun is renaming. The antecedent should be a noun or a pronoun, not a verb or an entire sentence.

Correct Vague Pronouns in Your Writing

____ Make sure there is no "want-to-be antecedent" — another person, place, or thing the pronoun could possibly refer to — that could cause confusion.

____ You can correct a vague pronoun by adding cues around it to let readers know what the pronoun refers to (for example, you might add a noun after *this* or *that* to make the pronoun into an adjective).

____ You can also correct a vague pronoun by rewording what comes before the pronoun so there is only *one* possible antecedent.

Lesson 12

*pron
ref*

The Bottom Line	When using a pronoun, be sure that **it** has a clear antecedent.

LESSON 13

I or *Me?* *She* or *Her?*
He or *Him?*

Error Sentences

CORRECTED SENTENCES APPEAR ON PAGE 142.

EXAMPLE 1: ✗ Kathy Wong and me took the same math class.

EXAMPLE 2: ✗ Frank sang a song for I alone.

What's the Problem?

Personal pronouns have a characteristic that most other **pronouns** and **nouns** do not have: their appearance can vary dramatically depending on how they are used. Only *you* and *it* have the same **subject** and **object** forms. The other personal pronouns have different subject and object forms:

SUBJECT FORM:	I	he	she	we	they
OBJECT FORM:	me	him	her	us	them

The subject form should be used (1) when the pronoun is the subject of a verb or (2) when the pronoun comes after a **linking verb** (such as *is, am, was, were, are*). Example 1 is an error because the subject form *I* should be used instead of *me*.

The object form is most often used (1) when the pronoun receives the action or (2) when the pronoun comes after a preposition. Example 2 is an error because the personal pronoun follows a preposition (*for*) and should be in the object form (*me*).

What Causes the Problem?

People often make errors in pronoun form when they "listen" to the words to decide which form "sounds" appropriate. For example, some people might say "It's *me*," but the correct pronoun form (after the linking verb *be*) is actually "It is I." Others might use *I* in formal situations because it sounds correct (see Example 2), when *me* is technically the correct choice. The problem of pronoun form is especially common in sentences that have compound objects (✗ *Pedro invited* <u>*Stasia and I*</u> *to dinner*).

In formal writing, however, writers—especially writers whose first language is not English—can't always trust the sound of the sentence or popular oral usage. Listening to how a sentence sounds can be helpful in determining whether it is clear and flows well, but don't rely on this approach to help you decide whether you have used the correct form of a personal pronoun.

ESL

Diagnostic Exercise

CORRECTED SENTENCES APPEAR ON PAGE 482.

Correct all errors in the following paragraph using the first correction as a model. The number in parentheses at the end of the paragraph indicates how many errors you should find.

My roommate and ~~me~~ *I* visited her friend Jeff, who lives in a

cabin he built from scratch. That's a formidable project for I.

My roommate asked Jeff whether he would mind if her and I stayed

at his place for a few days in the summer. He said that was fine if

we would help him build a new storeroom, and we quickly agreed to

help him out. I'm not much of a carpenter, but Jeff said he'd be patient

and help me learn. For an inexperienced builder such as I, building

even a small storeroom is a major challenge, but I am looking forward

to learning some carpentry skills. (3)

Fixing This Problem in Your Writing

Following are two tips for avoiding most errors involving the form of personal pronouns:

> **NEXT-WORD TIP:** Use the *subject form* of the pronoun if a **verb** comes right after it (or very soon after it).

> **PRECEDING-WORD TIP:** Use the *object form* of the pronoun if a **preposition** or a **verb** immediately precedes (comes before) the pronoun.

In Example 1, the verb *took* comes right after *me*. Also, there is no verb or preposition right before *me*. Thus, both tips show that the subject form of the personal pronoun should be used.

EXAMPLE 1:	✗ Kathy Wong and me took the same math class.

verb
↓
TIP APPLIED: ✗ Kathy Wong and me took the same math class.

I
CORRECTION: Kathy Wong and ~~me~~ took the same math class.
                                ^

Consider the term itself: *subject form*. A subject is a noun or pronoun that performs an action. Thus, use the subject form when the pronoun is the subject of a verb, as in *I took*.

In Example 2, the preposition *for* immediately precedes the pronoun. Therefore, the object form of the personal pronoun is correct.

EXAMPLE 2:	✗ Frank sang a song for I alone.

preposition
↓
TIP APPLIED: ✗ Frank sang a song for I alone.

me
CORRECTION: Frank sang a song for ~~I~~ alone.
                                      ^

Caution: The Preceding-Word Tip does not apply when the personal pronoun comes after a form of the verb *be,* as in *I am he.* In this construction, the subject form is the correct one to use. Such a sentence is more common in speech than in academic writing, but the exception is worth remembering.

Sentence Practice 1

CORRECTED SENTENCES APPEAR ON PAGE 482.

Underline all personal pronouns and correct all pronoun errors in the following sentences. Write *OK* above all pronouns that are used correctly.

EXAMPLE: I thought my cat was missing, but Marsha said <u>it</u>
                     her
            was with ~~she~~.
                      ^

(margin) Lesson 13 · pron case

1. The pharaoh visited the burial tomb intended for just he.

2. Janet and me are going out Saturday night.

3. We want him to go with us.

4. Her and her cat were rescued by the firefighters.

5. Mom promised to write, and today I received a card from she.

 For more practice using pronouns, go to **Exercise Central** at **bedfordstmartins.com/commonsense/5-13**.

Sentence Practice 2

CORRECTED SENTENCES APPEAR ON PAGE 483.

Underline all personal pronouns and correct all pronoun errors in the following sentences. Write *OK* above all pronouns that are used correctly.

> EXAMPLE: That table was reserved for Velda and ~~I~~. *me*

1. Just between you and I, we are having an unannounced quiz on Tuesday.

2. Robert and me will be calling you soon.

3. Are you ready to meet with her?

4. If not for I, you would not be having a birthday at all today.

5. Jill and him left yesterday for Atlanta.

Sentence Practice 3

Replace the underlined noun with the appropriate pronoun.

> EXAMPLE: I thought that Shirley and ~~Jake~~ were engaged. *he*

1. The landlord and <u>Ms. West</u> are meeting with us today about the security deposit.

2. That cake is for <u>the person</u> who is talking to you right now.

3. <u>Carl</u> and <u>Brad</u> will be arriving shortly.

4. The request was made by <u>Tom</u>, not <u>Sue</u>.

5. <u>Dr. Wang</u> asked her students to write a letter to the dean describing their concerns about his new policy.

Editing Practice 1

CORRECTED SENTENCES APPEAR ON PAGE 483.

Correct all errors in the following paragraphs using the first correction as a model. The number in parentheses at the end of each paragraph indicates how many errors you should find.

Writing has never been the easiest task for someone like *me* ~~I~~ who has not written a great deal in the past; however, I am gaining more experience in my technical writing class. Three other students and I are supposed to work on a group paper. One group member, Suzanne, and me are supposed to write a definition section of our paper, which is on ethical behavior in accounting. I have two friends who are accountants; I don't necessarily agree with they about morality or ethics but believe their input would be useful. My group agreed to supplement our library research by interviewing these two accountants. (2)

An objective analysis of the issue is supposed to be included in the section that Suzanne and me were assigned. The interviews were useful because the two accountants each presented different perspectives. They also admitted that the issue of ethics was confusing

for they as well as I. (3)

Editing Practice 2

CORRECTED SENTENCES APPEAR ON PAGE 483.

Correct all errors in the following paragraphs using the first correction as a
model. The number in parentheses at the end of each paragraph indicates
how many errors you should find.

My roommate, Rusty, asked me to join a money-making

enterprise concocted by he [*him*] and his father. The plan they devised

sounds simple: Rusty's dad would purchase fifty compact refrigerators

that we would lease out to college students living in the dorms.

Rusty's dad would supply the capital, while Rusty and me would

do the labor. When Rusty told me the plan, I was skeptical. I talked

it over with he and agreed to help because I figured I had little to

lose. (2)

Rusty's dad lives in town and owns a place where we could

store any refrigerators Rusty and me could not lease. We placed

ads and notices around town and in the school paper. The week

before class began, thirty students came by to do business. It wasn't

stressful, but we had to stay around all day waiting on people.

Rusty and me won't get rich from this business, but it helps pay

the bills. (2)

Editing Practice 3

Correct all errors in the following paragraphs using the first correction as a model. The number in parentheses at the end of each paragraph indicates how many errors you should find.

My parents were a great influence on me, but I was influenced
by family members besides ~~they~~ *them*. My sister Monica and Uncle Ed
taught me a great deal. Monica and me were close in age, and
we were inseparable. Her greatest influence is that she taught
me not to dwell on the bad things that happen. While her was
on a bike ride once, a car ran into her and broke her leg. She
eventually laughed it off and said she'd learn to wear brighter
clothes when riding. (2)

Uncle Ed was like a second dad. My dad and him were
very close, and I would join them on long walks in the summer.
When I was small, they would take turns carrying Monica and
I when we were tired. Next to my dad, Uncle Ed was the gentlest
man I've known. He taught me through example to control my
temper and care for the feelings of people other than I. (3)

Lesson 13

pron
case

Writing Practice

On your own paper, write a paragraph or two describing how two or three family members or friends have influenced you. Try to use any combination of the pronouns covered in this lesson (*I, me, she, her, he, him*). Use the Editing Checklist to correct any pronoun errors in your sentences.

Editing Checklist

Identify Errors in Pronoun Forms in Your Writing

____ Identify personal pronouns in your writing (*I, me, he, him, she, her, we, us, they, them*).

____ Look to see what words surround each personal pronoun. For each pronoun, check to see if it is followed by a verb or preceded by a verb or a preposition.

Correct Pronoun Forms in Your Writing

____ If a personal pronoun is followed by a verb, use the subject form of the pronoun: *I, he, she, we, they.*

____ If a personal pronoun is preceded by a verb or a preposition, use the object form of the pronoun: *me, him, her, us, them.*

____ In formal writing, use the subject form if the pronoun comes right after a form of *be* (such as *is, was, were,* and *are*).

Lesson 13

pron case

The Bottom Line	The subject forms of personal pronouns have a distinct characteristic: **They are followed** more often than not by verbs.

LESSON 14

Who, Whom, and *That*

Error Sentences

CORRECTED SENTENCES APPEAR ON PAGE 150.

EXAMPLE 1: ✗ The woman that read my paper liked it.

EXAMPLE 2: ✗ I met a person who you would like.

What's the Problem?

Who, whom, and *that* are **relative pronouns**—special **pronouns** that always refer to a preceding **noun**. Writers are often confused about which of these three pronouns to use in a sentence, and the rules are not altogether clear or consistent about such issues as whether or not *that* can refer to people. The safest choice is to use *that* to refer to ideas or things, not to people. For instance, many readers would consider *that* in Example 1 to be inappropriate because *that* refers to a person (*a woman*).

Many writers use only the relative pronouns *who* and *whom* to refer to people. But how do you know which of these two to use? Keep in mind that the subject of a sentence performs the action, and the object receives the action. Whenever the pronoun is a subject, use *who;* whenever the pronoun is an object, use *whom.* In Example 2, for example, *you* is the subject of the verb *would like* and *whom* is the object.

What Causes the Problem?

In the quick give-and-take of conversation, speakers often avoid the complicated choice between *who* and *whom* by using *that* to refer to people; or speakers use *who* when they should use *whom.* Listeners usually don't comment on any "error" that speakers might make in choosing the most appropriate pronoun form among *that, who,* or *whom.* For these reasons, many writers simply haven't become sensitive to the distinctions among these relative pronouns. Nonetheless, readers (unlike listeners) are often more than willing to point out errors of this kind, so we suggest that you use these pronouns carefully.

Diagnostic Exercise

CORRECTED SENTENCES APPEAR ON PAGE 483.

In the following paragraph, every *that* is underlined. Using the first correction as a model, change each inappropriately used *that* to *who* or *whom.* The number in parentheses at the end of the paragraph indicates how many errors you should find.

An experience <u>that</u> we all have had is working for a bad boss.

One boss <u>~~that~~</u> we have all had is the petty tyrant, a person <u>that</u> loves

    whom ^

to find fault with every employee <u>that</u> works in the building. It seems

<u>that</u> the petty tyrant is more interested in finding employees <u>that</u> he or

she can belittle than in getting the job done. Even worse than the petty

tyrant is a supervisor <u>that</u> is inconsistent. An inconsistent boss is a

person <u>that</u> the employees can never depend on. A game <u>that</u> this kind

of boss loves is playing favorites. One day, this boss is your best buddy;

the next day, the boss acts as if he or she doesn't know the name of a

person <u>that</u> has worked with the company for ten years. (6)

Fixing This Problem in Your Writing

To use the appropriate relative pronoun in formal writing, look at the noun the pronoun refers to. (The noun will always be the word right before *that.*) If the noun refers to a thing or an idea, use *that.* However, if the noun refers to a person, use either *who* or *whom.*

Use *who* if the relative pronoun is the subject of the following verb. But if the pronoun is *not* the subject of the following verb, use *whom.*

The following tips can help you make sense of these three relative pronouns:

THAT ANIMAL! TIP: Look at the word the pronoun renames. Use *that* only if this word refers to something nonhuman.

WHO/WHOM TIP: Look at the word immediately after *who* or *whom.* If this word is a *verb,* use *who.* But if this word is a *noun* or *pronoun,* use *whom.*

The *That Animal!* Tip indicates that Example 1 should be changed because *that* is inappropriately used to refer to a person. Next, the *Who/Whom* Tip indicates that the more appropriate pronoun is *who*, because a verb comes immediately after it.

<table>
<tr><td>EXAMPLE 1:</td><td>✗ The woman that read my paper liked it.</td></tr>
</table>

EXAMPLE 1: ✗ The woman that read my paper liked it.

THAT ANIMAL! TIP APPLIED: *human*
✗ The woman that read my paper liked it.

WHO/WHOM TIP APPLIED: *verb*
The woman that read my paper liked it.

CORRECTION: *who*
The woman ~~that~~ read my paper liked it.
                    ^

Lesson 14

pron case

In Example 2, the pronoun *you* immediately follows *who*, so we should change *who* to *whom:*

EXAMPLE 2: ✗ I met a person who you would like.

TIP APPLIED: *pronoun*
✗ I met a person who you would like.

CORRECTION: *whom*
I met a person ~~who~~ you would like.
              ^

Because *who* and *whom* can be especially tricky, here are two more sample sentences.

EXAMPLE 3: The clerk <u>who</u> was at the desk called the manager.

EXAMPLE 4: ✗ The clerk <u>who</u> Alicia called found a room for us.

Using the *Who/Whom* Tip, let's check Example 3. The word after *who* is *was* (verb), so the sentence is OK as is. *Who* is the subject of *was at the desk.* In Example 4, the word after *who* is *Alicia* (noun), so the sentence is incorrect. Change *who* to *whom*, because *whom* is the object of the verb *called.*

Sentence Practice 1

CORRECTED SENTENCES APPEAR ON PAGE 483.

In each of the following sentences, underline the word that *that* refers to. If *that* is used to refer to a thing or an idea, write *OK* above it. However, if *that* refers to a person, cross out *that* and write *who* or *whom* above it.

> *whom*
> EXAMPLE: A teacher ~~that~~ I had in high school is my instructor
> in English. ^

1. The person that answered the phone took my order for a cheese pizza.

2. Somebody that was here a minute ago left this pen.

3. I called the couple that had answered the ad.

4. The information that Robert had received proved to be incorrect.

5. A friend that was staying with us this weekend ate your candy.

> For more practice using pronouns, go to **Exercise Central** at
> **bedfordstmartins.com/commonsense/5-14**.

Lesson 14

*pron
case*

Sentence Practice 2

CORRECTED SENTENCES APPEAR ON PAGE 483.

In each of the following sentences, underline the word that *that* refers to. If *that* is used to refer to a thing or an idea, write *OK* above it. However, if *that* refers to a person, cross out *that* and write *who* or *whom* above it.

> *who*
> EXAMPLE: The person ~~that~~ wrote these instructions left out a
> vital step. ^

1. Here is the cake that you wanted me to bring.

2. I need to know the name of the mechanic that supposedly fixed your car.

3. A guy that I knew in high school sits next to me in my math class.

4. The first person that makes fun of my hat is going to be sorry.

5. Today, the newspaper that reported the mayor died issued a retraction.

Sentence Practice 3

Change the capitalized word(s) in the second sentence into *who* or *whom* and make the second sentence modify the underlined word in the first sentence.

> EXAMPLE: <u>Someone</u> called me up.
> I had never met SOMEONE before.

> ANSWER: Someone <u>whom I had never met before</u> called me up.

1. O. J. Simpson was the first professional football <u>player</u>.
   THE PLAYER ran for over 2,000 yards in a single season.

Lesson 14

*pron
case*

2. I found <u>someone</u>.
   SOMEONE will help me study.

3. We need to call the <u>person</u>.
   You spoke to THE PERSON.

4. Over there is the <u>man</u>.
   You want to avoid THE MAN.

5. The first Japanese-born player to play major league baseball in America was <u>Masanori Murakami</u>.
   MASANORI MURAKAMI pitched for the Giants in 1964 and 1965.
   [*Hint:* A comma is needed after the player's name.]

Editing Practice 1

CORRECTED SENTENCES APPEAR ON PAGE 484.

Correct all errors in the following paragraphs using the first correction as a model. The number in parentheses at the end of each paragraph indicates how many errors you should find.

I have several teachers ~~whom~~ *who* use some form of group work.

My freshman composition class involves group activities, but

Ms. Isaacs, whom teaches the course, uses groups in ways that are

new to me. (1)

Ms. Isaacs believes that we need to become accustomed to working in groups even though they are not effective when they comprise people that prefer to learn independently. Of course, any group is likely to have at least one person that would prefer to work alone, but usually the group can adjust when it's just one or two individuals that learn little from group activities. Early in the course, Ms. Isaacs asked us to write a brief essay describing how we have functioned in groups; she then used these essays to help assign us to groups. My group is composed of people with who I can work well. (4)

Lesson 14

pron
case

Editing Practice 2

CORRECTED SENTENCES APPEAR ON PAGE 484.

Correct all errors in the following paragraphs using the first correction as a model. The number in parentheses at the end of each paragraph indicates how many errors you should find.

Most Americans ~~that~~ *who* have a religious affiliation are Christians, but other religions are thriving within the United States. Jews are a relatively small minority in this country, but their religion is one who was already established by the time of the American Revolution. Muslims, whom are a growing presence in the United States, actually outnumber Christians worldwide. (2)

Some religious denominations are much smaller in terms of the number of people that subscribe to their beliefs, yet these religions have found a niche in American society. For instance, one small religious group, referred to as Ethical Culture, is composed of some 7,000 members and was founded in 1876 by Felix Adler,

a humanist philosopher that stressed the importance of ethics

and morality. (2)

Editing Practice 3

Correct all errors in the following paragraphs using the first correction as a model. The number in parentheses at the end of each paragraph indicates how many errors you should find.

Lesson 14

*pron
case*

>   *who*

      Dorothy L. Sayers was an English writer ~~that~~ wrote some of the best detective novels ever. She is best known for a series of novels that features Lord Peter Wimsey. In the British tradition, Lord Peter is not a police officer or private detective but an amateur sleuth that manages to become involved in an amazing number of murders that involve friends or relatives. (1)

      Lord Peter deliberately adopts the manners of an overrefined aristocrat that doesn't seem to have any brains. Other characters dismiss him as a person who they do not need to take seriously, a fact that often leads to the criminal's exposure. The author also uses Lord Peter's foolishness to satirize the artificiality of the members of the aristocracy that Lord Peter comes into contact with. (3)

Writing Practice

On your own paper, write a paragraph or two about your favorite detective or law officer from a book, movie, or TV series. Include as many uses of *who, whom,* and *that* as you can. Use the Editing Checklist to show that each use of *that* refers to ideas or things and that *who* and *whom* are used appropriately to refer to people.

Editing Checklist

Identify Errors in Using **Who, Whom,** *and* **That** *in Your Writing*

____ Look for the relative pronouns *who*, *whom*, and *that* in your writing.

____ Look closely at the words immediately before and immediately after the relative pronoun.

Correct Errors in Using **Who, Whom,** *and* **That** *in Your Writing*

____ If the word *immediately* following the relative pronoun is a verb, use *who*.

____ If the word *immediately* following the relative pronoun is a noun or a pronoun, use *whom*.

The Bottom Line	A writer **who** wishes to follow conventions for formal writing should use *who* or *whom* — not *that* — to refer to people.

LESSON 15
Eliminating Sexist Pronouns

Error Sentences
CORRECTED SENTENCES APPEAR ON PAGE 158.

EXAMPLE 1: ✗ Each person should try to do <u>his</u> best.

EXAMPLE 2: ✗ A kindergarten teacher helps <u>her</u> students gain social as well as academic skills.

Lesson 15

sexist pron

What's the Problem?

Sexist language, even when unintentional, is unacceptable in college writing. There are two major problems with using this kind of language. First, because it excludes one gender or the other, it is demeaning and perpetuates discrimination and stereotyping. Second, a writer who uses even a few examples of sexist language is likely to offend readers, who, in turn, will be less likely to respect the writer's overall point or less likely to react in the way the writer wishes. Sexist language, then, is not a grammar issue as much as a style or usage issue.

ESL

Native and non-native speakers of English alike must realize that sexist language takes many forms, but we will focus on one of the most common types: *gender-exclusive pronouns*. These are certain **personal pronouns** used in ways that inappropriately exclude one gender. That is, they are used in ways that suggest *only* males or *only* females are being discussed. The personal pronouns that can be misused in this way are *he, his, him, she,* and *her.*

Example 1, for example, suggests that only males should do their best, while Example 2 implies that only females are kindergarten teachers. Of course, a writer can use pronouns such as *he* or *her* when they logically refer only to males (a father) or only to females (a bride).

What Causes the Problem?

At one time, it seemed perfectly acceptable to use the generic *he* to refer to *all* people. The generic *he* is simply the use of the masculine pronoun to refer to words (such as *anyone* or *a parent*) that can describe females as well as males. It also once seemed appropriate to associate one gender with particular professions (such as nurses = women; doctors = men).

156

Today, however, people are aware of the subtle discrimination of using the generic *he,* and more people are entering professions that once seemed exclusively the domain of just one gender. In short, writers' language should reflect the changed attitudes of society toward the roles of males and females.

Diagnostic Exercise

CORRECTED SENTENCES APPEAR ON PAGE 484.

Correct all instances of sexist language in the following paragraph using the first correction as a model. The number in parentheses at the end of the paragraph indicates how many problems you should find.

My psychology teacher, Ms. Crystal, had each member of the

class complete a questionnaire that would help him *or her* consider an

appropriate career. I had already decided on a career, but she said

the questionnaire would offer options. I've always wanted to be an

electrical engineer because I like to design things; an engineer

spends much of his time drawing designs and writing specifications.

Ms. Crystal said my survey results indicated I should consider being

an accountant. She also told me, however, that the survey was just

one resource for choosing a career. I agree. Each person has to

consider what he knows better than anyone else: his own interests. (3)

Lesson 15

sexist pron

Fixing This Problem in Your Writing

Keep in mind that writers often do not intentionally use sexist language. Here is a way to check your writing for this problem.

GENERAL-REFERENCE TIP: *First,* look for abstract references to people (**nouns** and **pronouns** that refer not to actual individuals but to people in general). *Second,* see whether you later refer to this abstraction by using a personal pronoun that includes only one gender. If so, the language is probably sexist.

In Example 1, *person* is an abstract noun that does not refer to a specific individual, but the writer has used the masculine personal pronoun *his* to rename the abstract noun. The General-Reference Tip demonstrates that this sentence includes sexist language.

EXAMPLE 1: ✗ Each person should try to do his best.

Here are three ways to revise this sentence to avoid sexist language:

1. Use plural forms and "genderless" pronouns. Reword the sentence so that any abstract reference to people is in the plural form. Do the same with the personal pronoun.

   People   *their*
   CORRECTION: ~~Each person~~ should try to do ~~his~~ best.

2. Include both genders by substituting *his or her* for *his* or *her*. (Avoid using this revision strategy too many times in a single paper. Some readers find the phrase monotonous when it is used over and over.)

   or her
   CORRECTION: Each person should try to do his best.

3. Reword the sentence to avoid any personal pronoun.

   CORRECTION: Each person should put forth a 100 percent effort.

Use these three correction strategies on Example 2.

EXAMPLE 2: ✗ A kindergarten teacher helps her students gain social as well as academic skills.

   Kindergarten teachers   *their*
   CORRECTION: ~~A kindergarten teacher~~ helps ~~her~~ students gain social as well as academic skills.

Using the plural form of *teacher* avoids the implied message that all kindergarten teachers are female. Note that when you change the subject to make it plural, you also have to change the verb.

   his or
   CORRECTION: A kindergarten teacher helps her students gain social as well as academic skills.

This revised version also changes the "exclusive" implication of this sentence.

   CORRECTION: A kindergarten teacher helps students gain social as well as academic skills.

In this final sample, deleting the personal pronoun does not change the meaning of the sentence, but it does eliminate the sexist language.

Sentence Practice 1

CORRECTED SENTENCES APPEAR ON PAGE 484.

If a sentence contains sexist language, show where it is by underlining the noun and the gender-exclusive pronoun. Correct any instance of sexist language. If a sentence avoids sexist language, write *OK* above it.

> EXAMPLE: <u>Somebody</u> left ~~his~~ set of car keys on the television.
> *a*

Lesson 15

sexist
pron

1. A leader has to be responsible to his constituents.

2. Boxer Vic Towell once knocked down his opponent fourteen times within ten rounds of their championship fight.

3. We must hire a secretary, and she has to be organized and efficient.

4. My accountant said that he would meet with me tomorrow.

5. Everyone should cast his vote in the next election. [*Hint: Everyone* is singular, so avoid correcting the error by just changing *his* to the plural *their.*]

 For more practice eliminating sexist pronouns, go to **Exercise Central** at **bedfordstmartins.com/commonsense/5-15**.

Sentence Practice 2

CORRECTED SENTENCES APPEAR ON PAGE 484.

If a sentence contains sexist language, show where it is by underlining the noun and the gender-exclusive pronoun. Correct any instance of sexist language. If a sentence avoids sexist language, write *OK* above it.

> EXAMPLE: *Parents*   *their*
>   ~~A parent~~ should let ~~her~~ children have some independence.

1. A professional wrestler usually must practice not only his wrestling moves but his ability to speak to a crowd.

2. If you ever put your children into day care, meet the person who will watch your children, and see if she is patient.

3. Has nobody done his homework today?

4. A writer must choose his words carefully.

5. I've never met anyone who brushes his teeth as often as you.

Sentence Practice 3

In the spaces provided, add the appropriate personal pronouns. You may need to change the subject of some sentences and make other necessary adjustments.

> EXAMPLE: **Nobody in class did _____ homework.**
>
> ANSWER: **Nobody in class did <u>his or her</u> homework.**

1. Everybody watching the movie got _____ money's worth.

2. Each employee who uses the restroom must wash _____ hands before returning to work.

3. A good spouse knows when to keep _____ mouth shut.

4. I want everyone to stay in _____ seat until class is officially dismissed.

5. An officer must command the respect of _____ troops.

Editing Practice 1

CORRECTED SENTENCES APPEAR ON PAGE 484.

Correct all instances of sexist language in the following paragraphs using the first correction as a model. The number in parentheses at the end of each paragraph indicates how many problems you should find.

       College students have   *they*
    ~~A college student has~~ many options about what ~~he~~ might study.

I am torn between geology and teaching. On the one hand, I have long

been interested in being a geologist in the private sector, perhaps for an oil company. A geologist spends much of his time outdoors collecting samples, and I like working outdoors. A geologist also works in his office or lab, but I like this sort of work as well. (2)

On the other hand, my mother is a teacher and has encouraged me to follow in her footsteps. Almost every teacher has a good deal of stress put on her by students, parents, and administrators; however, a teacher also has many rewards, such as knowing that she has helped somebody succeed in his life and intellectual development. I am seriously considering teaching earth science so that I can combine my interest in teaching with geology. (3)

Lesson 15

sexist pron

Editing Practice 2

CORRECTED SENTENCES APPEAR ON PAGE 485.

Correct all instances of sexist language in the following paragraphs using the first correction as a model. The number in parentheses at the end of each paragraph indicates how many problems you should find.

At one time or another, almost everybody has wondered what
                              or she
it would be like if he were born at another time or place. I don't
                          ^
think a person is necessarily unhappy or out of place simply because he's had such thoughts. Perhaps it's a way to explore possibilities in his own present circumstances. (2)

When I was much younger, I wondered what it would be like to be an early colonist in the Americas. The life of a colonist was not easy; he had to cope with starvation, the wilderness, and financial ruin. When I was a teenager, I dreamed of being an astronaut—again, a person who often puts his life in danger to explore a new world. Even today

I think about such adventures, and perhaps it's all a clue that I would not be happy confined in an office. I'm not saying that being a businessperson is dull, but everyone needs to find the sorts of challenges and environments that reflect his own dreams and goals. I imagine that sounds like a cliché, but I often think many people consider jobs only in terms of how they'll affect their bank accounts. (3)

Lesson 15

sexist pron

Editing Practice 3

Correct all instances of sexist language in the following paragraph using the first corrected sentence as a model. The number in parentheses at the end of the paragraph indicates how many problems you should find.

Internet technology has created careers that did not exist

a generation ago. *People*

~~A person~~ who might have combined *their* ~~his~~

design skills with an interest in media may have become

book designers or project editors

~~a book designer or a project editor~~. Now he can be a Web

graphics designer or Webmaster. In the not-so-old days, an

advertising executive would sell ad space for a phone book or

a radio program; now he sells on-line ad space. A person interested

in languages can apply his skills as an HTML (Hypertext

Markup Language) programmer. Finally, someone who dreams

of a career in education could find himself in the field of distance

education, where students commute to school by logging on to

www-dot-something. When a person is exploring his job options,

he should consider opportunities created by new technologies.

With e-mail, e-commerce, and e-school, a solid résumé can land

you a great e-job! (6)

Writing Practice

On your own paper, write a paragraph or two explaining a particular job or hobby and the skills it requires. Try to use at least four abstract references to people followed by *he, his, him, she, her, they, them,* or *their.* Use the Editing Checklist to correct any sexist language in the sentences you write.

Editing Checklist

Identify Sexist Pronouns in Your Writing

_____ First, look for words that refer to people in an abstract or general way, rather than to specific individuals.

_____ Next, see whether you later refer to this abstract person (or people) by using a gender exclusive pronoun (*he, his, him, she, her*). If so, it is likely that your writing includes sexist language.

Eliminate Sexist Pronouns from Your Writing

_____ See whether you can make the subject of your sentence plural and change the gender-exclusive pronoun to the plural form (*they, them,* or *their*).

_____ Try substituting *his or her* for a gender-exclusive pronoun when the subject is singular.

_____ Revise the sentence to avoid using personal pronouns altogether.

Lesson 15

sexist pron

The Bottom Line	A writer can use language more effectively if **he or she** avoids using the generic *he.*

UNIT FIVE: Understanding Pronouns

Pronouns replace nouns (and sometimes other pronouns) in a sentence. This unit presented five common pronoun problems.

Pronoun Agreement

A personal pronoun should agree in number with its antecedent (the person, place, or thing the pronoun refers to). A singular antecedent requires a singular personal pronoun; a plural antecedent requires a plural personal pronoun. Use this tip to be sure that the antecedents and pronouns match in your writing.

ARE TIP: When using *they, their,* or *them,* be sure the antecedent is plural. One way to do so is to see whether this antecedent would take the plural verb *are* after it. If *are* does not seem to fit, the antecedent is probably *singular* and thus not in agreement with *they, their,* or *them.*

Vague Pronouns: *This, That,* and *It*

It is a writer's responsibility to make each pronoun reference clear to readers. Often a writer will use the pronoun *this, that,* or *it* vaguely, so that the reader has a hard time determining what *this, that,* or *it* refers to. Use this tip to help you make pronoun references clear in your writing.

ANTECEDENT TIP: Locate what you think the pronoun refers to (the antecedent). Make sure this antecedent is a person, place, or thing — not another part of speech or an entire sentence. Make sure there is no "want-to-be" antecedent — another person, place, or thing the pronoun could possibly be referring to.

I or *Me?* *She* or *Her?* *He* or *Him?*

A personal pronoun changes its form depending on whether it is used in the **subject** position (*I, he, she, we, they*) or the **object** position (*me, him, her, us, them*) in a sentence. Use the following tips to help you decide which form is appropriate in your sentence.

NEXT-WORD TIP: Use the *subject form* of the pronoun if a verb comes right after it (or very soon after it).

PRECEDING-WORD TIP: Use the *object form* of the pronoun if a preposition or a verb immediately precedes (comes before) it.

Who, Whom, and *That*

Who, whom, and *that* are relative pronouns—special pronouns that always refer to a preceding noun. Use *who* or *whom* when the preceding noun refers to people. Here is a tip that will help you determine which of these words is correct in your sentence.

WHO/WHOM TIP: Look at the word immediately following *who* or *whom.* If this word is a verb, use *who.* If this word is a noun or pronoun, use *whom.* Use *that* to refer to things or ideas (Think: *That animal!*).

THAT ANIMAL! TIP: Look at the word the pronoun renames. Use *that* only if this word refers to something nonhuman.

Eliminating Sexist Pronouns

At one time, it was common practice to use *he, his,* and *him* to refer to all people. Today, however, writers are more careful about how they use pronouns. This tip will help you edit your writing for any sexist use of pronouns:

GENERAL-REFERENCE TIP: *First,* look for abstract references to people (nouns and pronouns that refer to people in general, not to actual individuals). *Second,* if you later refer to this abstraction, see whether you have used a personal pronoun that includes only one gender. If so, the language is probably sexist.

Unit Five

review

Review Test

Correct all errors in the following paragraph using the first correction as a model. The number in parentheses at the end of the paragraph indicates how many errors you should find.

Unit Five

review

Yesterday, I received a call from my neighbor Elena, ~~whom~~ *who* wanted me to meet her friend Janie. She has just arrived in town and is staying with Elena for a short time. Elena and me have been friends a long time, so I was glad to meet a friend of hers. Janie, who is an electrician, is looking for a job, and I know a number of contractors that work in the area. An electrician can get a job if he is really experienced and willing to work his way up the pay scale. Typically, an electrician is experienced because their skills are so technical that they do a lot of hands-on learning. (6)

UNIT SIX
Placing and Punctuating Modifiers

OVERVIEW

Terms That Can Help You Understand Modifiers

If you are not familiar with any of the following terms, look them up in the Guide to Grammar Terminology beginning on page 1. The number in parentheses indicates the lessons in which each term appears.

adjective clause (17)
adverb (16)
adverb clause (16)
appositive (18)
dangling modifier (19)
elliptical adverb clause (16, 19)
essential adjective clause (17)
infinitive phrase (16)
introductory element (16)
modifier (19, 20)

nonessential adjective
   clause (17)
participial phrase (16, 19)
past participle (19)
prepositional phrase (16)
present participle (19)
proper noun (18)
relative pronoun (17)
subject (16)

Unit Six

overview

The Nuts and Bolts of Placing and Punctuating Modifiers

Modifiers describe or qualify other words in a sentence. This unit introduces some of the problems that arise when you use modifiers. These five lessons will help you to correctly place and punctuate modifiers in your writing.

Lesson 16 shows you how to punctuate introductory elements. Some introductory elements require a comma, while for others a comma is optional. Failure to use a comma with introductory elements is the single most common error in the writing of college students.

167

EXAMPLE: ✗ While I was revising my paper my hard drive crashed.

CORRECTION: While I was revising my paper, my hard drive crashed.

Lesson 17 shows you how to punctuate adjective clauses. If the adjective clause does not significantly alter the meaning of the noun it modifies, it is said to be **nonessential** to the meaning of the sentence. A nonessential adjective clause should be set off from the rest of the sentence with commas. If the adjective clause does significantly alter the meaning of the noun, it is said to be **essential** to the meaning of the sentence. Essential adjective clauses do not require commas.

EXAMPLE: ✗ I wanted to go to a place, where I could relax.

CORRECTION: I wanted to go to a place, where I could relax.

Unit Six

overview

Lesson 18 shows you how to punctuate appositives. **Appositives** are nouns or pronouns that rename or modify the nouns they follow. If the appositive does not significantly alter the meaning of the noun it renames, it is said to be **nonessential** to the meaning of the sentence. A nonessential appositive should be set off from the rest of the sentence with commas. If the appositive does significantly alter the meaning of the noun, it is said to be **essential** to the meaning of the sentence and does not require the use of commas.

EXAMPLE: ✗ I recently visited Julia my aunt.

CORRECTION: I recently visited Julia, my aunt.

Lesson 19 will help you to identify and correct dangling modifiers. Certain modifiers can be moved outside the main sentence to provide background information for understanding the main sentence. If these modifiers are not clearly connected to the words they describe, the meaning may be misunderstood. These modifiers are called **dangling modifiers** because they are not properly connected to the main sentence.

EXAMPLE: ✗ While still a student, Microsoft recruited my sister for a job as a programmer.

CORRECTION: While *my sister was* still a student, Microsoft recruited ~~my sister~~ *her* for a job as a programmer.

Lesson 20 will help you to identify and correct misplaced modifiers. **Adverbs** can be moved to different places in the sentence. Sometimes writers position them so that readers cannot easily tell what they are supposed to modify. Even worse, the reader will completely misinterpret what the writer meant to say. These incorrectly used adverbs are called **misplaced modifiers**.

EXAMPLE: ✗ I only found one Web site about Attention Deficit Disorder.

only

CORRECTION: I ~~only~~ found one Web site about Attention Deficit Disorder.

Can you detect incorrectly placed and mispunctuated modifiers?

CORRECTED SENTENCES APPEAR ON PAGE 485.

Using the first correction as a model, correct the incorrectly placed and mispunctuated modifiers. The number in parentheses at the end of the paragraph indicates how many errors you should find.

> I started college fifteen years ago but dropped out to have
>
> *Since my children are*
> children. ~~Being~~ able to take care of themselves now, I decided to
>
> go back to school. Back then, students wrote papers the old-fashioned
>
> way—they typed them. When I started back to school I realized
>
> I was completely out of date. The students were using computers
>
> to write their papers. At first I stuck by my faithful typewriter
>
> an old Royal. However, my writing class which required multiple
>
> drafts quickly changed my mind. Doing multiple revisions on a
>
> typewriter, my papers were taking way too much time. I broke
>
> down and bought an inexpensive computer. It only took me about
>
> a week to learn to use it. Now that I've gotten used to it I cannot
>
> imagine being without it. (7)

LESSON 16

Commas with
Introductory Elements

Error Sentences

CORRECTED SENTENCES APPEAR ON PAGES 172–73.

> EXAMPLE 1: ✗ When you called Tom was listening on the phone.
>
> EXAMPLE 2: ✗ Under my air mattress, was a large rock.

What's the Problem?

In formal writing, an **introductory element** is usually set off from the **subject**—the beginning part of the main sentence—with a comma. The comma tells the reader where the introductory element ends and the subject begins. Even when the introductory element is short, the comma can prevent the reader from being confused about where the introductory element ends and the subject begins. For instance, in Example 1, the introductory element *when you called* is short, but without the comma, the reader might think that the introductory element is *when you called Tom*. Sometimes part of the main sentence is put in an inverted order for emphasis. In this case, a comma should not be used. This is the error in Example 2.

What Causes the Problem?

There are two separate problems with introductory elements. The most common problem is not using a required comma with an introductory element. In part, this problem results from the fact that there are several different types of introductory elements; some require commas but others do not, or the use of a comma is optional.

The second, less common problem is using a comma with what is called an **inverted sentence**. Inverted sentences flip the last part of the sentence to the front for emphasis: the subject has been moved to follow the verb, and the part that would normally follow the verb has been put first.

The punctuation problem inverted sentences pose is that they can look like sentences with introductory elements, and writers mistakenly use commas with them.

Diagnostic Exercise

CORRECTED SENTENCES APPEAR ON PAGE 485.

Correct comma errors in the following paragraphs using the first correction as a model. The number in parentheses at the end of each paragraph indicates how many errors you should find.

To change a baby's diaper, follow these simple steps. First lay the
˄
baby on a flat surface. If the surface is off the ground use safety straps

to secure the baby. Unfasten the tapes, and remove the soiled diaper.

To clean the diaper area use a wet cloth or a disposable "baby wipe"

product. (To avoid an unexpected spray or puddle you may want to

cover the diaper area immediately.) While gently holding the baby's

ankles with one hand use your other hand to slip the back part of the

diaper under him or her. Bring the front part of the diaper between

the baby's legs, and fasten it on each side using the adhesive tapes. (5)

Changing a diaper is a fairly mechanical process. However the

process often causes great anxiety for new parents and nonparents. (1)

Fixing This Problem in Your Writing

Here are examples of the types of introductory elements that *always* require commas:

> <u>However</u>, you can go if you want to.
> (**Transitional term**—see Lesson 4)

> <u>Smiling broadly</u>, she closed her book.
> (**Participial phrase**—see Lesson 19)

> <u>To open the door</u>, you'll need a key.
> (**Infinitive phrase**)

> While checking my notes, I found a major error.
> (**Elliptical adverb clause**—see Lesson 19)

The following types of introductory elements normally require commas *unless* they are short and not confusing:

> After dinner is over, let's go to a movie.
> (**Adverb clause**—see Lesson 5)

> In the evenings after dinner, we would go for walks.
> (**Prepositional phrase**)

Commas with single-word adverbs are optional:

> Soon it began to rain. (**Adverb**)

The first step in correctly punctuating introductory elements is locating them. Use this tip to locate introductory elements:

> DELETION TIP: Delete any suspected introductory element. If what remains is a complete sentence, what you deleted is an introductory element.

Lesson 16

Here is the tip applied to the error in Example 1:

> EXAMPLE 1:   ✗ When you called Tom was listening on the phone.

> TIP APPLIED: Tom was listening on the phone.

The tip helps to determine that *When you called* is an introductory element since what is left is a complete sentence (see Lesson 1).

Because all introductory elements *can* be set off with a comma, the following tip always works:

> COMMAS WITH INTRODUCTORY ELEMENTS TIP: Use commas after *all* introductory elements.

> CORRECTION: When you called, Tom was listening on the phone.

The Deletion Tip will also help you identify inverted sentences. If what remains is not a complete sentence, then the introductory word group should not be set off with a comma. Here is the tip applied to the second sample error:

> EXAMPLE 2:   ✗ Under my air mattress, was a large rock.

> TIP APPLIED: ✗ Was a large rock.

The Deletion Tip shows that *under my air mattress* is not an introductory element and thus should not be set off with a comma.

> CORRECTION: Under my air mattress,/ was a large rock.

Sentence Practice 1

CORRECTED SENTENCES APPEAR ON PAGE 485.

Correct the following sentences. Confirm your answers by applying the Deletion Tip.

> EXAMPLE: ✗ When we got the test back nobody even thought about sleeping.
>
> ANSWER: When we got the test back, nobody even thought about sleeping.
>
> CONFIRMATION: Nobody even thought about sleeping.

1. Although Wally Amos is best known for his brand of cookies he was also the first African American talent agent for the William Morris Agency.

2. In France shepherds once carried small sundials as pocket watches.

3. Even though he was best known as an actor Jimmy Stewart was a brigadier general in the U.S. Air Force Reserve.

4. After eating our cat likes to nap.

5. Whenever I walk our dog likes to go with me.

 For more practice using commas, go to **Exercise Central** at **bedfordstmartins.com/commonsense/6-16**.

Lesson 16

,

Sentence Practice 2

CORRECTED SENTENCES APPEAR ON PAGE 486.

Correct the following sentences. Confirm your answer by applying the Deletion Tip.

> EXAMPLE: ✗ According to a recent study more women than men take Oreo cookies apart to eat the middle.
>
> ANSWER: According to a recent study, more women than men take Oreo cookies apart to eat the middle.

CONFIRMATION: **More women than men take Oreo cookies apart to eat the middle.**

1. To keep people from sneaking up on him Wild Bill Hickok placed crumpled newspapers around his bed.

2. Before his career was suddenly ended Jesse James robbed twelve banks and seven trains.

3. Therefore he was a successful criminal for a time.

4. Believe it or not the official state "gem" of Washington is petrified wood.

5. When she was in a high school band singer Dolly Parton played the snare drum.

Sentence Practice 3

Combine the following sentences by changing one sentence in each pair into an introductory element. Attach the introductory element to the other sentence and punctuate correctly. You may have to add a dependent word, as in the example.

EXAMPLE: **I put on a sweater.**
I was getting cold.

ANSWER: **Because I was getting cold, I put on a sweater.**

1. The house is too hot.
    The air conditioner is broken.

2. Claire must leave early.
    Claire has to go get a haircut.

3. I crept into the house.
    I moved slowly and cautiously.

4. We have to eat.
    We must eat as soon as class is over.

5. The vultures circled overhead.
    They were waiting for a wounded animal to die.

Editing Practice 1

CORRECTED SENTENCES APPEAR ON PAGE 486.

Correct the errors in the following paragraph using the first correction as a model. The number in parentheses at the end of the paragraph indicates how many errors you should find.

When I was much younger, I used to run marathons. Even for

my age-group I was never very fast. I did it for the exercise and for

the challenge of it. Beginning with walking just a few miles every day

I gradually worked myself up to running in full-fledged marathon

races—26 miles, 385 yards. Fortunately for slowpokes like me the

organizers of marathons tolerate very slow runners. In fact the

volunteers who do most of the work at marathons are remarkably

supportive of the noncompetitive runners. Waiting until the last

stragglers finally limp in to the finish line, the volunteers often have

to stay at the course for five or six hours. After the race, comes the

cleanup. It is utterly amazing what a mess several hundred runners

can make. The average runner probably uses a dozen paper cups, all

of which are thrown on the ground for some volunteer to pick up. (6)

Lesson 16

^
,

Editing Practice 2

CORRECTED SENTENCES APPEAR ON PAGE 486.

Correct the errors in the following paragraph using the first correction as a model. The number in parentheses at the end of the paragraph indicates how many errors you should find.

As you might expect, there are heavy physical demands on

marathon runners. In addition to the common problem of fatigue the

greatest problem marathon runners have is with their feet. Among all marathon runners the universal topic of conversation is shoes. Every brand is minutely compared in terms of weight, support, and cost. Since most runners train on asphalt running shoes wear out amazingly quickly. Replacing an expensive pair of shoes every few months gets to be pretty costly; nevertheless every runner has learned that running in worn shoes is asking for foot and ankle problems. Despite the fact that running shoes are tremendously expensive there is no doubt that they are getting better and better. The improved design of modern running shoes has eliminated many of the nagging foot and ankle problems that used to plague runners. For most runners the main issue in shoes is the trade-off between weight and support—the more weight, the more support; the less weight, the less support. (6)

Lesson 16

^
,

Editing Practice 3

Correct the errors in the following paragraph using the first correction as a model. The number in parentheses at the end of the paragraph indicates how many errors you should find.

After I had finished several marathons, I felt that I was ready to enter the Honolulu Marathon without totally embarrassing myself. The Honolulu Marathon is run in the middle of December. While December is a nice time to visit Hawaii it has the great disadvantage of requiring us mainlanders to train in cold weather. Running 50 miles a week on icy roads is not my idea of fun. Nevertheless I managed to do a barely adequate amount of training in November and early December. Off to Hawaii, went I with three pairs of running shoes in my suitcase. Especially for those of us from cold climates the biggest problem running the Honolulu Marathon is dehydration. When I ran the actual race I made a point of stopping every two miles to drink at least 8 ounces of water. As a result of stopping so often my time was abominable even by my low standards. On the other hand I actually finished the race. During the last five miles I passed literally hundreds of faster runners who had not stopped for water. They were all flat on the ground, under yellow blankets, with just their expensive running shoes sticking out. (8)

Writing Practice

On your own paper, write a paragraph or two about your experience in a contest of some kind. Try to use at least five introductory elements. Use the Editing Checklist to make sure each introductory element is set off with a comma.

Lesson 16

^
,

Editing Checklist

Identify Introductory Elements in Your Writing

_____ Use the Deletion Tip to identify introductory elements. Whatever you can delete from the beginning of a sentence without making the sentence ungrammatical is an introductory element. The Deletion Tip will also identify inverted sentences, which are not set off with commas.

Correctly Punctuate Introductory Elements in Your Writing

_____ Whether the comma is required or optional, your safest bet is to set off all introductory elements with commas.

The Bottom Line

When you use an introductory element, set it off with a comma.

LESSON 17
Commas with Adjective Clauses

Error Sentences

CORRECTED SENTENCES APPEAR ON PAGE 200.

EXAMPLE 1: ✗ I see the man, who wants to meet Alice.

EXAMPLE 2: ✗ I visited my mother who still lives in Tampa.

What's the Problem?

Adjective clauses (also called **relative clauses**) modify the nouns they follow. Adjective clauses begin with **relative pronouns** (*who, whom, whose, that, which*) or relative adverbs (*when, where*).

When an adjective clause changes the meaning of the noun it modifies by limiting or restricting it in a significant way, it is called an **essential** (or **restrictive**) clause and is NOT set off with commas. On the other hand, when an adjective gives additional information but does not change the meaning of the noun it modifies, it is called a **nonessential** (or **nonrestrictive**) clause and MUST be set off with commas. Sometimes writers mistakenly use commas with essential adjective clauses (as in Example 1) or fail to use commas with nonessential adjective clauses (as in Example 2).

What Causes the Problem?

There is no simple grammatical rule that writers can use to determine if an adjective clause is essential or nonessential. Instead, writers must think carefully about how the meaning of the adjective clause affects the noun it modifies. The following examples illustrate how meaning determines the distinction between essential and nonessential.

ESSENTIAL: **All my roommates <u>who went to the party</u> were late for class.**

178

NONESSENTIAL: **All my roommates, <u>who went to the party</u>, were late for class.**

In the first example, some roommates went to the party and some did not. The ones who were late for class were the ones who went to the party (not the ones who stayed home). In the second sentence, all the roommates went to the party, and thus all the roommates were late for class.

Diagnostic Exercise

CORRECTED SENTENCES APPEAR ON PAGE 486.

Correct all errors using the first correction as a model. The number in parentheses at the end of the paragraph indicates how many commas you should either add or delete.

It was strange going back to my tenth-year high school reunion,
_^

which was held last summer. Monica who was my best friend as a

senior didn't even recognize me. I guess she didn't expect to see me

bald. I also saw a friend, whom I've stayed in touch with over the

phone but haven't actually seen in years. He told me that he recently

moved to California where he plans to start a new business. Since

I now live in Oregon, we agreed to try to get together next summer.

After the reunion, I had dinner with him and Monica in a restaurant,

that we used to go to when we were in high school. (5)

Lesson 17

^
,

Fixing This Problem in Your Writing

Essential adjective clauses significantly alter the meaning of the nouns they modify. Since essential adjective clauses contain information necessary to understanding the intended meaning, they can never be cut off from those nouns by commas. Here is a tip that will help you recognize essential adjective clauses:

> *WHICH ONE* TIP: If the adjective clause redefines the meaning of the noun it modifies by telling *which one* it is, then that clause becomes an **essential** part of the meaning of that word and cannot be separated from it by commas.

Here is the tip applied to the first example error:

EXAMPLE 1: ✗ I see the man, who wants to meet Alice.

TIP APPLIED: **Which man did you see? (The man who wants to meet Alice.)**

The adjective clause *who wants to meet Alice* tells which man the writer is referring to. The adjective clause redefines the meaning of *man* by narrowing it down from all possible men to the one who wants to meet Alice. The comma is incorrect because it cuts off an essential modifier from the noun whose meaning it affects.

CORRECTION: **I see the man,/ who wants to meet Alice.**

This tip will help you identify nonessential adjective clauses:

> *DO I NEED THIS?* **TIP:** If you can leave out the adjective clause without changing the basic meaning of the noun it modifies, then the adjective clause is **nonessential** and must be set off with commas.

Here is the tip applied to the second example error:

EXAMPLE 2: ✗ I visited my mother who still lives in Tampa.

TIP APPLIED: **I visited my mother.**

The adjective clause *who still lives in Tampa* can be left out of the sentence without changing the basic meaning of the noun it modifies. My mother is still my mother whether she lives in Tampa or not. When we omit the adjective clause, we lose all the information it contains, but the question is whether the basic meaning of the *noun* changes when we omit the adjective clause. In Example 2, that is not the case. Therefore, the adjective clause is nonessential and must be set off with a comma:

CORRECTION: **I visited my mother, who still lives in Tampa.**

There is one special rule about nonessential adjective clauses that you will find very helpful:

> **PROPER NOUN TIP:** The adjective clauses that modify proper nouns are always nonessential.

A **proper noun** is the name of a specific person or place. (*Mrs. Nguyen, Chicago, Microsoft* are all proper nouns.) Since proper nouns are already specific, they can never be further narrowed or restricted by an essential adjective clause. Always use commas with modifiers of proper nouns.

ESL

If English is not your first language, you may find adjective clauses tricky. Keep these hints in mind:

- Adjective clauses always follow the nouns they modify.

- Adjective clauses always begin with relative pronouns (*who, whom, whose, that, which*) or relative adverbs (*when, where*).

- There is no need to repeat an object in an adjective clause.

> **He wanted to paint the bench that I was sitting on ~~it~~.**

(Since *that* is the object of the preposition *on*, there is no need for the pronoun *it*.)

Sentence Practice 1

CORRECTED SENTENCES APPEAR ON PAGE 486.

Label the underlined adjective clauses in the following sentences as *essential* or *nonessential* and punctuate accordingly. Confirm your answer by applying the appropriate tip.

Lesson 17

∧
,

EXAMPLE: *essential*
Houses <u>that are made of wood</u> often survive major earthquakes.

CONFIRMATION: **Which houses often survive major earthquakes? Houses that are made of wood.**

1. Bo is reading a novel <u>that was written by J. R. R. Tolkien</u>.

2. Bo is reading *The Silmarillion* <u>which was written by J. R. R. Tolkien</u>.

3. She wanted to go to a place <u>where she could be alone</u>.

4. This neighborhood cafe <u>which first opened in 1939</u> is one of my favorite places to drink coffee.

5. My parents were married in the Middle East country of Yemen <u>where a wedding feast can last three weeks</u>.

For more practice using commas, go to **Exercise Central** at **bedfordstmartins.com/commonsense/6-17**.

Sentence Practice 2

CORRECTED SENTENCES APPEAR ON PAGE 486.

Label the underlined adjective clauses in the following sentences as *essential* or *nonessential* and punctuate accordingly. Confirm your answer by applying the appropriate tip.

EXAMPLE: ✗ I bumped into my fifth grade teacher <u>whom I hadn't seen in years.</u>

CORRECTION: I bumped into my fifth grade teacher,
nonessential ^
<u>whom I hadn't seen in years.</u>

CONFIRMATION: I bumped into my fifth grade teacher.

Lesson 17

1.   My roommate is from Seattle <u>which is over 600 miles from here</u>.

2.   Queen Latifah <u>who is best known as a rap artist</u> has also been a television host and an actress.

3.   Do you know a lawyer <u>who can help you with your legal problem</u>?

4.   Meet me at the place <u>where you and I first met</u>.

5.   The only river that flows north and south of the equator <u>is the Congo River which crosses the equator twice</u>.

Sentence Practice 3

Combine the two short sentences by making the second sentence into an adjective clause that modifies the underlined word in the first sentence. Correctly punctuate each modifier.

EXAMPLE: The <u>truck</u> is mine.
The truck is parked in the driveway.

ANSWER: The truck that is parked in the driveway is mine.

1.   My roommate and I like to watch the <u>Dallas Cowboys</u>.
The Dallas Cowboys play near us this Sunday.

2. <u>People</u> often do not like dogs.
   People like cats.

3. <u>I</u> hope I do well on this biology test.
   I did not know we were having this test.

4. My friend from England likes to play <u>checkers</u>.
   Checkers is usually called "draughts" in Britain.

5. I know <u>someone</u>.
   Someone wants you to work for her.

Editing Practice 1

CORRECTED SENTENCES APPEAR ON PAGE 487.

Correct all errors in the following paragraphs using the first correction as a model. The number in parentheses at the end of each paragraph indicates how many commas you should add or delete.

Lesson 17

I went to high school in San Bernardino‚ which is not far from Los Angeles. It's been ten years since I graduated from high school, and I've rarely been back to my hometown since attending San Diego State University which is fairly far away. But I recently spent a week back at my hometown and was surprised at the changes at my high school. (1)

For one thing, my favorite teacher who taught world history is now the principal, and the principal, who was there when I attended, is now the school superintendent. About half the teachers whom I had classes with have left entirely, and several of the ones who are still there are considering retirement. I found the new cafeteria which is twice as big as the one I remember, and the classroom where I once took three English classes is now a detention hall. I can't help but wonder how many more changes will occur before I visit again. (5)

Editing Practice 2

CORRECTED SENTENCES APPEAR ON PAGE 487.

Correct all errors in the following paragraph using the first correction as a model. The number in parentheses at the end of the paragraph indicates how many commas you should add or delete.

I am presently rooming with Harold Lee, who is very practical. We couldn't afford to spend much for Christmas gifts this year, so we decided to can some vegetables. First, we made a relish, that was primarily composed of tomatoes, onions, and cabbage. The tomatoes which we bought at the local market had to be completely green. The jars had to be carefully sterilized, and the directions confused us. Luckily, we received advice from my mom whom I called in a panic. Once we understood the process better, we went on to asparagus which has always been my favorite. I'm not sure we saved much time or money, but the experience was fun. (5)

Editing Practice 3

Correct all errors in the following paragraph using the first correction as a model. The number in parentheses at the end of the paragraph indicates how many commas you should add or delete.

My husband and I recently took our son Griffin to get an X-ray of his collarbone, which is also called the "clavicle." Our son's pediatrician who tends to be cautious about injuries ordered the X-ray as soon as we arrived at his office. After we described Griffin's fall, he told us that people, who fall directly onto their shoulder, risk a clavicle fracture. We suspected something might have been broken because Griffin seemed to be in pain whenever he tried to move his arm. The doctor reassured us that fractures in toddlers who are still growing heal

Lesson 17

very quickly. A quick trip to the X-ray lab revealed no fracture, thank goodness. But when the technician laid Griffin down on the X-ray table which was ice cold you would have thought he'd broken every bone in his 26-pound body! (8)

Writing Practice

On your own paper, write a paragraph or two about an injury that you have experienced. Try to use three adjective clauses. Use the Editing Checklist to make sure you have correctly punctuated each adjective clause.

Editing Checklist

Identify Errors in Punctuating Adjective Clauses in Your Writing

_____ First, find the adjective clause in your sentence (an adjective clause begins with *who, whose, whom, that, which, when,* or *where*).

_____ Next, find the noun that the adjective clause is describing. This noun is usually right before the adjective clause.

_____ Ask yourself if the information you've given readers in the adjective clause is necessary to identify the noun being described.

Correctly Punctuate Adjective Clauses in Your Writing

_____ Do not use commas with essential adjective clauses that affect the meaning of the nouns they modify. Do use commas with nonessential adjective clauses, which you can omit without changing the meaning of the noun being modified.

_____ Never use commas with adjective clauses that modify proper nouns.

Lesson 17

∧
,

The Bottom Line

Nonessential clauses, **which can always be omitted,** are always set off with commas.

LESSON 18
Commas with Appositives

Error Sentences

CORRECTED SENTENCES APPEAR ON PAGES 188–89.

EXAMPLE 1: ✗ Shakespeare's play, *Hamlet,* has just been made into a movie.

EXAMPLE 2: ✗ The senior senator from Iowa a Republican voted for the bill.

What's the Problem?

An **appositive** is a noun or pronoun that renames the noun it follows. Like adjective clauses (see Lesson 17), appositives can be **essential** or **nonessential**. Essential appositives supply crucial information to the "meat" of the sentence; readers would be confused without these appositives. Nonessential appositives are more like "gravy"; they offer supplemental information or additional detail. Nonessential appositives are set off with commas, but essential appositives are not. The problem is that writers sometimes identify nonessential and essential appositives incorrectly and, as a result, use commas incorrectly with essential appositives (Example 1) or fail to use commas with nonessential appositives (Example 2).

What Causes the Problem?

Appositives are not always easy to identify. Once an appositive has been identified, the writer still has to decide whether the appositive is essential ("meat") or nonessential ("gravy") to the meaning of the sentence in order to punctuate it correctly.

186

Diagnostic Exercise

CORRECTED SENTENCES APPEAR ON PAGE 487.

Correct all errors using the first correction as a model. The number in parentheses at the end of the paragraph indicates how many appositive errors you should find. (Each error involves a pair of commas unless the appositive is at the end of a sentence.)

Every summer I try to visit my Aunt Margie, a vigorous

sixty year old. Aunt Margie lives in a small town in Minnesota a

state in the northern part of the American Midwest. Though I dearly

love Aunt Margie, there is one area that we have nearly come to blows

over coffee. Like most midwesterners, she drinks coffee all day long,

and, like most midwesterners, her coffee is very, very weak. The

trouble is that I am from Seattle the home of Starbucks. Starbucks

one of the fastest growing companies in the United States has made

espresso into a lifestyle choice. My favorite drink a double mocha

has the caffeine equivalent of a dozen cups of Aunt Margie's coffee.

The first (and only) time I made coffee at Aunt Margie's house, she

had a fit because it was so strong. She not only threw out all the

coffee I had made, she made me wash the pot. From then on,

she made the coffee the kind you can see through. (7)

Lesson 18

Fixing This Problem in Your Writing

You first need to be able to identify an appositive. Knowing that appositives are nouns and pronouns that rename the nouns they follow helps, but here is another practical way to identify appositives:

SWITCHING TIP: You can always switch an appositive and the noun it modifies. The resulting sentence will be grammatical and coherent.

The Switching Tip works because appositives and the nouns they rename must always mean the same thing; thus, they can be used in either order. Here is the tip applied to both example error sentences. Don't worry yet about commas; just see whether the words can be switched.

<table>
<tr><td>EXAMPLE 1:</td><td>✗ Shakespeare's play, *Hamlet,* has just been made into a movie.</td></tr>
<tr><td>TIP APPLIED:</td><td>*Hamlet,* Shakespeare's play, has just been made into a movie.</td></tr>
<tr><td>EXAMPLE 2:</td><td>✗ The senior senator from Iowa a Republican voted for the bill.</td></tr>
<tr><td>TIP APPLIED:</td><td>A Republican the senior senator from Iowa voted for the bill.</td></tr>
</table>

As the Switching Tip shows, both example sentences contain appositives.

Once you have detected an appositive, you can determine whether it is **nonessential** (requiring commas) or **essential** (no commas). The tips given in Lesson 17 for distinguishing nonessential adjective clauses from essential adjective clauses apply equally well to appositives:

> *WHICH ONE* **TIP:** If the appositive redefines the meaning of the noun it modifies by telling *which one* it is, then that clause becomes an **essential** part of the meaning of that word and cannot be separated from it by commas.

Here is the tip applied to the first sample error:

<table>
<tr><td>EXAMPLE 1:</td><td>✗ Shakespeare's play, *Hamlet,* has just been made into a movie.</td></tr>
<tr><td>TIP APPLIED:</td><td>Which Shakespeare play has just been made into a movie? *Hamlet.*</td></tr>
<tr><td>CORRECTION:</td><td>Shakespeare's play⁄ *Hamlet⁄* has just been made into a movie.</td></tr>
</table>

The appositive *Hamlet* tells which of Shakespeare's many plays the writer is referring to. Therefore, the comma is incorrect because it cuts off an essential modifier (*Hamlet*) from the noun (*play*) whose meaning it defines.

> *DO I NEED THIS?* **TIP:** If you can leave out the appositive without changing the basic meaning of the noun it modifies, then the appositive is **nonessential** and must be set off with commas.

Here is the tip applied to the second example error:

EXAMPLE 2: ✗ The senior senator from Iowa a Republican voted for the bill.

TIP APPLIED: The senior senator from Iowa voted for the bill.

CORRECTION: The senior senator from Iowa, a Republican, voted for the bill.

The appositive *a Republican* can be left out of the sentence without changing the basic meaning of *senator,* the noun it modifies. The senior senator from Iowa is still the same person whether he or she is a Republican or not. When we leave out the appositive, we naturally lose the information, but the basic identification of the noun is unchanged. Therefore, the appositive is nonessential and must be set off with a comma.

There is one special rule about nonessential appositives that you will find very helpful:

> **PROPER NOUN TIP:** Appositives that rename proper nouns are always nonessential.

A **proper noun** is the name of a specific person or place. (*Mrs. Nguyen, Chicago, Microsoft* are all proper nouns.) Since proper nouns are already specific, they can never be further narrowed or restricted by appositives. Always use commas with modifiers of proper nouns.

Sentence Practice 1

CORRECTED SENTENCES APPEAR ON PAGE 487.

All the appositives in the following sentences are nonessential. Underline each appositive and add the necessary commas. Confirm your answer by applying the Switching Tip.

EXAMPLE: ✗ The university is in the capital of Thailand Bangkok.

ANSWER: The university is in the capital of Thailand, Bangkok.

CONFIRMATION: The university is in Bangkok, the capital of Thailand.

1. Ian Fleming the creator of 007 named James Bond after the author of a book about birds.

2. Ian Fleming also wrote *Chitty Chitty Bang Bang* a popular children's book.

3. Tim's mother a registered nurse thinks I have a virus.

4. Richard a guy in my geology class fell asleep during the lecture.

5. Spanish Fort a small town in south Alabama was the site of one of the last battles of the Civil War.

> For more practice using commas, go to **Exercise Central** at **bedfordstmartins.com/commonsense/6-18**.

Lesson 18

∧
,

Sentence Practice 2

CORRECTED SENTENCES APPEAR ON PAGE 487.

Underline the appositives in the following sentences. Label them *essential* or *nonessential,* and punctuate them correctly. Confirm your answer by applying either the *Which One* Tip or the *Do I Need This?* Tip.

EXAMPLE: ✗ My English assignment a ten-page essay is due next week.

nonessential
ANSWER: My English assignment, a ten-page essay, is due next week.

CONFIRMATION: My English assignment is due next week. (It is due next week whether it is ten pages or not.)

1. My roommate a political science major plans to run for public office one day.

2. He has a date this Friday with Janet Spain the woman who sits next to you in History 101.

3.   This note is for your friend Natalie.

4.   Matthew Henson an African American codiscovered the North Pole with Robert Peary in 1909.

5.   I had to take Junior one of my cats to get his shots.

Sentence Practice 3

Combine the two short sentences by making the second sentence into an appositive that modifies the underlined words in the first sentence. Punctuate correctly.

> EXAMPLE: My grandparents still recall "Black Thursday."
> "Black Thursday" is the day the stock market crashed in 1929.

> ANSWER: My grandparents still recall "Black Thursday," the day the stock market crashed in 1929.

Lesson 18

1.   His mother has a revolver.
His mother is a police officer.

2.   Victoria Woodhull and Tennessee Cook were the first stockbrokers in New York.
Victoria Woodhull and Tennessee Cook were two sisters.

3.   Peter Jackson has just made the first installation in a film version of *The Lord of the Rings,* called *The Lord of the Rings: Fellowship of the Ring.*
Peter Jackson is the director.

4.   Janis Joplin left $2,500 in her will to pay for a party for her friends.
Janis Joplin was a female rock singer.

5.   I went to see my favorite musical.
My favorite musical is *Cats.*

Editing Practice 1

CORRECTED SENTENCES APPEAR ON PAGE 488.

Correct all errors in the following paragraph using the first correction as a model. The number in parentheses at the end of the paragraph indicates how many commas you should add or delete.

Gary, my nephew, called and suggested we throw a surprise
birthday party for my mother, who just turned sixty-five. I'm not
much for birthday parties, but I agreed to help. We asked my friend
Sharon to assist. Sharon an interior-design major has an excellent
eye for decorating, so she took charge of turning my living room
a very plain room into a more festive place for the occasion.
My mother, who has a notorious sweet tooth, is particularly
fond of chocolate, so we ordered an enormous cake made of
dark chocolate. Gary asked my oldest sister Stephanie to arrange
to bring my mom to my house tomorrow. Everything is just
about finished, and thirty-five people plan to attend the party. (6)

Lesson 18

Editing Practice 2

CORRECTED SENTENCES APPEAR ON PAGE 488.

Correct all errors in the following paragraphs using the first correction as a
model. The number in parentheses at the end of each paragraph indicates
how many commas you should either add or delete.

World War II, one of the best-known wars of all time, was
followed a few years later by a conflict that still is not well understood. The Korean War, a conflict between the United Nations and
North Korea, was never officially a war. Harry Truman the U.S.
president at the time of the conflict never asked Congress to
declare war. The U.S. troops fought as part of the United Nations
forces. The conflict was therefore called a "police action." (2)

This war caused many problems for the United States, possibly
because its status and purpose were not clear. General Douglas

MacArthur the commander of the U.N. forces was removed from office for insubordination to President Truman the Commander in Chief. After the landings at Inchon a major turning point the North Koreans were pushed back. Neither side completely achieved its goals, and a truce was signed in 1953. (5)

Editing Practice 3

Correct all errors in the following paragraphs using the first correction as a model. The number in parentheses at the end of each paragraph indicates how many commas you should either add or delete.

The Mason-Dixon line, a famous boundary line, was laid out
          ^   ^
in the 1760's by surveyors Charles Mason and Jeremiah Dixon. It separated Pennsylvania and Maryland two regions having unclear boundaries at the time. However, it became symbolic of something else, the political divisions between North and South. (1)

Until the Civil War ended, the Mason-Dixon line was a distinct border between slaveholding states and free states. It's from this line that we get the name, *Dixie,* to designate the South and the Confederacy. Although Maryland is south of the boundary, it never seceded from the Union and is not considered part of the South. Today, the Mason-Dixon line a boundary rarely designated on a map seems to be gradually fading from use. With more and more people moving from one part of the country to another, it is becoming harder to find sharp regional divisions. (4)

Writing Practice

Consider boundaries in your hometown. On your own paper, write a paragraph or two explaining boundaries that are either on a map or that people consider significant (like track crossings or neighborhood boundaries). Try to use at least three appositives. Use the Editing Checklist to correct any punctuation errors in the sentences you write.

Editing Checklist

Identify Errors in Punctuating Appositives in Your Writing

_____ To help you determine whether a word or word group is an appositive, see if you can switch it with the word it renames. If the resulting test sentence is grammatically complete and coherent, the word or word group is an appositive.

_____ Cover up the appositive and ask, "Would readers be confused if the appositive were deleted?"

Correctly Punctuate Appositives in Your Writing

_____ If readers would be confused, do not put commas around the appositive, since it is essential to the meaning of the sentence.

_____ If readers would not be confused, set the appositive off with commas, since it is nonessential to the meaning of the sentence.

Lesson 18

^
,

| The Bottom Line | A nonessential appositive, the optional "gravy," is always set off with commas. |

LESSON 19
Dangling Modifiers

Error Sentences
CORRECTED SENTENCES APPEAR ON PAGE 197.

EXAMPLE 1: ✗ Damaged beyond all repair, I threw my watch away.

EXAMPLE 2: ✗ While waiting for the bus, it began to rain.

What's the Problem?

Modifiers are words that describe or give more information about other words. Some modifiers can be moved outside the main sentence (usually in front of the main sentence) to give relevant background information. If an opening modifier is not immediately followed by the word it describes, it is called a **dangling modifier**. This lesson focuses on the two most common types of dangling modifiers: dangling **participial phrases** (Example 1) and dangling **elliptical adverb clauses** (Example 2).

What Causes the Problem?

Sometimes writers are not careful with modifiers because they assume that the meaning of their sentence is clear or obvious. An error occurs when a modifier cannot logically modify the noun that follows it. If a modifier is not logically related to its main clause, it is said to be a **dangling modifier**. For clarity, modifiers should be placed close to the person, place, thing, or action they describe. In the following examples, the modifiers are correctly and logically attached to the main clause.

> Working all night, Pasquale finished his paper on time.

> Exhausted by her work, Harriet slept through class.

These examples include participial phrases. Participial phrases contain either **present participles** (verbs ending in *-ing*) or **past participles** (verbs usually ending in *-ed*).

195

> Since getting his assignment, Carl has been very busy.
>
> Although pleased by her progress so far, Luisa was slipping behind schedule.

These examples include elliptical adverb clauses (adverb clauses from which the subject has been deleted). These clauses also contain either a present or a past participle.

Diagnostic Exercise

CORRECTED SENTENCES APPEAR ON PAGE 488.

Correct all errors using the first correction as a model. The number in parentheses at the end of the paragraph indicates how many dangling modifier errors you should find.

Studying for hours, ~~my eyes grew tired~~ . I felt I could not read

I felt my eyes grow tired

another word. I walked to the snack bar for a cup of coffee. When

getting there, the place was closed. Deciding against walking a

mile to another place, the thought crossed my mind that maybe

I should just quit for a while and get some sleep. I returned to my

room and tried to decide what to do. Torn between the need to

sleep and the need to study, the alarm clock went off and made me

realize it was time for class. After struggling to stay awake in class,

my decision was to get some sleep and then get back to work. (4)

Lesson 19

dm

Fixing This Problem in Your Writing

Both types of dangling modifiers share the same problem: they are not logically related to their main sentences. Here is a tip that will help you to identify dangling modifiers:

> **RESTORED SUBJECT TIP:** Turn the modifier into a complete sentence by using the subject of the main sentence as the subject of the modifier and making the necessary changes in the verb. If the new sentence does not make sense, then the modifier is dangling.

Here is the tip applied to both example sentences:

EXAMPLE 1: ✗ Damaged beyond all repair, I threw my watch away.

TIP APPLIED: ✗ I was damaged beyond all repair.

Since the new complete sentence does not make sense (the *watch* was damaged, not *I*), the original sentence has a dangling modifier. You can correct dangling modifiers by rewriting the main sentence so that the subject of the main sentence is the same as the subject of the modifier:

CORRECTION: Damaged beyond all repair, <u>my watch</u> had to be thrown away.

EXAMPLE 2: ✗ While waiting for the bus, it began to rain.

TIP APPLIED: ✗ It waited for the bus.

Since *it* cannot be the subject of *waited for the bus*, the modifier must be dangling. Here is a correction made by changing the subject of the main sentence:

CORRECTION: While waiting for the bus, <u>I</u> got caught in the rain.

Another way to correct an elliptical adverb clause is to make it into a complete clause with a subject different from the one in the main clause. Here is an example:

EXAMPLE 2: ✗ While waiting for the bus, it began to rain.

CORRECTION: While waiting for the bus, *I was* it began to rain.

Lesson 19

dm

Sentence Practice 1

CORRECTED SENTENCES APPEAR ON PAGE 488.

Underline the dangling modifier and confirm your answer by applying the Restored Subject Tip. Then, correct the sentence.

EXAMPLE: ✗ <u>Surprised by the explosion</u>, panic spread through the crowd.

CONFIRMATION: ✗ The panic was surprised by the explosion.

CORRECTION: Surprised by the explosion, the crowd panicked.

1. Realizing that it was time to eat, lunch was served to the hungry students.

2. Hoping there was plenty of air in her tank, the sunken wreck was explored a bit longer by the scuba diver.

3. After seeing the wreck, Sharon's day was ruined.

4. While reading my e-mail, somebody knocked at the door.

5. Running up the stairs, Colleen's nose broke as she fell.

 For more practice with dangling modifiers, go to **Exercise Central** at **bedfordstmartins.com/commonsense/6-19**.

Lesson 19

dm

Sentence Practice 2

CORRECTED SENTENCES APPEAR ON PAGE 488.

Underline the dangling modifier, and confirm your answer by applying the Restored Subject Tip. Then, correct the sentence.

EXAMPLE: ✗ <u>When traveling overseas</u>, hepatitis A shots are a good idea.

CONFIRMATION: ✗ Hepatitis A shots are traveling overseas.

CORRECTION: **When you are traveling overseas, hepatitis A shots are a good idea.**

1. Reading the contract carefully, it was decided to wait a few days before both parties would sign.

2. While relaxing in the sun, dark clouds suddenly appeared.

3. Enraged by his pitiful score, Ted's tennis rackets were hurled across the court.

4. Breaking the pencil in anger, Ted's bad temper again revealed itself.

5. Feeling hungry because I skipped lunch, eating supper seemed a really good idea.

Sentence Practice 3

Combine the two short sentences by making the second sentence into a participial phrase or elliptical adverb clause that can be moved in front of the underlined subject. Punctuate appropriately.

EXAMPLE: The <u>chicken</u> was injured by a speeding truck.
The chicken was crossing the road.

ANSWER: <u>While crossing the road</u>, the chicken was injured by a speeding truck.

1. The <u>cat</u> seemed nervous.
   The cat heard the panting of a dog.

2. <u>We</u> left the party early.
   We were disgusted by the obnoxious behavior of the host.

3. <u>Carl</u> easily jumped over the barricade.
   Carl was in excellent shape.

4. <u>The chicken</u> looked both ways.
   The chicken was concerned about the heavy traffic.

5. <u>The chicken</u> decided never to cross the road again.
   The chicken was frightened by his near-death experience.

Lesson 19

dm

Editing Practice 1

CORRECTED SENTENCES APPEAR ON PAGE 488.

Correct all errors in the following paragraphs using the first correction as a model. The number in parentheses at the end of each paragraph indicates how many errors you should find.

Worried that he would be late for class, ~~Oliver's leisurely walk turned~~ *Oliver turned his leisurely walk* into a trot. He quickly entered the science building. Whenever late for class, his chemistry teacher always seemed to notice. Meeting an old friend who wanted to chat, his chances of arriving on time diminished. Oliver didn't want to be rude, so he left as soon as he could. While thinking about skipping his class altogether, several options went through his mind. He decided he would simply try to walk in without being noticed. (3)

Opening the classroom door as quietly as possible, no one seemed to notice him. But then Dr. Wilson said, "Oh, I hope it wasn't too much trouble for you to join us today, Oliver." While attempting to explain why he was unavoidably detained, his excuses only made him look even more foolish. Walking to his assigned seat, his books slipped out of his damp hands. Oliver resolved to come to class on time or not at all. (3)

Editing Practice 2

CORRECTED SENTENCES APPEAR ON PAGE 489.

Correct all errors in the following paragraphs using the first correction as a model. The number in parentheses at the end of each paragraph indicates how many errors you should find.

Having a horrible time finding a birthday present for her boy-
friend Shane, ~~his few hobbies provided little inspiration for Rose.~~ *Rose realized that his few hobbies provided little inspiration*
Remembering that he had once said he liked electronic "toys," her decision was to go to an electronics store. She would not leave until she found something. Looking up electronics stores in the yellow pages, a nearby mall seemed to have an ideal store. (2)

While looking through aisles of merchandise, Rose's curiosity was aroused by a foot-long racing car with antennae. Since there was a demo model available, she took it for a spin down the aisle. Running into a wall, the car's hood flew off. While quietly attempting to put the car back together without anyone's noticing, its two front wheels broke off. She decided that this particular model was not quite sturdy enough. Discouraged by her adventures with electronic toys, a new set of speakers seemed a good choice. (4)

Editing Practice 3

Correct all errors in the following paragraphs using the first correction as a model. The number in parentheses at the end of each paragraph indicates how many errors you should find.

Jacquita realized that her day just wasn't going well
Irritated by the recent turn of events, ~~the day just wasn't going well for Jacquita~~. She had no control over the virus that plagued her, but she really couldn't afford to miss the economics study session. She decided to ask a classmate to take notes for her. Calling her friend Jerry, her plan was shot down when he said that he was sick too. Realizing that she didn't have anyone else's phone number, her only option was to drag herself to the study session. (2)

Getting about halfway to the classroom, the need for a quick detour to the rest room interrupted her. She soon decided that having a stomach virus was not going to be a crowd-pleaser, so she headed back to her dorm. Overcome by fatigue and illness, sleep came to her immediately. When Jacquita woke up, she called her teacher, but the teacher wasn't in. When talking to her friends the next day, they told her that the study session had been canceled because the teacher was sick with a stomach flu. (3)

Lesson 19

dm

Writing Practice

On your own paper, write a paragraph or two describing an awkward or funny classroom experience. Try to use several participial phrases and elliptical adverb clauses as introductory modifiers. Use the Editing Checklist to make sure your writing contains no dangling modifiers.

Editing Checklist

Identify Dangling Modifiers in Your Writing

_____ Use the Restored Subject Tip to identify dangling modifiers in sentences that begin with an introductory participial phrase or elliptical adverb clause.

Correct Dangling Modifiers in Your Writing

_____ If the dangling modifier is a participial phrase, change the subject of the main sentence to fit the modifier.

_____ If the dangling modifier is an elliptical adverb clause, you can either change the subject of the main sentence or add a subject to the modifier to make it a complete clause.

Lesson 19

dm

| **The Bottom Line** | When written correctly, introductory modifiers are very effective. |

LESSON 20
Misplaced Modifiers

Error Sentences

CORRECTED SENTENCES APPEAR ON PAGE 205.

EXAMPLE 1: ✗ Carole barely took ten minutes to finish the American history test.

EXAMPLE 2: ✗ The landlord told me yesterday the rent was due.

What's the Problem?

A **modifier** is a word or group of words that describes something, somebody, or an action. A modifier should be positioned in a sentence so that readers can easily determine what the modifier is describing. For instance, *angry* and *quickly* are modifiers in *The angry teacher quickly left the room.* The word *angry* clearly modifies the subject *teacher,* while *quickly* clearly modifies the verb *left.*

A misplaced modifier occurs when readers cannot easily determine what a modifier is supposed to be describing. In Example 1, *barely* isn't describing how Carole *took;* instead, *barely* is placing a limit on the amount of time—not quite ten minutes. In Example 2, it is not clear whether *yesterday* describes *when the landlord said something* or indicates *when the rent was due.*

In this lesson, we focus on single-word modifiers that are frequently misplaced. A related problem is the dangling modifier, which typically involves groups of words at the beginning of a sentence (see Lesson 19).

What Causes the Problem?

Misplaced modifiers are difficult to detect because they often do not make a sentence ungrammatical; that is, the sentence structure can look perfectly OK. The problem is that the sentence may not accurately reflect the writer's intended meaning. The meaning of a sentence can change dramatically depending on where a modifier is placed. Compare, for instance, *Only I love you* and *I love only you.*

Diagnostic Exercise

CORRECTED SENTENCES APPEAR ON PAGE 489.

Correct all errors in the following paragraph using the first correction as a model. The number in parentheses at the end of the paragraph indicates how many errors you should find.

today

My brother called and said he would travel to Europe ~~today~~.

He plans to go as soon as school is out this summer. A travel agent told him it would only cost $400 for a round-trip ticket to London. The agent he spoke with enthusiastically said that he should take advantage of this price. My brother asked whether I wanted to go with him, but I have already committed myself to a summer job. He almost talked for an hour before I convinced him I couldn't go with him. (3)

Fixing This Problem in Your Writing

Start by locating any modifiers that have the potential to be misplaced. This is not an easy task, but the following tip will help you pick out such modifiers.

> *OFTEN* TIP: Look for each use of *often* or for any word that could be replaced by *often* (such as *just, simply, hardly, barely, only,* and *nearly*). You might change the meaning of the overall sentence by doing the *often* substitution, but the sentence should still be grammatical.

Once you have located these modifiers, closely examine each one to see whether it is placed so that it clearly modifies the word it most logically describes. For instance, Example 1 could easily be reworded as follows:

EXAMPLE 1: ✗ Carole barely took ten minutes to finish the American history test.

TIP APPLIED: Carole <u>often</u> took ten minutes to finish the American history test.

Now that you have located a *possible* problem, you must decide whether *barely* is misplaced. Look at all the possible words that the modifier could be describing, and reword the sentence so that readers will not be confused about what is being modified. Often, all you need to do is move the modifier. Since *barely* is placing a limit on *time* (not on *taking*), you should reword Example 1 as follows:

> *barely*
> CORRECTION: Carole ~~barely~~ took ten minutes to finish the
> American history t̂est.

By applying the *Often* Tip to Example 2, we see that *yesterday* is indeed a modifier.

> EXAMPLE 2: ✗ The landlord told me yesterday the rent was due.

> TIP APPLIED: The landlord told me <u>often</u> the rent was due.

But is *yesterday* misplaced? It could be describing *told* or it could be indicating when the rent was due. No one can know how to correct Example 2 without knowing what the writer intended, but either of these next two revisions would correct the problem.

> *Yesterday, the*
> CORRECTION: ~~The~~ landlord told me ~~yesterday~~ the rent was due.
> ^

> *yesterday*
> CORRECTION: The landlord told me ~~yesterday~~ the rent was due .
> ^

If English is not your first language, you may have difficulty determining where to put modifiers in your writing. Keep in mind that adverbs (words that modify verbs) cannot be placed between a verb and its object.

ESL

> EXAMPLE 3: ✗ Marco checked carefully the subway map before
> boarding the B train.

> *carefully*
> CORRECTION: Marco checked ~~carefully~~ the subway map before
> ^
> boarding the B train.

Sentence Practice 1

CORRECTED SENTENCES APPEAR ON PAGE 489.

First, locate *potential* misplaced modifiers by determining whether any words could be replaced by *often*. Next, write *OK* above each correct sentence, or correct the sentence by moving any misplaced modifier to a position that clarifies what the modifier describes. Your correction might depend on how you interpret the sentence.

>   *slowly*   *often*
> EXAMPLE: **The man who had been dancing** ~~slowly~~ **began**
>   **laughing.**

1. Professor Washington almost gave us a quiz over the homework.

2. Hamsters are only pregnant for sixteen days.

3. We almost read forty short stories in my American literature class.

4. My biology teacher said that there are 138,000 varieties of butterflies and moths yesterday.

5. She nearly hit the ball out of the park.

> For more practice correcting misplaced modifiers, go to **Exercise Central** at **bedfordstmartins.com/commonsense/6-20**.

Sentence Practice 2

CORRECTED SENTENCES APPEAR ON PAGE 489.

First, locate *potential* misplaced modifiers by determining whether any words could be replaced by *often*. Next, write *OK* above each correct sentence, or correct the sentence by moving any misplaced modifier to a position that clarifies what the modifier describes. Your correction might depend on how you interpret the sentence.

>   *often*   *nearly*
> EXAMPLE: **Jean** ~~nearly~~ **talked for two hours on the phone.**

1. The man reading slowly asked me to to turn off my radio.

2. Iva said yesterday she found my keys.

3. He only bought that DVD for ten dollars.

4. We located just three sources for our group paper.

5. Gardening often gives me both relaxation and time alone.

Sentence Practice 3

For each of the following sentences, place the word in parentheses into the sentence so that it is clear what the word modifies.

1. José lost his hearing last month as a result of an accident at the factory. (nearly)

2. On my income tax statement, I can deduct half of my travel expenses. (only)

3. His study group met to discuss the goals of the project. (quickly)

4. She goes to the gym after class. (often)

5. WebTech Corporation did not lose revenue once in the past fiscal year. (even)

Lesson 20

mm

Editing Practice 1

CORRECTED SENTENCES APPEAR ON PAGE 489.

Correct all errors in the following paragraphs using the first correction as a model. The number in parentheses at the end of each paragraph indicates how many errors you should find.

regularly

My friend Janet tells me what her literature teacher discusses
regularly. Janet said yesterday her literature teacher discussed
comic books. That topic does not seem appropriate for a college-
level course, but the teacher brought comics up while covering
popular literature because comics reveal the values of a culture
as well as helping promote these values. (1)

Take, for instance, the popular character Batman. The
character today is violent and even scary to law-abiding citizens.
The fact that he lurks in the shadows and is a creature of the
night frequently is interesting. Perhaps readers envy Batman

for being outside the law. Indeed, heroes who border on being lawbreakers commonly are best-selling characters in the comics—a trend suggesting that readers barely seem satisfied with governmental law enforcement and yearn to take matters into their own hands. (3)

Editing Practice 2

CORRECTED SENTENCES APPEAR ON PAGE 489.

Correct all errors in the following paragraph using the first correction as a model. The number in parentheses at the end of the paragraph indicates how many errors you should find.

Lesson 20

mm

Generally, a

~~A~~ person whose brain is damaged ~~generally~~ runs the risk of aphasia. Sometimes, this disorder, called *dysphasia,* happens when damage occurs to the part of the brain devoted to language production or comprehension. All people with aphasia have some language ability remaining, but it has been impaired in some way. Strokes almost account for 85 percent of aphasia cases. Eating an unhealthy diet, avoiding exercise, or smoking frequently can cause arteries to become clogged, a situation that can lead to strokes. Another cause of aphasia is head injuries from accidents. About a quarter of all penetrating head injuries result in aphasia, with males accounting for most cases. However, nearly a quarter of all cases involve short-term aphasia, with recovery occurring within three months. After six months, though, full recovery is unlikely. (2)

Editing Practice 3

Correct all errors in the following paragraphs using the first correction as a model. The number in parentheses at the end of each paragraph indicates how many errors you should find.

While going to class, I saw a friend who was talking to two

men. I discovered ~~later~~ *later* Hank was upset because the two men had

been handing out leaflets and warning people abruptly the world

would end. I found out that they claimed yesterday the world

would be destroyed around 2001. (2)

Hank had politely disagreed with them and asked them

for evidence. He said that he had never seen such belligerence on

campus; the two men had angered several students by yelling at

them and even blocking their paths. Hank told the two men he

would call campus administrators to prevent such harassment, and

that is when they decided loudly to speak to him. Eventually, they

began shouting at Hank. Hank was concerned that these two

people would cause students to be annoyed with anyone who

wishes graciously to share his or her beliefs on campus. (2)

Lesson 20

mm

Writing Practice

On your own paper, write a paragraph or two about something that took place at school and bothered you. Use the Editing Checklist to find and correct any misplaced modifiers in your writing.

Editing Checklist

Identify Misplaced Modifiers in Your Writing

_____ Look for any use of *often* or any word that could be replaced by *often* (the meaning will change, but the sentence will make sense). These words have the potential to be misplaced modifiers.

_____ Once you locate these words, closely examine each to see whether it is placed so that it is clearly modifying the word you want it to describe.

Correct Misplaced Modifiers in Your Writing

_____ To correct a misplaced modifier, you might simply need to move it to a position closer to the word it modifies — and away from any other word that it could possibly modify.

The Bottom Line

Modifiers are **usually** placed
close to the words they **best** describe.

UNIT SIX: Placing and Punctuating Modifiers

REVIEW

Using modifiers correctly is a key step in writing clearly. When writers misplace or mispunctuate modifiers, they may confuse readers, who will not understand their intended meaning. This unit introduced five problems writers encounter in placing and punctuating modifiers.

Commas with Introductory Elements

Introductory elements should be set off from the main sentence by commas. Here is a tip that will help you identify introductory elements:

> DELETION TIP: Delete any suspected introductory element. If what remains is a complete sentence, what you deleted is an introductory element.

Because all introductory elements *can* be set off with a comma, the following tip always works:

> COMMAS WITH INTRODUCTORY ELEMENTS TIP: Use commas after *all* introductory elements.

Commas with Adjective Clauses

Essential adjective clauses affect the meaning of the nouns they modify; they are not set off with commas. Nonessential adjective clauses merely rename the nouns they modify and do not affect their meanings; they are set off with commas. Here are three tips to help you to decide whether an adjective clause is essential or nonessential. The first tip helps identify essential adjective clauses:

> *WHICH ONE* TIP: If the adjective clause redefines the meaning of the noun it modifies by telling *which one* it is, then that clause becomes an essential part of the meaning of that word and cannot be separated from it by commas.

211

The second tip helps identify nonessential adjective clauses:

> *DO I NEED THIS?* TIP: If you can leave out the adjective clause without changing the basic meaning of the noun it modifies, then the adjective clause is nonessential and must be set off with commas.

The third tip is an important special rule for proper nouns:

> PROPER NOUN TIP: The adjective clauses that modify proper nouns are always nonessential. They always require commas.

Commas with Appositives

Essential appositives affect the meaning of the nouns they modify and are not set off with commas. Nonessential appositives merely rename the nouns they follow and do not affect their meaning. Nonessential appositives are set off with commas. Here is the basic tip for recognizing appositives:

> SWITCHING TIP: You can always switch an appositive and the noun it modifies. The resulting sentence will be grammatical and coherent.

Once you have detected an appositive, you can determine whether it is nonessential (requiring commas) or essential (no commas) by using one of the following three tips. The first tip helps identify essential appositives:

> *WHICH ONE* TIP: If the appositive redefines the meaning of the noun it modifies by telling *which one* it is, then that clause becomes an essential part of the meaning of that word and cannot be separated from it by commas.

The second tip helps identify nonessential appositives:

> *DO I NEED THIS?* TIP: If you can leave out the appositive without changing the basic meaning of the noun it modifies, then the appositive is nonessential and must be set off with commas.

The third tip is an important special rule for proper nouns:

> PROPER NOUN TIP: Appositives that modify proper nouns are always nonessential.

Dangling Modifiers

Certain types of modifiers are placed outside the main part of the sentence to give background information about it. If these modifiers are not logically connected to the main sentence, they are called dangling modifiers. Here is the basic tip for telling when a modifier is dangling:

> **RESTORED SUBJECT TIP:** Turn the modifier into a complete sentence by using the subject of the main sentence as the subject of the modifier and making the necessary changes in the verb. If the new sentence does not make sense, then the modifier is dangling.

Misplaced Modifiers

If adverb modifiers are put in the wrong place in a sentence, the reader will not be able to tell what the adverb is supposed to modify. Even worse, the reader may think the adverb modifies a word that is completely different from the one the writer intended. Here is a tip that will help you identify the adverb modifiers that are most likely to be misplaced:

> *OFTEN* **TIP:** Look for each use of *often* or for any word that could be replaced by *often* (such as *just, simply, hardly, barely, only,* and *nearly*). You might change the meaning of the overall sentence by doing the *often* substitution, but the sentence should still be grammatical.

Unit Six

review

Review Test

Correct all errors involving misplaced or mispunctuated modifiers using the first correction as a model. The number in parentheses at the end of the paragraph indicates how many errors you should find.

Jobs today have a common feature, endless meetings. In my

workplace the number of meetings, that I have to attend, has doubled

in the last three years. While trying to cope with increasing job

demands, meetings actually decrease the amount of time we have

to do our job. To a degree, I understand the need for increased

communication within the organization. Our jobs have become

much more interconnected; what one person often does affects many other workers. While meetings can play an important role in communication all too often they do not. For example, my boss who is a good and kind man does not know how to conduct a meeting. While attending a meeting, notes are never kept of our decisions. As a result, everybody has a different memory of what was decided a week later, so we have to have another meeting to resolve the conflicts. (7)

Unit Six

review

Using Apostrophes Correctly

Terms That Can Help You Understand Apostrophes

If you are not familiar with any of the following terms, look them up in the Guide to Grammar Terminology beginning on page 1. The numbers in parentheses indicate the lessons in which each term appears.

contraction (21)
gerund (23)
indefinite pronouns (22)
possessive apostrophe (22)

The Nuts and Bolts of Using Apostrophes Correctly

An apostrophe (') is a mark of punctuation used to indicate that letters are missing in a contraction and to show possession or ownership. Your writing may be unclear to your readers if you misplace or misuse apostrophes.

Lesson 21 shows you the proper way to build contractions with apostrophes. Contractions are shortened forms of words. For example, *I'll* is short for *I will; didn't* is short for *did not;* and *what's* is short for *what is.* Writers use an apostrophe to take the place of the letters dropped from a contracted word.

EXAMPLE: ✗ Wasnt that course canceled last semester?

CORRECTION: Wasn't that course canceled last semester?

Lesson 22 covers the use of possessive apostrophes. Writers use an apostrophe to show that someone possesses something. The placement of the apostrophe depends upon whether the "owner" is singular (the *girl's* *books* = the books of one girl) or plural (the *girls' books* = the books of two or more girls). This lesson covers the use of apostrophes and spelling of contractions.

EXAMPLE: ✗ Five students cars were towed from the parking lot.

CORRECTION: Five students' cars were towed from the parking lot.

Lesson 23 covers other uses of the apostrophe, the most common of which involves expressions of time or measure.

EXAMPLE: ✗ I can carry over a weeks worth of vacation at the end of the year.

CORRECTION: I can carry over a week's worth of vacation at the end of the year.

Lesson 24 shows you when *not* to use an apostrophe. Sometimes writers use an apostrophe when there is no need for one.

EXAMPLE: ✗ Your sentence has too many apostrophe's.

CORRECTION: Your sentence has too many apostrophes.

Unit Seven

overview

Can you detect problems with apostrophes?

CORRECTED SENTENCES APPEAR ON PAGE 490.

Correct all errors in the following paragraph using the first correction as a model. The number in parentheses at the end of the paragraph indicates how many errors you should find.

    During last ~~years~~ *year's* summer break, I spent two weeks' traveling in Italy. My big adventure was renting a car and driving in Italian traffic. I had heard everyones jokes about Italian drivers. For example, a friends Italian cousin told him that it was OK to go the wrong way on a one-way street as long as you drove backward. But I found that Italians driving was no worse or better than Americans driving.

Nevertheless, there are some real differences. We are used to Americans complaining about the price of gasoline, but we need to count our blessings. Gasoline in Italy costs about $5 a gallon. Roads are surprisingly well maintained; Im sure there are more potholes in New York City than in all of Italy put together. The biggest problem I encountered was parking. The older towns, narrow streets, and lack of open space meant that there often was absolutely no place to park inside the cities walls. (7)

Unit Seven

overview

LESSON 21

Apostrophes in Contractions

Error Sentences

CORRECTED SENTENCES APPEAR ON PAGE 220.

EXAMPLE 1: ✗ Pacifism is the belief that warfare isnt justified.

EXAMPLE 2: ✗ The ethics committee announced that its no longer supporting the senator's decision to remain in office.

What's the Problem?

Contractions are shortened forms of words, and — for better or worse — they add an informal tone to writing, as well as some conciseness. Many readers prefer that writers not use contractions in formal writing, so one way to avoid contraction errors is simply to avoid using contractions. However, many writers want to use contractions, so here we describe how they can be correctly "assembled."

An error occurs when a contraction lacks an apostrophe or when the apostrophe is in the wrong place. We focus on the first situation, since it is by far the more frequent error. An apostrophe offers a cue to readers, letting them know that you are using a contraction (and letting them know you fully realize the word is a contraction).

Example 1 has a contraction error because *isnt* ("is not") lacks an apostrophe between the *n* and the *t*. Similarly, Example 2 requires an apostrophe to show that *its* stands for "it is."

What Causes the Problem?

Contractions are especially common in speech. In fact, many writers use contractions to lend their writing the relaxed, natural tone found in conversation. Thus, it is easy to overlook the apostrophe, since we do not worry about it in speech. In addition, some contractions are used so often, we forget that they are contractions.

Lesson 21

And then there is the confusion between the contraction *it's* ("it is") and the possessive *its* (as in *The fish ate its neighbor*). Many writers—even experienced ones—often confuse these two words.

Diagnostic Exercise

CORRECTED SENTENCES APPEAR ON PAGE 490.

Correct all errors in the following paragraph using the first correction as a model. The number in parentheses at the end of the paragraph indicates how many errors you should find.

The student government announced today the election results

for representation in the student senate. Almost half the students

didn't
~~didnt~~ vote at all, and there werent many candidates running. Im
 ^

not sure why, but apathy was widespread. My guess is that many

students dont think the senators have much real power, or perhaps the

candidates' qualifications and goals were unclear. Its clear that students

arent enthusiastic about our student government, so perhaps we should

consider large-scale changes to the system. (5)

Fixing This Problem in Your Writing

For writers who have a habit of overlooking a contraction, here is an editing tip.

> CONTRACTION TIP: Reread to see whether you can "expand" any one word by filling in missing letters (or numbers, as in *the class of '04*). If so, you probably have a contraction, which needs an apostrophe to show that letters or numbers are missing.

For instance, note how the following words can all be expanded and how the apostrophe replaces the missing letters:

they're = they <u>are</u>   didn't = did n<u>o</u>t   '01 = <u>20</u>01   let's = let <u>us</u>

The Contraction Tip almost always works, but non-native speakers of English may not know that *won't* is an irregular contraction in which *will not* becomes *won't*.

ESL

In Examples 1 and 2, we can easily expand the words *isnt* and *its* to *is not* and *it is*. Thus, they are contractions, and we can either write them out completely or put the apostrophe in the right place.

EXAMPLE 1:   ✗ Pacifism is the belief that warfare isnt justified.

TIP APPLIED: Pacifism is the belief that warfare <u>is not</u> justified.

CORRECTION: Pacifism is the belief that warfare isn't justified.

EXAMPLE 2:   ✗ The ethics committee announced that its no
                  longer supporting the senator's decision to remain
                  in office.

TIP APPLIED: The ethics committee announced that <u>it is</u> no
                  longer supporting the senator's decision to remain
                  in office.

CORRECTION: The ethics committee announced that ~~its~~ *it's* no
                  longer supporting the senator's decision to remain
                  in office.

Lesson 21

The most troublesome contraction is *it's* ("it is"). The contraction *it's* is often confused with *its*—which shows possession and is not a contraction. To help you determine whether you are using the contraction *it's*, use the *It's* Tip.

> *IT'S* TIP: Look at the apostrophe in *it's* and think of it as the little dot above the letter *i*—the letter that just happens to be the one the apostrophe stands for in *it's*.

In other words, if you see *it's* you should be able to imagine *it is* as well. If *it is* fits into the sentence, your choice of *it's* is correct. The word *its* should always refer to possession (as in *the dog bit its tail*).

Try the *It's* Tip to see whether the following sentence is correctly punctuated:

It's about time the bell rang.

The apostrophe in *it's* should make you think of the dot above the letter *i*—the missing letter. Indeed, you could replace *It's* with *It is*, so the sentence is correct.

Sentence Practice 1

CORRECTED SENTENCES APPEAR ON PAGE 490.

If a sentence does not have a contraction error, write *OK* above it. If there is an error, cross it out. Then, write out the full form of the word or words to show that the original is a contraction. In addition, supply the correct form of the contraction.

EXAMPLE: I think ~~its~~ time to leave.

it is
it's

1. Lets get one thing straight.

2. It wont be a problem.

3. Im afraid that we werent ready for the test.

4. Theyre ready for you now.

5. Even if it's raining, we still have to go.

 For more practice using contractions, go to **Exercise Central** at **bedfordstmartins.com/commonsense/7-21**.

Lesson 21

Sentence Practice 2

CORRECTED SENTENCES APPEAR ON PAGE 490.

If a sentence does not have a contraction error, write *OK* above it. If there is an error, cross it out. Then, write out the full form of the word or words to show that the original is a contraction. In addition, supply the correct form of the contraction.

EXAMPLE: ~~Theres~~ no business like show business.

There is
There's

1. I think that's OK.

2. Youre really in trouble now.

3. Do you want to come; were going to the early show.

4. Theres nothing wrong with my punctuation.

5. Its six of one, and half a dozen of the other. (traditional saying)

Sentence Practice 3

Rewrite the sentences below using at least one contraction in each sentence.

> EXAMPLE: **I do not see the problem.**
>
> ANSWER: **I don't see the problem.**

1. I could not agree with you more.

2. Here is another fine mess you have gotten me into!

3. I am sorry; there is nothing I can do about it.

4. They will not do that, will they?

5. They are sure that they are acting in its best interests.

Editing Practice 1

CORRECTED SENTENCES APPEAR ON PAGE 490.

Correct all errors in the following paragraphs using the first correction as a model. The number in parentheses at the end of each paragraph indicates how many errors you should find.

       don't
People ~~dont~~ think often about where their favorite foods come from, but the subject can be interesting. For instance, there isnt much evidence that waffles originated in Belgium. The waffle seems so popular that many countries claim its origin is with them. The Scots say that the waffle resulted accidentally when Sir Giles Whimple sat on a fresh oatcake while wearing a suit of chain mail. (1)

In France, waffles go back to at least the fifteenth century. Street vendors would sell them in front of churches during religious festivals. Theyd cook waffles with shapes reflecting religious themes to attract the attention of the celebrators. In modern Mexico, waffles are topped with cinnamon and sugar. In tropical countries, theyll often be topped with exotic fruits, while northern countries use whipped cream. For whatever reason, though, *Belgian waffle* has come to be a worldwide term referring to thick waffles. (2)

Editing Practice 2

CORRECTED SENTENCES APPEAR ON PAGE 490.

Correct all errors in the following paragraphs using the first correction as a model. The number in parentheses at the end of each paragraph indicates how many errors you should find.

Lesson 21

Many holidays are celebrated around the globe, but ~~theyre~~ *they're* often celebrated in diverse ways. For example, Christmas is celebrated in many countries, but each culture has it's own Christmas traditions. In France, for example, the Noël celebration begins right after December 6 (the feast day of St. Nicholas) and doesnt end until January 6. Many French have a grand meal that isnt served until after midnight mass on Christmas Eve. (3)

In Brazil, Christmas isnt simply a product of one culture; it represents a blend of Portuguese, African, and indigenous Indian cultures. On Christmas Eve, for instance, a traditional dinner includes a stuffing thats made out of a potato-like root from the indigenous Indians' diet. On December 31, many Brazilians go to the beach to celebrate the festival of a religious group that reflects

both Roman Catholic and African beliefs. (2)

Editing Practice 3

Correct all errors in the following paragraphs using the first correction as a model. The number in parentheses at the end of each paragraph indicates how many errors you should find.

Margaret Mead's book, *Coming of Age in Samoa,* is an

observer's account of life in Samoa, and ~~its~~ ^{it's} standard reading in

many anthropology courses. In 1928, this book revolutionized the

field of anthropology. Mead didnt stress the effects of biological

factors on people's behavior. Rather, she emphasized the effects of

social conventions and culture. (1)

Her findings arent the only revolutionary aspect of the book;

her methods were also new. Although many social scientists assume

that observers should be detached from what theyre studying, Mead

argued that its impossible to understand people and their culture

fully unless observers have an insider's perspective. Accordingly,

she tried to integrate herself into a Samoan community as much as

possible. Her approach has its drawbacks but is generally well

respected and often used today. (3)

Writing Practice

On your own paper, write a paragraph or two explaining an experience you had among a group of people who seemed quite different from you. Try to use at least three contractions. Use the Editing Checklist to correct any contraction errors in your writing.

Editing Checklist

Identify Apostrophe Errors in Your Writing

____ Proofread your words to see whether any one word can be "expanded" into two words. If so, it is probably a contraction.

____ Check carefully each use of *its* and *it's* in your writing. If you are indicating possession, there is no need for an apostrophe. However, if you are using a shortened form of *it is,* you need an apostrophe to take the place of the missing letter.

Correct Apostrophe Errors in Your Writing

____ In each contraction, position the apostrophe over the place where you have left out a letter or number.

____ Alternatively, you might choose to avoid the contraction entirely and use the expanded form instead (especially in formal writing).

____ Use *it's* only when *it is* would also fit in your sentence. *It's* is always a contraction — never a possessive pronoun.

The Bottom Line

If you use a contraction, it'll need an apostrophe.

LESSON 22
Apostrophes Showing Possession

Error Sentences

CORRECTED SENTENCES APPEAR ON PAGES 228–29.

EXAMPLE 1: ✗ The quarterbacks pass was incomplete.

EXAMPLE 2: ✗ The problem of pollution is everyones concern.

EXAMPLE 3: ✗ I get tired of picking up the childrens' toys.

What's the Problem?

ESL

In English, writers normally add an apostrophe and an *s* to show that some-one or something possesses something else. Apostrophes are used with the possessive *s* forms of nouns and with **indefinite pronouns** (words like *any-body, someone, nobody*) to distinguish the possessive *s* form from the more common plural *s* form. Some writers incorrectly leave out the apostrophe when they use possessive nouns (as in Example 1) or indefinite pronouns (as in Example 2).

A second problem is deciding where the apostrophe should be placed—before or after the *s*. Generally, an *'s* is added to singular nouns, and an *s'* is added to plural nouns. However, if the plural form of a word does not end in *s* (as in Example 3), an *'s* is used to indicate possession.

What Causes the Problem?

In speech, the various kinds of possessive apostrophes sound exactly alike, so writers who try to punctuate by ear have no way to tell which form of the possessive apostrophe to use. Even if writers have correctly identified a pos-sessive *s,* they are sometimes confused by the complicated rules about where the apostrophe goes and how the possessive word is spelled.

Diagnostic Exercise

CORRECTED SENTENCES APPEAR ON PAGE 491.

Correct all errors in the following paragraph using the first correction as a model. The number in parentheses at the end of the paragraph indicates how many errors you should find.

Paul Ortega has been one of my ~~families'~~ *family's* friends over the years. Although he was born in Mexico, he speaks English like a native because his fathers' employer relocated his family to Arizona when Paul was six. By the time he graduated from high school in Phoenix, Pauls' English was as good as anyones. Nearly every summer, however, Paul and his sisters' went back to Mexico City, where they stayed at a relatives' house. As a result, he is completely at home in either countries' culture. He and my father have been business partner's for years. Their companies' success has been due largely to Paul's ability to conduct business in both Mexico and the United States. (8)

Lesson 22

Fixing This Problem in Your Writing

Here is a good way to tell whether a noun or an indefinite pronoun needs a possessive *s* ending. This tip also tells you whether the noun is singular (you usually add an *'s*) or plural (you usually add an *s'*).

> *OF* TIP: See whether you can reword the phrase containing the *s* by reversing the words and adding *of* to show that something belongs to somebody. If you can, then you have a possessive *s* that needs to be marked by an apostrophe. The paraphrase will also show you whether the modifying word is singular or plural so you can punctuate it correctly.

The *Of* Tip can be applied to Example 1.

EXAMPLE 1:   ✗ The quarterbacks pass was incomplete.

TIP APPLIED: The <u>pass of the quarterback</u> was incomplete.

The *Of* Tip tells you two things: *quarterback* is indeed a possessive modifier requiring a possessive apostrophe, and *quarterback* is a singular noun. Now you can make the following correction:

CORRECTION: The quarterback's pass was incomplete.

Here is a similar example with a plural noun:

EXAMPLE: ✗ Both quarterbacks passes were inaccurate.

TIP APPLIED: The <u>passes of both quarterbacks</u> were inaccurate.

The *Of* Tip tells you that *quarterbacks* is a plural possessive noun, which requires an *s'* ending.

CORRECTION: Both quarterbacks' passes were inaccurate.

Here is the *Of* Tip applied to Example 2:

EXAMPLE 2:   ✗ The problem of pollution is everyones concern.

TIP APPLIED: The problem of pollution is <u>a concern of everyone</u>.

The *Of* Tip tells you that the indefinite pronoun *everyone* is a singular possessive modifier.

CORRECTION: The problem of pollution is everyone's concern.

Note: Sometimes the *Of* Tip produces what is called a "double-possessive." This is a structure that has both *of* AND a possessive apostrophe. Here are some examples: *Jim's friend = a friend of Jim's; Mozart's pupil = a pupil of Mozart's*. This double-possessive structure is perfectly grammatical.

The rules governing the spelling of the possessive seem rather complicated, but if you look at them this way they make sense:

> **DOUBLE DUTY *S'* TIP:** *s'* must always do TWO things together: (1) change a regular singular noun into a plural, AND (2) make the noun possessive.
> If the Double Duty *s'* Tip does not apply because either the possessive noun is singular, or the possessive noun has an irregular plural, do not use *s'*.
> Use *'s* instead.

Lesson 22

'
∨

Here is the Double Duty *s'* Tip applied to a regular noun:

> **the girls' books**
> (s' makes *girl* **both** plural **and** possessive)

The Double Duty *s'* Tip cannot be applied to irregular nouns because irregular nouns don't use an *s* ending to form plurals. For example, *women* is a plural irregular noun. If we were to add *s'* to *women*, the result would be incorrect because it was already plural before we added the *s'*.

> ✗ the womens' books

The Double Duty *s'* Tip prevents this error and gives the correct spelling:

> **the women's books**

Let's look at Example 3.

> EXAMPLE 3:   ✗ I get tired of picking up the childrens' toys.

We cannot add *s'* to make *children* plural because *children* is already plural. To make *children* possessive, we only need to add *'s*:

> TIP APPLIED: **I get tired of picking up the children's toys.**

Nouns ending in *-y* that change *y* to *i* and add *es* follow the normal Double Duty *s'* Tip because they form their plural with an *s*. Notice the spelling of *spy* in the following examples:

> SINGULAR: **A spy gathers secrets.**
>
> SINGULAR POSSESSIVE: .**The spy's assignment was dangerous.**
>
> PLURAL: **The spies were arrested.**
>
> PLURAL POSSESSIVE: **The spies' activities were made public.**

Here is one exception to the apostrophe rule: when a proper name ends in two closely occurring *s* sounds, use just the apostrophe alone rather than *'s* to avoid bunching three *s* sounds in a row:

> **Moses' commandments**
>
> **Ulysses' voyages**
>
> **Jesus' teachings**

Lesson 22

Sentence Practice 1

CORRECTED SENTENCES APPEAR ON PAGE 491.

Correct the apostrophe error in each of the following sentences. Confirm your correction by applying the *Of* Tip.

>   *visitors'*
> EXAMPLE: They put all the ~~visitors~~ suitcases out in the hall.
>
> CONFIRMATION: They put <u>the suitcases of all the visitors</u> out in the hall.

1. Its nobodys business.

2. I really like that guitars sound.

3. The ladders rungs were covered with paint.

4. Platos dialogues are still an important part of philosophy.

5. The team met to discuss the tumors treatment.

> For more practice using apostrophes, go to **Exercise Central** at **bedfordstmartins.com/commonsense/7-22**.

Lesson 22

Sentence Practice 2

CORRECTED SENTENCES APPEAR ON PAGE 491.

Correct the apostrophe error in each of the following sentences. Confirm your correction by applying the *Of* Tip.

>   *couple's*
> EXAMPLE: The ~~couples~~ car was parked in the driveway.
>
> CONFIRMATION: <u>The car of the couple</u> was parked in the driveway.

1. The whole community was opposed to the bridges destruction.

2. Some of Wagners operas are the longest ever written.

3. I hastily scribbled my notes on the envelopes back.

4.   We were met by the hospitals administrator.

5.   An Englishmans home is his castle.

Sentence Practice 3

Turn the *of* structures in the following sentences into possessive structures.

> EXAMPLE: <u>The collapse of Enron</u> sent shock waves throughout the energy sector.
>
> POSSESSIVE: <u>Enron's collapse</u> sent shock waves throughout the energy sector.

1.   Black Bart took <u>the advice of the sheriff</u> seriously.

2.   <u>The waterfront of Brooklyn</u> used to be one of the busiest in the country.

3.   <u>The last episode of the soap opera</u> was a complete waste of time.

4.   <u>The tempo of the conductor</u> was really too fast for the orchestra.

5.   <u>The strength of the euro</u> is directly tied to <u>the value of the dollar</u>.

Lesson 22

Editing Practice 1

CORRECTED SENTENCES APPEAR ON PAGE 491.

Correct all errors in the following paragraph using the first correction as a model. The number in parentheses at the end of the paragraph indicates how many errors you should find.

Many years ago, when soccer was not so widely played,

I volunteered to be our elementary <u>~~schools~~</u> *school's* soccer coach.

Although I enjoyed watching soccer, I had never actually played

it myself. My situation was like everybodys. Without parent's

participation, there simply would have been no kid's soccer then.

Fortunately, the American Youth Soccer Organization ran clinics for beginning coaches. They correctly assumed that we didn't

know the rules or even the basics of building players soccer skills.

In many ways, it was a good time to be involved. We were there

strictly for the kids benefit. We didn't keep track of a teams'

win-and-loss record. Each game was played for its own sake.

I think the kids got a lot out of it because they knew it was for

them. They were not just acting out their fathers and mothers

past athletic successes. (8)

Editing Practice 2

CORRECTED SENTENCES APPEAR ON PAGE 491.

Correct all errors in the following paragraph using the first correction as a
model. The number in parentheses at the end of the paragraph indicates
how many errors you should find.

Lesson 22

Last summer we spent a week at Tanglewood, the Boston

Symphony's

~~Symphonys~~ summer home. That week featured contemporary

composer's works. Contemporary classical music is not every-

ones favorite music. It is demanding music to listen to because

of the musics reliance on dissonance rather than harmony.

The most interesting concert was by the pianist Ursula Oppens.

Several of the pieces she played had been commissioned by

her, and several of the other composers pieces had been dedi-

cated to her. Clearly, she was a contemporary musicians'

musician. While I really found the music she played to be

very difficult to get into, I couldn't help liking her. She engaged

everybodys attention, even people like me who are not fans of contemporary classical music. She played some of the most difficult piano music I have ever heard at breathtaking speed. Even though she took the music very seriously, she was also having such a great time playing it that the audiences enthusiasm matched hers. (7)

Editing Practice 3

Correct all errors in the following paragraph using the first correction as a model. The number in parentheses at the end of the paragraph indicates how many errors you should find.

Although I have been using the Internet more and more, I have quite mixed feelings about the ~~Internets~~ *Internet's* usefulness. I don't know about other peoples experience, but I get frustrated by how time-consuming it is. Part of the trouble is that my universitys' server is so overloaded that it just crawls. My parents commercial service is even worse. Half the time, they can't even get online. When they do get online, their companys server is so slow that it takes about a minute for each screen to download. When you are paying for the telephone line, every minutes delay is costing you more money. My other gripe is that when you do reach somebodys Web site, all too often it is completely out of date. It looks like the company presidents nerdy cousin set up the Web site three years ago, and no one has touched it since. It is especially frustrating to wait ten minutes for their fancy five-color logo to download only to find that none of the buttons on the page are actually connected to anything. Nevertheless, despite everyones complaints, the Internet is here to stay. Excuse me while I check my e-mail. (8)

Lesson 22

Writing Practice

On your own paper, write a paragraph or two describing how you use the Internet. How has it been most useful to you? What has been your biggest frustration in using it? Try to use as many possessive nouns and pronouns as possible. Use the Editing Checklist to ensure that you have used apostrophes correctly.

Editing Checklist

Identify Possessive Apostrophe Errors in Your Writing

____ Use the *Of* Tip to identify possessive nouns and indefinite pronouns requiring a possessive apostrophe.

____ Use the *Of* Tip to decide whether the possessive noun is singular or plural.

Correct Possessive Apostrophe Errors in Your Writing

____ To make a singular regular noun possessive, add *'s.* To make a plural regular noun possessive, add *s'.*

____ To make a plural irregular noun (one that does not end in *s* in the plural) possessive, add *'s.*

Lesson 22

The Bottom Line

Use the *Of* Tip to check
everybody's possessive apostrophes.

LESSON 23
Other Uses of the Apostrophe

Error Sentences

CORRECTED SENTENCES APPEAR ON PAGE 237.

EXAMPLE 1:   ✗ Todays high temperature was 94°F.

EXAMPLE 2:   ✗ We were worried about Johns being late.

What's the Problem?

The apostrophe has two other uses besides indicating a contraction (Lesson 21) and showing possession (Lesson 22). One use is in expressions of time or measure, for example: **today's** *newspaper, last* **year's** *schedule, your* **money's** *worth, at* **arm's** *length.* The second, altogether different use of the apostrophe is with the subjects of **gerund phrases**. A **gerund** is the *-ing* form of a verb used as a noun; a gerund phrase is the gerund and whatever else goes with it. For example, in the sentence

ESL

Lesson 23

> *Carla's rejecting the offer* surprised us,

Carla's is the subject of the gerund phrase *rejecting the offer.* Sometimes writers fail to use the apostrophe with expressions of time or measure (as in Example 1) and with the subjects of gerunds (as in Example 2).

What Causes the Problem?

Since neither time/measure expressions nor the subjects of gerunds are possessive, some writers may be unaware that they require apostrophes just as possessives do.

Diagnostic Exercise

CORRECTED SENTENCES APPEAR ON PAGE 492.

Correct all errors in the following paragraph. The number in parentheses at the end of the paragraph indicates how many errors you should find.

Economists'

~~Economists~~ recommending that we tie Social Security benefits
‸
to the stock market has started a fierce debate. In the long run,

advocates argue, retired persons would more than get their moneys

worth from retirees putting their money in the stock market.

For the last fifty years, the argument goes, the value of stocks has

increased an average of 10 percent a year. At that rate of return,

money doubles in seven years time. Social Securitys increasing

only 1 or 2 percent a year cannot compare with money invested

in the stock market. With just Social Security, retired persons

outliving their incomes is a major long-term issue. On the other

hand, what retiree wants to stay up nights worrying about whether

the stock markets going into free fall, as it sometimes has? (6)

Lesson 23

Fixing This Problem in Your Writing

The *Of* Tip presented in Lesson 22 is also a very useful way to identify
expressions of time/measure that require an apostrophe.

> *OF* TIP: See whether you can reword the time/measure expression by
> reversing the words and adding *of*. If you can, then you need to add
> an apostrophe. The *Of* Tip will also show you whether the modifying
> time/measure word is singular or plural so you will know whether to
> use *'s* or *s'*.
>
> (See the Double Duty *s'* Tip in Lesson 22 for help in placing the
> apostrophe.)

Here is the *Of* Tip applied to a time/measure expression:

EXAMPLE 1: ✗ Todays high temperature was 94°F.

TIP APPLIED: The <u>high temperature of today</u> was 94°F.

The *Of* Tip shows that we need an apostrophe and that *today* is singular.

CORRECTION: Today's high temperature was 94°F.

Subjects of gerund phrases must always be possessive. If the subject of a gerund phrase is a noun or an indefinite pronoun, then you must show that it is possessive by using an apostrophe. Identifying gerund phrases is not easy, especially when the gerund phrase is the object of a verb or preposition. Gerund phrases are much easier to spot when they are the subjects of sentences. Here is a tip that will help you spot them by making the gerund phrases into subjects.

> _____-*ING SURPRISED ME* TIP: Put -*ing* phrases into this test frame:
> "_____ surprised me." If the resulting sentence is OK, then it has a gerund phrase. You need to make its subject possessive.
>   (See the Double Duty *s'* Tip in Lesson 22 for help in placing the apostrophe.)

Here is the _____-*ing Surprised Me* Tip applied to Example 2:

EXAMPLE 2:   ✗ We were worried about Johns being late.

TIP APPLIED: John's being late surprised me.

The tip shows us that *John's being late* is a gerund and that *John's* must be used in the possessive form.

CORRECTION: We were worried about John's being late.

Lesson 23

Sentence Practice 1

CORRECTED SENTENCES APPEAR ON PAGE 492.

Correct the possessive apostrophe errors in the following sentences. Confirm your corrections by applying the *Of* Tip to expressions of time/measure and the _____-*ing Surprised Me* Tip to the subjects of gerunds.

                                              union's
EXAMPLE: The company blamed the ~~unions~~ refusing to
                 negotiate for the strike.

CONFIRMATION: The union's refusing to negotiate surprised me.

1. Wilbur hated Orvilles flying all those kites.

2. I didn't get Sundays newspaper.

3. The restaurants being open so late in Spain was a shock.

4. This weeks lesson is from St. Paul.

5. They are debating this years budget.

> ▨ For more practice using apostrophes, go to **Exercise Central** at
> **bedfordstmartins.com/commonsense/7-23**.

Sentence Practice 2

CORRECTED SENTENCES APPEAR ON PAGE 492.

Correct the possessive apostrophe errors in the following sentences. Confirm your corrections by applying the *Of* Tip or the _____-*ing Surprised Me* Tip.

> EXAMPLE: It is a problem in ~~todays~~ *today's* fast-paced society.
>   ^
> CONFIRMATION: It is a problem in the <u>fast-paced society of today</u>.

Lesson 23

1. The attack of September 11 was this centurys first major U.S. crisis.

2. I don't know if it was worth two weeks wages.

3. That is tomorrows problem.

4. Donalds selling Boardwalk turned out to be a big mistake.

5. I can't do it on a minutes notice.

Sentence Practice 3

Turn the second sentence into a gerund phrase by changing the verb into an -*ing* form and making the subject possessive. Then put the entire gerund phrase into the first sentence in place of the IT.

> EXAMPLE: IT was a common theme in Shakespeare's time.
>   A ghost called for revenge.
>
> COMBINED: <u>A ghost's calling for revenge</u> was a common theme in Shakespeare's time.

1. IT is something new.
    The school offered girl's soccer.

2. IT is probably a myth.
    Lincoln walked miles to return two pennies.

3. IT was amazing.
    The parrot knew classical Greek.

4. The union hadn't expected IT so quickly.
    The company agreed to their offer.

5. We were worried about IT.
    The girls stayed out so late.

Editing Practice 1

CORRECTED SENTENCES APPEAR ON PAGE 492.

Correct all errors in the following paragraph using the first correction as a model. The number in parentheses at the end of the paragraph indicates how many errors you should find.

Lesson 23

       today's
In ~~todays~~ political climate, we are discovering that
      ^

never has so much money been spent on so few voters. We have

all been dismayed by politicians spending so much money

on campaigns. In just four years time, the amount of money

spent on political campaigns has nearly doubled. The entire

credibility of the political system is being threatened by

politicians endlessly seeking financial support. It demeans

politicians, who are forced to devote most of their time

to fundraising. Political parties depending on special

interest groups erodes our confidence in the fairness of the

political system. One symptom of the publics disengaging

from the political process is the fact that the turnout in

this years election was the lowest in a hundred years. (6)

Editing Practice 2

CORRECTED SENTENCES APPEAR ON PAGE 492.

Correct all errors in the following paragraph using the first correction as a model. The number in parentheses at the end of the paragraph indicates how many errors you should find.

          people's

There was an article about young ~~peoples~~ eating habits

in todays paper. According to the article, American children are

fat and getting fatter. The article blamed the situation on a number

of causes: childrens eating habits, teenagers eating more and

more fast food, and everybodys failing to get enough exercise.

The article talked about high school students getting over half

their daily calories from soft drinks. Adults fussing about their

childrens eating habits is nothing new, but clearly the magnitude

of the problem has changed. For example, every week our paper

runs an old photograph of local interest. This weeks photo-

graph was of a high school dance from 1950. There were about

two hundred teenagers in the photograph, and every single person

was skinny by todays standards! (9)

Lesson 23

'
v

Editing Practice 3

Correct all errors in the following paragraphs using the first correction as a model. The number in parentheses at the end of each paragraph indicates how many errors you should find.

            summer's

With the savings from this ~~summers~~ extra jobs, I decided

to buy a motorcycle, despite my moms warning me that they

were dangerous. I took a two-week course in motorcycle safety.

I learned a lot. For example, I learned about riders impairing

their rear vision by mirrors being too small. It is also important

for passengers to have unobstructed views since passengers

seeing a hazard sometimes helps the driver avoid an

accident. (4)

    In last weeks class, we got very conflicting safety advice.

One school of thought advises against motorcyclists driving

down the center of the lane because that is where oil collects.

Another group of safety experts argues for cyclists driving

down the center because motorists can see cyclists better in

their rearview mirrors. In a couple of months time, I will have

the experience to offer my own advice. (4)

Lesson 23

Writing Practice

On your own paper, write a paragraph or two describing some good (or remarkably bad) advice you have been given. Try to use several gerunds and time/measure expressions that use apostrophes. Use the Editing Checklist to ensure that you are punctuating correctly.

Editing Checklist

Identify Apostrophe Errors in Your Writing

____ Proofread your writing for time/measure expressions and for gerunds (*-ing* words used as nouns).

____ Use the *Of* Tip to determine whether time/measure expressions need an apostrophe.

____ Use the _____*-ing Surprised Me* Tip to identify the subjects of gerund phrases.

Correct Apostrophe Errors in Your Writing

____ To make a singular regular noun possessive, add *'s*. To make a plural regular noun possessive, add *s'*.

____ To make a plural irregular noun (one that does not end in *s* in the plural) possessive, add *'s*.

Lesson 23

,
ˇ

The Bottom Line

Writers' using the *Of* Tip helps them punctuate words with apostrophes correctly.

LESSON 24
Unnecessary Apostrophes

Error Sentences

CORRECTED SENTENCES APPEAR ON PAGES 244–45.

EXAMPLE 1: ✗ Your sentence has three comma's.

EXAMPLE 2: ✗ Two Adams' were elected president.

What's the Problem?

The apostrophe (') is commonly used to show that letters have been left out of a word to form a **contraction** (see Lesson 21) or to show **possession** (see Lesson 22). For almost all words, it is incorrect to use an apostrophe to indicate *plurality*. That is, rarely will an apostrophe be used to show that there is more than one of something. This is the problem in Example 1.

Many people add an apostrophe and an *s* to form the plural of a last name, but this is *not* one of those rare occasions when an apostrophe is used to show plurality. For instance, the plural of the name *Clinton* is *Clintons*. If a last name ends in the letter *s*, the plural is formed by adding *es*, not an apostrophe as in Example 2.

What Causes the Problem?

One reason apostrophe errors occur is that people associate apostrophes with adding an *s*. However, there are two reasons to add an *s*, and only one of these involves an apostrophe.

The first reason to add an *s* is to indicate that there is more than one of something (as in *five books*). The second reason is to show that something belongs to somebody (as in *Bob's car*). *Only* in the second situation should the writer add an apostrophe with the *s*. An error occurs when writers confuse these two situations and add an apostrophe each time they add an *s* to a word.

Diagnostic Exercise

CORRECTED SENTENCES APPEAR ON PAGE 492.

Correct all errors in the following paragraph using the first correction as a model. The number in parentheses at the end of the paragraph indicates how many errors you should find.

> *friends*
> Some old ~~friend's~~ of mine stopped by my apartment for
>
> coffee. My roommate's coffee pot was broken, so I made them
>
> some instant coffee. I'm not good at making coffee, but everybody
>
> had two cup's apiece. The coffee was pretty old, yet nobody seemed
>
> to care. We talked about our schedule's for next semester, and
>
> we all decided we should try to leave some time open for getting
>
> together every now and then. (2)

Lesson 24

no ⌄

Fixing This Problem in Your Writing

Suppose you use an apostrophe, and you want to determine whether you actually need one. Here are three tips you can use.

> *OF* TIP: See whether you can reword the phrase containing the *s* by reversing the words and adding *of* to show that something belongs to somebody. If you can, then you have a possessive *s* that needs to be marked by an apostrophe. The paraphrase will also show you whether the modifying word is singular or plural so that you can punctuate it correctly.

Let's try to apply this tip to Example 1.

EXAMPLE 1: ✗ Your sentence has three comma's.

This sentence does not indicate that *comma* possesses anything, so it is impossible to use the *Of* Tip and rearrange the words to make sense. In this sentence, then, there is no need for an apostrophe, since there is no possession. The word *comma* is merely plural.

CORRECTION: Your sentence has three comma/s.

CONTRACTION TIP: Reread to see whether you can "expand" any one word by filling in missing letters or numbers. If so, you probably have a contraction, which needs an apostrophe to show that letters or numbers are missing.

Let's try to apply this tip to Example 2.

EXAMPLE 2: ✗ Two Adams' were elected president.

It isn't possible to expand *Adams'* because there are no contracted words implied here. In this sentence, then, there is no need for an apostrophe, since there is no possession. The word *Adams* is merely plural.

Adamses
CORRECTION: Two ~~Adams'~~ were elected president.
                              ^

Only very rarely should you use an apostrophe to show that there is more than one of something. One occasion is when both an apostrophe and an *s* are added to abbreviations, numbers, or letters, as in *Three students earned A's on the last test.* Except for this rare situation, avoid using an apostrophe to show that there is more than one of something.

SPECIAL-WORD TIP: Use the apostrophe to indicate plurality *only* with numbers, letters, or abbreviations.

Lesson 24

no ,̬

  1920's   four *m*'s   two VCR's   some perfect 10's

Sentence Practice 1

CORRECTED SENTENCES APPEAR ON PAGE 493.

Refer to the three tips to label each correct apostrophe as "contraction," "possession," or "special word." If there is an error, make the necessary change by deleting the apostrophe.

possession
EXAMPLE: The company's acquisition was helped by the news

reports
~~report's~~ .
      ^

1. I can't wait to turn my essay's in.

2. We bought some maple bar's at Trudy's Cash-and-Carry.

3. The 1930's was one of the darkest period's in America's history.

4. I got two A's and two B's on four grammar test's.

5. Gary's excuses were the lamest reason's I've ever heard.

   For more practice using apostrophes, go to **Exercise Central** at
bedfordstmartins.com/commonsense/7-24.

Sentence Practice 2

CORRECTED SENTENCES APPEAR ON PAGE 493.

Refer to the three tips to label each correct apostrophe as "contraction,"
"possession," or "special word." If there is an error, make the necessary
change by deleting the apostrophe.

special word   *cases*
EXAMPLE: **The CD's were still in their ~~case's~~.**

Lesson 24

no ˅'

1. I can't believe that classes' were canceled today.

2. The president's remarks certainly raised some eyebrow's around the
    table.

3. Now that I have everyone's attention, I'd like to begin.

4. There're four s's in "possession."

5. Do you want to ask the Flores' to give us a ride to Paolo's party this
    weekend?

Sentence Practice 3

Rewrite the underlined *of* expression to produce a correct possessive apostrophe.

The election's outcome
EXAMPLE: ~~The outcome of the election~~ was still in doubt.

1. The success of the team was completely unexpected.

2. The coastline of Canada is absolutely immense.

3. An accident was averted thanks to the vigilance of the crew.

4. We got caught up in the excitement of the children.

5. The worth of the stamps was difficult to establish.

Editing Practice 1

CORRECTED SENTENCES APPEAR ON PAGE 493.

Correct all errors in the following paragraphs using the first correction as a model. The number in parentheses at the end of each paragraph indicates how many errors you should find.

My nephew's birthday was a few day's *days* ago, and I wasn't sure what to get him. Jimmy just turned four, and he likes all kind's of games and toys. However, I wanted to give him something that would stand out. (1)

The toy store's I visited, however, carried the usual stuff: monster toys, superhero dolls, assorted airplanes and cars, and hundreds of computer game's. I wasn't terribly inspired, so I decided to look at some of my old toys from the late 1970's. They were all broken. However, I went through my mother's attic and found three old military-type action figure's from the 1960's. Unlike today's tiny toy figures, these were about 10 inches high and had movable arms and legs. They were also in good condition. I gave them to Jimmy, and I'm hoping he'll pass them along in decent shape to some other family members. (3)

Lesson 24

no ,

Editing Practice 2

CORRECTED SENTENCES APPEAR ON PAGE 493.

Correct all errors in the following paragraphs using the first correction as a model. The number in parentheses at the end of each paragraph indicates how many errors you should find.

> Edith Wharton was one of the best-known ~~novelist's~~ *novelists* of the
> early 1900's, but much of her fame in the late 1990's results
> from movie version's of her books *Ethan Frome* and *The Age of*
> *Innocence.* Many of Wharton's stories focus on the wealth and
> elegance of high society. (1)

> Undoubtedly, her settings and themes were influenced by
> her parents' lifestyle. Not only were the Wharton's well-off
> financially, but their ancestry could also be traced back to
> prestigious New Yorker's. Her childhood was spent among the
> well-to-do socialite's of New York City, Rhode Island, and various
> parts of Europe. Despite her upbringing, Wharton's stories often
> presented satiric portrait's of the rich that questioned their
> extravagant lifestyles. (4)

Lesson 24

no '

Editing Practice 3

Correct all errors in the following paragraphs using the first correction as a model. The number in parentheses at the end of each paragraph indicates how many errors you should find.

> The term *sexual revolution* refers to the shift in how people,
> especially ~~American's~~ *Americans*, view sexual behavior. Starting in the
> 1960's, the sexual revolution called for a less conservative view

of sex. Sex outside marriage wasn't seen as always wrong, nor
did partners necessarily need to love one another to have a
sexual relationship. The use of birth control pill's fostered the
revolution; they offered an inexpensive, generally reliable way of
preventing pregnancies'. (2)

One of the effect's of the sexual revolution is that there are
fewer restriction's on nudity in magazines and movies. Another
effect is found in fashion; with the introduction of the mini-
skirt, clothes' became skimpier and more provocative.
People's views on nudity (or near nudity) differ, but society
in general has become accustomed to scantily clad models
and actresses. The sexual revolution has slowed considerably,
largely because of the spread of AIDS. However, society's
views on sex may never return to what they were before the
sexual revolution. (3)

Lesson 24

no

Writing Practice

On your own paper, write a paragraph or two explaining a cultural movement or historical event that has affected you. Try to use at least four apostrophes. Use the Editing Checklist to see whether each sentence you write is
punctuated correctly.

Editing Checklist

Identify Unnecessary Apostrophes in Your Writing

_____ This unit has presented three reasons to include an apostrophe in your writing: contraction (*you're a winner*), possession (*the engineer's lab notes*), and special words (*there are three 8's in my phone number*). Use the Contraction Tip, the *Of* Tip, and the Special-Word Tip to determine if your word needs an apostrophe.

Correct Apostrophe Errors in Your Writing

_____ Remove apostrophes that don't fit one of the three situations described above. Most likely, you simply need to make your word plural.

The Bottom Line	Writers often add unnecessary apostrophes to plural words, but only numbers, letters, or abbreviations use apostrophes to form plurals.	

Lesson 24

UNIT SEVEN: Using Apostrophes Correctly

Apostrophes (') are used for several quite different purposes. This unit presented situations in which apostrophes are required and those in which apostrophes are unnecessary.

Apostrophes in Contractions

The most common purpose of the apostrophe is to show where letters (or numbers) have been left out in a contraction. Here is the tip for identifying contractions:

> **CONTRACTION TIP:** Reread to see whether you can "expand" any one word by filling in missing letters or numbers. If so, you probably have a contraction, which needs an apostrophe to show that letters or numbers are missing.

This tip works even for the confusing pair *its/it's*. If you can expand *its* to *it is*, then you need to add the apostrophe to fill in the missing letter: *it's*.

Apostrophes Showing Possession

The second most common use of the apostrophe is to identify the possessive *s* in noun and indefinite pronoun modifiers. Here is a tip that will help you identify these possessive forms:

> *OF* **TIP:** See whether you can reword the phrase containing the *s* by reversing the words and adding *of* to show that something belongs to somebody. If you can, then you have a possessive *s* that needs to be marked by an apostrophe. The paraphrase will also show you whether the modifying word is singular or plural so that you can punctuate it correctly.

Other Uses of the Apostrophe

The *Of* Tip also works well for writers who fail to use apostrophes in time or measure expressions (such as *a moment's notice* and *today's news*).

A related problem with possessive nouns and nouns used in expressing time or measure is knowing where to put the apostrophe—before or after the possessive *s*. Here is a tip that will help you make that determination:

> **DOUBLE DUTY *S'* TIP:** *s'* must always do TWO things together: (1) change a regular singular noun into a plural, AND (2) make the noun possessive. If the Double Duty *s'* Tip does not apply because either the possessive noun is singular, or the possessive noun has an irregular plural, then do not use *s'*. Use *'s* instead.

Another use of apostrophes is with the subjects of gerund phrases. Here is a way to recognize a gerund phrase:

> **_____-*ING SURPRISED ME* TIP:** Put -*ing* phrases into this test frame: "_____ surprised me." If the resulting sentence is OK, then it has a gerund phrase. You need to make its subject possessive.

Unnecessary Apostrophes

The final use of the apostrophe is to indicate plurality with numbers, letters, or abbreviations: *1950's, three x's, two TV's*. Some writers consider this use of the apostrophe to be optional.

> **SPECIAL-WORD TIP:** Use the apostrophe to indicate plurality *only* with numbers, letters, or abbreviations.

Unit Seven

review

Review Test

Correct all errors in the following paragraphs using the first correction as a model. The number in parentheses at the end of each paragraph indicates how many errors you should find.

                     Americans'
~~American's~~ attitude toward flying has changed since the

industry was deregulated. In the day's when fares and routes were

strictly regulated, airlines could compete with each other only in

terms of each airlines service and convenience. Customers preference

for airlines was often decided by the quality of meal service. I can

remember airlines serving three-course meals with free wine on

linen tablecloths to coach customer's. Coach passengers meals on

international flights were often rather elegant, more like first-class passengers meals today. Many airplanes on international flights had a passengers lounge with armchairs, couches, and an open bar for everyones use. (9)

In the world of todays deregulated industry, things are very different. Deregulations main effect was to force airlines into direct, open competition. Since airlines revenue is highly sensitive to passenger load (the average percentage of seats' occupied on each flight), airlines began cutting prices to ensure that every planes seating capacity was maximized. The more people on a flight, the more profitable it was. Airlines concerns about passengers leg room quickly became a thing of the past. Airlines attracting passengers by offering the lowest fare means that airlines have to cut costs at every turn. One of the fare wars first casualties was meal service. Southwest Airlines even jokes about it's "two-course" meals—peanuts and pretzels. (10)

Unit Seven

review

UNIT EIGHT
Using Other Punctuation and Capitalizing Certain Words

Terms That Can Help You Understand Other Punctuation and Capitalization

If you are not familiar with any of the following terms, look them up in the Guide to Grammar Terminology beginning on page 1. The numbers in parentheses indicate the lessons in which each term appears.

complete sentence (27)   **proper adjective (29)**
direct quotation (25)   **proper noun (29)**
indirect quotation (25)   **quotation (25)**
paraphrase (25)

Unit Eight

overview
The Nuts and Bolts of Other Punctuation and Capitalization

This unit covers capitalization and the remaining marks of punctuation most likely to cause problems for writers.

Lesson 25 shows you how to use quotation marks with direct quotations and paraphrases. Using someone's words exactly as they said or wrote them is called **direct quotation**. Direct quotation requires the use of quotation marks. Summarizing or otherwise altering someone's words is called **paraphrase** (or **indirect quotation**). Paraphrase does not require the use of quotation marks.

EXAMPLE: ✗ Camryn said that "she wanted to buy a
               laptop computer."

254

CORRECTION: Camryn said that ʌshe wanted to buy a laptop
computer.ʌ (Correct this way if you are paraphrasing
Camryn's words.)

CORRECTION: Camryn said, ~~that~~ *"I want* "~~she wanted~~ to buy a laptop
computer." (Correct this way if those were Camryn's
exact words.)

Lesson 26 shows you how to use periods, commas, semicolons, and other
punctuation with quotation marks.

EXAMPLE: ✗ The instructor warned, "This next test will be
harder than the last one".

CORRECTION: The instructor warned, "This next test will be
harder than the last ~~one".~~ *one."*

Lesson 27 shows you how to use semicolons correctly in your writing.
Semicolons have the same function as periods. They are both used to signal
the end of a complete sentence. Semicolons are sometimes confused with
colons.

EXAMPLE: ✗ Soy sauce contains the following ingredients; water,
extract of soya beans, wheat flour, and salt.

CORRECTION: Soy sauce contains the following ingredients: water,
extract of soya beans, wheat flour, and salt.

Unit Eight

overview

Lesson 28 shows you how to use colons correctly in your writing. The
most common use of a colon is to introduce a list. It is not surprising that a
common mistake is to use a colon to introduce a list that is actually a
required part of the sentence. In this case, the colon is incorrect.

EXAMPLE: ✗ To remove this wallpaper, I will need: a sponge,
a bucket of warm water, a commercial stripping
solution, and a 4-inch putty knife.

CORRECTION: To remove this wallpaper, I will need a sponge,
a bucket of warm water, a commercial stripping
solution, and a 4-inch putty knife.

Lesson 29 gives you some guidelines for capitalizing certain words. **Proper nouns** and **proper adjectives** are capitalized to show that they are the "official" names of specific, individual persons, places, or institutions. Other special capitalization rules govern, for example, names of ethnic groups, languages, and certain academic courses.

EXAMPLE: ✗ Gustavo barra, my Professor, has taught english and french in brazil, bolivia, and los Angeles.

CORRECTION:
$$\overset{B}{\text{Gustavo}}\ \underset{\wedge}{\text{barra}},\ \text{my}\ \overset{p}{\underset{\wedge}{\text{P}}\text{rofessor}},\ \text{has taught}\ \overset{E}{\underset{\wedge}{\text{e}}\text{nglish}}$$

$$\text{and}\ \overset{F}{\underset{\wedge}{\text{f}}\text{rench}}\ \text{in}\ \overset{B}{\underset{\wedge}{\text{b}}\text{razil}},\ \overset{B}{\underset{\wedge}{\text{b}}\text{olivia}},\ \text{and}\ \overset{L}{\underset{\wedge}{\text{l}}\text{os Angeles}}.$$

Can you detect punctuation and capitalization problems?

CORRECTED SENTENCES APPEAR ON PAGE 493.

Correct all errors in the following paragraph using the first correction as a model. The number in parentheses at the end of the paragraph indicates how many errors you should find. (Count a pair of quotation marks as one error.)

Because my ~~History~~ *history* class ends at 11:30 and my Math class begins at noon, I have little time to eat lunch. I can still hear my Mother saying, you need a nutritious lunch, so I try to eat something quick that is still filling and at least remotely healthy, such as: vegetable soup, a whole-wheat roll, and fruit juice. Luckily, several vendors on campus sell ethnic food; which is usually more nutritious than hamburgers and fries. Yesterday, my friend sarah asked me "where we could go to get a quick bite to eat." I told her, "Let's go to the student union for gyros"! She was surprised to learn that they contain: meat, salad, and yogurt. She was also surprised to learn; how good they taste. (11)

LESSON 25

Quotation Marks with Direct Quotations and Paraphrases

Error Sentences

CORRECTED SENTENCES APPEAR ON PAGES 259–60.

EXAMPLE 1:　✗ In 1854, Chief Joseph of the Nez Percé tribe met with white leaders and said every part of this soil is sacred to my people.

EXAMPLE 2:　✗ Iva said that "it was cold now in her part of the world."

What's the Problem?

A primary function of quotation marks (" ") is to indicate *exactly* what a person has said or written—a **direct quotation**.

An alternative to quoting someone exactly is to use a **paraphrase** (or **indirect quotation**), which means putting most or all of somebody else's words in your own words. A paraphrase does not need quotation marks because a paraphrase *substantially* changes the words and the sentence structure of the original material. By paraphrasing, you signal to your readers that you are presenting your interpretation of someone else's idea. A paraphrase, however, should not change the meaning of the source. Both direct quotations and paraphrases should give credit to the source of the ideas you are using.

Often, you can't simply look at a sentence and tell whether quotation marks are needed; you have to know exactly what the original passage says to see whether it is being quoted word for word. Still, the two sample sentences seem to have errors. An error occurs if a direct quotation lacks quotation marks (as in Example 1) or if a paraphrase has quotation marks around paraphrased material (as in Example 2).

Keep in mind that quotation marks have other functions besides indicating a direct quotation. As shown in several places in this lesson, for instance, quotation marks are used around titles of songs, poems, short stories, and other brief works.

Lesson 25

" "

What Causes the Problem?

Quotation marks are an aspect of writing that doesn't exist in speech. Thus, writers have to consider an issue they don't normally associate with quoting someone. Another reason for errors is that people often think they can avoid using quotation marks merely by changing a word or two of the original.

Diagnostic Exercise

CORRECTED SENTENCES APPEAR ON PAGE 493.

Correct all errors in the following paragraph using the first correction as a model. The number in parentheses at the end of the paragraph indicates how many errors you should find. (Count a pair of quotation marks as one error.)

Until recently, poor picture quality and a high price tag have prevented consumers from purchasing digital cameras. Industry analyst Kevin Kane recently said, ~~the~~ "The next several years will be key in determining what part digital cameras will play in leisure and business budgets." Kane also reported that "digital cameras are now becoming affordable enough for the average consumer." Like PC's, fax machines, and cellular phones, digital cameras first attracted the interest of technology enthusiasts. But recreational photographers like Sanjei Rohan of Spokane, Washington, just appreciate the convenience. As a rock climber, I have seen some amazing landscapes, he says. I take pictures, download them to my computer, and e-mail them to my cousins in Nebraska, where they have fewer rocks to climb. "Industry analysts predict a sharp growth in consumer enthusiasm." (4)

Lesson25

" "

Fixing This Problem in Your Writing

If you wish to paraphrase, cover up the original sentence and begin writing (and rewriting) your own interpretation, going back to the original when you're done to make sure your paraphrase means about the same thing.

Also, keep in mind that even though only a direct quotation requires quotation marks, both a direct quotation and a paraphrase should indicate whose ideas or words you are using.

Here is one convention widely used to signal an indirect quotation:

> *THAT* TIP: Use *that* to begin a paraphrase, but do not use *that* to begin a direct quotation. Although it is not absolutely essential to use *that* before a paraphrase, inserting *that* will never change the meaning of a paraphrase. Inserting *that* before a direct quotation might change the meaning.

Often, such use of *that* comes naturally, but the tip helps you remember when to use quotation marks and when not to use them. Make sure that you don't use quotation marks when paraphrasing and that you do use them when quoting directly. In Example 1, there is no *that,* and inserting one seems to change the meaning of the sentence.

EXAMPLE 1:   ✗ In 1854, Chief Joseph of the Nez Percé tribe met with white leaders and said every part of this soil is sacred to my people.

TIP APPLIED: In 1854, Chief Joseph of the Nez Percé tribe met with white leaders and said <u>that</u> every part of this soil is sacred to my people.

The *that* version suddenly makes *my* refer to the writer, not to Chief Joseph. Since *that* doesn't work, this sentence must have a direct quotation needing quotation marks. You also need to add a comma before the quote and to capitalize its first word (see Lesson 26 about using quotation marks combined with commas and other punctuation).

CORRECTION: In 1854, Chief Joseph of the Nez Percé tribe met with white leaders and said , "Every ~~every~~ part of this soil is sacred to my people."

You can also correct Example 1 by changing the direct quotation to an indirect quotation.

CORRECTION: In 1854, Chief Joseph of the Nez Percé tribe met with white leaders and said that every part of this soil was ~~is~~ sacred to his my people.

Example 2 has a *that* before quoted material, suggesting a paraphrase. Also, why would Iva use the word *her* to refer to herself? She probably wouldn't,

Lesson 25

" "

so there is reason to believe that the material in quotation marks is not really a direct quotation.

EXAMPLE 2:   ✗ Iva said that "it was cold now in her part of the world."

We can't be positive unless we see *exactly* what Iva said. A writer should be able to track down the original material, so we've provided Iva's original statement:

Where I live, it's very cold now.

Example 2 has the same meaning as the original statement, but the wording is much different. Therefore, Example 2 is, indeed, a paraphrase and should *not* have quotation marks.

CORRECTION: Iva said that ⸝it was cold now in her part of the world.⸝

Sentence Practice 1

CORRECTED SENTENCES APPEAR ON PAGE 494.

First, use each of the following statements as a direct quotation in a sentence of your own (additional information is in brackets). Second, turn the direct quotation into a paraphrase starting with *that*.

Lesson 25

" "

Thomas Paine once wrote, "These

EXAMPLE: ~~These~~ are the times that try men's souls."
[Thomas Paine, writing about the need to fight the British in 1776]

PARAPHRASE: *Thomas Paine believed that circumstances in his day tested people's convictions.*

1.   I want to seize fate by the throat. [Composer Ludwig van Beethoven, in a letter he wrote in 1801]

2.   From where the sun now stands, I will fight no more forever. [Chief Joseph, speaking to his Nez Percé tribe]

3.   The covers of this book are too far apart. [Ambrose Bierce, in a review of another writer's book]

4. I beheld the wretch—the miserable monster whom I had created. [Mary Wollstonecraft Shelley, in her 1818 novel, *Frankenstein*]

5. Talk low, talk slow, and don't say too much. [John Wayne, giving advice on acting]

 For more practice using quotation marks, go to **Exercise Central** at **bedfordstmartins.com/commonsense/8-25**.

Sentence Practice 2

CORRECTED SENTENCES APPEAR ON PAGE 494.

First, use each of the following statements as a direct quotation in a sentence of your own (additional information is in brackets). Second, turn the direct quotation into a paraphrase starting with *that*.

EXAMPLE: *The poet Robert Frost once remarked, "The*
~~The~~ brain is a wonderful organ. It starts working the moment you get up and does not stop until you get into the office." [Poet Robert Frost]

PARAPHRASE: *The poet Robert Frost said sarcastically that the brain, though functioning constantly, seems to shut down when a person gets to work.*

1. The reason I'm going ahead with this attempt now is because I just cannot wait any longer to impress you. [Letter by John Hinckley to actress Jodie Foster, on the day he shot President Reagan]

2. The trouble with some women is they get all excited about nothing, and then they marry him. [Cher, singer and actress]

3. My life had its beginning in the midst of the most miserable, desolate, and discouraging surroundings. [Former slave Booker T. Washington, writing in 1901 about the effects of slavery]

4. When I'm good, I'm very good, but when I'm bad, I'm better. [Actress Mae West, in the movie *I'm No Angel*]

5. I see one-third of a nation ill-housed, ill-clad, ill-nourished. [Franklin Roosevelt, referring to the Great Depression in 1937]

Sentence Practice 3

Combine the following sentences by turning the direct quote in the second sentence into an indirect quote in the first sentence.

> EXAMPLE: Simple Simon said IT.
> "I met a pie-man going to the fair."

> ANSWER: Simple Simon said <u>that</u> he met a pie-man going to the fair.

1. Sharon said IT.
   "I have to leave soon."

2. Virginia Woolf said IT.
   "As a woman my country is the whole world."

3. Dominique said IT.
   "This book is the best I have ever read."

4. Mark Twain supposedly said IT.
   "Everybody talks about the weather, but nobody does anything about it."

5. Cal said IT.
   "The sky is falling!"

Lesson25

" "

Editing Practice 1

CORRECTED SENTENCES APPEAR ON PAGE 494.

Correct all errors in the following paragraphs using the first correction as a model. The number in parentheses at the end of each paragraph indicates how many errors you should find. Count a pair of quotation marks as one error.

Many Americans have spoken or written of the need for the United States to provide fair treatment to women. In 1850, for instance, Sojourner Truth, a former slave, said of the feminist cause, "If the first woman God ever made was strong enough to turn the world upside down all alone, these women together ought to be able to turn it back and get it right side up again!" A few years later, Lucy Stone said that From the first years to which my memory

stretches, I have been a disappointed woman. She went on to explain

that education, the professions, and religion were often closed to

her and other women. (1)

The women's movement became increasingly active after the

Civil War. After being arrested for leading the fight for women's

right to vote, Susan B. Anthony said, "It was we, the people—not

we, the white male citizens, nor we, the male citizens—but we

the whole people who formed this Union." She went on to argue

that "she and all women should be allowed to vote based on

the amendments made to the Constitution as a result of the

Civil War." (1)

Editing Practice 2

CORRECTED SENTENCES APPEAR ON PAGE 495.

Correct all errors in the following paragraphs using the first correction as a model. The number in parentheses at the end of each paragraph indicates how many errors you should find. Count a pair of quotation marks as one error.

The music of the 1960's often reflected a belief that ˮchange

should—and would—occur if people were willing to act and to

work together.ˮ Some popular songs of that period became theme

songs of the civil rights movement. For example, "We Shall

Overcome," which was an African American spiritual song of the

nineteenth century, became an anthem of the protest marchers. One

key statement is repeated over and over in the song: We shall overcome.

That is the best-known line, but the civil rights workers singing this

song also said that they were unafraid. (1)

"O Freedom" was another African American spiritual that became a protest song of the 1960's. This song proclaims before I'd be a slave, I'd be buried in my grave. As popular hits, protest songs conveyed important messages. (1)

Editing Practice 3

Correct all errors in the following paragraphs using the first correction as a model. The number in parentheses at the end of each paragraph indicates how many errors you should find. Count a pair of quotation marks as one error.

My brother Pete once said that "he wouldn't give up any of his bad habits." He lately had a disagreement with his fiancée, Lynn, who doesn't smoke and wants to avoid the health risks of second-hand smoke. She once said that "she wouldn't allow smoking at their home once they were married." Today, though, she said, "Pete can smoke as long as he does so on the back porch, where I rarely go." Later, she told me that she preferred he not smoke at all but that she knew when they got engaged that he was a heavy smoker. (1)

I think they're coming to an agreement. Pete said I will soon be sharing a home with Lynn and will have to compromise. He read an article that confirmed that "researchers have found that nonsmokers are at risk if they inhale smoke of people smoking around them." (2)

Lesson 25

" "

Writing Practice

Write a paragraph or two explaining a disagreement you had with someone. Try to use at least two direct quotations and two paraphrases. Use the Editing Checklist to correct any errors in the sentences you write.

Editing Checklist

Identify Errors in Using Quotation Marks in Your Writing

____ Use the *That* Tip to help you determine whether a quotation is a direct or an indirect quotation.

Correct Errors in Using Quotation Marks in Your Writing

____ When you quote someone word for word (a direct quotation), the quoted material should have quotation marks around it. Do not use quotation marks around a paraphrase.

____ If you can use *that* before the material you want to quote, without changing the meaning, the material is likely to be a paraphrase. A direct quotation should not be preceded by *that*.

____ Finally, remember that both a direct quotation and a paraphrase should indicate whose ideas or words you are using.

The Bottom Line

As we said earlier in this lesson, "Make sure that you don't use quotation marks when paraphrasing and that you do use them when quoting directly."

Lesson 25

" "

LESSON 26
Quotation Marks
with Other Punctuation

Error Sentences

CORRECTED SENTENCES APPEAR ON PAGES 267–68.

EXAMPLE 1: ✗ Edgar Allan Poe wrote "The Raven", "Annabel Lee", and "The Bells".

EXAMPLE 2: ✗ Rosa asked, "Do you want to play tennis"?

What's the Problem?

According to preferred American punctuation style, periods and commas go *inside* closing quotation marks—no matter whether the quotation marks are used for a quoted statement or the name of a brief work. In Example 1, the writer has incorrectly placed the period and commas. Colons (:) and semi-colons (;) go *outside* closing quotation marks—no matter what the quotation marks are used for.

Question marks and exclamation points can go either inside or outside, depending on how they are used. They go inside if the material inside the quotation marks is a question or an exclamation. For instance, the material inside quotation marks in Example 2 is a question, so the question mark belongs inside the closing quotation mark.

What Causes the Problem?

One reason for this type of error is that spoken English offers no clues about correct placement of punctuation with quotation marks in writing. Another reason for this error is that there is no compelling logical reason to put punctuation marks either inside or outside the closing quotation mark. Adding to the problem is that placement of question marks and exclamation marks depends on the meaning of the entire sentence.

CORRECTED SENTENCES APPEAR ON PAGE 495.

Diagnostic Exercise

Correct all errors in the following paragraph using the first correction as a model. The number in parentheses at the end of the paragraph indicates how many errors you should find.

Yesterday, my literature teacher asked, "Who can name three
Americans?"
poems written by African ~~Americans~~"? I was able to come up with
　　　　　　　　　　　　　　^

"Incident," which was written by Countee Cullen. Herman, the guy

who sits next to me, named Langston Hughes's "Harlem". I started to

bring up "Letter from Birmingham Jail;" however, I quickly recalled

that is an *essay* by Martin Luther King, Jr. Then, somebody in the

back row mentioned Hughes's "Same in Blues", and somebody else

remembered Richard Wright's "Between the World and Me". Our

teacher seemed glad that it didn't take very long for us to answer.

I don't know about any of the other students, but in my high school

English classes we studied quite a few African American poets. (4)

Lesson 26

" "

Fixing This Problem in Your Writing

For better or worse, you simply need to memorize the rules stated earlier. In particular, remember that periods and commas go *inside* the closing quotation mark. So, Example 1 needs commas inside the quotation marks following the first two titles and a period inside the quotation mark following the last title.

EXAMPLE 1:　　✗ Edgar Allan Poe wrote "The Raven", "Annabel Lee", and "The Bells".

CORRECTION:　　Edgar Allan Poe wrote "The Raven," "Annabel Lee," and "The Bells."
　　　　　　　　　　　　　　　　　　^　　　　　　　^
　　　　　　　^

What about question marks and exclamation points? The following tip will help you correctly use these marks of punctuation with quotation marks.

> **MOVEMENT TIP:** Take whatever is inside the quotation marks out of the sentence and out of quotation marks. Now what sort of punctuation would you use? If you use a question mark or an exclamation point, this same punctuation belongs *inside* the closing quotation mark in the original sentence.

For instance, Example 2 has an error because we would use a question mark if the group of words was taken out of quotation marks.

EXAMPLE 2:   ✗ Rosa asked, "Do you want to play tennis"?

TIP APPLIED: Do you want to play tennis?

CORRECTION: Rosa asked, "Do you want to play ~~tennis"?~~ *tennis?"*

Because the quoted material is a question, the question mark belongs with the quoted material — *inside* the quotation mark.

The tip holds true even for this example, in which both the whole sentence and the quoted material are questions.

CORRECT: Who said, "Can we leave early?"

TIP APPLIED: Can we leave early?

Only one closing punctuation mark (a period, question mark, or exclamation point) should appear after the last word in a sentence.

Sentence Practice 1

CORRECTED SENTENCES APPEAR ON PAGE 495.

For each sentence, take the material that is inside quotation marks out of quotation marks. If the test material requires a question mark or an exclamation point, then the original sentence needs that same punctuation *inside* the closing quotation mark. Write *OK* if the sentence is correct, and correct any sentence that has punctuation errors.

Letter from Birmingham Jail
EXAMPLE: Who wrote "Letter from Birmingham Jail?"?

1. Grace asked, "When will we get our tests back"?

2. The title of my paper is "Can There Be Peace in the Middle East?"

3. The platoon leader yelled at the top of her lungs, "Move it!"

4. The title of the first chapter is "Where Do We Go Next"?

5. Charlene responded, "Why are you following me"?

 For more practice using quotation marks, go to **Exercise Central** at
bedfordstmartins.com/commonsense/8-26.

Sentence Practice 2

CORRECTED SENTENCES APPEAR ON PAGE 495.

For each sentence, take the material that is inside quotation marks out of
quotation marks. If the test material requires a question mark or an exclamation point, then the original sentence needs that same punctuation *inside* the
closing quotation mark. Write *OK* if the sentence is correct, and correct any
sentence that has punctuation errors.

EXAMPLE: Can you tell me the meaning of the word "alliteration~~?~~"~~?~~

Lesson 26

66   99

1. Did she say, "The store opens at noon?"

2. Didn't W. H. Auden write "The Unknown Citizen"?

3. Who wrote the song entitled, "Are You Lonesome Tonight?"

4. A panicked man yelled, "Don't push that button"!

5. Will you tell me who asked, "Will you leave?"

Sentence Practice 3

Combine the following sentences by using the title or quotation in the second sentence in place of the IT in the first sentence.

EXAMPLE: I have never heard IT.
          "Brother, Can You Spare a Dime?" [popular song in 1930's]

ANSWER: I have never heard "Brother, Can You Spare a Dime?"

1. The chair sang IT.
    "Amazing Grace"

2. She shouted IT.
    "Look out for that train!"

3. Wendy asked IT.
    "Are we there yet?"

4. The teacher asked IT.
    "Are you sick?"

5. Jane yelled IT.
    "Look out for that tree!"

Editing Practice 1

CORRECTED SENTENCES APPEAR ON PAGE 495.

Correct all errors in the following paragraph using the first correction as a model. The number in parentheses at the end of the paragraph indicates how many errors you should find.

Lesson 26

" "

Have you ever heard the song "Dixie?"? Most Americans

have heard this song but have not considered its usefulness as

a source of information about the Civil War. Other songs of that

time, for instance, the spirituals sung by slaves, offer a personal

look at the slaves' lives and hardships. In "Go Down, Moses", the

lyrics refer to attempts by Moses to free his people from slavery,

yet the song is also a poignant cry for the freedom of African

Americans. In contrast to this melancholy spiritual is "Dixie."

This battle hymn of the Confederacy, with its upbeat tempo,

is a celebration of the South. Other songs, such as "The Bonnie

Blue Flag", were even more explicit about loyalty to the

Confederacy, but the one most remembered today is

"Dixie". (3)

Editing Practice 2

CORRECTED SENTENCES APPEAR ON PAGE 495.

Correct all errors in the following paragraph using the first correction as a model. The number in parentheses at the end of the paragraph indicates how many errors you should find.

Many conflicts have given rise to what might be called "war

songs."/ Each war, it seems, becomes the subject of popular music.

World War I, for example, had its protest songs, such as "I Didn't

Raise My Boy to Be a Soldier". This song captured many Americans'

desire to stay out of the war. Once the United States entered the war,

though, many songs served to rally the troops and the general public.

One of the most famous is "Over There". All good American parents

and "sweethearts," according to this song, should be proud and eager

to send their loved ones to fight in the war. George M. Cohan received

a Congressional Medal of Honor for composing this immensely

popular song. In Irving Berlin's "Oh, How I Hate to Get Up in the

Morning", however, the singer is less enthusiastic about fighting in

the trenches, taking a lighthearted view of military life but still

celebrating victory. (3)

Lesson 26

" "

Editing Practice 3

Correct all errors in the following paragraphs using the first correction as a model. The number in parentheses at the end of each paragraph indicates how many errors you should find.

My literature class read an essay entitled "What If Shakespeare Had a Sister?"? It deals with obstacles that female authors have encountered. During the discussion, Paul asked, "Are women writers still discriminated against"? It depends on what one means by "discrimination," but I imagine women certainly have a harder time if they want to write certain types of material, such as sports stories. However, a male author might have a harder time publishing the so-called love story. We still haven't gotten past all of our biases. (2)

We also read Kate Chopin's "The Storm." Our professor asked, "Do you see any similarity between this story and the essay"? Somebody answered, "Both deal with the treatment of women in our society, but the story seems a bit more optimistic." I admit the story didn't seem so hopeful to me, but then we discussed how it suggests that women have the same rights to passion and romance as men do. For tomorrow, we're reading "The Girls in Their Summer Dresses", which also deals with how men and women approach romance. (2)

Lesson 26

" "

Writing Practice

On your own paper, write six sentences, each having quotation marks plus another form of punctuation. Try to vary the type of punctuation that occurs with the quotation marks. Use the Editing Checklist to see whether each sentence you write is punctuated correctly.

Editing Checklist

*Identify Errors in Using Quotation Marks with
Other Punctuation in Your Writing*

_____ Examine your writing for quotation marks. Wherever you use
quotation marks, check to see if you have used other marks of
punctuation (periods, commas, colons, semicolons, question marks,
and exclamation points) correctly.

*Correct Errors in Using Quotation Marks with
Other Punctuation in Your Writing*

_____ Place periods and commas *inside* quotation marks.

_____ Place colons and semicolons *outside* quotation marks.

_____ Use the Movement Tip to test whether material inside the quotation
marks needs a question mark or an exclamation point. If it does, then
place the punctuation *inside* the quotation marks.

**The
Bottom
Line**

As advised, "Periods and commas go
inside quotation marks."

LESSON 27
Semicolons

Error Sentences

CORRECTED SENTENCES APPEAR ON PAGES 275–76.

EXAMPLE 1: ✗ Sam brought the drinks; lemonade, Coke, and iced tea.

EXAMPLE 2: ✗ Unfortunately, he forgot something; glasses to drink them from.

What's the Problem?

Sometimes writers confuse semicolons with colons (as in Example 1) and incorrectly use semicolons to introduce lists. (See Lesson 28 for the correct use of colons.) Sometimes semicolons are mistakenly treated as a stylistic alternative to commas (as in Example 2).

What Causes the Problem?

Quite simply, many writers don't really understand the function of a semicolon. The main use of a semicolon is to separate two related groups of words in a sentence when each group could stand alone as a **complete sentence**. In other words, semicolons are very similar to periods—they can both be used to punctuate complete sentences.

Lesson 27

;

Diagnostic Exercise

CORRECTED SENTENCES APPEAR ON PAGE 496.

Correct all errors using the first correction as a model. The number in parentheses at the end of the paragraph indicates how many errors you should find.

In the early 1900's; "pulp" magazines were extremely popular.

These magazines were named for the cheap pulp paper they were printed on. They contained various types of stories; adventures, detective stories, romance tales, and Western stories. One of the most successful pulp publishers was Street and Smith; this firm sold millions of magazines. Most old issues; however, have been destroyed or lost. Higher quality magazines were printed on glossy paper; which gave them the nickname "slicks." The terms "pulp" and "slicks" are still used today to distinguish simple action-oriented fiction from the more sophisticated writing that might appear in more upscale magazines such as the following; *Cosmopolitan, Esquire,* and *Harper's.* (4)

Fixing This Problem in Your Writing

The following tip will help you determine whether you have used a semi-colon correctly.

> **IMAGINARY PERIOD TIP:** Replace the semicolon with an imaginary period. If there is a complete sentence on both sides of the imaginary period, the semicolon is correct. If you are left with a fragment on either side of the imaginary period, the semicolon is incorrect.

Lesson 27

;

The Imaginary Period Tip shows that both example sentences are incorrect:

EXAMPLE 1: ✗ Sam brought the drinks; lemonade, Coke, and iced tea.

TIP APPLIED: Sam brought the drinks. ✗ Lemonade, Coke, and iced tea.

The part of the original sentence that follows the imaginary period cannot stand alone; thus, the semicolon is incorrect. In this case, the writer has confused the semicolon with a colon.

CORRECTION: Sam brought the drinks;/: lemonade, Coke, and iced tea.

EXAMPLE 2:   ✗ Unfortunately, he forgot something; glasses
              to drink them from.

TIP APPLIED: Unfortunately, he forgot something. ✗Glasses
               to drink them from.

The part of the original sentence that follows the imaginary period cannot stand alone, so the semicolon is incorrect. In this case, the writer has confused the semicolon with a comma.

CORRECTION: Unfortunately, he forgot something;, glasses
               to drink them from.

Writers use semicolons to keep closely related ideas within a single sentence. Semicolons are typically used to show a

> **Cause-and-effect** relation between two ideas:
> The attic had not been cleaned in years; it smelled of dust
> and mold.
> **Generalization-and-example** relation between two ideas:
> Telephone solicitors always call at dinnertime; last night we
> were interrupted twice during our meal.
> **Statement-and-comment** relation between two ideas:
> My wife considers the *Three Stooges* to be utterly moronic; I still
> think they are pretty funny.

In addition, semicolons are often used with **transitional terms**—words like *however, thus, nevertheless, moreover.* These words help the reader see how the idea in the second part of a sentence is related to the idea in the first part. (See Lesson 4 for a discussion of using semicolons with transitional terms.)

Lesson 27

;

Sentence Practice 1

CORRECTED SENTENCES APPEAR ON PAGE 496.

Using the Imaginary Period Tip, examine the part of the sentence before the semicolon and the part after the semicolon. If one part can stand alone as a complete sentence, write *OK* above it. If the other part cannot stand alone as a complete sentence, write *X* above it. If either part cannot stand alone, correct the semicolon error.

EXAMPLE: David wanted to borrow my book; the one about
            home improvement.

                            OK   X
TIP APPLIED: David wanted to borrow my book. The one about
                home improvement.

ANSWER: David wanted to borrow my book⸴, the one about home improvement.

1. Next week, we will have a major test; one that will be difficult.

2. Delaware's nickname is First State; it was the first state to ratify the Constitution.

3. My car is too loud; I think it needs a new muffler.

4. Allyson and I went to the same high school; Pine Tree High School.

5. Ken brought several items; napkins, glasses, and forks.

 For more practice using semicolons, go to **Exercise Central** at **bedfordstmartins.com/commonsense/8-27**.

Sentence Practice 2

CORRECTED SENTENCES APPEAR ON PAGE 496.

Using the Imaginary Period Tip, examine the part of the sentence before the semicolon and the part after the semicolon. If one part can stand alone as a complete sentence, write *OK* above it. If the other part cannot stand alone as a complete sentence, write *X* above it. If either part cannot stand alone, correct the semicolon error.

EXAMPLE: I hate three things; soggy pancakes, runny eggs, and burnt toast.

                          OK   *X*
TIP APPLIED: I hate three things. Soggy pancakes, runny eggs, and burnt toast.

ANSWER: I hate three things⸴: soggy pancakes, runny eggs, and burnt toast.

1. Her truck failed to start; because the battery was dead.

2. I read an article about Ralph Bunche; the first African American to win the Nobel Peace Prize.

3. Annie ordered a parfait; a dessert made of ice cream, fruit, and syrup.

Lesson 27

;

4. Actor Spencer Tracy was asked to play the Penguin on the TV show *Batman*; he declined when he was told he could not kill Batman.

5. I need to go to the store; which is only about one mile away.

Sentence Practice 3

Combine the two ideas in each of the following items using a semicolon where appropriate. (A semicolon is *not* appropriate in all cases.)

> EXAMPLE: **Allan's sister called for him.**
> **As usual, he was not around.**

> ANSWER: **Allan's sister called for him; as usual, he was not around.**

1. Sara hated the movie.
    It was too violent for her.

2. I live in Daphne.
    Which is a small town near Mobile, Alabama.

3. The song "I'd Like to Teach the World to Sing" originated as a Coca-Cola ad.
    The song was a Top 10 hit in 1972.

4. Pineapples are associated with Hawaii.
    They originated, however, in South America.

5. Blue M&M candies replaced tan ones in 1995.
    Because blue was voted the overwhelming favorite in a contest.

Editing Practice 1

CORRECTED SENTENCES APPEAR ON PAGE 496.

Correct all errors in the following paragraphs using the first correction as a model. The number in parentheses at the end of each paragraph indicates how many errors you should find.

Langston Hughes is one of the best-known African American

poets;, his fame having begun in 1915, when he was thirteen.

At that time, he was elected poet of his graduating class; an unusual

selection not merely because he was one of only two African

American students in his class but because he had never written any poems. Hughes explained that nobody else in the class had written any poetry either. His classmates elected him; however, because they assumed that poetry requires rhythm and that he must have rhythm because of his ethnicity. (2)

Even though such reasoning had an element of stereotyping, Hughes was inspired; and wrote a graduation poem that the teachers and students enthusiastically received. He went on to publish many types of writing; poems, plays, short stories, children's books, histories, and song lyrics, just to name a few. (2)

Editing Practice 2

CORRECTED SENTENCES APPEAR ON PAGE 496.

Correct all errors in the following paragraphs using the first correction as a model. The number in parentheses at the end of each paragraph indicates how many errors you should find.

Some science projects can take time. Others;, however, are relatively easy. A terrarium is a small environment that is built for living plants and animals; it is not terribly difficult to make. It can be built out of containers such as; a large glass jug, a plastic container, or even a glass baking pan covered with plastic wrap. A particularly good container; however, is an aquarium, even if it has minor cracks or holes. (2)

The bottom of the container must be lined with a shallow layer of pebbles; this layer allows for good drainage. A couple of inches of a sand and soil mixture go on top of the pebbles. The terrarium then needs a small dish of water placed into the soil; so that the rim of

Lesson 27

;

the dish is level with the top of the soil. Then a variety of plants and minerals can be added, including; ferns, moss, rotting bark, and a few rocks. The terrarium must be covered with glass or plastic; and placed out of direct sunlight. You can also put lizards, toads, or other small animals into the environment; just give them the appropriate food. (3)

Editing Practice 3

Correct all errors in the following paragraphs using the first correction as a model. The number in parentheses at the end of each paragraph indicates how many errors you should find.

Our football team won most of its games last year; all except one. The one loss was a 21-to-7 bowl game. Before that game; we were ranked fourth in the nation; our opponent was ranked fifth. Needless to say, it was a big game. We were well prepared; however, the other team was even better prepared. (1)

Unfortunately, we dropped to tenth in the nation after the big loss; that was the lowest ranking we had all year. This year, the preseason polls put us in the top twenty; we are ranked by one poll as seventeenth and by another as twentieth. Most people I have talked to; however, think we have a chance to end up in the top five. Some are even saying; that we might compete for the national championship. We'll wait and see; I don't want to get my hopes up. (2)

Writing Practice

On your own paper, write a paragraph or two describing a sports team you like or dislike (or perhaps a paragraph about why you *don't* have a favorite team). Try to use three semicolons. Use the Editing Checklist to correct any semicolon errors in the sentences you have written.

Lesson 27

;

Editing Checklist

Identify Semicolon Errors in Your Writing

____ Each time you use a semicolon, use the Imaginary Period Tip to
see whether what comes before it and what comes after it can
stand as complete sentences.

____ If either part of your sentence cannot stand alone as a complete
sentence, you cannot use a semicolon.

Correct Semicolon Errors in Your Writing

____ Delete unnecessary semicolons, and add the correct punctuation.
If you are introducing a list, use a colon. If one part of your
sentence cannot stand on its own, you may need a comma or
no punctuation at all.

The Bottom Line

See if the part of the sentence before the
semicolon can stand alone; do the same thing
with the part after the semicolon.

Lesson 27

;

LESSON 28
Colons

Error Sentences

CORRECTED SENTENCES APPEAR ON PAGE 284.

EXAMPLE 1: ✗ Sarah bought: milk, bread, and crackers.

EXAMPLE 2: ✗ For the trip, be sure to bring such items as: books, clothes, and lots of money.

What's the Problem?

A colon has several functions. One is to introduce a quotation. Another common but often misunderstood function of the colon is to introduce *certain types* of lists. A colon is used to introduce a list that is *not* needed for the sentence to be grammatically complete. In the following example, the colon is used correctly because the sentence would be complete even if you left out the list.

EXAMPLE: At the football game, I met three friends: José, Tyrone, and Mark.

A colon *cannot* introduce a list *if* the list is needed for the sentence to be complete. In Examples 1 and 2, the lists are necessary. Therefore, these lists should not be introduced by a colon.

In some ways, a colon is similar to "end punctuation" (to a period or question mark, for instance). A colon—just like a period—is usually used only at the end of a grammatically complete set of words.

What Causes the Problem?

The colon is used to introduce certain types of lists, but many people over-generalize this use and mistakenly put a colon before any sort of list. The only type of list that should be introduced by a colon is one that is "expendable" (in other words, one that you can do without). It is expendable because, though it may make your sentence clearer or more specific, it is grammatically unnecessary.

Diagnostic Exercise

CORRECTED SENTENCES APPEAR ON PAGE 497.

Correct all errors in the following paragraph using the first correction as a model. The number in parentheses at the end of the paragraph indicates how many errors you should find.

My roommate, who is shopping for a new car, looked at several types, including / Fords, Nissans, and Mazdas. She knew which features she wanted, like: automatic transmission, cruise control, and leather seats. However, she quickly discovered that such features were not within her budget. To get the best deal for her money, I suggested that she consult sources such as: her mechanic or *Consumer Reports* magazine. She did some research, but she seemed disappointed because there was no clear choice. She finally narrowed her choices to: a Ford Taurus and a Nissan Altima. She hasn't gotten much further than that. (3)

Fixing This Problem in Your Writing

Here is a tip that can help you see whether a colon is *incorrectly* used to introduce a list.

> IMAGINARY PERIOD TIP: Imagine that you have used a period instead of the colon. If what comes *before* this period could stand alone as a complete sentence, the colon should be correct. Otherwise, there is probably an error.

Why does this tip work? It shows whether or not the list is a necessary part of the sentence. If the list is necessary, it should *not* be separated from the rest of the sentence by a colon. For instance, the colon in Example 1 fails the test because *Sarah bought* is not a complete sentence. (See Lessons 1 and 2 about recognizing complete sentences.)

EXAMPLE 1:   ✗ Sarah bought: milk, bread, and crackers.

TIP APPLIED: ✗ Sarah bought.

To correct this sentence, simply leave out the colon.

CORRECTION: Sarah bought⁄ milk, bread, and crackers.

In Example 2, what comes before the colon could *not* stand alone as a complete sentence.

EXAMPLE 2:   ✗ For the trip, be sure to bring such items as: books, clothes, and lots of money.

TIP APPLIED: ✗ For the trip, be sure to bring such items as.

CORRECTION: For the trip, be sure to bring such items as⁄ books, clothes, and lots of money.

The test sentence proves that the list is necessary. Thus, the original sentence should not have a colon.

In the following two correct examples, however, colons are truly needed. In the test sentences, what comes before the periods could stand alone, so the colons are necessary.

CORRECT: I'm taking two science courses: Physics 101 and Biology 210.

TIP APPLIED: I'm taking two science courses.

CORRECT: My roommate, who is shopping for a new car, looked at several types: Fords, Nissans, and Mazdas.

TIP APPLIED: My roommate, who is shopping for a new car, looked at several types.

Lesson 28

Sentence Practice 1

CORRECTED SENTENCES APPEAR ON PAGE 497.

Determine whether the colon is correct by applying the Imaginary Period Tip. Write *OK* above colons that are used correctly. Correctly punctuate the incorrect sentences.

EXAMPLE: To mend these pants, I will need: scissors, thread, a needle, and a little gratitude.

TIP APPLIED:	✗ To mend these pants, I will need. ✗ Scissors, thread, a needle, and a little gratitude.
CORRECTION:	To mend these pants, I will need ⫶ scissors, thread, a needle, and a little gratitude.

1. Many farmers in this area grow: cotton, grain, and turnips.

2. Kamilah and Doug saved enough money to travel throughout: Denmark, Germany, and Belgium.

3. My college will not offer several courses I need, such as: English 100 and Math 201.

4. We will need to buy: a textbook, gloves, and a dissecting kit.

5. Some actors who changed their names are: Jane Wyman, Raquel Welch, and Rudolph Valentino.

 For more practice using colons, go to **Exercise Central** at **bedfordstmartins.com/commonsense/8-28**.

Sentence Practice 2

CORRECTED SENTENCES APPEAR ON PAGE 497.

Determine whether the colon is correct by applying the Imaginary Period Tip. Write *OK* above colons that are used correctly. Correctly punctuate the incorrect sentences.

Lesson 28

EXAMPLE:	The subjects I like to read about are: Chinese history, dog breeding, and personal finance.
TIP APPLIED:	✗ The subjects I like to read about are. ✗ Chinese history, dog breeding, and personal finance.
CORRECTION:	The subjects I like to read about are ⫶ Chinese history, dog breeding, and personal finance.

1. Some famous people had dyslexia, such as: Leonardo da Vinci, Winston Churchill, Albert Einstein, and George Patton.

2. Remember to buy everything we need to clean the apartment: soap, detergent, and a mop.

3. Native Americans added many words to English: totem, tomahawk, hickory, raccoon, and other common terms.

4. Many languages have contributed to English, especially: French, Latin, Persian, and German.

5. New words in English arise from many sources, including: gang culture, popular music, and the computer industry.

Sentence Practice 3

Combine the sentences by using a colon.

> EXAMPLE: **They had three flavors.**
> **The flavors were chocolate, strawberry, and vanilla.**

> ANSWER: **They had three flavors: chocolate, strawberry, and vanilla.**

1. The movies you must view are as follows.
   The movies are *The Patriot, Gone with the Wind,* and *Braveheart.*

2. Our football team has three plays.
   These three plays are punt, pass, and pray.

3. There are two things you must remember.
   These two things are call me when you arrive, and bring me back a gift.

4. We only close the store for three holidays.
   The holidays are Thanksgiving, Christmas, and Martin Luther King, Jr. Day.

5. I encourage you to take two classes this summer.
   These two classes are English 226 and History 102.

Editing Practice 1

CORRECTED SENTENCES APPEAR ON PAGE 497.

Correct all errors in the following paragraph using the first correction as a model. The number in parentheses at the end of the paragraph indicates how many errors you should find.

In the past, my English teachers discussed various types of writing, including/ poetry, drama, and short stories. In my present English class, the teacher discussed the writing we'll do this semester. She discussed three other types of writing that my previous teachers had not covered: expressive essays, arguments, and informative papers. She mentioned that there are many ways a writer can develop an essay, such as using: narration, comparison and contrast, and definition. For her class, we are required to write: six long papers, three fairly short papers, and several in-class paragraphs. Some of these assignments will allow us to pick our own topics, but a few will not. She has already mentioned that we will write about the following: educational reform, male-female relation-ships, and discrimination. The class seems challenging, but I'm looking forward to it. Next semester, I am looking forward to taking: a technical writing class or a creative writing class. (3)

Editing Practice 2

CORRECTED SENTENCES APPEAR ON PAGE 497.

Correct all errors in the following paragraphs using the first correction as a model. The number in parentheses at the end of each paragraph indicates how many errors you should find.

Many people try to get rid of "tummy" fat so they'll feel better about/ their appearance, their self-image, and even their relationships with significant others. However, fat has also been linked to health risks such as: heart disease, high blood pressure, and strokes. The most dangerous type of abdominal fat can't even be seen; it's the fat around vital organs like: the intestines and liver. (2)

Lesson 28

:

Two factors that determine how much fat a person has are:

gender and habits. Almost all males have more lean tissue per

pound than do females, and lean tissue helps burn fat. Thus,

females typically have to exercise more to rid themselves of fat.

Several bad habits can lead to more fat: smoking, drinking, and

partying. Although some people say these habits help them

deal with stress, such habits also have been correlated with larger

waist-to-hip ratios. (1)

Editing Practice 3

Correct all errors in the following paragraphs using the first correction as a model. The number in parentheses at the end of each paragraph indicates how many errors you should find.

The Wizard of Oz may seem terribly old-fashioned, but it's

still one of my favorite movies. Even though some people consider it

just a kids' movie, most adults know⫽ Dorothy, the Wicked Witch, the

Tin Man, the Scarecrow, the Cowardly Lion, and the Wizard (and

Toto too!). I'm not sure why the movie has become such a classic.

Maybe its popularity has something to do with: the colorful

characters, the enduring theme of "going home again," and the

way in which several scenes are memorable. (1)

Two scenes in particular are etched in my memory: the first

appearance of the Wicked Witch and her final scene, when she

melts into oblivion. I bet most Americans don't even need these

scenes described to them. A couple of other favorite parts are: the

discovery of the Cowardly Lion in the dark forest and the farewell scene in which Dorothy clicks her ruby slippers. Next week, this movie will be on TV for the umpteenth time, but I will be watching it yet again! (1)

Writing Practice

On your own paper, write about your favorite scenes from your favorite movies. Try to use three or four colons to introduce lists. Use the Editing Checklist to correct any colon errors in the sentences you have written.

Editing Checklist

Identify Colon Errors in Your Writing

_____ Each time you use a colon to introduce a list, see whether what comes *before* the colon could stand alone as a complete, grammatical sentence.

Correct Colon Errors in Your Writing

_____ If what comes before the colon *cannot* stand alone, you do *not* need the colon.

_____ If it *can* stand alone, then using the colon should be *correct*.

The Bottom Line

When using a colon to introduce a list, remember these two steps: (1) imagine using a period instead of the colon, and (2) see whether what comes before this imaginary period would be a complete sentence.

LESSON 29
Capitalization

Error Sentences

CORRECTED SENTENCES APPEAR ON PAGES 292–94.

EXAMPLE 1: ✗ My english teacher said that we would read stories by Flannery O'Connor and other writers from the south.

EXAMPLE 2: ✗ Did your Math classes in High School include writing assignments?

What's the Problem?

Some words (**proper nouns** and **proper adjectives**) should be capitalized to show they are the "official" names or nicknames of specific persons, places, things, or events. In addition, many words are capitalized because they are derived from official names. In Example 1, *English* must be capitalized because it is derived from the name of a country (England). Also, *South* should be capitalized since people widely recognize it as the name of a specific area.

More general words are not capitalized. In Example 2, *math* should *not* be capitalized because it is a general term for a type of class; *high school* also is a general term and is *not* the name of a specific school. Compare these two terms with *Calculus I* and *Lewis and Clark High School.*

What Causes the Problem?

Capitalization is not an issue in spoken language, so the rules can be difficult to learn. Compounding the problem is the fact that capitalization "rules" are not always consistent. For instance, many words are capitalized or not capitalized depending on how they are used (compare *My <u>uncle</u> is here* with *I saw <u>Uncle</u> Brett there*).

Although capitalization errors can easily occur, it is important to avoid them. Frequently, capitalization errors—like spelling errors—jump out and distract readers from what a writer is saying. On occasion, errors in

Lesson 29

cap

capitalization can confuse readers by sending the wrong message about whether a word is the specific name of somebody (or something) or whether the word is just a general description.

Diagnostic Exercise

CORRECTED SENTENCES APPEAR ON PAGE 498.

Correct all errors in the following paragraph using the first correction as a model. The number in parentheses at the end of the paragraph indicates how many errors you should find.

community college

My sister is attending a ~~Community College~~ in Kansas City,

and we've been comparing our courses. Her spanish class is much

different from mine because hers includes discussion of hispanic and

latino cultures. Her teacher, professor Gonzales, believes students

are more interested in learning a language when they appreciate

the culture connected with that language. (4)

Fixing This Problem in Your Writing

Concerning capitalization, try to consult the handbook, style guide, or dictionary suggested by your teacher or readers. When such a resource isn't available or suggested, use the following capitalization tips.

> **PERSON TIP:** Capitalize a person's title or a family term (like *Uncle, Senator,* or *Mother*) when it is followed by a name (like *Randy* or *Johnson*) *or* when you could use a name instead of the title or family term.

Lesson 29

cap

In these four sentences, a name could take the place of the family terms and titles, so they are correctly capitalized.

These sentences . . .	Can be reworded as . . .
Are you ready, Senator?	Are you ready, Randy?
I called Mother last night.	I called Sue last night.
Was Governor Bush re-elected?	Was Janet Bush re-elected?
Wasn't that Officer Bean?	Wasn't that Fred Bean?

However, the same words are not capitalized in the next four examples because these words cannot be replaced with a person's name.

These sentences . . .	*Cannot* be reworded as . . .
We need a new senator.	We need a new Randy.
Is your mother really sick?	Is your Sue really sick?
The governor of Iowa is here.	The Janet of Iowa is here.
The officer gave me a ticket.	The Fred gave me a ticket.

GROUP TIP: Capitalize a term accepted by a group of people as describing their culture, nationality, religion, ethnic background, or language (as with *Latino, German, Muslim, Asian,* and *Yiddish*).

PLACE TIP: Capitalize any name that you'd find on a map or that is widely recognized as a *distinct* place or region. Thus, not only would names of cities be capitalized but so would places such as *Rocky Mountains, Pacific Ocean, Middle East, Dixie, Cape Cod, Oak Street,* and *the West.* Don't capitalize directions (*Go north*) or general locations (*I live in northern Iowa*).

SCHOOL TIP: Capitalize the name of a specific school or course (such as *Kilgore Community College* or *Math 101*). Don't capitalize a more general term. You can usually place *a, some,* or a possessive term (such as *my*) in front of general terms.

Lesson 29

cap

Let's look at Example 1.

EXAMPLE 1:   ✗ My english teacher said that we would read stories by Flannery O'Connor and other writers from the south.

GROUP TIP
APPLIED: My English teacher . . .

Even though here it refers to a subject someone teaches, *English* is also the name of a group of people and the name of a language.

PLACE TIP
APPLIED: . . . and other writers from the South.

The *South* is widely recognized as a distinct region of the United States.

CORRECTION: My ~~english~~ *English* teacher said that we would read stories by Flannery O'Connor and other writers from the ~~south~~ *South*.

Use the School Tip to correct Example 2.

EXAMPLE 2: ✗ Did your Math classes in High School include writing assignments?

math   *high school*
TIP APPLIED: Did your ~~Math~~ classes in ~~High School~~ include writing assignments?

Note that here a possessive term comes before *math,* indicating that in this sentence *math* refers to a general term and not to a specific course. High school should not be capitalized in this sentence because the reference is not to a specific high school; *your* could be placed in front of it as well.

Sentence Practice 1

CORRECTED SENTENCES APPEAR ON PAGE 498.

If the underlined word is correct in terms of capitalization, write *OK* over it. Correct any error, and write a brief explanation of why the word should or shouldn't be capitalized by referring to the four tips.

General   *OK*   *OK*
EXAMPLE: Yes, ~~general~~, your uncle called from Boston today.

Person Tip: "General" is a title that could be replaced by a name.

cap

1. My father has a job teaching Biology in eastern Delaware.

2. Theodore Roosevelt was once governor of New York.

3. Much of the southwestern United States was once Mexican territory.

4. Students write in almost every class at this University, even Physical Education courses.

5. Tenskwatawa was a native american leader who encouraged his people to give up alcohol along with european clothing and tools.

For more practice using capitalization, go to **Exercise Central** at **bedfordstmartins.com/commonsense/8-29**.

Sentence Practice 2

CORRECTED SENTENCES APPEAR ON PAGE 498.

If the underlined word is correct in terms of capitalization, write *OK* over it. Correct any error, and write a brief explanation of why the word should or shouldn't be capitalized by referring to the four tips.

> *geology*
> EXAMPLE: I have to take my ~~Geology~~ class again.
> ^
>
> *School Tip: The term geology is not the name of a specific class (the word "my" in front indicates a general term).*

1.   In the 1860's, Montana's present <u>Capital</u>, <u>Helena</u>, was named <u>Last Chance Gulch</u>.

2.   Citizens of <u>Rio de Janeiro</u> are normally called *cariocas*. [*Hint:* Minor words such as *de* are usually not capitalized when part of proper nouns.]

3.   Did you say that <u>aunt</u> Iva is arriving today?

4.   The <u>rhone river</u> and the <u>rhine river</u> both rise out of the <u>Alps</u> of <u>Switzerland</u>.

5.   My <u>Grandmother</u> believes she can meet with the <u>Pope</u> during our visit to <u>Rome</u>.

Lesson 29

cap

Sentence Practice 3

Combine the sentence with each of the following words or word groups. (You will be writing two sentences for each item.) First, replace the word in italics with the word or words, and then capitalize correctly.

> EXAMPLE: They interviewed *her* on television.
> governor whitman
> the governor
>
> ANSWER: They interviewed <u>Governor Whitman</u> on television.
> They interviewed <u>the governor</u> on television.

1. She telephoned her yesterday.
    ms. perkins
    my boss

2. I graduated from it in 2001.
    fairhope high school
    a nearby high school

3. Sam learned a great deal from it.
    english 100
    my english class

4. Farmers ship millions of bushels of wheat on it.
    the columbia river
    this river

5. He is a member of it.
    the nez percé
    a local tribe

Editing Practice 1

CORRECTED SENTENCES APPEAR ON PAGE 498.

Correct all errors in the following paragraphs using the first correction as a model. The number in parentheses at the end of each paragraph indicates how many errors you should find.

Molly

Mary, also called ~~molly~~, Dewson was a pioneer in encouraging

women to be active in Politics and the Federal Government.

In the 1928 presidential campaign, she worked for candidate

Al Smith and helped mobilize female supporters. Smith never

became president, but Dewson did not abandon her Feminist

efforts. (4)

In 1930, Dewson continued to mobilize women to campaign for Franklin Roosevelt's successful bid for governor of New York. Later, she worked for his Presidential campaigns. Perhaps her greatest accomplishment, though, was becoming Head of the Democratic Party's efforts to recruit women for Government jobs. She also worked with Democrats in training women to serve in election campaigns. Though she died in 1962, her legacy lives on, and millions of men as well as women have been affected positively by her efforts to involve women in the Democratic process. (5)

Editing Practice 2

CORRECTED SENTENCES APPEAR ON PAGE 498.

Correct all errors in the following paragraphs using the first correction as a model. The number in parentheses at the end of each paragraph indicates how many errors you should find.

Lesson 29

cap

Last week, the ~~University~~ *university* I'm attending announced that all history majors would be guaranteed that they could receive a degree in History in no more than four years. As a Sophomore planning to be a history major, I was interested in this announcement and looked into it. (2)

I spoke with an advisor, professor Hearns, about the guarantee. She said the College would do its part in regularly offering courses that are most in demand. In particular, she said that each semester the department would offer several sections of American history I and cultural history of Asia. (5)

Editing Practice 3

Correct all errors in the following paragraphs using the first correction as a model. The number in parentheses at the end of each paragraph indicates how many errors you should find.

One reason why ~~english~~ *English* is a complex and often confusing language is that it is heavily based on many languages and cultures. The english language did not even exist when Julius Caesar invaded britain in 55 B.C. However, the Celts who lived there had an impact on what later became english. Later, the germanic tribes that sailed across the North sea settled in Britain and passed along their farming vocabulary (such as *ox, swine,* and *sheep*). (5)

Another influence was Christianity, for pope Gregory the great sent monks who added many religious words to English, including *angel, mass,* and *shrine.* Still later, the Vikings sailed from scandinavia to raid Britain and brought more words, especially many beginning with *sk* (such as *sky* and *skin*). When the normans conquered England in 1066, their language influenced English. For some time, there were three competing languages in England: latin for the church, french for the rulers, and english for the commoners. Eventually, though, english absorbed the other two, especially the french language. (9)

Lesson 29

cap

Writing Practice

On your own paper, write a paragraph discussing the three most helpful courses you have taken. Use at least four different words that should be capitalized (other than words that begin sentences). Use the Editing Checklist to correct any capitalization errors in the sentences you wrote.

Editing Checklist

Identify Capitalization Errors in Your Writing

_____ Proofread your writing for references to individuals, groups, schools, courses, subjects, and places. Use the tips in this lesson to help you determine whether each word you've identified needs to be capitalized.

Correct Capitalization Errors in Your Writing

_____ Capitalize a professional title or family term only if (1) it is immediately followed by a name or (2) you could use a name in place of the title or family term.

_____ Capitalize any term that a group of people accept as describing their culture, language, nationality, religion, or ethnic background.

_____ Capitalize the names of actual courses, schools, and subjects. Do not capitalize when you are making a general reference.

_____ Capitalize any name on a map or region recognized as a distinct area.

Lesson 29

cap

The Bottom Line

According to rules for formal **English**, words that are "official" names, titles, or nicknames are capitalized.

UNIT EIGHT: Using Other Punctuation and Capitalizing Certain Words

Punctuation marks and capitalization form an important part of standard written English. The following is a review of the punctuation and capitalization tips in this unit.

Quotation Marks with Direct Quotations and Paraphrases

Quotation marks are most often used to distinguish direct quotations (those that use a source's exact words) from indirect quotations (those that paraphrase a source's words). This tip will help you recognize indirect quotations:

> *THAT* TIP: Use *that* to begin a paraphrase, but do not use *that* to begin a direct quotation. Although it is not absolutely essential to use *that* before a paraphrase, inserting *that* will never change the meaning of a paraphrase. Inserting *that* before a direct quotation might change the meaning.

Quotation Marks with Other Punctuation

Periods and commas always go inside quotation marks. Semicolons and colons always go outside quotation marks. The following tip shows how to treat question marks and exclamation points when they are used with quotation marks:

> MOVEMENT TIP: Take whatever is inside the quotation marks out of the sentence and out of quotation marks. Now what sort of punctuation would you use? If you use a question mark or an exclamation point, this same punctuation belongs *inside* the closing quotation mark in the original sentence.

Semicolons

Semicolons are an alternative to periods when you want to connect two closely related complete ideas. Here is a way to determine the correct use of a semicolon:

> **IMAGINARY PERIOD TIP:** Replace the semicolon with an imaginary period. If there is a complete sentence on both sides of the imaginary period, the semicolon is correct. If you are left with a fragment on either side of the imaginary period, the semicolon is incorrect.

Colons

The main function of colons is to introduce certain kinds of lists. A variation of the Imaginary Period Tip works to determine whether you've used a colon correctly.

> **IMAGINARY PERIOD TIP:** Imagine that you have used a period instead of the colon. If what comes *before* this period could stand alone as a complete sentence, the colon should be correct. Otherwise, there is probably an error.

Capitalization

Capitalize proper nouns and proper adjectives. The following two tips help you identify nouns and adjectives that are "official" names or nicknames of specific people or places:

Unit Eight

review

> **PERSON TIP:** Capitalize a person's title or a family term (like *Uncle, Senator,* or *Mother*) when it is followed by a name (like *Randy* or *Johnson*) *or* when you could use a name instead of the title or family term.

> **PLACE TIP:** Capitalize any name that you'd find on a map or that is widely recognized as a *distinct* place or region. Thus, not only would names of cities be capitalized but so would places such as *Rocky Mountains, Pacific Ocean, Middle East, Dixie, Cape Cod, Oak Street,* and *the West.* Don't capitalize directions (*Go north*) or general locations (*I live in northern Iowa*).

The remaining two tips deal with the capitalization of important special categories:

> **GROUP TIP:** Capitalize a term accepted by a group of people as describing their culture, nationality, religion, ethnic background, or language (as with *Latino, German, Muslim, Asian,* and *Yiddish*).

SCHOOL TIP: Capitalize the name of a specific school or course (such as *Kilgore Community College* or *Math 101*). Don't capitalize a more general term. You can usually place *a, some,* or a possessive term (such as *my*) in front of general terms.

Review Test

Correct all errors in the following paragraph using the first correction as a model. The number in parentheses at the end of the paragraph indicates how many errors you should find. (Treat a pair of quotation marks as one error.)

         roommate
   My ~~Roommate~~ Troy invited me to visit his hometown, College Station, Texas. I had never been to the south before, much less to Texas over Christmas break. Since I had grown up in boston, the prospect of visiting a new part of the Country was pretty exciting. Troy said that "We would have to drive East for twelve hours to reach College Station; which is in the Central part of the state." College Station is really just a college town, but it also has: cotton, retail, and cattle. (8)

Unit Eight

review

UNIT NINE
Writing Clear Sentences

Terms That Can Help You Understand How to Write Clear Sentences

If you are not familiar with any of the following terms, look them up in the Guide to Grammar Terminology beginning on page 1. The numbers in parentheses indicate the lessons in which each term appears.

active (31)
coordinating conjunction (30)
faulty parallelism (30)
gerund (30)
helping verb (31)
infinitive (30)

parallelism (30)
passive (31)
past participle (31)
verb (30, 31)
voice (31)

The Nuts and Bolts of Writing Clear Sentences

This unit covers two topics that can make your writing unclear: faulty parallelism and the passive voice.

Lesson 30 shows you how to create parallel sentences. **Parallelism** refers to a series of two or more identical grammatical structures joined by a **coordinating conjunction** (usually *and* or *or*). The most common parallelism errors involve verb forms that either end in *-ing* (**gerunds**) or appear after *to* (**infinitives**). **Faulty parallelism** results when items in a series are not all in the same grammatical form.

EXAMPLE: ✗ Sylvia likes reading poetry, listening to music, and to collect spiders.

CORRECTION: Sylvia likes reading poetry, listening to music, and collecting spiders.

Lesson 31 shows you how to revise passive voice sentences. In most sentences, the subject of the sentence performs the action of the verb. This

302

type of sentence is said to be in the **active voice**. In the **passive voice**, the subject of the sentence does not perform the action; instead, it receives the action of the verb. Although using the passive voice is not incorrect, active voice sentences are clearer and stronger.

EXAMPLE (PASSIVE VOICE):   The new parking rule was criticized by the students.

EXAMPLE (ACTIVE VOICE):   The students criticized the new parking rule.

Can you detect problems with faulty parallelism and the passive voice?

CORRECTED SENTENCES APPEAR ON PAGE 498.

Correct all errors of faulty parallelism, and change all passive voice structures to active voice. The number in parentheses at the end of the paragraph indicates how many errors you should find.

I planned a trip recently.
~~A trip was planned by me recently.~~ While I enjoy traveling,

I really hate packing. I must choose what to take, pick the

appropriate luggage, and trying to cram everything in. It's not

too bad if I am going to a single place for a single purpose.

The problem is when I want to do different things: walk in the

country, to dress up for a nice dinner, and meet business

colleagues. The wrong things can be taken, or I can easily

end up with three wardrobes to carry around. The biggest

problem for me is shoes because they are heavy and take up

so much space in my suitcase. The shoes that are chosen never

seem to be the right ones. What I should do before I pack is

close my eyes, take a deep breath, and to take three pain

relievers. (5)

Unit Nine

overview

LESSON 30
Parallelism

Error Sentences

CORRECTED SENTENCES APPEAR ON PAGE 306.

EXAMPLE 1: ✗ I like to bike, swim, and to go on camping trips.

EXAMPLE 2: ✗ It is hard to make a mistake and starting over again.

What's the Problem?

The term **parallelism** refers to a series of two or more grammatical elements of the same type joined by the **coordinating conjunction** *and* (or, sometimes, by *or*). When one of the elements breaks the pattern set up by the other elements, the error is called **faulty parallelism**.

The most common type of faulty parallelism involves different forms of verbs. In Example 1, there are three verbs in the **infinitive**: *to bike, swim,* and *to go.* However, the forms of their infinitives are not parallel—*to* is used with the first and third verbs but not with the second. In Example 2, *to make* is an infinitive, but *starting* is a **gerund** (the *-ing* form of a verb that is used as a noun). Inconsistency is the problem in both sentences.

Lesson 30

//

What Causes the Problem?

Faulty parallelism usually occurs when writers join elements together with *and* but fail to check whether the elements all have the same form. The error is most likely to occur when there is a choice between forms and it does not make any difference which form is used. For instance, in Example 1, it makes no difference whether or not we repeat the *to* with a series of infinitive verbs; either choice is fine. In Example 2, we could choose the infinitives *to make* and *to start* or the gerunds *making* and *starting.* However, we must be consistent in whatever choice we make.

Diagnostic Exercise

CORRECTED SENTENCES APPEAR ON PAGE 499.

Correct all errors in the following paragraph using the first correction as a model. The number in parentheses at the end of the paragraph indicates how many errors you should find.

We all go to college for different reasons—to get an education, meet new people, and ~~to~~ gain the skills for a job. The best programs are ones that reach several of these goals at the same time. I like to take courses that interest me and building skills that will lead to a job. For example, it is great to read about something in a class and then applying it in a practical situation. That is why I am doing an internship program. I have the opportunity to get credits, develop professional skills, and to make important contacts. The internship will be worthwhile even if I have to go to school an extra semester to earn all the credits I need to graduate. (3)

Fixing This Problem in Your Writing

Lesson 30

//

Every time you use an *and* (or an *or*), you are creating parallel elements. You always need to check to see that the parallel elements have exactly the same form. You need to be especially careful to check for parallel elements when you use *and* with an infinitive (the *to* form of a verb) or a gerund (the *-ing* form of a verb).

AND TIP: Whenever you use an infinitive or a gerund after an *and* (or an *or*), look to the left side of the *and* and check every single infinitive or gerund to see that each has the *exact same form* as the infinitive or gerund on the right side of the *and*. If the form(s) on the left side of the *and* are not exactly the same as the form on the right side of the *and*, then you have faulty parallelism.

Correcting a case of faulty parallelism once you have found it is not very difficult. Often either form will work, since the problem is usually one of inconsistency in your choice between two equally valid alternatives.

Here is how we would apply the *And* Tip to the two examples.

EXAMPLE 1:   ✗ I like to bike, swim, and to go on camping trips.

The infinitive after *and* is *to go,* which uses *to.* Starting on the left side of the *and,* work backward through the sentence looking at the exact form of each infinitive to see whether or not it also uses *to.* Correct the faulty parallelism by using *to* with each of the infinitives or by using *to* only once, with the first, to apply to all three verbs equally.

TIP APPLIED: I like to bike, ^to^ swim, and to go on camping trips.
I like to bike, ^swim, and ~~to~~ go on camping trips.

In Example 2, there is a gerund (*starting*) after the *and.*

EXAMPLE 2:   ✗ It is hard to make a mistake and starting over again.

Beginning on the left side of the *and,* work backward through the sentence looking for a matching gerund. Since *to make* is an infinitive, the sentence contains faulty parallelism. Rewrite the sentence using parallel infinitives or parallel gerunds.

TIP APPLIED: It is hard to make a mistake and ~~starting~~ ^to start^ over again.
It is hard ~~to make~~ ^making^ a mistake and starting over again.

Sentence Practice 1

CORRECTED SENTENCES APPEAR ON PAGE 499.

Underline the verb forms used before and after *and.* If the verb forms are parallel, write *OK.* Correct sentences that contain faulty parallelism.

EXAMPLE: I want to improve my skills, go online, and ~~to~~
surf the Internet.

1. Before leaving, I have to call my mother, write a report, and to pay my bills.

2. College gives us a chance to be away from home and gaining independence.

3. This book will teach you ways to write better, make good grades, and to amuse your friends.

4. A standard formula for speeches is beginning with a joke and to conclude with a summary.

5. Student representatives on committees are required to attend all meetings, take notes, and to report to the student government.

 For more practice using parallelism, go to **Exercise Central** at **bedfordstmartins.com/commonsense/9-30**.

Sentence Practice 2

CORRECTED SENTENCES APPEAR ON PAGE 499.

Underline the verb forms used before and after *and* or *or*. If the verb forms are parallel, write *OK*. Correct sentences that contain faulty parallelism.

> EXAMPLE: Japanese cranes need about 30 feet <u>to run</u>,
> <u>flap their wings</u>, and <del>to</del> <u>fly away</u>.

1. The porters began sorting the baggage and clearing a space for us to assemble.

2. I have to put the cat out, water the plants, and to leave a house key with a friend.

3. This semester, I started working at home in the mornings and to do my school work later in the afternoons.

4. I do not want you to lose the directions and becoming lost.

5. I remembered filling out the form, handing it to the clerk, and asking her to check it.

Lesson 30

//

Sentence Practice 3

Combine each of the following groups of sentences. Use parallel forms of the verbs in parentheses.

> EXAMPLE: The children are eager (open) their presents.
> The children are eager (play) with their toys.
> The children are eager (show) them off.

ANSWER: The children are eager to open their presents, play with their toys, and show them off.

1.   My boss is eager (get) the costs for the new product.
     My boss is eager (begin) selling it.
     My boss is eager (see) profits.

2.   (Brush) your teeth correctly is important.
     (Floss) regularly is important.
     (Visit) a dentist twice a year is important.

3.   I cannot stand it when friends (make) complicated plans.
     I cannot stand it when friends (call) me at the last second.
     I cannot stand it when friends (expect) me to be ready on time.

4.   Texas Slim likes (drink) Lone Star Beer.
     Texas Slim likes (eat) barbecue.
     Texas Slim likes (watch) Martha Stewart on TV.

5.   You should try (prepare) nutritious meals.
     You should try (watch) your weight.
     You should try (get) enough sleep.

Editing Practice 1

CORRECTED SENTENCES APPEAR ON PAGE 499.

Lesson 30

//

Correct all errors in the following paragraph using the first correction as a model. The number in parentheses at the end of the paragraph indicates how many errors you should find.

It used to be that schools just taught students to read, write,

and ~~to~~ do arithmetic, and that was it. When students left school,

there were plenty of blue-collar jobs, for example, on the automobile

assembly line. The assembly line required workers who were

willing to be punctual, work at a steady pace, and to follow

instructions. These jobs often paid pretty well—well enough for

a worker to support a family, to buy a new car, and make the
down payment on a house. Because the work was broken down
into tiny routines, workers never needed to receive any training
more sophisticated than basic first aid or even developing technical
knowledge relevant to the industry. The work was designed to be
simple, make little demand on the workers, and to ensure that
nearly anybody could do the job. (4)

Editing Practice 2

CORRECTED SENTENCES APPEAR ON PAGE 499.

Correct all errors in the following paragraphs using the first correction as a model. The number in parentheses at the end of each paragraph indicates how many errors you should find.

Nowadays, there are far fewer manufacturing jobs around
because companies are able to subcontract to the cheapest bidder,
get components manufactured overseas, and ~~to~~ do the same
work with fewer workers because of automation. These developments leave Americans jobs that require workers to meet
extremely short deadlines, produce customized products, and
to do high technology. Routine jobs will be done overseas or
by machines. (1)

These changes in the workplace mean that American
workers must become much more sophisticated to function in
a high-tech world. For example, they need to learn to read technical
manuals, communicate with many different technical specialists,
and to be able to upgrade themselves constantly. What companies

Lesson 30

//

need are students who are able to read, write, and to engage in critical thinking. It is a strange paradox: the more high-tech and specialized our society becomes, the more general our education needs to be. (2)

Editing Practice 3

Correct all errors in the following paragraph using the first correction as a model. The number in parentheses at the end of the paragraph indicates how many errors you should find.

Train robberies in the United States reached their peak in January of 1885, when on average they occurred once every four days. It cost so much money to locate, apprehend, and ~~convicting~~ convict the robbers that it was often more economical to ignore them. Efforts to stop the robberies were hindered by such things as quarreling over word usage, dealing with unscrupulous lawyers, and trying to get Congress to pass effective legislation. In California, a lawyer successfully argued that his client did not rob a train; rather, he managed to derail a train, to turn it into a mangled heap of cars, and take money from a "wreck" (technically, not a "train"). Another lawyer argued that it was impossible to "rob" a train — that only people can be robbed. In 1902 Congress finally managed to agree on wording, to define terms clearly, and pass the Train Robbery Act, which spelled out the law on this issue. (2)

Lesson 30

//

Writing Practice

On your own paper, write a paragraph or two about the kinds of education you think you will need for your career. Try to use several parallel verb forms. Use the Editing Checklist to check for parallelism.

Editing Checklist

Identify Faulty Parallelism in Your Writing

____ As you reread your writing, check for verb forms (or other grammatical elements) in a series.

____ Once you've identified a series of verbs (or other grammatical elements), check to see whether each is in the same form.

Correct Faulty Parallelism in Your Writing

____ Match the form of every verb (or other grammatical element) on one side of *and* or *or* with the forms on the other side of *and* or *or*. If you begin your series with an infinitive (*to* form), use infinitives throughout. If you begin your series with a gerund (*-ing* form), use gerunds throughout.

The Bottom Line	Make verb forms parallel by **using** the gerund (*-ing*) form for verbs in a series or by **making** the verbs infinitives (used with *to*).

Lesson 30

//

LESSON 31
Passive Voice

Error Sentences

CORRECTED SENTENCES APPEAR ON PAGE 314.

> EXAMPLE 1: ✗ The ball was kicked by me.

> EXAMPLE 2: ✗ A report was written.

What's the Problem?

The passive voice occurs when the grammatical **subject** is the thing that *receives* the action, not the thing that *performs* it. In Example 1, for instance, the *ball* didn't do the kicking; the ball was the thing that *received* the kick. Sentences in the passive voice often use the word *by* to indicate who performed an action.

Using the passive voice is not really an error, because there is no universal rule against using it. However, many readers prefer that writers avoid passive voice. As the name suggests, the *passive* voice can lead to a dull style because it does not stress action. Also, it can "hide" the person or thing doing an action. For instance, Example 2 does not indicate *who* wrote the report. Generally, writers should avoid using the passive voice unless they can justify doing so.

What Causes the Problem?

ESL Non-native speakers of English should know that sometimes people use the passive voice because they think it sounds formal and objective. People also sometimes use it to be polite. For instance, compare *You must avoid these errors* with the passive-voice version: *These errors must be avoided.* Still, overusing the passive voice can easily lead to boring, unclear writing; so this lesson focuses on how to recognize the passive voice and how to convert it to the active voice.

Diagnostic Exercise

Using the first correction as a model, change all passive-voice verbs to the active voice. The number in parentheses at the end of the paragraph indicates how many errors you should find.

Matt's apartment manager called him, wanting

~~Matt was called by his apartment manager, who wanted~~ to

know why he played his music so loudly. Matt was surprised by the

phone call; he didn't think his music was loud. He apologized, but

he said his radio was playing at only a fourth of its potential volume.

Apparently, the manager was satisfied by this response. Matt was told

by her that she would speak with the people who complained. I have

heard that they have a history of complaining. (3)

Fixing This Problem in Your Writing

You can recognize the passive voice by applying the following tip:

> **FORMULA TIP:** The passive voice is produced by a definite formula:
> a *to be* helping verb + a past participle form of another verb = passive voice.

Let's look at each of these two parts of this formula in more detail. Here are the only *to be* verbs in formal English:

is	was	were	are	am	be	being	been

A sentence is *not* in the passive voice just because it has a *to be* verb. There must also be a **past participle** form of another verb. Usually, this immediately follows the *to be* verb.

Verb	**Past participle form**
eat	eaten
write	written
borrow	borrowed
sing	sung

Lesson 31

pass

To eliminate the passive voice, use the following tip:

> **FLIP-FLOP TIP:** Revise passive sentences by flip-flopping what comes before the passive verb with what comes after the passive verb. Move the subject so that it *receives* the action and make the person, place, or thing that *performs* the action the new subject.

We know that the two example sentences are in the passive voice because they follow the passive voice formula. Each can be revised using the Flip-flop Tip.

to be verb + past participle

EXAMPLE 1: ✗ The ball <u>was kicked</u> by me.

To revise the sample error, flip-flop *ball* and *me*, and change *me* to the subject form *I*. Then delete the *to be* verb, and make any other minor changes needed for the sentence to make sense.

TIP APPLIED: **I kicked the ball.**

Sometimes a passive voice sentence will not indicate who or what performed the action.

to be verb + past participle

EXAMPLE 2: ✗ A report <u>was written</u>.

TIP APPLIED: **Somebody wrote a report.**

In this revision, we added the subject *somebody* because the original sentence did not specify who wrote the report.

Lesson 31

pass

Sentence Practice 1

CORRECTED SENTENCES APPEAR ON PAGE 500.

In each of the following sentences, underline the *to be* verb and the past participle verb that comes after it. Then change the passive sentence into an active one by flip-flopping what comes before and after the verbs you've underlined.

The gardener carelessly left a rake in the yard.

EXAMPLE: **A rake** <u>*was*</u> **carelessly** <u>*left*</u> **in the yard by the gardener.**

1. The plants were uprooted by those kids.

2. The children are frightened by your shouting.

3.   The television was broken by you.

4.   I am hurt by your actions.

5.   The story was written by Eudora Welty.

 For more practice using the passive voice, go to **Exercise Central** at **bedfordstmartins.com/commonsense/9-31**.

Sentence Practice 2

CORRECTED SENTENCES APPEAR ON PAGE 500.

In each of the following sentences, underline the *to be* verb and the past-participle verb that comes after it. Then change the passive sentence into an active one by flip-flopping what comes before and after the verbs you've underlined.

> *The Naked Chef, Jamie Oliver, presented a cooking demonstration.*
>
> EXAMPLE: **A cooking demonstration** <u>*was presented*</u> **by the Naked Chef, Jamie Oliver.**

1.   The meal was quickly eaten by the hungry workers.

2.   On Monday, my van was hit by a driver who pulled in front of me.

3.   All rooms were cleaned over the weekend by the custodians.

4.   My dancing partner was violently bumped by another dancer.

5.   The pesticide was sprayed by the farmers.

Sentence Practice 3

In each item below there are two nouns and a verb. Use the first noun as the subject of an active sentence; then use the second noun as the subject of a passive sentence.

> EXAMPLE: **the Senate**
> **the bill**
> **pass**
>
> ANSWER: Active: **The Senate passed the bill.**
> Passive: **The bill was passed by the Senate.**

Lesson 31

pass

1. our governor
    the new law
    supported

2. the voters
    the results
    protested

3. my pet bird
    potato chips
    likes

4. the class
    test
    finished

5. our professor
    papers
    graded

Editing Practice 1

CORRECTED SENTENCES APPEAR ON PAGE 500.

Change all passive-voice sentences in the following paragraphs to the active voice using the first correction as a model. The number in parentheses at the end of each paragraph indicates how many passive-voice verbs you should find.

Lesson 31

pass

My parents greatly influenced me
~~I was greatly influenced by my parents~~ to love reading. Both
⌃

of them are avid readers, yet I was rarely hassled by them to read.

Rather, they let me read at my own pace and pick what I wished

to read. (1)

Almost every type of reading material has an appeal for me, but

science-fiction stories are most often read by me. They were consumed

by me during my teenage years; often, one a week would be read.

Now that I'm in college, I have less time to spend on pleasure reading, but some time was carved out of my schedule by me to devote to reading a good book every now and then. (4)

Editing Practice 2

CORRECTED SENTENCES APPEAR ON PAGE 500

Change all passive-voice sentences in the following paragraphs to the active voice using the first correction as a model. The number in parentheses at the end of each paragraph indicates how many passive-voice verbs you should find.

I consider parking on this campus
~~Parking on this campus is considered by me~~ to be a real
^
problem. The school is in the middle of a large city, and available parking places are searched for by students, teachers, and people working in the city. When more classrooms were needed by the school, the parking lots it once had disappeared. As the city grew, the parking places gave way to more and more stores. All this growth has its advantages, but parking needs were not considered carefully by the school or the city. (3)

Parking permits can be bought by students, but the better lots are expensive. Riding the bus is encouraged by the school and the city, but it can take forever to get to class from where I live. Most schools seem to have parking problems, but the problem is even worse when the school is in the middle of a busy down-town area. (2)

Lesson 31

pass

Editing Practice 3

Change all passive-voice sentences in the following paragraphs to the active voice using the first correction as a model. The number in parentheses at the end of each paragraph indicates how many passive-voice verbs you should find.

A pair of travelers were on the side of a dusty road, resting
their sore feet. ~~They were seen by me,~~ *I saw them,* so I walked up to them and
asked them where they were going. My question was not answered.
My question was asked again. This time, one man said, "We are
traveling north to Maine." I was surprised by this response
because I was going to Maine as well. (3)

The travelers said that I could travel with them, so we
soon left. The long road was traveled all day by us. Our feet were
hurt by the hot gravel. We were not in a hurry, so we stopped
frequently to rest. A driver stopped to see whether we wanted a
ride. He was friendly and offered directions. Our feelings were
hurt by him. He told us that we were crazy to walk a thousand
miles to Maine. (3)

Writing Practice

Lesson 31

pass

On your own paper write a paragraph or two describing a recent car trip,
walk, or bike ride. Use the Editing Checklist to see whether any of your
sentences are in the passive voice. If so, change each passive-voice sentence
to the active voice unless there is a strong reason to use the passive voice.

Editing Checklist

Identify the Passive Voice in Your Writing

_____ Look at the verbs in your sentences and see how many follow the passive-voice formula: a *to be* helping verb + a past participle form of another verb = the passive voice.

Correct the Passive Voice in Your Writing

_____ Turn passive sentences into active sentences by flip-flopping them so that the subjects are moved to follow the verbs.

_____ Make any other minor changes necessary so that the new sentences are grammatical and haven't changed their meaning.

The Bottom Line	Writers use active voice when the subject of the sentence actually performs the action indicated by the verb of the sentence.

UNIT NINE: Writing Clear Sentences

This unit presented sentence structures that can be misused (in the case of faulty parallelism) or inappropriately used (in the case of the passive voice). So that your writing will be clear to your readers, use parallel structures and the active voice.

Parallelism

Writers create faulty parallelism when elements in a series are not balanced. The most common error involves mixing infinitives (*to* verb form) and gerunds (*-ing* verb form). Use this tip to help balance your sentences.

> *AND* TIP: Whenever you use an infinitive or a gerund after an *and* (or an *or*), look to the left side of the *and*, and check every single infinitive or gerund to see that each has the *exact same form* as the infinitive or gerund on the right side of the *and*. If the form(s) on the left side of the *and* is not exactly the same as the form on the right side of the *and*, then you have faulty parallelism.

Passive Voice

The passive voice is not ungrammatical, but it might distract and annoy readers because it sounds dull and can make your meaning unclear. The first tip in this lesson helps you identify the passive voice in your own writing:

> FORMULA TIP: The passive voice is produced by a definite formula: a *to be* helping verb + a past participle form of another verb = passive voice.

The second tip helps you revise passive voice sentences into active voice sentences.

> FLIP-FLOP TIP: Revise passive sentences by flip-flopping what comes before the passive verb with what comes after the passive verb. Move the subject so that it *receives* the action, and make the person, place, or thing that *performs* the action the new subject.

Unit Nine

review

Review Test

Correct all errors in the following paragraphs using the first correction as a model. The number in parentheses at the end of each paragraph indicates how many errors you should find.

This summer, I took a bowling class and learned how to select a comfortable ball, ~~to~~ be consistent in my approach, and aim the ball. I have always liked to bowl or watching my friends bowl. Since I had to take a PE course anyway, the requirement was satisfied by a bowling course. Most of my bad habits were corrected by this course. (3)

Some of my worst habits were to vary my approach almost every time I bowled and throwing the ball with all my strength. I was shown by my instructor that I did not need to hurl the ball at the pins. The pins can easily be knocked down by a slower, more controlled release. Amazingly, it just takes a little effort to knock a pin over and starting a chain reaction that can knock them all down. My scores have been greatly improved by my more deliberate approach. (5)

Choosing the Right Article

Terms That Can Help You Understand Articles

If you are not familiar with any of the following terms that appear in this unit, look them up in the Guide to Grammar Terminology beginning on page 1. The numbers in parentheses indicate the lessons in which each term appears.

article (32, 33, 34)	**definite article** (33, 34)
common noun (32, 33)	**indefinite article** (33, 34)
count noun (32, 33, 34)	**noncount noun** (32, 33, 34)

The Nuts and Bolts of
ESL **Choosing the Right Article**

One of the most complicated and confusing aspects of English for non-native speakers is the use of **articles**. There are two types of articles, **definite** (*the*) and **indefinite** (*a* and *an*, together with *some*, which behaves like an indefinite article). The choice among these articles—and the additional option of using no article at all—is determined by the nature of the noun the article modifies. This unit will examine how both the form of nouns and the meaning of nouns affect the choice of articles.

There are two main groups of nouns: proper nouns and common nouns. **Proper nouns** name particular people, places, and institutions and are usually capitalized. Most categories of proper nouns do not involve the use of articles. For example:

PEOPLE: Ms. Chin, Martin Luther King, Jr., Oprah Winfrey

PLACES: Chicago, State Street, Niagara Falls, China, Mexico City

INSTITUTIONS: General Motors, Apple Computer, Columbia University

However, some proper nouns are used with the definite article *the*. While many such uses are completely idiomatic, some uses of *the* actually follow rules of their own. Just for fun, see whether you can figure out the rules for using *the* with certain classes of proper nouns, based on the following examples. (*Hint:* Think about the difference in meaning between the nouns that don't use articles and the ones that use *the*.)

(ANSWERS APPEAR ON PAGE 500.)

No article	**Used with *the***
Mt. Everest, Mt. McKinley, Pikes Peak, Mt. Hood, Mt. Washington	the Alps, the Rockies, the Sierra Nevadas, the Andes, the Himalayas
Lake Como, Golden Pond, Lake Ontario, Walden Pond	the Atlantic, the Mediterranean Sea, the Pacific, the Indian Ocean

This unit focuses on the other type of nouns — common nouns. **Common nouns** are not capitalized and are not the names of particular people, places, or institutions. For example, *Ms. Chin* is the name of a particular person, but the common noun *woman* is not. The choice of which article to use with a common noun (or whether to use any article at all) depends on three questions, each of which is discussed in its own lesson.

Lesson 32 helps you to answer the question *What is the form of the noun?* The choice of which article to use depends, in part, on whether the noun is singular or plural and whether it is a count noun or a noncount noun.

EXAMPLE: ✗ Our team manager loaded all the equipments onto the bus before the game.

CORRECTION: Our team manager loaded all the equipments̸ onto the bus before the game.

Lesson 33 helps you to answer the question *Does the reader know which specific noun I am referring to?* The choice of which article to use depends, in part, on whether the writer is referring to a specific person, place, or thing that is known to the reader.

EXAMPLE: ✗ Let's go to a coffee shop at the corner of Main Street and Maple.

CORRECTION: Let's go to a̸ *the* coffee shop at the corner of Main Street and Maple.

Lesson 34 helps you to answer the question *Am I using the noun to make a generalization?* The choice of which article to use depends, in part, on whether the noun is being used to make a generalization—a broad statement or conclusion—about something.

EXAMPLE: ✗ The nutritionists now believe that eating soybeans may help stop calcium loss and prevent osteoporosis.

CORRECTION: *Nutritionists*
~~The nutritionists~~ now believe that eating soybeans may help̂ stop calcium loss and prevent osteoporosis.

This unit is somewhat different from other units in the book. In the other units, the lessons are loosely connected. Usually, you can do one lesson in a unit without doing any other lessons first. In this unit, however, this is not the case; the three lessons are tightly connected. You should do all three lessons in order. They work together to give you a specific technique called a *decision tree* for deciding which article (if any) you should use with a given common noun. This technique is found in the Unit Ten review.

Can you detect problems involving articles?

CORRECTED SENTENCES APPEAR ON PAGE 500.

Correct all errors in the following paragraphs using the first correction as a model. The number in parentheses at the end of each paragraph indicates how many errors you should find.

a
We live in ~~the~~ time of the great technological change. The engine

that is driving this change is the computer. It is hard to believe how

quickly the computers have become the absolutely essential part of

our personal and professional lives. Many of us first used computers

as the greatly improved typewriters. With computers, we were able to

edit and revise the essays with a few keyboard commands without

going to trouble of having to retype entire document over again. In business world, computers were first used as the greatly improved

desk calculators. With computers, we could create spreadsheets that

would do tiresome calculations for us. (9)

As the computers have become more common and more

powerful, they have begun to redefine what it means to write and

to calculate. For example, it used to be that distinction between

writing term paper and publishing book was as different as day and

night. That is no longer the case. What I write at my computer in my

office can be sent out over Internet and be more widely distributed

than any published book ever was. It used to be that jobs of book-

keeper and the financial planner were completely different. That is

no longer the case. With the financial planning software, I can do

analysis of dozens of alternative business choices and decide which

one works best, and even throw in strategy for minimizing taxes

at the same time. (10)

Unit Ten

overview
ESL

LESSON 32

ESL

Incorrect Plurals and
Articles with Noncount Nouns

Error Sentences

CORRECTED SENTENCES APPEAR ON PAGE 328.

EXAMPLE 1:   ✗ There have been many studies about the effects of violences on children watching TV.

EXAMPLE 2:   ✗ The customs agent might ask to see a luggage.

What's the Problem?

A large group of nouns in English cannot be used in the plural. For instance, the word *violences* in Example 1 has incorrectly been made plural. Another peculiarity of this group of nouns is that they cannot be used with the article *a* or *an*. For instance, in Example 2, *a luggage* is incorrect.

What Causes the Problem?

A noun that cannot be used in the plural and that cannot be used with the article *a* or *an* is called a **noncount noun** (or a *mass noun*). Since non-native speakers of English have great difficulty in recognizing noncount nouns, they are likely to treat a noncount noun as though it were a regular **count noun** and incorrectly pluralize it or use the article *a* or *an* with it.

Diagnostic Exercise

CORRECTED SENTENCES APPEAR ON PAGE 501.

Correct all errors in the following paragraph using the first correction as a model. The number in parentheses at the end of the paragraph indicates how many errors you should find.

modernization

The ~~modernizations~~ of agriculture has meant a huge increase

in just a few crops—wheats and rices for a human consumption, corns

for an animal consumption, and cottons for industrial productions. This

specialization in a few crops is called a *monoculture.* A monoculture

has some disadvantages: it reduces a biodiversity and requires huge

amounts of energies and fertilizer. (11)

Fixing This Problem in Your Writing

The reason nouns in this group are called "noncount" is that they cannot be counted with number words like *one, two, three.* For example, we cannot say "one luggage, two luggages." This fact also explains why we cannot use the article *a* or *an* with noncount nouns. Historically, the articles *a* and *an* come from the word for the number *one.*

> **PLURAL TIP:** The easiest way to test whether a word is a noncount noun is to make the noun plural. If the plural of the word is not grammatical or does not make sense in the context of the sentence, then the word is a noncount noun. (Note that when the tested noun is a subject, the verb will change to agree with it.)

In the expression *Talk is cheap,* for example, *talk* is a noncount noun because the plural *Talks are cheap* is not grammatical without completely changing the meaning of the expression. However, in the sentence *I went to the talk,* the noun *talk* is a count noun because we can make it plural: *I went to the talks.* In the first sentence, the noncount noun *talk* means "the process of talking." In the second sentence, the count noun *talk* means a "lecture."

Although it is difficult to predict which nouns are noncount nouns, many noncount nouns do occur in relatively well-defined classes based on their meaning. Here are some common examples:

Abstractions (the largest single group of noncount nouns): faith, hope, charity, beauty, luck, peace, flexibility, knowledge, reliability, intelligence

Liquids and gases: water, coffee, tea, wine, blood, gasoline, air, oxygen

Materials: gold, silver, paper, wool, silk, wood, glass, chalk, sand, plastic

Food: bread, butter, rice, cheese, meat, jam, chicken, beef, salt, sugar

Languages: English, Chinese, Spanish, Russian

Academic fields: anthropology, chemistry, physics, literature

Sports and games: tennis, bridge, soccer, football, baseball, chess

Gerunds (words ending in *-ing* used as nouns): smiling, wishing, walking

Weather words: weather, fog, snow, rain, pollution, thunder, wind, hail

Natural phenomena: gravity, electricity, space, energy, matter

People tend to use abstract noncount nouns to make generalizations about categories of things or events. Conversely, when talking about some particular thing or event, people tend to use count nouns.

> GENERALIZATION TIP: A noun used to make a generalization — especially if the noun refers to an abstraction — is often a noncount noun.

In Example 1, the noun *violence* is an abstraction used to make a generalization. In other words, *violence* does not refer to one specific violent act but to the idea in general. The Generalization Tip tells us that this sort of noun cannot be made plural.

EXAMPLE 1:   ✗ There have been many studies about the effects of violences on children watching TV.

CORRECTION: There have been many studies about the effects of violence̸ on children watching TV.

In Example 2, *luggage* does not refer to the individual bags and suitcases you might carry on a trip but to the whole general category, whether there are ten suitcases or one suitcase. As a noncount noun, *luggage* cannot be made plural or used with the indefinite articles *a* or *an*.

EXAMPLE 2:   ✗ The customs agent might ask to see a luggage.

CORRECTION: The customs agent might ask to see a̸ luggage.

Noncount nouns have one other odd feature. While they cannot have a plural meaning, sometimes they can be used with the plural marker *-s* to mean something like "different kinds of." For example, *tea* is a noncount noun; when it is used with an *-s,* it means "different kinds of teas," as in the sentence *That store carries* <u>*teas*</u> *from all over the world.* In this sentence, *teas* is still a noncount noun because it does not have a plural meaning.

Sentence Practice 1

CORRECTED SENTENCES APPEAR ON PAGE 501.

In the following sentences, many noncount nouns have been incorrectly used in the plural or with the article *a* or *an.* Underline the incorrectly used noncount nouns and make any necessary corrections.

familiarity

    EXAMPLE: **They demonstrated their <u>familiarities</u> with the topics.**

^

1. We studied the country's system of transportations.

2. The company hoped to improve their productivities.

3. The desks were made out of metals.

4. We helped the campers get their gears out of the trucks.

5. The amount of trade directly affects the prosperities of nations.

> For more practice with noncount nouns, go to **Exercise Central** at **bedfordstmartins.com/commonsense/10-32**.

Sentence Practice 2

CORRECTED SENTENCES APPEAR ON PAGE 501.

In the following sentences, many noncount nouns have been incorrectly used in the plural or with the article *a* or *an.* Underline the incorrectly used noncount nouns, and make any necessary corrections.

    EXAMPLE: **~~An~~ <u>anxiety</u> about the future is a normal thing.**

1. Good plannings gave us good results.

2. During winter we didn't get a sunlight for days.

Lesson 32

art
ESL

3. His idea was a complete nonsense.

4. We were not able to get a good information on those topics.

5. News reportings during wartime are always confusing and misleading.

Sentence Practice 3

The following sentence has two very different meanings because the word *lamb* can be used as either a noncount noun or a count noun:

EXAMPLE: The lamb is too hot to eat.

Can you explain the two different meanings of *lamb*?

Below are other nouns that can be used either as noncount or as count nouns, though often with considerably different meanings. Use each noun in two different sentences—once as a noncount noun and once as a plural count noun. Explain the difference in meaning.

EXAMPLE :   **paper**

ANSWER:

NONCOUNT: **The book is printed on very cheap** paper. **[Paper is a raw material.]**

COUNT: **I read two** papers **this morning. [Papers means "newspapers" or "essays."]**

1. Baseball

2. Coffee

3. Bridge

4. Iron

5. Nickel

Lesson 32

art
ESL

Editing Practice 1

CORRECTED SENTENCES APPEAR ON PAGE 501.

Correct all errors in the following paragraphs using the first correction as a model. Make whatever other changes are necessary. The number in parentheses at the end of each paragraph indicates how many errors you should find.

Gold has long been one of the most valued of metals. A̶ ̶j̶e̶w̶e̶l̶r̶y̶ *Jewelry*
made of gold has been discovered at an excavation in Iraq that
dates from 3500 B.C. The high level of artistries in the workmanships
suggests that the craft of working golds had been evolving for
centuries before then. (3)

From ancient times to today, gold has been highly prized for
a number of reasons. Its soft yellow color makes it intrinsically
beautiful; unlike irons, coppers, and most other metal, a gold does
not rust; and gold can be easily shaped into any desired form. (3)

Editing Practice 2

CORRECTED SENTENCES APPEAR ON PAGE 501.

Correct all errors in the following paragraphs using the first correction as a
model. Make whatever other changes are necessary. The number in parentheses at the end of each paragraph indicates how many errors you should find.

One of the most remarkable Americans who ever lived
was Benjamin Franklin. He was born in 1706 in Boston. His
education was
e̶d̶u̶c̶a̶t̶i̶o̶n̶s̶ ̶w̶e̶r̶e̶ quite limited because his father, who made
candles and soap, was unable to send him to school beyond the age
of ten. It is amazing that one of the most educated men in the Age of
Reasons was entirely self-taught. Franklin learned to be printer, and
by the time he was twenty-four, Franklin was the owner of his own
print shop in Philadelphia. He began publishing a highly successful
newspaper, writing much of the materials himself as his own editor.
Through the newspaper and other publishings, Franklin became one of
the most important public figures in the thirteen colonies. (4)

Lesson 32

art
ESL

Adding to his already substantial fames was his work as an inventor and scientist. Two of his most famous inventions were bifocal eyeglasses and a much more efficient stove, called the Franklin Stove. His research on electricities made him world famous. (2)

Franklin's great personal reputations and knowledge of civic affairs made him a natural political leader. He had enormous influences on the Revolutionary War. For example, he helped draft the Declaration of Independence and was one of its signers. However, his most important impacts on the war were his role in obtaining the diplomatic supports and eventual military intervention of France on the side of the colonies. After the war, Franklin's wisdoms and common senses played a key role in resolving fundamental conflicts in the creations of the Constitution. (7)

Editing Practice 3

Correct all errors in the following paragraphs using the first correction as a model. Make whatever other changes are necessary. The number in parentheses at the end of each paragraph indicates how many errors you should find.

Probably the most important aspect of gold is its rareness.
The fact that there ~~are~~ *is* always more ~~demands~~ *demand* for gold than there is availability of gold means that gold has great economic values. Several times in histories, our quest for gold has led to several great discoveries (albeit accidentally). For example, in the Middle Ages in Europe, alchemists, half-scientists and half-magicians, believed that inexpensive metals like leads could be turned into gold. The works of the alchemists never succeeded, but their researches were the foundation for the science of chemistries. The search for gold was also the main motivation for the early exploration of the New World and Australia. (6)

Lesson 32

art
ESL

Today, we do not use gold for a money. Instead, gold is used to stand behind paper currency. Some economists have urged the United States to return to the gold standard, a system in which the government agrees to redeem its paper money for a fixed amount of gold. The advantage of the gold standard is that it prevents an inflation. (2)

Writing Practice

On your own paper, write a paragraph or two describing the qualities you look for in a good friend or companion. Try to use at least four noncount nouns. Use the Editing Checklist to see whether you have used noncount nouns correctly.

Editing Checklist

Identify Noncount Noun Errors in Your Writing

_____ To see whether a word is a noncount noun, try making it plural. Noncount nouns will sound ungrammatical in the plural. They will also sound ungrammatical when used with *a* or *an*.

_____ Determine which nouns in your paper refer to abstract ideas (like *violence* or *knowledge*) or general categories (like *luggage* or *equipment*). These words cannot be made plural or used with *a* or *an*.

Correct Noncount Noun Errors in Your Writing

_____ Edit noncount nouns by removing the plural -*s* ending or removing the indefinite article *a* or *an*.

Lesson 32

art
ESL

The Bottom Line

Count **nouns** can be made plural,
but noncount nouns cannot be made plural.

LESSON 33

Using *A/An, Some,* and *The*

Error Sentences

CORRECTED SENTENCES APPEAR ON PAGE 336.

EXAMPLE 1:   ✗ Masanori had the good idea.

EXAMPLE 2:   ✗ Effie went into a phone booth and picked up a receiver.

What's the Problem?

English has two fundamentally different types of articles: **definite** and **indefinite**. Every time you use an article, you must correctly decide which type is appropriate. Since the factors that govern the choice between definite and indefinite articles are complex and subtle, it is easy to make an incorrect choice that sends a message you do not really intend. However, before discussing the problems of article selection, let's clarify some terminology.

The **definite article** is always *the,* which is used with all types of **common nouns**: singular and plural, **count** and **noncount**. The indefinite article is more complicated. The **indefinite articles** *a* and *an* are used *only* with singular count nouns. With plural count nouns and all noncount nouns, the word *some* is used. Since the rules that govern *some* are exactly parallel to the rules that govern *a* and *an,* this lesson will group them all together as indefinite articles.

What Causes the Problem?

Many writers whose native language is not English may have difficulty understanding how articles help to convey meaning to readers. Let's illustrate the basic distinction between definite and indefinite articles with the singular count noun *truck.*

> Using the definite article *the* (*the truck*) means two things, *both* of which must be true: (1) the writer has a particular truck in mind, *and* (2) the writer can reasonably assume that the reader can identify *which* truck the writer has in mind.

Using the indefinite article *a* or *an* (*a truck*) means *either* (1) that the writer does *not* have a particular truck in mind *or* (2) that, even if the writer has a particular truck in mind, he or she does not assume that the reader can identify *which* truck that is.

When deciding between using a definite article or an indefinite article, ask yourself whether the intended meaning of the noun is known to the reader or new to the reader. For instance, in Example 1, the reader has no idea what Masanori's good idea is, so the definite article *the* is incorrect. In Example 2, the writer can reasonably assume that the reader knows which receiver the writer has in mind, so the indefinite article *a* is incorrect.

Diagnostic Exercise

CORRECTED SENTENCES APPEAR ON PAGE 502.

Correct all errors in the following paragraph using the first correction as a model. The number in parentheses at the end of the paragraph indicates how many errors you should find.

Doctors have long known that we need to have iron in our diet. Recently, however, ~~the~~ *a* new study has revealed that we may be getting too much iron. The human body keeps all an iron it digests. An only way we lose stored iron in a body is through bleeding. John Murray, the researcher at the University of Minnesota, discovered that people who live on the very low iron diet may have the greatly reduced risk of the heart attack. Another study found that diets high in meat have the strong correlation with a high risk of heart disease. Apparently, when people have the high level of iron, excess iron may worsen the effect of cholesterol. (9)

Lesson 33

art
ESL

Fixing This Problem in Your Writing

Here is a useful strategy for testing your use of definite and indefinite articles: if you have a specific person, place, or thing in mind when you use a noun, ask yourself whether you can reasonably assume that the reader will be able to identify which meaning you have in mind. If this assumption can be met, use *the;* if this assumption cannot be met, then you must use an indefinite article, either *some* or *a* or *an* depending on the initial sound of the noun being modified. Here are some tips that will help you decide whether you can reasonably assume the reader will be able to identify which meaning you have in mind:

> **PREVIOUS-MENTION TIP:** Use the definite article if you have already mentioned the noun.

Suppose Example 1 occurred in the following context:

> When he found himself locked out of his house, Masanori
>
> began to panic. He had to make a presentation for class, but all
>
> his materials were in his study in the basement. He thought for
>
> a while. ✗ **Masanori had the good idea.** The screens of the
>
> basement windows were locked, but he used the scissors on
>
> his Swiss army knife to cut one open. In no time, he was off to
>
> class again.

Since Masanori's good idea has not been mentioned previously, the definite article *the* is incorrect.

>   *a*
> TIP APPLIED: **Masanori had ~~the~~ good idea.**
>   ^

> **NORMAL-EXPECTATIONS TIP:** Use the definite article if the noun meets our normal expectations about the way things work.

> EXAMPLE 2:   ✗ **Effie went into a phone booth and picked up a receiver.**

Even though the receiver has not been mentioned, you would use the definite article *the* because the reader expects phone booths to contain telephones with receivers.

>   *the*
> CORRECTION: **Effie went into a phone booth and picked up ~~a~~ receiver.**
>   ^

> **DEFINED-BY-MODIFIERS TIP:** Use the definite article if the noun is followed by modifiers that uniquely identify the noun.

TIP APPLIED: **There was an accident at <u>the</u> corner of Fifth Street and Riverside Drive.**

The reader can tell which corner the writer has in mind because the modifier *of Fifth Street and Riverside Drive* automatically defines the corner.

> **UNIQUENESS TIP:** Use the definite article if the noun has a uniqueness that everybody would be expected to know about.

TIP APPLIED: **<u>The</u> sun was beginning to rise above <u>the</u> horizon.**

Unless you are writing science-fiction, our planet has only one sun and only one horizon, and everybody already knows about them.

Sentence Practice 1

CORRECTED SENTENCES APPEAR ON PAGE 502.

The following sentences contain one or more correct uses of the word *the* (underlined). Assume that there is no previous context that these sentences refer to. In each case, indicate which of the four tips in this lesson provides your reason for using the definite article.

EXAMPLE: **I love my new car, although <u>the</u> brakes are pretty noisy.**

REASON: **Normal expectations. We expect cars to have brakes.**

1. We didn't get lost because we could see <u>the</u> North Star.
   Reason:

2. <u>The</u> walnuts you brought have not been shelled.
   Reason:

3. When we got to their house, <u>the</u> lights were all off.
   Reason:

4. Have you heard <u>the</u> rumor about what Harry and Sally did?
   Reason:

5. When people visit a castle, they always want to see <u>the</u> dungeon.
   Reason:

Lesson 33

art
ESL

> For more practice using articles, go to **Exercise Central** at **bedfordstmartins.com/commonsense/10-33**.

Sentence Practice 2

CORRECTED SENTENCES APPEAR ON PAGE 502.

The following sentences contain one or more correct uses of the word *the* (underlined). Assume that there is no previous context that these sentences refer to. In each case, indicate which of the four tips in this lesson provides your reason for using the definite article.

> EXAMPLE: We saw <u>the</u> movie version of *The Lord of the Rings.*

> REASON: Defined-by-modifiers. The modifying prepositional phrase tells which movie we saw.

1. If you really liked a movie, you can usually buy <u>the</u> sound track.
   Reason:

2. Before we start on a long hike, we always check <u>the</u> weather.
   Reason:

3. <u>The</u> joke that Louise told was not very funny.
   Reason:

4. A storm far out to sea was making <u>the</u> waves higher than normal.
   Reason:

5. <u>The</u> article that Professor Chou assigned was pretty interesting.
   Reason:

Sentence Practice 3

Fill in the blanks with the correct article: *the* or *a/an.*

Lesson 33

art
ESL

> EXAMPLE: I took ____*a*____ picture of ____*the*____ New York skyline.

1. We got _____ city map and found _____ location of _____ restaurant we were going to.

2. I made _____ mistake on _____ first question on _____ exam in chemistry.

3. When they got to _____ airport in Denver, they had to wait _____ hour.

4. There was _____ truck parked in _____ parking lot next to Safeway.

5. After I got home, I went into _____ kitchen and fixed myself _____ sandwich.

Editing Practice 1

CORRECTED SENTENCES APPEAR ON PAGE 502.

Correct all errors in the following paragraph using the first correction as a model. The number in parentheses at the end of the paragraph indicates how many errors you should find.

All of us have seen movies that were completely forgettable except for ~~the~~ ^a single scene. For some reason, this scene has always stuck in our minds. Often, a scene is not even a major part of a plot. It is usually some little piece of character development that struck us, or it is the funny or whimsical episode. For example, a few years ago I saw the French film whose title I can no longer even recall. In this otherwise forgettable movie, there was the long scene that showed someone fixing dinner and chopping the big pile of garlic while carrying on the long and animated conversation with the dinner guests. Everything in a scene was perfectly normal except that the cook was wearing the mask and snorkel while he prepared a garlic. (10)

Editing Practice 2

CORRECTED SENTENCES APPEAR ON PAGE 502.

Correct all errors in the following paragraph using the first correction as a model. The number in parentheses at the end of the paragraph indicates how many errors you should find.

My nomination for the Unforgettable Scenes from Forgettable Movies Award is ~~the~~ ^a scene in one of Humphrey Bogart's last movies,

Lesson 33

art
ESL

Beat the Devil. A movie is set in rural Italy on the Amalfi Coast. Bogart and Sydney Greenstreet are taking the taxi up the narrow mountain road. Just below a top, a taxi stalls, and they have to get out to push it. A driver walks alongside a driver's seat and steers as Bogart and Sydney Greenstreet push from behind. Bogart and Greenstreet get into the terrible argument as they are pushing, and a taxi driver is dying to hear what they are talking about. All three men get so involved in an argument that they forget what they are doing. (10)

Editing Practice 3

Correct all errors in the following paragraphs using the first correction as a model. The number in parentheses at the end of each paragraph indicates how many errors you should find.

Probably ~~a~~ **the** classic example of an unforgettable episode from a less-than-memorable movie is the cartoon characters created for the opening credits in the Peter Sellers movie *The Pink Panther*. As you may or may not recall, there are no panthers in a movie, pink or otherwise. A term *Pink Panther* refers to the fabulous diamond. It is called the Pink Panther because a diamond has the pink shadow in its center. In the movie, Peter Sellers plays Inspector Clouseau, the comically inept Parisian policeman. Clouseau is after the international jewel thief, who, of course, is intent on stealing a Pink Panther. (8)

The Pink Panther cartoon was so popular that a whole series of Inspector Clouseau comedies starring Peter Sellers are now known as the Pink Panther movies. A Pink Panther character has taken on the life

of its own, independent of an original movie. (3)

Writing Practice

On your own paper, write a paragraph or two that describes your favorite unforgettable scene from a forgettable movie. Use the Editing Checklist to examine all the definite and indefinite articles in your essay and to make certain they are correct.

Editing Checklist

Identify Errors in Using Definite and Indefinite Articles

____ As you proofread your paper, ask yourself these questions each time you come across *a, an, some,* or *the:* Am I referring to a specific person, place, or thing? If so, can I reasonably assume that the reader knows which specific person, place, or thing I am referring to?

Correct Errors in Using Definite and Indefinite Articles

____ If you answered yes to both questions above, use the definite article *the* before your noun.

____ If you answered no to one or both questions above, use *a* or *an* with singular count nouns, and use *some* with plural count nouns and all noncount nouns.

The Bottom Line	Use *the* only when **the** reader knows what **the** noun refers to.

LESSON 34

ESL

Making Generalizations
without Articles

Error Sentences

CORRECTED SENTENCES APPEAR ON PAGE 343.

EXAMPLE 1: ✗ The barn is always full of some cats.

EXAMPLE 2: ✗ Our family usually has the fish for dinner on Fridays.

What's the Problem?

Generally speaking, nouns in English must be preceded by an **article** or some similar modifier. However, there is one major exception to this rule: to signal a generalization about a noun, use no article or other noun modifier with a **noncount noun** or a plural **count noun**.

For instance, in Example 1, the writer uses the plural count noun *cats*. In this sentence, the word *cats* does not refer to any actual cats; instead, the writer is making a generalization about the category of animals that inhabit the barn. Therefore, Example 1 should not include the indefinite article *some*. (See Lesson 33 for an explanation of why *some* is treated as a kind of indefinite article.)

In Example 2, the writer uses the definite article *the* with the noun *fish*. In this sentence, the word *fish* does not refer to any actual fish the family ate on any particular day. Example 2 is a generalization about the family's typical meal on Fridays. Therefore, Example 2 should not include the article *the*.

What Causes the Problem?

Non-native speakers of English (and sometimes native speakers) incorrectly use an **article** with a **noncount noun** or with a plural **count noun** to make a generalization.

Lesson 34

art
ESL

342

Diagnostic Exercise

CORRECTED SENTENCES APPEAR ON PAGE 502.

Correct all errors in the following paragraph using the first correction as a model. The number in parentheses at the end of the paragraph indicates how many errors you should find.

Scientists
~~The scientists~~ have long known that the honeybees are some-
^
how able to tell some other bees where to look for some food.

In the 1940's, Karl von Frisch of the University of Munich discovered

that the type of the dance that the bees make when they return to their

beehive is significant. It seems that the honeybees are able to signal

both the direction of the food that they found and its approximate

distance from their hive to the bees who had remained at the hive. (6)

Fixing This Problem in Your Writing

Anytime writers use a noncount noun or a plural count noun, they must monitor the meaning of the noun to see whether they are using that noun to make a generalization. If that is the case, then they should not use an article. Following are some tips that may help you recognize when a noun is being used in a general sense.

> **ADVERB-OF-FREQUENCY TIP:** Look for such adverbs of frequency as *always, often, generally, frequently,* or *usually.*

Adverbs of frequency are often used in sentences that describe habitual or repeated actions — typically a sign of a generalization. Notice that both of the example sentences use adverbs of frequency.

EXAMPLE 1: ✗ The barn is always full of some cats.

TIP APPLIED: The barn is always full of ~~some~~ cats.

EXAMPLE 2: ✗ Our family usually has the fish for dinner on Fridays.

TIP APPLIED: Our family usually has ~~the~~ fish for dinner on Fridays.

Lesson 34

art
ESL

> **PRESENT TENSE TIP:** Sentences used for making generalizations are often written in the present tense.

Writers usually use the present tense to make generalizations (see Lesson 9: Present, Past, and Tense Shifting), so be especially sure to check non-count nouns and plural count nouns in sentences that use the present tense to see whether these nouns are being used to make generalizations. Notice, for instance, that both of the example sentences are in the present tense.

> ***MOST* TIP:** A noun that can be modified by the word *most* is probably being used to make a generalization.

For example, you can modify the noun in the sentence *Textbooks have really gotten to be expensive* with the word *most* to confirm that you are using *textbooks* as a generalization. *Textbooks*, therefore, should be used without any article.

> TIP APPLIED: **Most textbooks have really gotten to be expensive.**

> **NO-MODIFIERS TIP:** A noun used for making a generalization is not usually restricted by any modifiers that follow the noun.

Modifiers after a noun usually restrict the meaning of the noun so that it is not a generalization.

Compare the following two sentences:

> NO MODIFIER AFTER THE NOUN: **Cheese is very salty.**

> MODIFIER AFTER THE NOUN: **The cheese in the refrigerator is very salty.**

The first sentence is an unrestricted generalization about all cheese; therefore, you do not use an article. The second sentence is talking only about the cheese that is in the refrigerator. Since you are referring to a particular piece of cheese, you must use the definite article *the* in this sentence.

Lesson 34

art
ESL

Sentence Practice 1

CORRECTED SENTENCES APPEAR ON PAGE 503.

In the following sentences, underline any noncount nouns and plural count nouns that are used for making generalizations. Cross out any articles incorrectly used with these nouns. Assume that there is no previous context that these sentences refer to.

> EXAMPLE: ~~The~~ <u>sticks and stones</u> may break my bones, but ~~the~~ <u>words</u> will never hurt me. [traditional saying]

1. Most countries tax the cigarettes and the alcohol heavily.

2. During a heavy storm, the streams often are blocked by the leaves and the other trash.

3. Typically, the employers look for the skilled and trained workers.

4. The researchers have found that the American diets contain the excess fats.

5. The detergents work by making the water super wet.

 For more practice using nouns, go to **Exercise Central** at **bedfordstmartins.com/commonsense/10-34**.

Sentence Practice 2

CORRECTED SENTENCES APPEAR ON PAGE 503.

In the following sentences, underline any noncount nouns and plural count nouns that are used for making generalizations. Cross out any articles incorrectly used with these nouns. Assume that there is no previous context that these sentences refer to.

> EXAMPLE: ~~The~~ <u>fools</u> and their money are soon parted. [traditional saying]

1. The substitutions in the recipes often lead to the disasters.

2. The global warming is becoming a common topic in the academic conferences.

Lesson 34

art
ESL

3. Increasingly, the tourism is an important source for the national budgets.

4. The classical painting is normally divided into the landscapes, the still lifes, and the portraits.

5. In America, unlike the many countries, you can usually get the prescriptions filled at the grocery stores.

Sentence Practice 3

Combine the following sentences by adding the underlined information in the second sentence to the underlined noun in the first sentence. The added modification restricts the noun so that it is no longer a generalization. Make the necessary changes in articles.

> EXAMPLE: **Pianos** are pretty expensive.
> They are **used in public performances**.
>
> ANSWER: **The pianos used in public performances** are pretty expensive.

1. Seniors are excused from class.
    They are in the school play.

2. Clouds were threatening rain.
    They were in the west.

3. Disputes are hard to resolve.
    They were involved in property rights cases.

4. Tea comes from Japan.
    They serve in this restaurant.

5. Malls are now too small.
    They were built in the '70's and '80's.

Lesson 34

art
ESL

Editing Practice 1

CORRECTED SENTENCES APPEAR ON PAGE 503.

Correct all errors in the following paragraph using the first correction as a model. The number in parentheses at the end of the paragraph indicates how many errors you should find.

The history of ~~the~~ furniture reflects the history of the culture. Relatively little is known about the furniture of the ancient societies, simply because furniture is usually made of the perishable materials — wood and sometimes fabric — that have not survived. Our limited knowledge of Egyptian, Greek, and Roman furniture is based mostly on the paintings and the sculptures. The only actual surviving pieces of furniture are from the burials. For example, King Tut's tomb in Egypt contained piles of elegantly decorated royal furniture. About the only surviving examples of everyday Roman furniture are from the two cities near Naples that were buried under the tons of volcanic ash from the eruption of Mt. Vesuvius on August 24, 79 A.D. (8)

Editing Practice 2

CORRECTED SENTENCES APPEAR ON PAGE 503.

Correct all errors in the following paragraphs using the first correction as a model. The number in parentheses at the end of each paragraph indicates how many errors you should find.

The American linguist Deborah Tannen is best known for her books about the differences in the language of ~~the~~ men and women. Her books show that the men tend to use language in a very competitive way. For example, the conversations among a group of men are marked by some competition to be the center of the attention. (3)

Women tend to be careful about taking the turns in the conversations. Even in the animated conversations, the interruptions tend to be supportive rather than confrontational. (3)

Lesson 34

art
ESL

Editing Practice 3

Correct all errors in the following paragraphs using the first correction as a model. The number in parentheses at the end of each paragraph indicates how many errors you should find.

Dr. Tannen maintains that ~~the~~ conversational styles are generally the result of the way that children grow up. The little boys and little girls have the very different forms of the social interaction. The different conversational styles that they learn to use are a natural result of their different social needs. For example, until the puberty, the sexes are largely self-segregated—boys play with boys, and girls play with girls. The nature of their play is quite different. Boys' play is based on the competition. Girls' play is much more cooperative and democratic. (5)

Dr. Tannen believes that neither form of the conversation is superior to the other. However, there are often some big problems when the men and women talk to each other, because each group assumes that the other group plays by the same rules that it does—but the other group doesn't! (2)

Writing Practice

On a separate sheet of paper, write a paragraph or two generalizing the differences in male and female language that you have observed. If you come from another country, do you think that Dr. Tannen's observations about Americans' conversational styles can be applied to your country? Use the Editing Checklist to identify every noncount noun and plural count noun in your short essay and see whether they are used for making generalizations. Correct any errors you might have made.

Editing Checklist

Identify Errors in Using Articles in Your Writing

_____ Whenever you use a noncount noun or a plural count noun, be sure to check to see whether you are using that noun to make a generalization. You can check by using one or more of the tips presented in this chapter.

Correct Errors in Using Articles in Your Writing

_____ If you are using a noncount noun or a plural count noun to make a generalization, do not use an article with that noun.

The Bottom Line	Noncount and plural count **nouns** that are used to make a *generalization* do not need *articles*.

UNIT TEN ESL:
Choosing the Right Article

Every time you use a common noun, you must decide whether or not you need to use an article; if you do need to use an article, you must choose which one it should be. Your choice should be governed by four decisions:

- Decision 1: *Generalization?* Is the noun (whether a noncount noun or a plural count noun) being used to make a generalization (see Lesson 34)? If the answer is yes, use *no* article at all. If the answer is no, then you must make the following decision.

- Decision 2: *Known or New?* Is your intended meaning of the noun "known" to the reader or is it "new" (see Lesson 33)? If the intended meaning is known to the reader, use the definite article *the*. If the meaning will be new, use an indefinite article: *a, an,* or *some.* The choice of indefinite article is determined by the next two decisions.

- Decision 3: *Plural or Singular?* If the new noun is plural, then you must use *some.* If the new noun is singular, then you must decide whether it is a count or a noncount noun. That brings you to the final decision.

- Decision 4: *Count or Noncount?* If the singular noun is a count noun, then you must use the indefinite article *a.* If the singular noun is a noncount noun, use *some* (see Lesson 32).

Use one or more of these tips to help you make Decision 1:

ADVERB-OF-FREQUENCY TIP: Look for such adverbs of frequency as *always, often, generally, frequently,* or *usually.*

PRESENT TENSE TIP: Sentences used for making generalizations are often written in the present tense.

MOST TIP: A noun that can be modified by the word *most* is probably being used to make a generalization.

NO-MODIFIERS TIP: A noun used for making a generalization is not usually restricted by any modifiers that follow the noun.

Use one or more of these tips to help you make Decision 2:

PREVIOUS-MENTION TIP: Use the definite article if you have already mentioned the noun.

DEFINED-BY-MODIFIERS TIP: Use the definite article if the noun is followed by modifiers that uniquely identify the noun.

NORMAL-EXPECTATIONS TIP: Use the definite article if the noun meets our normal expectations about the way things work.

UNIQUENESS TIP: Use the definite article if the noun has a uniqueness that everybody would be expected to know about.

Use these tips to help you make Decisions 3 and 4:

PLURAL TIP: The easiest way to test whether a word is a noncount noun is to make the noun plural. If the plural of the word is not grammatical or does not make sense in the context of the sentence, then the word is a noncount noun. (Note that when the tested noun is a subject, the verb will change to agree with it.)

GENERALIZATION TIP: A noun used to make a generalization — especially if the noun refers to an abstraction — is often a noncount noun.

Unit Ten

review
ESL

Use a decision tree to help you choose the right article

This *decision tree* maps out a process for choosing the right article for each common noun in your writing. Using this tool, you can proceed step-by-step from Decision 1 to Decision 4.

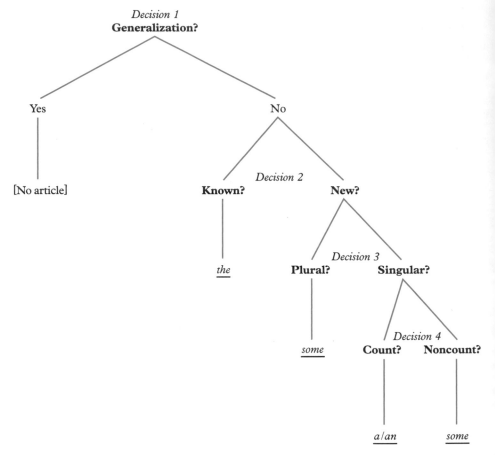

Review Test

The *decision tree* on page 352 shows you how these four sets of decisions flow step by step from Decision 1 to Decision 4. Use the decision tree to edit the following paragraphs for correct use of articles. The number in parentheses at the end of each paragraph indicates how many errors you should find.

Some cellular phones can certainly come in handy in a emergency. If the driver witnesses an accident or is involved in an accident, he or she can call a State Police without having to waste crucial time. In the event of the flat tire or dead battery, a driver can call tow truck without having to walk a mile or two— or more—to a phone. Wireless technology has allowed the family members to reach loved ones in an emergency, even if the person whom they are trying to reach is at the business meeting or a baseball game. (8)

For me, a beauty of having the cell phone is being able to maximize my time. I like having a flexibility to make the important phone calls either when I'm home or as I'm driving home. (4)

UNIT ELEVEN ESL
Using Verbs Correctly

Terms That Can Help You Understand Verbs

If you are not familiar with any of the following terms that appear in this unit, look them up in the Guide to Grammar Terminology beginning on page 1. The numbers in parentheses indicate the lessons in which each term appears.

adjective (36)	past participle (36)
adverb (37)	phrasal verb (37)
future progressive (35)	present participle (35, 36)
helping verb (35)	preposition (37)
information question (38)	progressive tense (35)
inseparable phrasal verb (37)	separable phrasal verb (37)
noun clause (39)	verb (35, 36, 37, 38, 39)
participle (35, 36)	

The Nuts and Bolts of Verbs

ESL

All of the lessons in this unit deal with various aspects of **verb** use that are likely to be troublesome for non-native speakers. The first lesson deals with use of the **progressive tense**. The second lesson deals with the way **present** and **past participle** verb forms can be used to form **adjectives**. The third lesson deals with **phrasal verbs**, two-word verbs whose meanings are often idiomatic and unpredictable. The last two lessons discuss related problems of verb word order in **information questions** and **noun clauses**.

Unit Eleven

overview
ESL

Lesson 35 shows you how to use the **progressive tenses**, which are made with the helping verb *be* (in some form) followed by a verb in the **present participle** form (*-ing*). If you use a present tense form of *be* (*am, is, are*), you create a **present progressive** verb (*Rina **is watching** TV now*). If you use the past tense forms *was* or *were*, you create a **past progressive** verb (*Rina **was watching** TV when you called*). If you use *will be*, you create a **future**

354

progressive verb (*Rina **will be watching** TV later*). Some writers do not use the progressive tense when they should, or use it when they shouldn't. Others mistakenly use the progressive tense with certain verbs that do not allow the use of progressive tenses. Here is an example of the first kind of mistake.

EXAMPLE: Dr. Hernandez can't see you right now. ✗ She sees another patient.

CORRECTION: Dr. Hernandez can't see you right now. She ~~sees~~ *is seeing* another patient.

Lesson 36 shows you how to use present and past participles as adjectives. When these two types of participles are used as adjectives, they mean very different things. For example, there is a world of difference between *a **boring** teacher* (the teacher bores the students) and *a **bored** teacher* (the students bore the teacher). This lesson will show you how to decide which participle to use as an adjective.

EXAMPLE: ✗ The movie we saw had a surprised ending.

CORRECTION: The movie we saw had a ~~surprised~~ *surprising* ending.

Lesson 37 shows you how to use phrasal verbs. **Phrasal verbs** are compounds (often with idiomatic meanings) made from verb + adverb or verb + preposition combinations. When a phrasal verb is made with an adverb, it is called a **separable** phrasal verb because the adverb can be separated from the verb. That is, it can be moved after the object (*Jamie **looked up** the word* / *Jamie **looked** the word **up***). When the compound is made with a preposition, it is called an **inseparable** phrasal verb because the preposition can never be moved away from the verb (*Ben **depended on** Maria* / ✗ *Ben **depended** Maria **on***). Sometimes writers confuse the two types of phrasal verbs and don't move adverbs when they should, or they move prepositions when they shouldn't.

EXAMPLE: ✗ I didn't know her phone number, so I looked up it.

CORRECTION: I didn't know her phone number, so I ~~looked up it~~ *looked it up*.

Lesson 38 shows you how to check for the proper word order in **information questions**. Information questions are questions that begin with words that require a detailed response like *who, where,* and *why* (as opposed

Unit Eleven

overview
ESL

to simple questions that can be answered with *yes* or *no*). Sometimes non-native speakers fail to invert the helping verb and the subject word when forming information questions.

EXAMPLE: ✗ Where you want to go after class?

                  did you want
CORRECTION: Where ~~you want~~ to go after class?

Lesson 39 shows you how you can avoid the reverse mistake of inverting the helping verb and the subject, which is appropriate for information questions, when you are creating certain types of **noun clauses**.

EXAMPLE: ✗ We found out where should we go after class.

                          we should go
CORRECTION: We found out where ~~should we go~~ after class.

Can you detect problems with verbs?

CORRECTED SENTENCES APPEAR ON PAGE 503.

Correct all errors in the following paragraph using the first correction as a model. The number in parentheses at the end of the paragraph indicates how many errors you should find.

                the most photographed city in the world is
Do you know what ~~is the most often photographed city in the world~~? It is Venice. Venice is being one of the most unusual cities in the world. This fascinated city is built on thousands of small muddy islands in a marshy lagoon. Why anybody would choose to live on these swampy, mosquito-infesting islands? Nobody sought out them for their ocean views. The first settlers in the lagoon were refugees from the Italian mainland, fleeing Attila the Hun after the fall of Rome. What did the islands give them was protection from anyone not intimately familiar with the area. The lagoon is filled with mud banks that are invisible in

the muddy water even at high tide. Unless you are knowing exactly where are the channels, it is impossible to navigate through them. The early settlers marked the channels with poles, and when they were threatened by invaders, they simply pulled up them. When the invaders' fleets got stuck on mud banks, the settlers would attack the invaders' stranded boats one at a time and completely wipe out them. (10)

Unit Eleven

overview
ESL

LESSON 35

The Progressive Tenses

Error Sentences

CORRECTED SENTENCES APPEAR ON PAGES 360–61.

> EXAMPLE 1: I can't talk to you right now. ✗ I study for my exams.
>
> EXAMPLE 2: ✗ I am knowing the answer.
>
> EXAMPLE 3: ✗ Ms. Higa was owning a house in the country last year.

What's the Problem?

The **progressive tenses** are formed by using some form of the helping verb *be* with a **present participle** (a verb form ending in *-ing*). These tenses are used to indicate continuous activity.

The tense is *present progressive* when the helping verb *be* is in one of its three present tense forms (*am, are, is*); for example: *I am smiling; They are smiling; She is smiling.*

The tense is *past progressive* when the helping verb *be* is in one of its two past tense forms (*was, were*); for example: *He was smiling; They were smiling.*

The tense is *future progressive* when the helping verb *be* is used with *will;* for example: *They will be smiling.*

There are two sources of mistakes in using the progressive tense. The first one is using the present tense when the progressive tense is called for, as in Example 1. The second one is using the progressive tense with certain English verbs that do not have a progressive form. We call these *steady-state verbs. Know* and *own* in Examples 2 and 3 are both this type of verb.

What Causes the Problem?

Most verbs cannot be used in the present tense without sounding stilted or even ungrammatical *unless* they are used to make "timeless" statements (see Lesson 9). To describe an action that is ongoing at some moment in time, writers use the present, the past, or the future progressive, as appropriate.

However, some writers, especially those who are not native speakers of English, may not know how to form the progressive tenses or which verbs can and cannot be made progressive.

Diagnostic Exercise

CORRECTED SENTENCES APPEAR ON PAGE 504.

Correct all errors in the following paragraph using the first correction as a model. The number in parentheses at the end of the paragraph indicates how many errors you should find.

Every weekday morning at 6 A.M., my alarm is going *goes* off. By 6:15, the breakfast dishes are on the table, and the coffee brews. I always am getting the children up next. It is very hard for them to get going. On Mondays, they are resembling bears coming out of hibernation. While they take their showers with their eyes still closed, I get everyone's clothes ready. Since the youngest child still is needing a lot of help getting dressed, I usually am spending some extra time with her talking about the day's events. By 7 A.M., we all sit at the table for breakfast. The children are loving pancakes and waffles, but there just isn't time to make them except on weekends. Breakfast goes by quickly, unless somebody is spilling the milk or juice. I am wishing we had more time in the morning, but every morning I am being amazed when I am looking back and realizing that we got it all done again. (13)

Fixing This Problem in Your Writing

The basic function of the progressive tenses is to signal an action or a condition that is in *progress* (as the name of the tense indicates) at some point in time or over some period of time. Since the action in progressive sentences is linked to some point or period of time, it communicates a sense of being temporary. This temporariness is particularly important in distinguishing

Lesson 35

vt
ESL

between the "timeless" nature of the present tense and the "temporary" nature of the present progressive.

For example, compare the following two sentences:

PRESENT: I <u>live</u> in Santa Cruz.

PRESENT
PROGRESSIVE: I <u>am living</u> in Santa Cruz.

Both sentences are grammatical, but they mean slightly different things. In the first sentence, the present tense implies that the writer is a permanent resident of Santa Cruz, while in the second sentence, the present progressive implies that the writer is only there "for now"—in other words, that the writer is there only temporarily. Here is a tip to help you remember when to use a progressive tense:

> **PROGRESSIVE TENSE TIP:** Use the progressive tense when you are describing an event that is taking place at a particular moment, either now (present progressive), during some past moment (past progressive), or during some future moment (future progressive).

Here, the Progressive Tense Tip is applied to Example 1.

EXAMPLE 1:   I can't talk to you right now. ✗ I study for my exams.

TIP APPLIED: I can't talk to you right now. I ~~study~~ *am studying* for my exams.

In this example, the present progressive indicates that the action (*studying*) is ongoing at the present moment.

Consider two additional examples:

EXAMPLE: Sorry I couldn't talk to you last night. I <u>was studying</u> for my exams.

In this example, the past progressive indicates that the action was ongoing at a particular moment of time in the past (*last night,* in this case).

EXAMPLE: I can't meet you for dinner tonight. I <u>will be studying</u> for my exams.

In this example, the future progressive indicates that the action will be ongoing at a particular moment of time in the future (*tonight,* in this case).

Because the progressive tenses indicate action that is temporary in nature, the use of the progressive tenses is incompatible with certain steady-state verbs whose meaning implies a continuous condition or state.

Lesson 35

vt
ESL

> **STEADY-STATE VERB TIP:** Verbs that refer to unchanging, steady-state conditions are incompatible with the progressive tenses. These verbs tend to fall into certain broad categories: mental activity, emotional condition, and possession.

Steady-state verbs tend to fall into three broad categories:

- **Mental activity:** *believe, doubt, forget, imagine, know, mean*
- **Emotional condition:** *appreciate, care, dislike, envy, fear, hate, like, love, need, prefer, want*
- **Possession:** *belong, contain, consist of, own, possess*

This list is far from complete. Moreover, many verbs are incompatible with the progressive tenses in some meanings but not in others. For example, verbs of perception cannot be used in the progressive when they describe something (✗ *The soup is tasting salty*), but they can be used in the progressive when a subject performs the action of the verb (*The cook is tasting the soup to see whether it is ready to serve*).

In Examples 2 and 3, steady-state verbs are incorrectly used in the progressive tenses.

EXAMPLE 2:   ✗ I am knowing the answer.

TIP APPLIED: I ~~am knowing~~ *know* the answer.

When a person knows the answer to a question, that knowledge is not tied to just a specific moment in time; a person does not know something one minute and then not know it the next. Taking the verb out of its progressive form makes the sentence grammatical as a simple statement of fact.

EXAMPLE 3:   ✗ Ms. Higa was owning a house in the country last year.

TIP APPLIED: Ms. Higa ~~was owning~~ *owned* a house in the country last year.

The verb *own* is incompatible with the progressive tenses. The verb *own* implies that ownership is not limited to a set period of time. Even though we can assume that Ms. Higa no longer owns the house now, her right of ownership *when she owned the house* was not temporary. Taking the verb out of its progressive form makes the sentence grammatical as a statement about the past.

Lesson 35

vt
ESL

Sentence Practice 1

CORRECTED SENTENCES APPEAR ON PAGE 504.

The following sentences contain verbs in their dictionary form (underlined). Above each underlined verb, write the correct form of the verb using either the present tense, the past tense, or one of the three progressive tenses, as appropriate.

EXAMPLE: I couldn't hear you. The TV *was playing* play too loudly.

1.   Hurry up! The train <u>leave</u> now.

2.   I couldn't come to the phone because we <u>eat</u> dinner when you called.

3.   Disco <u>be</u> still wildly popular in some places in Europe.

4.   The book <u>belong</u> to one of my friends.

5.   The book <u>be</u> used by one of my friends at the moment.

> For more practice with verb tense, go to **Exercise Central** at
> **bedfordstmartins.com/commonsense/11-35**.

Sentence Practice 2

CORRECTED SENTENCES APPEAR ON PAGE 504.

The following sentences contain verbs in their dictionary form (underlined). Above each underlined verb, write the correct form of the verb using either the present tense, the past tense, or one of the three progressive tenses, as appropriate.

EXAMPLE: During the whole exam, somebody *was coughing* <u>cough</u> his head off.

Lesson 35

vt
ESL

1.   By this time next year, I <u>work</u> in New York.

2.   As of now, that <u>seem</u> to be the best alternative.

3.   My roommate always <u>hate</u> to get up in the morning.

4. She <u>run</u> an errand right now, but she will be back in just a minute.

5. Hi! I <u>return</u> your phone call.

Sentence Practice 3

Combine the following sentences by adding the underlined information in the second sentence to the first sentence. Change the past tense of the first sentence to the appropriate progressive tense.

> EXAMPLE: I flew to Chicago.
> It will be <u>this time tomorrow</u>.

> ANSWER: I <u>will be flying</u> to Chicago this time tomorrow.

1. I'm sorry. She met with another client.
    It is <u>now</u>.

2. She met with another client.
    It was <u>when you called</u>.

3. We painted the garage.
    We did it <u>when the rain storm hit</u>.

4. I slept soundly.
    I did it <u>when the alarm went off</u>.

5. I took my last exam.
    It will happen <u>when you get here</u>.

Editing Practice 1

CORRECTED SENTENCES APPEAR ON PAGE 504.

Correct all errors in the following paragraphs using the first correction as a model. The number in parentheses at the end of each paragraph indicates how many errors you should find.

> *know*
> You all ~~are knowing~~ the old joke that research is showing that

the amount of sleep that we are needing is always five minutes more.

I am never using the snooze button on my alarm clock because I am hitting it without actually waking up. In fact, I am finding that I must put my clock clear across the room so that I am being forced to actually get out of bed to turn it off. (6)

I am not a morning person, to put it mildly. I am hating getting up, and I am being nauseated by the thought of breakfast. Since I am so dopey in the mornings, I have learned to be methodical. While the water warms up in the shower, I set my clothes out. I fix two pieces of toast while I make the coffee. As I leave for the office, I grab the morning paper to read on the bus while I ride to work. When I finally do get to work, I am almost resembling a normal person. (7)

Editing Practice 2

CORRECTED SENTENCES APPEAR ON PAGE 504.

Correct all errors in the following paragraphs using the first correction as a model. The number in parentheses at the end of each paragraph indicates how many errors you should find.

This year, both my husband and I *~~go~~* *are going* to school in programs that are requiring a lot of writing. We are both pretty good writers and are tending to get good grades on our papers. However, we are going about the process of writing in completely different ways. He is compulsive about how he writes his papers. First, he is brainstorming the topic and grouping all his thoughts into clusters. From the clusters, he makes a list of topics that he is wanting to include in his paper. Then, he writes draft after draft until he gets it right. (6)

I am completely the opposite. I am thinking that I would go crazy if I wrote the way my husband does. I am spending just as much time on my papers as he does, but I write in a completely different way. I am spending my time thinking about my papers before I ever write a word. I write my papers in my head. When I am feeling that I know what I want to say, I sit down and write a complete draft. I am needing to go over this draft for mechanical errors and punctuation, but I rarely make any big changes. (5)

Editing Practice 3

Correct all errors in the following paragraphs using the first correction as a model. The number in parentheses at the end of each paragraph indicates how many errors you should find.

I really enjoy cooking. Even though it is something that we

need

~~are needing~~ to do every day, I find it very relaxing. I am liking
^

to cook Italian food. When I was living in Italy, I was loving eating in restaurants. In Italy, people are going out to restaurants to try foods from different regions in Italy. Soon I was knowing something about the different regional dishes. I was appreciating most the importance of fresh ingredients. (5)

In my own cooking, I am liking to keep things relatively simple. Also, since I am trying to eat a low-fat diet, I am not liking the creamy dishes of northern Italy. Instead, I am preferring to cook the country dishes from the south, especially the ones that are having a lot of vegetables. The only problem that I have with these recipes is that they are using a lot of cheese. And, much as I am loving cheese, its fat content makes it a killer. (5)

Lesson 35

vt
ESL

Writing Practice

On your own paper, write about some process that is familiar to you, such as your morning routine, your writing process, or how you cook. Use the Editing Checklist below to make sure that you have used the present and progressive tenses correctly.

Editing Checklist

Identify Errors in Using the Progressive Tenses

____ Identify the verb in your sentence.

____ Ask yourself whether you are describing continuous or ongoing activity in your sentence.

____ Check your verb to see whether it expresses a continuous condition or state.

Correct Errors in Using the Progressive Tenses

____ If you are describing some action that is ongoing at the current moment, use the present progressive tense (present tense of *be* + a verb ending in *-ing*)

____ If you are describing some action that was ongoing at a particular moment in the past, use the past progressive tense (past tense of *be* + a verb ending in *-ing*)

____ If you are describing some action that will be ongoing at a particular moment in the future, use the future progressive tense (*will* + *be* + a verb ending in *-ing*)

____ Change all steady-state verbs to present or past tense.

Lesson 35

vt
ESL

The Bottom Line

Use the progressive tenses only for events that **are taking** place at a particular moment or period of time.

LESSON 36
Using Participles as Adjectives

ESL

Error Sentences

CORRECTED SENTENCES APPEAR ON PAGE 369.

EXAMPLE 1: ✗ The movie was about a frightened old house.

EXAMPLE 2: ✗ After the three-hour exam, there was a break for the exhausting students.

What's the Problem?

A **participle** is a verb used as an **adjective**, a word that modifies (describes or gives more information about) a noun. There are two routes by which most verbs can be turned into adjectives:

- Verbal adjectives that end in -*ing* are called **present participles**.

- Verbal adjectives that end in -*ed* are called **past participles**. (A relatively small number of verbs have irregular past participle forms.)

The problem is that the two different types of participles mean completely different things. In Examples 1 and 2, the writer has used the wrong participle. As a result, the meaning in each of these sentences is unclear.

What Causes the Problem?

Every participle comes from a verb. In using a participle to modify a noun, a writer is making a statement about the relationship of the noun to that underlying verb. That noun is either the subject of the underlying verb or the object of the underlying verb. For example, the present participle phrase *a boring teacher* means that the teacher (subject) is boring the students; however, the past participle phrase *a bored teacher* means just the opposite—that the students are boring the teacher (object).

Writers who are not careful to work out the correct relationship between the noun and the verb underlying the participle may use the wrong participle to express the intended meaning.

Lesson 36

vf
ESL

367

As this *bored/boring* example shows, you may be able to write a grammatical sentence using either the past participle form or the present participle form of the verb, but the *meaning* of the sentence will depend on which one you choose.

Diagnostic Exercise

CORRECTED SENTENCES APPEAR ON PAGE 504.

Correct all errors in the following paragraph using the first correction as a model. The number in parentheses at the end of the paragraph indicates how many errors you should find.

       The Smithsonian Institution is an ~~amazed~~ *amazing* system of museums and art galleries in Washington, D.C. The Smithsonian is a requiring stop for every concerning visitor to Washington. Recently, I spent a fascinated day at the National Museum of Natural History. The only problem is that there is so much to see that the overwhelming visitors find themselves frantically rushing from one interested exhibit to another without taking the time to understand all the information in the exhibits. One solution to this frustrated problem is to take a tour. The guide points out important highlights of the show. (6)

Fixing This Problem in Your Writing

To find out whether you have used the right participle, examine the relationship between the participle and the noun it modifies. The easiest way to do this is to change the participle back into its underlying verb form; see what role—subject or object—the noun plays, and then, choose the participle form accordingly.

Lesson 36

vf
ESL

> **SUBJECT TIP:** Use the present participle form (*-ing*) if the noun being modified plays the role of the subject of the verb underlying the participle.

Now apply this tip to Example 1:

EXAMPLE 1: ✗ The movie was about a frightened old house.

Once you have identified the underlying verb (*frighten*), ask yourself this question: Is *house* the subject of *frighten*? Can old houses frighten people? Clearly, the answer is yes, they can. Now ask yourself the opposite question with *house* as the object of *frighten:* Can people frighten an old house? No, they can't, so *house* can't be the object of *frighten.*

TIP APPLIED: The movie was about a ~~frightened~~ old house.
                                              frightening
                                              ^

Here is another tip that will help you choose the correct participle form for your meaning:

> **OBJECT TIP:** Use the past participle form (*-ed*) if the noun being modified plays the role of the object of the verb underlying the participle.

Now apply this tip to Example 2:

EXAMPLE 2: ✗ After the three-hour exam, there was a break for the exhausting students.

Once you have identified the underlying verb (*exhaust*), ask yourself this question: Did something exhaust the students? Or were the students exhausting something? Clearly, a yes answer to the first question, in which *students* is the object, makes more sense. When the noun being modified is the object, then you must use the *-ed* past participle.

TIP APPLIED: After the three-hour exam, there was a break for the
             exhausted
             ~~exhausting~~ students.
             ^

Let's apply these two tips to the following sentence:

EXAMPLE: ✗ After their thrilled ride through the rapids, the exhausting rafters rested for a while in calmer water.

Thrilled ride is incorrect because *ride* is the subject of the verb *thrill* (*The ride thrilled the rafters*); it is not the object (✗ *The rafters thrilled the ride*). You must use the present participle *-ing: thrilling ride.*

Likewise, *exhausting rafters* is incorrect because *rafters* is the object of the underlying verb *exhaust* (*The ride exhausted the rafters*); it is not the subject (✗ *The rafters exhausted the ride*).

You must use the past participle *-ed: exhausted rafters.*

CORRECTION: After their ~~thrilled~~ *thrilling* ride through the rapids, the ^
exhausted
~~exhausting~~ rafters rested for a while in calmer water.
^

Sentence Practice 1

CORRECTED SENTENCES APPEAR ON PAGE 505.

The following sentences contain underlined participles. If the participle is wrong, replace it with the correct one. If the participle is correct, write *OK* above it. Confirm correct answers by turning the participle into a verb and using the noun as a subject or an object, as appropriate.

People deserted the gloomy factory building.

EXAMPLE: The movie was set in a gloomy ~~deserting~~ *deserted* factory building.   ^

1. The speaker ignored the <u>interrupted</u> noises.

2. The new bridge was an <u>amazing</u> structure.

3. The riders struggled to keep their balance on the <u>rocked</u> train.

4. He grinned and proudly waved his newly <u>stamping</u> passport.

5. Be sure you take just the <u>prescribing</u> dose of the medicine.

> For more practice using participles, go to **Exercise Central** at
> **bedfordstmartins.com/commonsense/11-36**.

Lesson 36

vf
ESL

Sentence Practice 2

CORRECTED SENTENCES APPEAR ON PAGE 505.

The following sentences contain underlined participles. If the participle is wrong, replace it with the correct one. Confirm correct answers by turning the participle into a verb and using the noun as a subject or object, as appropriate.

> *The tide advanced.*
>
> EXAMPLE: Our sandcastles were soon washed away by the ~~advanced~~ *advancing*
> tide.   ^

1. It was a very <u>alarmed</u> experience.

2. We walked carefully beside the newly <u>plowing</u> fields.

3. I was lucky to get by with nothing worse than a <u>scraped</u> knee and some bruises.

4. It was a very <u>tempted</u> offer.

5. We began classifying the <u>cataloging</u> samples.

Sentence Practice 3

Combine the following sentences by adding the correct participle form of the verb in parentheses in the second sentence to the underlined noun in the first sentence.

> EXAMPLE: The teachers took pity on the <u>students</u>.
> The students were (shiver).
>
> ANSWER: The teachers took pity on the shivering students.

1. Sherlock Holmes examined the <u>body</u> carefully.
   The body was (disfigure).

2. Fold the <u>pieces</u>.
   The pieces were (trim).

3. The Russians quickly followed Napoleon's <u>army</u>.
   The army was (retreat).

4. I held my hands over my <u>ears</u>.
   My ears were (ring).

5. We were told to stay away from all <u>areas</u>.
   The areas were (restrict).

Lesson 36

vf
ESL

Editing Practice 1

CORRECTED SENTENCES APPEAR ON PAGE 505.

Correct all errors in the following paragraphs using the first correction as a model. The number in parentheses at the end of each paragraph indicates how many errors you should find.

           conflicting

I have quite ~~conflicted~~ feelings about the National Museum of Natural History. On the one hand, it is in a depressed building. Even a casual visitor can't help noticing the water-staining walls and crumbled plaster in the remote hallways. Clearly, a penny-pinched Congress has not adequately provided the museum with the needing funds. One recent report said that repairing storm-damaging roofs alone would absorb the whole maintenance budget for the year. (6)

On the other hand, the new exhibits are lively and colorful. We can only hope that in these difficult times, Congress can develop a balancing plan that maintains the old building and provides for excited new exhibits. (2)

Editing Practice 2

CORRECTED SENTENCES APPEAR ON PAGE 505.

Correct all errors in the following paragraph using the first correction as a model. The number in parentheses at the end of the paragraph indicates how many errors you should find.

                          amazing

One of the things that strikes visitors to Hawaii is the ~~amazed~~ variation in climate. Waikiki Beach, for example, has only about 20 inches of rain a year. Without irrigation, Waikiki would be a dusty plain, as it was shown in photographs from missionary times. However, Manoa Valley, the valley behind the beach, has gradually increased amounts of rainfall until, at the back of the valley, less than 10 miles

from Waikiki Beach, there is an astonished 130 inches a year. Another

interested fact about the valleys in Hawaii is that, despite the

astonished rainfall at the backs of the valleys, there are only a few

rivers. The reason for this surprised fact is that the volcanic soil is

remarkably porous. The rain is absorbed into the ground before it

can run off. In most places in the world, such overwhelmed rain could

not be held by the saturating soil and would create streams and rivers

to carry off the excess water. (7)

Editing Practice 3

Correct all errors in the following paragraphs using the first correction as a model. The number in parentheses at the end of each paragraph indicates how many errors you should find.

                                      undisputed
Milan has become Italy's ~~undisputing~~ financial capital. Despite
                                     ^

its central role in modern Italy, Milan is not a recognizing tourist

destination comparable to Venice, Rome, or Florence. Milan is not a

well-preserving Renaissance city; it is a modern industrializing city

that seems more German than Mediterranean. (3)

    Milan does have one undisputing claim to fame: Leonardo da Vinci's

Last Supper. The painting is in an otherwise undistinguishing building

attached to the church of Santa Maria delle Grazie. There are several

astonished features about the painting. First is its surprised size: it covers

the entire end of the building. Second, it incorporates existed features

of the building. For example, the beams that support the building appear

to continue right into the creating room in the painting. (6)

Writing Practice

On your own paper, write about a visit to a museum or other famous place and your reactions to it. Use as many present and past participles as you can. Then, use the Editing Checklist to show that your use of present and past participles is correct.

Editing Checklist

Identify Errors in Using Participles in Your Writing

____ Identify any participles in your writing. Look for words ending in *-ing* or *-ed* that modify (describe or give more information about) nouns.

____ Identify the underlying verb for each participle.

Correct Errors in Using Participles in Your Writing

____ Use the *-ing* present participle if the noun being modified is the *subject* that is doing the action of the underlying verb.

____ Use the *-ed* past participle when the noun being modified is the *object* of the underlying verb.

The Bottom Line

Use -ing if the noun **being** modified serves as the subject. Use -ed if the noun being **modified** serves as the object.

LESSON 37
Phrasal Verbs

ESL

[Note: See pages 467–69 for a glossary of one hundred of the most frequently used phrasal verbs.]

Error Sentences

CORRECTED SENTENCES APPEAR ON PAGE 378.

> EXAMPLE 1: ✗ Roland called up her.

> EXAMPLE 2: ✗ Misako turned down him.

What's the Problem?

Some verbs in English combine with an adverb or a preposition to form a **phrasal verb**. These two-word verbs can be troublesome for some writers because their meanings are often idiomatic. In other words, it is difficult to predict the meaning of the expression based on the meanings of the individual words. Consider these phrasal verbs: *turn down* (verb + adverb) and *turn against* (verb + preposition).

> EXAMPLE: The prince **turned down** the king.
> (*turned down* = rejected)

> EXAMPLE: The prince **turned against** the king.
> (*turned against* = became an enemy of)

Because they are unpredictable, all phrasal verbs pose considerable problems (especially for non-native speakers of English), but the ones formed with adverbs pose an additional grammatical problem. When a phrasal verb + adverb is followed by an object *noun,* the adverb can be moved from its position after the verb to one after the object noun. For example,

> The prince **turned** the king **down**.

Since the adverb can be separated from the verb, this type of phrasal verb is often called **separable**. When the object following the adverb is a *pronoun,* instead of a noun, the adverb MUST be moved:

> The prince **turned** him **down**.

Lesson 37

vf
ESL

375

Failure to move the adverb makes the sentence ungrammatical (✗ *The prince turned down him*). This is the error in both example sentences.

Phrasal verbs with prepositions are **inseparable**. Prepositions must always come before their objects. They can never be moved.

What Causes the Problem?

The problem is that separable and inseparable phrasal verbs look so much alike, it is hard to tell them apart, especially if a writer is unfamiliar with the idiomatic nature of two-word verbs. Nevertheless, writers need to be able to tell which phrasal verbs are separable because these verbs work differently when the object is a pronoun.

Diagnostic Exercise

CORRECTED SENTENCES APPEAR ON PAGE 505.

Correct all phrasal verb errors in the following paragraph using the first correction as a model. The number in parentheses at the end of the paragraph indicates how many errors you should find.

It used to be that making a plane reservation was a simple matter. You found a travel agency and ~~called up it~~ *called it up* . Since the agency didn't work for any airlines, it looked for the best fare and found out it. There was no direct cost to you, since the airlines paid the commission; they built in it to the price of your ticket. After the airlines were deregulated, however, this system began to fall apart. Faced with much greater competition, airlines identified commission costs as an unnecessary expense, and they cut down them by reducing the commission they paid agencies. Some airlines, like Southwest, even cut out them entirely. As a result, most travel agencies stopped selling tickets to those airlines. If you want to know about their fares you must deal with each of the airlines separately. The catch, of course, is that if you call one of them, they can talk only about their fares, and you have no way to check out it to see if you have the best bargain. (5)

Fixing This Problem in Your Writing

Here are the ten most common adverbs used in separable phrasal verb constructions:

apart	*away*	*down*	*over*	*together*
around	*back*	*off*	*out*	*up*

When you see one of these ten words in a two-word verb, you can be fairly certain you are looking at a separable phrasal verb. The point to keep in mind is that when a two-word verb is followed by an object *noun,* you have the option of separating the verb and the adverb, but when the two-word verb is followed by an object *pronoun,* you MUST separate the verb and the adverb. Look at the following examples of separable phrasal verb sentences. Notice the difference in the position of the verb and the adverb when the sentence has a noun object and when it has a pronoun object.

VERB + ADVERB	MEANING	EXAMPLE
take apart	disassemble	We **took apart** the bicycle. We **took** it **apart**.
show around	give a tour to	We **showed around** the visitors. We **showed** them **around**.
throw away	discard	We **threw away** the boxes. We **threw** them **away**.
put back	replace	We **put back** the books. We **put** them **back**.
break down	categorize	We **broke down** the addresses by zip code. We **broke** them **down** by zip code.
call off	cancel	We **called off** the meeting. We **called** it **off**.
find out	discover	We **found out** the truth. We **found** it **out**.
talk over	discuss	We **talked over** the situation. We **talked** it **over**.
keep together	group/bunch	We **kept together** all the loose papers. We **kept** them **together**.
hang up	disconnect	We **hung up** the phone. We **hung** it **up**.

Short of simply memorizing the list of separable adverbs, is there any way to remember which words in phrasal verb compounds are adverbs (separable) and which are prepositions (inseparable)? Probably the most useful way is to see if the word following the phrasal verb can be used in a **prepositional phrase**. If it can, it is a preposition; if it can't, it is an adverb. A good noun to use in testing the phrasal verb is *movies*.

> *THE MOVIES* TIP: If the second word in a phrasal verb can be used to form a prepositional phrase with *the movies,* it is a preposition and thus, inseparable from the verb. If it cannot form a prepositional phrase with *the movies,* it is an adverb and thus, separable from the verb.

Here is *The Movies* Tip applied to the two example sentences:

EXAMPLE 1:   ✗ Roland called up her.

TIP APPLIED: ✗ up the movies

The failure of *The Movies* Tip indicates that *up* is not a preposition. Thus, *up* is an adverb and must follow a pronoun object:

called her up
CORRECTION: Roland ~~called up her~~.
                              ^

EXAMPLE 2:   ✗ Misako turned down him.

TIP APPLIED: ✗ down the movies

The failure of *The Movies* Tip indicates that *down* is not a preposition. Thus, *down* is an adverb and must follow a pronoun object:

turned him down
CORRECTION: Misako ~~turned down him~~.
                              ^

Two additional words—*in* and *on*—are commonly used in phrasal verbs, either as adverbs in separable phrasal verb constructions or as prepositions in inseparable phrasal verb constructions. You will need to learn phrasal verb combinations with *in* or *on* one at a time. Here are some examples.

In and *on* as adverbs (separable):

turn in	submit	We **turned in** our papers.
		We **turned** them **in**.
turn on	activate	We **turned on** the radio.
		We **turned** it **on**.

Lesson 37

vf
ESL

In and *on* as prepositions (inseparable):

look into	investigate	The FBI will **look into** the bombing.
		The FBI will **look into** it.
call on	visit	We **called on** some friends.
		We **called on** them.

Unfortunately, *The Movies* Tip does not help with two-word verbs that use *in* or *on,* since these words can be either adverbs or prepositions. By listening to native speakers use these words and by using them in your own speaking and writing, you will soon learn the correct uses of two-word verbs with *in* and *on.*

Sentence Practice 1

CORRECTED SENTENCES APPEAR ON PAGE 506.

Correct the errors in the underlined phrasal verb constructions by drawing a line through the error and putting the corrected form above it. If the sentence is correct as is, write *OK* above it. Use *The Movies* Tip to confirm your answer.

EXAMPLE: I took my books to the desk to ~~check out them~~.
(above: check them out)

CONFIRMATION: *out the movies*

1. She emphasized the point to <u>get across it</u>.

2. The children <u>argued about it</u>.

3. I promised to <u>pay back them</u>.

4. The news <u>cheered up them</u> enormously.

5. We promised to <u>bring back them</u> as soon as we could.

For more practice using phrasal verbs, go to **Exercise Central** at **bedfordstmartins.com/commonsense/11-37** .

Sentence Practice 2

CORRECTED SENTENCES APPEAR ON PAGE 506.

Correct the errors in the underlined phrasal verb constructions by drawing a line through the error and putting the corrected form above it. If the sentence is correct as is, write *OK* above it. Use *The Movies* Tip to confirm your answer.

EXAMPLE: *OK*
              It never <u>occurred to me</u>.

CONFIRMATION: *to the movies*

1. Jason really liked her, so he <u>asked out her</u>.

2. I don't believe what he said. I think he just <u>dreamed up it</u>.

3. They are afraid that they <u>let down us</u>.

4. The project didn't get full funding, so we had to <u>scale back it</u>.

5. He was <u>punished it for</u>.

Sentence Practice 3

Replace the underlined objects with an appropriate pronoun. If the pronoun follows a separable phrasal verb (verb + adverb), then move the adverb to follow the pronoun. If the pronoun follows an inseparable phrasal verb (verb + preposition), do not move it.

EXAMPLE: Round up <u>the usual suspects</u>.

ANSWER: Round <u>them</u> up.

Lesson 37

vf
ESL

1. I was done, so I put away <u>my books</u>.

2. The flashlight kept slipping from <u>my fingers</u>.

3. I really couldn't figure out <u>the problem</u>.

4. Did you back up <u>your essay?</u>

5. We were just talking about <u>the assignment</u>.

Editing Practice 1

CORRECTED SENTENCES APPEAR ON PAGE 506.

Correct all phrasal verb errors in the following paragraph using the first correction as a model. The number in parentheses at the end of the paragraph indicates how many errors you should find.

    Nineteen ninety-eight was the year of cable TV. It was the first

year in which more American TV viewers ~~tuned in it~~ *tuned it in* than watched

the three major networks — ABC, CBS, and NBC. In the old days

before cable, the three networks had a captive audience that had to

turn on them. In those days, the networks competed for prime-time

viewers by trying to get viewers to keep on them during the whole

evening. They believed that if they could get viewers to watch a

hit show, then the viewers would tend to tune in them for the rest

of the evening. For this strategy to work, the networks had to first

come up with a highly popular "anchor" program for each evening,

and then they had to turn programs out that were compatible with

it. A classic example for this strategy is ABC's *Monday Night*

Football. Monday Night Football pulls in a large percentage of male

viewers. To keep this audience from changing channels, ABC always

Lesson 37

vf
ESL

follows up it with programs aimed at male viewers. The other

two networks have essentially abandoned the Monday-night male

audience to ABC. (4)

Editing Practice 2

CORRECTED SENTENCES APPEAR ON PAGE 506.

Correct all errors in the following paragraph using the first correction as a model. The number in parentheses at the end of the paragraph indicates how many errors you should find.

We all should try to eat healthy foods, but it is hard to
balance them out
~~balance out them~~. I know I don't eat as well as I should. There

is probably way too much fat in my meals and snacks, but I try

to fix up them with salads and fresh fruit. I don't eat enough

vegetables because it is so hard to fit in them to my hectic

schedule, though I suspect that the real reason is that it is so

easy to leave off them my shopping list. Since so many of us

have to eat on the run, I wish it were easier to get healthier fast

food. A cheeseburger and an order of fries is over 2,000 calories.

You would have to exercise all day to burn off it. Usually the

only alternative is a generic salad bar with head lettuce and

sad-looking carrot sticks. You see people getting a plate and

then loading up it with lettuce, which they then drench with salad

dressing that probably has more calories than a steak dinner.

I suppose the only real alternative is to fix a good lunch at home,

pack up it, and take it with you. (6)

Lesson 37

vf
ESL

Editing Practice 3

Correct all errors in the following paragraph using the first correction as a model. The number in parentheses at the end of the paragraph indicates how many errors you should find.

I have two papers due this week. I can't just ~~dash off them~~ *dash them off* like some people. I have to really plan out them. I need to get a bunch of ideas together and then write down them. Then, I have to work up them into some kind of logical order. Once I have satisfied myself that I have a coherent and interesting thesis, I try to write down it in a few short sentences. Then I try to tear apart it. I want to find out right away if there are going to be any major problems with my argument. When I begin to write the paper, I focus on stating exactly what the issue or topic is. I learned a long time ago that whenever I couldn't get a paper started, it was because the topic wasn't really clear in my own mind—I hadn't thought it out. I had several competing topics, and I hadn't really sorted out them. For me at least, if I know what I want to say, I can write down it. (8)

Writing Practice

On a separate piece of paper, write a paragraph describing two or three ways in which you have tried to change your diet in recent years. See pages 467–69 for a glossary of frequently used phrasal verbs. Try to use several phrasal verbs. Then, use the Editing Checklist to show that your use of phrasal verbs is correct.

Lesson 37

vf
ESL

Editing Checklist

Identify Errors in Using Phrasal Verbs in Your Writing

_____ Use *The Movies* Tip to help distinguish between separable (verb + adverb) and inseparable (verb + preposition) phrasal verb constructions.

Correct Phrasal Verb Errors in Your Writing

_____ If a separable phrasal verb is followed by an object pronoun, move the adverb to follow the pronoun.

_____ If a separable phrasal verb is followed by an object noun, you have the option of placing the adverb before or after the noun.

_____ Inseparable phrasal verbs must never be separated by nouns or pronouns.

| **The Bottom Line** | Adverbs in separable phrasal verb constructions are unique. We can **move** them **around**. |

LESSON 38
Information Questions

ESL

Error Sentences

CORRECTED SENTENCES APPEAR ON PAGE 388.

EXAMPLE 1:   ✗ Where we can park?

EXAMPLE 2:   ✗ What you want to see?

What's the Problem?

Information questions begin with a question word, for example: *who, what, where, why, when, how often, whose* + noun, *which* + noun or pronoun. Sometimes non-native speakers form information questions incorrectly by failing to move a **helping verb** to the right place, or to use *do* (in some form — *do, does, did*) when it is required. Compare the incorrect and corrected forms of information questions, first with a helping verb that has not been moved to the right place, and then with a missing *do*:

Helping verb not moved:

EXAMPLE: ✗ How often you <u>can</u> work?

CORRECTION: How often <u>can</u> you work?

As you can see in the corrected example, the helping verb *can* has been moved right after the question words *how often*.

Missing *do*:

EXAMPLE: ✗ Where Liu go? or Where Liu went?

CORRECTION: Where <u>did</u> Liu go?

As you can see in the corrected example, the verb *did* (the past tense of *do*) has been added right after the question word *where*.

Lesson 38

info ?s
ESL

What Causes the Problem?

Imagine that underlying the question *Where should Liu go?* is the statement *Liu should go where.* In most languages in the world, the information question would be formed in one step by simply moving the question word (*where* in this case) to the beginning of the sentence: *Where Liu should go?*

In English, we need to move BOTH the question word and the helping verb *should:* ***Where should*** *Liu go?* The problem with English is that it is very difficult for our brains to process two movement operations at the same time. It is like juggling too many balls in the air at one time. Learners simplify the complexity by just moving the question word to the beginning of the sentence. As a result, we get the incorrectly formed information question *Where Liu should go?* instead of the correct *Where should Liu go?*

The situation is even more complicated when the underlying sentence does not have a helping verb to be moved. In this case, we must put some form of the verb *do* as a kind of substitute or dummy helping verb into the sentence. For example, from the underlying statement *They say what,* we form the information question by moving the question word *what* and adding *do* (*did* in this case): ***What did*** *they say?*

Diagnostic Exercise

CORRECTED SENTENCES APPEAR ON PAGE 506.

Correct all errors in the following dialogue using the first correction as a model. The number in parentheses at the end of the dialogue indicates how many errors you should find.

Dialogue between Anna and her sister Maria.

> *does your flight leave*
> ANNA: When ~~your flight leave~~?
>   ^
>
> MARIA: At 6:15. Why are so you worried? We're not going to be late, are we?

> ANNA: I don't think so, but how long it takes to get to the airport?
>
> MARIA: It depends on the traffic. If the roads are crowded, it will take an hour.
>
> ANNA: How soon you will be ready to leave?

MARIA: Don't get upset. I'm nearly done packing now. Have you seen my alarm clock?

ANNA: I don't know where it is. When you used it last?

MARIA: For my interview, two days ago. Here it is in the dresser drawer.

ANNA: Where I left the car keys?

MARIA: Come on! Now you're the one who is going to make us late. Why we didn't get started sooner? (6)

Fixing This Problem in Your Writing

Correcting this type of error requires you to do two things. The first thing is to see if there is an error by checking that the question word is immediately followed by a verb. If the question word is followed by *anything* except a verb, then the information question is incorrectly formed.

> **THE QUESTION WORD + VERB TIP:** Whenever you ask an information question, check to see if the question word is immediately followed by a verb. If it is not followed by a verb, then the information question is incorrectly formed, and you must supply a verb.

Which verb you supply depends on the rest of the sentence. There are two possibilities:

(1) If the information question contains a **helping verb**, then move that helping verb right after the question word. (The helping verbs are any form of *be* or *have* plus the verbs *can, could, may, might, must, shall, should, will,* or *would.*) Here is an example of an incorrect information question with a helping verb:

EXAMPLE: ✗ Where we <u>are</u> going?

The question word *where* is not followed by a verb. Since the sentence contains the helping verb *are*, we must move *are* (a form of *be*) right after the question word:

CORRECTION: **Where <u>are</u> we going?**

(2) If the information question does not contain a helping verb, then we must add the appropriate form of *do* (*do, does, did*) as a helping verb substitute. When we add *do*, we must use the form of *do* that agrees with

Lesson 38

info ?s
ESL

the subject. Here is an example of an incorrect information question without a helping verb:

EXAMPLE: ✗ Where he went?

The question word *where* is not followed by a verb. Since the sentence does not contain a helping verb, we must add some form of the verb *do* (*did*, in this case) right after the question word:

CORRECTION: Where <u>did</u> he go?

(Notice that the verb *went* changes to the infinitive or base form *go* because it no longer is the verb that agrees with the subject.)

> **VERB PLACEMENT TIP:** If the verb following the question word in an information question is missing, place a verb after the information question either by (1) moving the helping verb if there is one or (2) adding the appropriate form of *do* if there is no helping verb (and changing the main verb if necessary).

Here are the two tips applied to the example sentences:

EXAMPLE 1:   ✗ Where we can park?

The Question Word + Verb Tip tells us that this information question is wrong because the question word *where* is not followed by a verb. We can correct the error by applying the Verb Placement Tip: since the helping verb *can* is in the sentence, we must move *can* after the question word *where*:

TIP APPLIED: Where <u>can</u> we park?

EXAMPLE 2:   ✗ What you want to see?

The Question Word + Verb Tip tells us that this information question is wrong because the question word *what* is not followed by a verb. We can correct the error by applying the Verb Placement Tip: since there is no helping verb in the sentence, we must put *do* in the appropriate form after the question word.

TIP APPLIED: What <u>do</u> you want to see?

In all the examples of information questions we have examined so far, the question word has played the role of an adverb (for instance, the *where* in Example 1) or an object (for instance, the *what* in Example 2). What would happen if the question word played the role of the **subject** of the sentence? Would the Question Word + Verb Tip still work correctly? The answer is yes. Here are two examples of correctly formed information questions with the question word playing the role of subject:

EXAMPLE: <u>Who</u> answered the phone?

<u>What</u> confused them?

The Question Word + Verb Tip tells us that both these sentences are correct since a verb immediately follows the question word. These questions may look odd because they do not use either a helping verb or the verb *do* as most information questions do. The reason we don't move a helping verb or add *do* is that these questions don't need them: the verb is already in the right place, after the question word.

Sentence Practice 1

CORRECTED SENTENCES APPEAR ON PAGE 507.

Correct the information questions by applying the two tips. Remember, if you add *do*, you may need to change the main verb.

EXAMPLE: ✗ When they came here before?

Question Word + Verb Tip: The question is incorrect because the question word *when* is followed by *they*, which is not a verb.

Verb Placement Tip: Since there is no helping verb already in the sentence, add *do* and change the main verb.

CORRECTION: When <u>did</u> they <u>come</u> here before?

1.   Who you talked to?

2.   Where Sara found the books?

3.   When we plan to leave?

4.   Why they didn't bring their lunches?

5.   How soon you can be ready?

Lesson 38

info ?s
ESL

For more practice with information questions, go to **Exercise Central** at **bedfordstmartins.com/commonsense/11-38**.

Sentence Practice 2

CORRECTED SENTENCES APPEAR ON PAGE 507.

Correct the information questions by supplying the proper form of the missing helping verb and making any other necessary changes to the main verb. If the question is already correctly formed, write *OK* above it.

> EXAMPLE: ✗ Whose car we can use?
>
> CORRECTION: Whose car <u>can</u> we use?

1. Why the library closed early last Saturday?

2. Who we should thank for the party?

3. Where you parked the car?

4. Why you not ask?

5. Who knows the answer?

Sentence Practice 3

Turn the following statements into information questions by moving the underlined question word to the beginning of the sentence and making the necessary changes to the verb.

> EXAMPLE: ✗ The Weather Channel predicted rain <u>when</u>.
>
> ANSWER: When **did** the Weather Channel **predict** rain?

1. The chicken crossed the road <u>why</u>.

2. The garage changes the oil <u>how often</u>.

3. You wanted to see <u>who(m)</u>.

4. They picked <u>which one</u>.

5. They can't come <u>why</u>.

Lesson 38

info ?s
ESL

Editing Practice 1

CORRECTED SENTENCES APPEAR ON PAGE 507.

Correct all information question errors using the first correction as a model. The number in parentheses at the end of the dialogue indicates how many errors you should find.

Dialogue between Anna and her sister Maria at the airport:

ANNA: Which terminal *should we go to* ~~we should go to~~?

MARIA: I think we go to Terminal ^C. Most international flights leave from there.

ANNA: Where we parked last time?

MARIA::   In the short-term lot outside Terminal C. How long you can park there?

ANNA: As long as you want, but you must pay by the hour. Sometimes it is full, though.

MARIA: Why you not just drop me off at the curb?

ANNA: Don't be silly. You've got too many bags. Which parking space that car leave from?

MARIA: Over there on the left. How much money the meter take?

ANNA: Don't worry, I have a lot of change. What gate your flight leave from? (6)

Editing Practice 2

CORRECTED SENTENCES APPEAR ON PAGE 507.

Correct all information question errors using the first correction as a model. The number in parentheses at the end of the dialogue indicates how many errors you should find.

Dialogue between Anna and her sister Maria at the airport:

ANNA: What airline *are you taking* ~~you are taking~~?

MARIA: United. Where its ^counter is?

ANNA: I see it. Let's get in line.

Lesson 38

info ?s
ESL

MARIA: How long we will have to wait? I wanted to go to the duty-free shop.

ANNA: I told you we should have left earlier. When leaves the next flight?

MARIA: Don't get so upset. There is plenty of time. Why you be in such a big rush? Are you going somewhere tonight?

ANNA: Don't be silly. Where I would go on a Monday night?

MARIA: I don't know. Who you talked to on the phone just before we left?

ANNA: Never mind. Let's talk about something else. (6)

Editing Practice 3

Correct all information question errors using the first correction as a model. The number in parentheses at the end of the dialogue indicates how many errors you should find.

Dialogue between Anna and her sister Maria at the airport:

ANNA: Which bags ~~you want to check~~? *do you want to check*

MARIA: The two big ones.

ANNA: They are really heavy! What you have in them, rocks?

MARIA: I have a lot of school books.

ANNA: Why you want them? You don't even read them when you are here.

MARIA: I do too. I have to write a big term paper for my sociology class.

ANNA: What it is about?

MARIA: Wealth and class distinctions in Latin America.

ANNA: When you will find time to do it at home?

MARIA: I don't know, but I will have to make time for it.

ANNA: When it is due?

MARIA: Just as soon as I get back.

ANNA: Uh-oh. You're in trouble.

MARIA: Look who's talking. How often you work all night finishing your papers?

ANNA: At least I get them in on time. Which bag your passport is in?

MARIA: Oh no. I forgot it. Can you drive back and get it? Just joking. (7)

Writing Practice

On a separate piece of paper, write a short dialogue about an experience you have had at an airport. Use as many information questions as possible. Use the Editing Checklist to make sure that the questions are formed correctly.

Editing Checklist

Identify Information Question Errors in Your Writing

_____ Look at the word immediately following the question word. If it is not a verb, then the information question is incorrectly formed.

Correct Information Question Errors in Your Writing

_____ To correct the error, you must place a verb after the question word.

_____ If the sentence contains a helping verb, move that verb after the question word.

_____ If the sentence does not contain a helping verb, add the appropriate form of the verb *do*, and change the main verb if necessary since the main verb no longer agrees with the subject.

The Bottom Line

Where **does** the helping verb go in information questions?

ESL

LESSON 39
Word Order in Noun Clauses

Error Sentences

CORRECTED SENTENCES APPEAR ON PAGE 397.

EXAMPLE 1: ✗ I know where can you get it.

EXAMPLE 2: ✗ What does he want is anybody's guess.

What's the Problem?

A **noun clause** is a clause that functions as a noun. Noun clauses can play the major noun roles of subject of a sentence, object of a verb, and object of a preposition. Here is an example of a noun clause (underlined) in each of these roles:

SUBJECT: <u>What they said</u> is none of our business.

OBJECT OF A VERB: We know <u>how you feel about it</u>.

OBJECT OF A PREPOSITION: I asked about <u>where we could eat</u>.

Notice that noun clauses have normal statement word order with no moved helping verb or added *do*.

Sometimes non-native speakers incorrectly move a helping verb after the word that begins the noun clause or add an unnecessary *do* (in some form). For example, look at the underlined noun clause in the following sentence: ✗ *I asked <u>what **should** I bring to the party</u>.* The noun clause is incorrectly formed because the helping verb *should* has been mistakenly moved after the *what* that begins the noun clause. The helping verb belongs back in its normal place between the subject and the main verb of the noun clause: *I asked <u>what I **should** bring to the party</u>.*

Here is an example of a noun clause with an unnecessary *do*: ✗ *<u>Why **did** they act like that</u> was a mystery to me.* The added *do* must be deleted and the main verb changed to the appropriate present or past tense form: *<u>Why they **acted** like that</u> was a mystery to me.*

What Causes the Problem?

The cause of the problem is easy to identify: non-native speakers mistakenly apply the much more common Question Word + Helping Verb or Question Word + *do* patterns of information questions to noun clauses. The confusion of noun clauses with information questions is understandable. Information questions and noun clauses look somewhat alike because both information questions and noun clauses can begin with the same words—*who, what, when, where, why, how, which* + noun, and *whose* + noun or pronoun.

As we saw in Lesson 38, we create information questions by moving the helping verb from its normal place between the subject and main verb to a new position immediately after the question word, or else we add *do* (in some form) if there is no helping verb. However, a noun clause is not part of a question, so the helping verb cannot be moved and the *do* is unnecessary. For example, the correct placement of the helping verb *could* in the information question below might cause us to incorrectly copy that same Question Word + Helping Verb pattern in a similar looking noun clause.

INFORMATION QUESTION: Where **could** we go?

INCORRECT NOUN CLAUSE (UNDERLINED):   I wondered <u>where **could** we go</u>.

Since the sentence with a noun clause is not a question, we must put the helping verb *could* back in its normal place between the subject and the main verb:

CORRECTED NOUN CLAUSE (UNDERLINED):   I wondered <u>where we **could** go</u>.

Here is a comparable example with *do* incorrectly added to a noun clause:

INFORMATION QUESTION: What **did** he say?

INCORRECT NOUN CLAUSE (UNDERLINED):   I told them <u>what **did** he say</u>.

Since the sentence with a noun clause is not a question, we must delete the added *did* and change the main verb of the noun clause into the appropriate present or past tense form.

CORRECTED NOUN CLAUSE (UNDERLINED):   I told them <u>what he **said**</u>.

Lesson 39

w.o.
ESL

Diagnostic Exercise

CORRECTED SENTENCES APPEAR ON PAGE 507.

Correct all noun clause errors in the following paragraph using the first correction as a model. The number in parentheses at the end of the paragraph indicates how many errors you should find.

the American court system is so cumbersome

Many non-Americans ask why ~~is the American court system so cumbersome~~. To understand that, you need to know something about where did it come from and how did it evolve. Until the Revolutionary War, the American legal system was exactly what was the British legal system. Despite the many advantages of the British legal system, colonial Americans felt that the British had used the powers of the government to override the rights of individual citizens. This deep distrust of the ability of the government to use its power fairly explains why is the American system so heavily weighted in favor of the defendant. Often court cases in the United States are fought on the ground of what is admissible government evidence. (5)

Fixing This Problem in Your Writing

The key to using correct word order in noun clauses is avoiding the habit of automatically using the verbs appropriate to an information question whenever we use a noun clause. To do so, first we need to be sure if we are asking a genuine information question or not. If we are, we must move the helping verb after the question word or add *do*. If we are not asking an information question, then we have a noun clause. If so, we must put the helping verb back in its normal position between the subject and the main verb of the noun clause, or delete the added *do* and change the main verb of the noun clause appropriately. The following tip is a way to consciously check if we are really dealing with an information question.

Lesson 39

w.o.

ESL

THE REAL QUESTION/REAL ANSWER TIP: Anytime you use *who, what, when, where, why, how, which* + noun, or *whose* + noun or pronoun, check if they are genuine question words used to ask an information question. A good way to do this is to see if you can actually give an appropriate answer to the information question. If you can give a valid answer, then the information question form is correct. If you cannot give a valid answer, then you are dealing with a noun clause.

Here is the Real Question/Real Answer Tip applied to a genuine information question.

EXAMPLE: Where can I get the bus?

TIP APPLIED: Question: Where can I get the bus?
Answer: You can get it at the corner.

Since there is a valid answer, we know that there was a valid information question. As such, the Question Word + Helping Verb word order is correct.

Now here is the Real Question/Real Answer Tip applied to the two example sentences:

EXAMPLE 1: ✗ I know where can you get it.

TIP APPLIED: Question: I know where can you get it?
Answer: (None possible)

Therefore, Example 1 is not a valid information question. Instead, it contains a noun clause, which we must restore to its normal statement form. In this case, we must move the helping verb *can* back to its normal position between the subject and the main verb of the noun clause.

CORRECTION: I know <u>where you **can** get</u> it.

EXAMPLE 2: ✗ What does he want is anybody's guess.

TIP APPLIED: Question: What does he want is anybody's guess?
Answer: (None possible)

Therefore, Example 2 is not a valid information question. Instead, it contains a noun clause, which we must restore to its normal statement form. In this case, we must delete *does* and change the main verb *want* back to its appropriate form.

CORRECTION: <u>What he **wants**</u> is anybody's guess.

Lesson 39

w.o.
ESL

The difference between information questions and noun clauses is obvious once we stop to check. The problem is that if we don't stop and consciously check, we can unconsciously let the more common pattern of the information question incorrectly influence how we form the somewhat similar looking noun clause.

Sentence Practice 1

CORRECTED SENTENCES APPEAR ON PAGE 507.

All of the following sentences contain incorrectly formed noun clauses. First underline the noun clauses, and then restore the noun clauses to their proper forms.

EXAMPLE: ✗ I found out where did they go.

NOUN CLAUSE UNDERLINED: I found out <u>where did they go</u>.

NOUN CLAUSE CORRECTED: I found out <u>~~where did they go~~</u>. *where they went*

1. I realized what did I need to do.

2. We couldn't agree on which movie did we want to see.

3. They asked us when did the plane leave.

4. Why is that a wrong answer seemed obvious to the whole class.

5. How do you dress tells a lot about you.

> For more practice with word order, go to **Exercise Central** at **bedfordstmartins.com/commonsense/11-39**.

Sentence Practice 2

CORRECTED SENTENCES APPEAR ON PAGE 508.

Apply the Real Question/Real Answer Tip to the following unpunctuated sentences. If the tip shows that a sentence is not a valid information question, underline the noun clause and make the necessary corrections.

EXAMPLE: ✗ They guessed what was the right answer

REAL QUESTION/   Question: They guessed what was the right answer?
REAL ANSWER TIP: Answer: (None possible)

NOUN CLAUSE   They guessed <u>what was the right answer</u>
UNDERLINED:

                     what the right answer was

CORRECTION: They guessed ~~what was the right answer~~.

1. It depends on how did you feel about it

2. How can I be of help to you

3. You can leave what don't you like

4. We were surprised at how late was it

5. What did they do was very important to all of us

Sentence Practice 3

Turn the following information questions into noun clauses, and insert them in place of the IT in the statements below the questions.

EXAMPLE: **Where did you go?**
                      Tell me IT.

ANSWER: **Tell me <u>where you went</u>.**

1. Why was he so late?
   I wondered IT.

2. What did the sign say?
   I couldn't make out IT.

3. How did Hermione do it?
   Harry finally figured out IT.

4. Who is the guilty party?
   It is up to the court to determine IT.

5. Where did we go wrong?
   IT is obvious to us now.

Lesson 39

W.O.
ESL

Editing Practice 1

CORRECTED SENTENCES APPEAR ON PAGE 508.

Correct all noun clause errors using the first correction as a model. The number in parentheses at the end of the paragraph indicates how many errors you should find.

In my Film as Literature class, we have had many discussions
about ~~what is the difference~~ *what the difference is* between a book and the filmed version
of it. What do I like about the class is that we all have such different

ideas. Some students don't really care about what is the movie like.

They feel that no movie can be as good as the book it came from.

What don't they like is the movie's simplification of the book. I don't

think what are they saying is fair. We need to remember how much

shorter is a movie than a book. Can you imagine sitting through a

movie that lasts as long as it would take to read the book? I believe

what do movies show us is the director's interpretation of the book.

Sometimes that interpretation is more interesting than the book it

came from. (6)

Editing Practice 2

CORRECTED SENTENCES APPEAR ON PAGE 508.

Correct all noun clause errors using the first correction as a model. The number in parentheses at the end of the paragraph indicates how many errors you should find.

How students are taught writing
~~How are students taught writing~~ has changed greatly in the

past decade. Back in the dark ages, when I went to school, writing

wasn't really taught as a topic in its own right. Professors almost never

explained why was your writing good or bad. It seemed completely

Lesson 39

W.O.
ESL

subjective—either they liked what did you write or they didn't. There didn't seem to be anything else to say. One of the big changes has been to look at writing as a process that can be studied. How do good writers write is substantially different from how do bad writers write. The biggest single mistake that poor writers make is to try to do too much at one time. They try to figure out what are they trying to say at the same time as they are trying to write a finished paper. Usually when they do this, they end up writing the first sentence over and over, thinking that if they just could find the "right" first sentence, their paper would flow effortlessly. Good writers first explore the topic, working out what do they want to say before they ever try to actually write a finished product. (6)

Editing Practice 3

Correct all noun clause errors using the first correction as a model. The number in parentheses at the end of the paragraph indicates how many errors you should find.

Do you know ~~what is~~ "writing across the curriculum"? It is
what "writing across the curriculum" is

another important change in how is writing taught. The key idea is how can writing be taught outside the English classroom. For example, students in a history class are asked to write a paper imagining what was it like to live in a different time. Science classes are natural places for writing across the curriculum because nearly all steps in the scientific process lend themselves to writing. For example, students can write about how did they set up and conduct an experiment. They can write about what did they observe. What they can conclude

Lesson 39

w.o.
ESL

from the experiment is also a natural topic. An effective use of writing in math classes is asking students to explain how did they arrive at their answers. (7)

Writing Practice

On your own paper, write a paragraph describing what process you actually use when you write an essay. Use as many noun clauses as possible. Use the Editing Checklist to make sure that the noun clauses are formed correctly.

Editing Checklist

Identify Noun Clause Errors in Your Writing

_____ Whenever you use a noun clause, check that the introductory words such as *who, what, when, where, why, how, which* + noun, and *whose* + noun or pronoun are not followed by an incorrectly moved helping verb or added *do*. A good way to do this is to see if you have asked a real information question that has a real answer. If you have not asked a real information question, then you have written a noun clause that must have normal statement word order.

Correct Noun Clause Errors in Your Writing

_____ If the noun clause contains a helping verb that has been moved, move that verb back to its normal place between the subject and the main verb.

_____ If the noun clause has an added *do* (in any form), delete it and make the appropriate change in the main verb of the noun clause.

The Bottom Line

You should know why the **subject** goes before the **verb** in noun clauses.

UNIT ELEVEN ESL:
Using Verbs Correctly

Unit Eleven contains five lessons, each of which deals with an aspect of verb use that non-native speakers have found to be particularly troublesome. The first lesson shows when to use (and when not to use) the progressive tense. The second lesson shows you how to correctly change a verb into an adjective. The third lesson deals with phrasal verbs, highly idiomatic verb + preposition and verb + adverb compounds. The fourth and fifth lessons deal with interrelated problems of where to place the verbs in information questions and noun clauses.

The Progressive Tenses

The progressive tenses describe ongoing actions that are "in progress" at a particular moment in time. Unlike the present tense, which is used for making "timeless" statements of fact and for generalizations, the progressive tenses are used for "temporary" conditions. Use the following tip to help you remember when to use one of the progressive tenses:

> **PROGRESSIVE TENSE TIP:** Use the progressive tense when you are describing an event that is taking place at a particular moment, either now (present progressive), during some past moment (past progressive), or during some future moment (future progressive).

The progressive tenses cannot be used with a family of verbs called "steady-state" verbs. Here are some examples of verbs in this family: *appreciate, believe, belong, care, contain, doubt, envy, fear, forget, hate, imagine, know, like, love, need, own, prefer, want.* The following tip helps you remember the types of verb that cannot be used with the progressive tenses:

> **STEADY-STATE VERB TIP:** Verbs that refer to unchanging, steady-state conditions are incompatible with the progressive tenses. These verbs tend to fall into certain broad categories: mental activity, emotional condition, and possession.

Unit Eleven

review
ESL

Using Participles as Adjectives

Participles are verb forms. In English (unlike some languages), there are two forms of participles: present participles and past participles. Participles can be turned into adjectives that modify nouns. An example of a present participle used as an adjective is *an **amusing** child*. An example of a past participle used as an adjective is *an **amused** child*. The choice of participle depends on the relation of the noun being modified to the verb that underlies the participle (*amuse* in the case of the two examples above). The two tips below will help you decide which participle to use:

> SUBJECT TIP: Use the present participle form (*-ing*) if the noun being modified plays the role of the subject of the verb underlying the participle.

> OBJECT TIP: Use the past participle form (*-ed*) if the noun being modified plays the role of the object of the verb underlying the participle.

Phrasal Verbs

Many verbs combine with either an adverb or a preposition to form a compound with a new (and sometimes quite unexpected) meaning. These combinations are called phrasal verbs, or two-word verbs. The combination of verb + adverb poses a special problem because the adverb can be separated from the verb by the object. If the object is a pronoun, the adverb MUST be separated. The verb + preposition combination, on the other hand, is inseparable. It is very hard for non-native speakers to know which phrasal verbs are separable and which are inseparable. The following tip will help you decide:

> *THE MOVIES* TIP: If the second word in a phrasal verb can be used to form a prepositional phrase with *the movies*, then it is a preposition and is, thus, inseparable. If it cannot form a prepositional phrase with *the movies*, then it is an adverb and is, thus, separable.

Unit Eleven

review
ESL

Information Questions

Information questions begin with a question word, for example: *who, what, where, why, when, how often, whose* + noun, or *which* + noun or pronoun. Sometimes non-native speakers form information questions incorrectly by failing to move a helping verb in front of the subject, or by not adding a helping verb substitute (some form of the verb *do*) if there is no helping verb.

Correcting this type of error requires you to do two things. The first thing is to see if there is an error by checking that the question word is immediately followed by a verb. If the question word is followed by *anything* except a verb, then the information question is incorrectly formed.

> **THE QUESTION WORD + VERB TIP:** Whenever you ask an information question, check to see if the question word is immediately followed by a verb. If it is not followed by a verb, then the information question is incorrectly formed, and you must supply a verb.

The second thing to do is to correct the error.

> **VERB PLACEMENT TIP:** If the verb following the question word in an information question is missing, place a verb after the information question either by (1) moving the helping verb if there is one or (2) adding the appropriate form of *do* if there is no helping verb (and changing the main verb if necessary).

Word Order in Noun Clauses

Sometimes non-native speakers have problems with word order in noun clauses that begin with words like *who, what, where, why, when, how often, whose* + noun, or *which* + noun or pronoun. Non-native speakers mistakenly move a helping verb or add some form of the verb *do* after the word that begins the noun clause because they are following the much more common pattern for forming information questions. The key to using correct word order in noun clauses is avoiding the habit of automatically using the verbs appropriate to an information question whenever we use a noun clause. To do so, we need to be sure if we are asking a genuine information question or not.

> **THE REAL QUESTION/REAL ANSWER TIP:** Anytime you use *who, what, when, where, why, how, which* + noun, or *whose* + noun or pronoun, check if they are genuine question words used to ask an information question. A good way to do this is to see if you can actually give an appropriate answer to the information question. If you can give a valid answer, then the information question form is correct. If you cannot give a valid answer, then you are dealing with a noun clause. In this case you must use normal subject-verb word order.

Unit Eleven

review
ESL

Review Test

Correct the verb errors in the following paragraphs using the first correction as a model. The number in parentheses at the end of each paragraph indicates how many errors you should find.

quickly learn
When people visit Venice they ~~are quickly learning~~ about how
many problems does the modern city face. The most publicizing problem is flooding. Several times every year, the water is rising to flood parts of the city in several feet of water. Even the famous Piazza San Marco must be closed because water covers up it. The flooding is caused by a variety of factors. What most people think is the main cause? You get a different answer from nearly every expert you are asking. What do many people believe is that the canals no longer drain properly because people have filled in them. As a result, rainwater and the water from rivers flowing into the top of the lagoon are blocked; the islands have dammed up them. (9)

Another problem that everybody is recognizing is that parts of the city are simply sinking into the lagoon under their own weight. For example, consider the Piazza San Marco. In this square are two absolutely enormous stone buildings: the Basilica of San Marco, one of the most amazed churches in the world, and the Ducal Palace. How many hundreds of thousands of tons you think they each weigh? When you look closely at the Ducal Palace, you will notice something odd about the proportions of the stone columns on the ground floor. They are too short. It looks like something has worn down them. In fact, just the opposite is the case. Over the centuries the palace has sunk about five feet, and the ground has been filled them around. What do you see in paintings of the Ducal Palace made 200 years ago is that the columns are noticeably taller than they are today. (6)

UNIT TWELVE
A Commonsense Writing Guide

Though we focus primarily on grammar and usage in this book, we do not want to suggest that you should focus *only* on grammar and usage. So this final unit offers a concise guide to writing. This unit also covers valuable information you need to know about the reading process. Here you will find some practical, commonsense strategies for improving your paragraphs and essays.

Here are two points you should know before you start.

- This unit emphasizes an often overlooked fact: teachers have expectations that affect what student writers should do. A writer's situation always affects his or her choices, and teachers are a normal part of a student writer's situation.

- This section offers no formulas for writing. Instead, we encourage you to develop questions to ask yourself, your teacher, or anyone giving you feedback about your writing. Developing a habit of asking yourself critical questions throughout your writing process is one of the most important steps you can take toward improving your writing.

What Readers Look For: Basic Standards

Since writing is meant to be read, begin by thinking about what readers typically expect. Here we present some general expectations that apply to most writing, especially writing done in school. If you know what readers consider when evaluating writing, you can use this information as you write.

Though definitions of "good writing" differ from culture to culture, here are five *basic standards* that readers in the United States use to evaluate writing. Keep in mind that you might have to adjust these standards based on your own specific situation, audience, and assignment.

Unit Twelve

overview

407

Basic Standards for Evaluating Writing

PURPOSE: Readers expect a paper to be focused, based on a clear and appropriate purpose. A focused paper

- stays on one subject
- makes a specific point about this subject
- considers its audience
- is narrow enough to fulfill its purpose within the assignment's page-length requirements

SUPPORT: Readers expect a paper to contain enough supporting detail to fulfill its purpose. A well-supported paper

- gives readers a clear understanding of the paper's subject matter
- explains or proves the paper's one main point with details, examples, and evidence
- offers in-depth thinking, not just obvious or superficial generalizations

ORGANIZATION: Readers expect a paper to have a sense of order. This typically means that

- the paper has an introduction, a body, and a conclusion
- each paragraph has one major point
- paragraphs are arranged so they clearly build on one another
- individual sentences flow from one to another

STYLE: Readers expect writers to use words and sentence patterns that suit their purpose and topic. For most college papers, style means that

- the writing is *either* formal *or* informal, depending on the paper's purpose
- sentences should not be too choppy or too awkward
- writers choose the words that most clearly and precisely convey ideas to a particular audience

MECHANICS: Readers expect that writers follow the conventions and rules of standard English. This expectation means that writers should carefully consider the guidelines given in the first part of this book (Units 1 through 11).

Unit Twelve

overview

These five basic standards provide a *starting place*. They are criteria for you to consider no matter what type of formal writing you are doing. The remainder of this chapter offers strategies you can use so that your paper reflects these five standards. Because the main part of this book focuses on style and mechanics, this unit will concentrate on purpose, support, and organization.

What Writers Do:
Reading, the Writing Process, and Situation

Reading and writing: What is the connection? Reading is more closely connected to writing than many students assume. Both writing and reading involve processes—ever-evolving steps and actions you go through to understand and create information. Reading as well as writing depends on your situation. For example, you do not read a physics textbook the same way you read e-mail from a friend. Nor do you go through the same steps to create a grocery list as you would a research paper. Writing not only depends on reading (and vice versa), but both are shaped by specific processes and situations.

Thus, the next four lessons discuss how to read and write more effectively by considering certain situations, especially those common in higher education, and processes. You already know how to read and write, but these lessons will help you read and write better in college—a situation that likely you are not highly familiar with yet.

This unit begins with a discussion of reading, for many (perhaps most) writing assignments in college are closely connected with reading material that you are either assigned or that you must find yourself. Even if your reading skills are strong, we encourage you to study Lesson 40 so you will better understand concepts of and tips for reading that also relate to writing. This lesson only briefly discusses writing and the writing process; Lessons 41–43 discuss writing more fully.

What is a *writing process*? At one time or another, most of us have written a paper all at once. Sometimes, the result was acceptable or even good; other times, the paper didn't reflect our best thinking. For most people, their "best thinking" isn't what comes off the top of their heads. Rather, it is the result of a process. Using a *process* in writing means coming up with good ideas, developing plans, trying out your best ideas, making improvements, and sharing ideas with readers. There is no one right way to proceed, and the route can even be messy. It would be convenient if there were a formula, but the truth is that each writer, situation, purpose, and audience requires a unique approach. You can, however, think about three general stages.

Unit Twelve

overview

GENERAL STAGES IN THE WRITING PROCESS

Planning ———▶ Drafting ———▶ Revising

Writing is not always a neat step-by-step process. When you revise a paragraph to make it descriptive, for instance, you might also do more planning. Keep in mind as well that writing is not just drafting. You need to plan, write, rewrite, and make improvements. You can consider editing as the final stage, using the other parts of this book to guide you.

What is a *writing situation*?   Your exact writing process will depend on your situation. A writer's situation is a combination of everything that directly affects a given piece of writing. Here are the basic elements:

Assignment	Readers (Audience)	Tools for Writing
Purpose	Deadline	Physical Environment

Your writing situation will change with every assignment. For example, some assignments may require research. Others may require that you consider a community or a corporate (rather than an academic) audience. Some writing assignments begin and end in the classroom during an exam. Others may be long-term and require several trips to the library or computer lab. How you prepare to write is affected by your overall writing situation.

Unit Twelve

overview

LESSON 40
Reading

Writing depends upon reading. At the very least, you yourself read everything you write, and your teacher and classmates frequently read your writing as well. And as we all know, one way to improve your writing ability is to read, read, read.

There is one other reason why you need to consider the connections between reading and writing. In college, you will find that many teachers base their writing assignments around something they will ask you to read—such as a textbook, novel, journal article, or item from the Internet. College requires you to read a range of items—from textbooks, to literature, to government documents (just to name a few). There are also different ways to write about these diverse reading selections. Thus, this lesson will offer *general* strategies for reading and writing about what you read. In later lessons, we will focus more on the actual process of writing and more specific types of assignments you will encounter in college.

Types of Assignments

There are *many* ways to write about something you have been assigned to read. Thus, you first need to understand some of the most common "writing about reading" assignments and their differences.

College teachers often make writing assignments such as the following, although they might call these assignments by different names:

COMMON TYPES OF ASSIGNMENTS

Objective Summary: This is a brief description of what a reading selection covers—its most important ideas. Your own opinions about the selection and its topic are kept out as much as possible.

Evaluative Summary: This also is a brief description of what an author covers in a reading selection, but you are allowed to offer more of your own opinions and reflections about the selection or the topic.

Critique (or Review): This is not always brief, nor is your specific purpose to summarize. Instead, your purpose is to evaluate a reading selection. Your paper would describe its strengths or weaknesses (or

411

both) and then provide reasons to support your evaluation. The goal is to convince your readers that your evaluation is valid and reasonable.

Reflection: Like a critique, the purpose is not to summarize. Compared to a critique, a reflection is less formal and does not focus on convincing readers. The reflection is a more personal response that makes a connection between you and what the author writes. For instance, you might discuss what you learned from the reading selection or how it relates to your own experiences.

Explanation (or Analysis): This assignment is most often used when the reading selection is a work of fiction or literature—such as a poem, short story, or novel. Your purpose is to offer an explanation about the meaning of the reading selection. This type of writing is particularly broad, covering many specific forms. One common form involves answering a particular question about the author's work; this question could be one you develop or one the teacher assigns. Another common form is describing the overall point or theme of a work of literature.

Research Paper: Although many teachers avoid this particular name, the so-called research paper is a lengthy paper that first requires you to find out how much has been written on a topic in books, magazines, newspaper articles, or on the Internet. Then, you select the best sources and use them to support your own point or position. Some papers might use two or three sources, while others might require a dozen or more.

Lesson 41 will describe how you must determine your general purpose in writing a paper. When writing about something you've read, you will usually find that this purpose fits into one of the above categories.

COMMONSENSE TIP: Do not overlook this first step of identifying the purpose of the assignment. Many students seem to think that all "writing about reading" assignments are the same, but it is a crucial mistake to write, for example, a reflective essay when the teacher expects a research paper.

Understanding What You Read

No matter what the assignment is, you need to read something well if you are to write about it. One misconception many people have is that reading is easy—something that people learn in elementary school. College students face some of the most challenging, complex reading selections that can be

Lesson 40

read

found (one would hope so, in fact, if college is supposed to help students understand the most complex challenges facing society).

Let's face it—just skimming or casually reading an article or book will work well enough in some situations (such as when you're reading for pleasure). But college requires you to have a better understanding of what you read, in addition to requiring you to read more complex selections. Keep in mind that "reading" something does not simply mean being able to sound out the words. Reading means *understanding* what is written. If you do not understand what you have "read," then you really have not read it.

Here are four practical suggestions for helping you read (and understand) more effectively.

Tip #1: Do not worry about reading quickly.

Many people feel they are poor readers because they do not read quickly, and such an attitude typically lowers their confidence (and, thus, their ability to read well). In truth, many of your professors read slowly, taking time to consider fully what they are reading. Many people "read" quickly but are unable to understand the material, so have they really read it at all?

Certainly, there are occasions when time is essential, and college students usually feel a shortage of time. Avoid thinking that every situation calls for a quick reading. Indeed, reading too quickly can eventually take more time if it results in such a poor understanding that you are unable to write. In sum, find time—ample time—to devote to reading.

Tip #2: Preview what you are going to read.

Just as you should plan what to write, you should plan to read. Research has shown that if you have an idea of what is coming up next in a reading selection, you will better understand what you read.

Take a few moments or more to look through the reading material for "signposts" such as the following. These indicate what is coming up next in the reading selection.

- An introductory paragraph in which the author indicates his/her purpose

- Information indicating where and when the selection originally appeared (some articles and essays in textbooks originally appeared elsewhere, and knowing this information can provide useful background for what you are about to read)

- Preface (many essays, articles, and books start with an overview or description of the reading selection)

- Headings and sub-headings (these often indicate what the author considers to be important topics)

Lesson 40

read

- Visual cues, such as pictures, diagrams, and lists

- Words or phrases that are emphasized (boldface, underlining, italics, capitalization)

- A conclusion or summary

- Review or discussion questions at the end (these often tell you what you are supposed to know by the time you finish, so look for the answers *as* you read)

Tip #3: Don't skip the introduction; don't focus just on the ending.   Some authors recognize that readers need to understand what is coming up next in a reading selection. Consequently, authors often explicitly provide a preview in the introduction of, say, a particular chapter. The odd thing is that many college students consider this preview to be "fluff" and skip it. Avoid the temptation to skip this preview, even if it seems dull. The author is basically doing the readers' work for them by providing a preview, and one would hope that the author's own preview of what is important in the selection is, indeed, important.

In contrast, some readers assume that the summary or conclusion is basically all they need to know, and they skim (or skip) everything else. Even the best-written summary is just a *general* description of an author's ideas, and many college teachers—realizing what the conclusion does not cover—want students to understand the important details, not just the simple basics.

Tip #4: Use writing to reinforce your reading.   Researchers who study reading and writing have found that people who write *as* they read (or soon afterward) better understand what they read. Suppose that a teacher has required you to write an analysis of something you were asked to read. Even in this situation, you have not exhausted the ways in which other types of writing can help you better understand a reading assignment. Here are a few more ways in which writing can help you more fully understand and remember what you read:

- **Highlighting.** Is this a form of "writing"? It is writing in the sense that you produce markings to indicate a type of meaning (even if you are just emphasizing somebody else's ideas). Highlighting not only helps you identify important portions of a text, it also keeps you less passive and more active during the reading process, making you more alert and receptive.

  One problem with highlighting is that many students rely on just this one simple strategy. Although helpful, it can be a bit superficial in terms of engaging the reader in understanding, interpreting, and critiquing a text. Other strategies, such as those below, require more work but usually result in a better understanding.

- **Note taking.** For many students, one of the most useful strategies is taking notes while they read — brief comments, questions, definitions, explanations, or evaluations. Notes can even make connections to what the teacher or others have said (especially if there is disagreement). Such notes can be put in the margin (if it's your book), on cards, on paper, or on the computer. The format isn't as important as the act: take notes that help clarify what you read or help you identify problematic portions.

COMMONSENSE TIP: Many students buy used textbooks in which another student wrote notes or highlighted. Do *not* assume the previous owner of the book was accurate or logical in terms of his/her highlighting or note taking! In addition, relying on somebody else's markings or notes does little to increase your own active involvement in the act of reading.

- **Summarizing.** A study conducted several years ago found that students in a psychology course received better test scores when they wrote summaries of chapters assigned from their psychology textbook. For whatever reason, people remember and better understand something after they write a summary of it. Even if you are not required to write an objective summary (a type of writing described earlier in this lesson), writing a brief, straightforward summary will help you understand whatever you summarize. In doing so, you will likely reread the selection, which alone helps you better understand the material.

  This strategy can be a time-consuming way to improve your comprehension of what you read, and you cannot use it for every reading situation. Most students have to be selective about what they summarize. Having the summary will also help when you study for a test. If it is not practical to write a summary, at least consider an oral summary — summarizing aloud, perhaps in a study group.

- **Rereading and Reviewing.** As you read, you will naturally find yourself not truly understanding some parts. Don't feel as though rereading is a waste of time. Often, in fact, people almost "doze off" when reading and are not really reading at all, even if they are sounding out the words in their mind. Whether your attention is drifting or whether you just don't follow what the author is writing, don't continue until you have reread the troublesome sentence, passage, or page.

  What happens if rereading does not help? In such cases, it is best to backtrack to earlier portions that might have set up the troublesome

Lesson 40

read

portion of the text. If that does not help, *then* you should proceed in hopes that the subsequent sections will clarify the author's message.

The reviewing stage of reading is similar to revising a paper: you look through the text and make decisions about the meaning. Many people consider their reading done when they reach the last words of a text. In some situations, though, the act of reading—of really understanding the text—has only begun at that point. Making sense of a reading selection means understanding, evaluating, and questioning the material, and these acts can best be done *after* an initial reading of the text. Reviewing might mean, in fact, rereading some or all of the reading selection, or it might mean taking notes or highlighting significant portions. The important point to remember is that reading often means taking time to reflect on what you read—time to absorb, critique, and reconsider the message.

Below, we offer additional advice on what you might do after (or perhaps during) the process of reading.

Questions for Readers

Many people are confused about what they should do to "reflect" on something they read. This is a highly individualistic activity that depends on what you read, why you are reading it, and who you are. However, we wish to end this lesson by noting several questions that most students can use to help them understand, evaluate, and write about a reading selection.

- What does the author's purpose seem to be? What is his/her thesis, claim, or position?
- Do you agree with the author's major point? Do you think most people would?
- Can you think of something current or historical that is relevant to the major topic of this passage?
- How does this reading selection relate to your life? That is, is it relevant to your past, present, or future?
- What about other people—is the selection relevant to most people? For whom is it *not* relevant?
- What does the selection fail to include even though it is related to the topic, and was it reasonable for the author to leave out this material?
- Find two or three sentences you found memorable, insightful, or interesting. Why are these notable or important to you?
- Is there something else you have read (or heard or seen) that supports or contradicts this reading selection?

- Consider how the reading selection is organized—what comes first and last, and how it can otherwise be divided into different sections. How well does the author's arrangement work?
- Consider the author's word choice and the way s/he puts sentences together. Are these effective choices?
- If the reading selection involves a story, consider the characters, setting, and actions. How do all or any of these contribute to a particular interpretation of the story?
- What sort of person does the author appear to be? Consider the author's tone, word choice, and the types of reasons or information provided to readers.
- Could some people find the reading selection offensive at times? Immoral? Useless?
- If the author is making an argument or recommendation, what would be the results if society were to accept it? What is needed in order to turn the author's ideas into something concrete and useful?
- No matter whether you agree or disagree with the author, why do you respect or not respect the way s/he writes?

For additional questions, consider the questions found in Lesson 41 dealing with purpose and standards. Although intended for writers, those questions are also relevant to reading.

Above all, do not merely accept what another person has put down in writing. College readers should not only understand a reading selection, they should also question it, evaluate it, and consider if and how the author's ideas can contribute to readers' lives.

Lesson 40

read

LESSON 41
Planning

Whether you are assigned an in-class essay or a long-term research project, start by determining your purpose. Determining your purpose means more than completing the sentence, "What I want to do in this paper is...." It also involves answering these questions:

- What effect do I want to have on readers?
- What do I want to get out of this paper—besides a good grade?
- How will my paper reflect the task that the teacher assigned?
- What does the teacher want me to learn from doing this task?

Working your way through questions like these can be overwhelming, so we suggest first thinking about purpose in two ways:

> Your *general purpose* is the basic goal of the paper according to the assignment.

> Your *specific purpose* is the general purpose plus your narrowed topic and the point you want to make.

Determine Your General Purpose

Your first step in the planning stage is determining your general purpose— what you are required to do with the subject or topic.

> **COMMONSENSE TIP:** Don't assume that your paper meets the assignment simply because it is "on topic." In this early stage of writing, many people mistakenly place more emphasis on staying on the topic than on making sure they understand the general purpose of the assignment.

What is a *general purpose*?   Rarely will teachers say simply, "Write a paper on the pyramids." Although some teachers will assign just a subject, most teachers have additional expectations about what you should do with this subject. They will also indicate the general effect your paper should have. Take a look at the following three assignments. All involve the same subject—the pyramids—but each has a different general purpose.

ASSIGNMENT	GENERAL PURPOSE
What relevance does this story about a woman's trip to see the pyramids have to your life?	To express yourself
Write a paper that explains the origins of the pyramids.	To inform readers
Should the pyramids be preserved? Take a stand.	To persuade readers

Three types of general purposes.   Most college writing has one of three general purposes: to express yourself, to inform readers, or to persuade readers.

Expressing Yourself.   The goal is to express your authentic and personal reactions and feelings. The emphasis is on you and your individual response to a subject. A personal narrative, a paper describing an event in your life that has special significance to you, is a common type of expressive writing assignment.

Informing Readers.   The goal is to explain or describe something in a clear, accurate, thorough way. Usually you should try to be objective and keep your personal feelings out of the assignment. Like a reporter, you are focusing on the subject and on providing information that would be new to readers.

Persuading Readers.   The goal is to convince readers to accept your claim or position. In most of the persuasive writing you do in college, you should concentrate on logic, not emotions. The desired effect of persuasion is to convince readers to agree with you.

COMMONSENSE TIP: If you believe your teacher has given you a wide-open assignment, you might be able to pick any subject or general purpose, but double-check to see if the paper can *really* do anything you want. Usually teachers (like most readers) have some expectations about a written assignment.

Suppose your teacher has assigned a paper that asks you to summarize the plot of a novel. This paper is likely to have an informative purpose. But

Lesson 41

plan

suppose your paper winds up describing how you personally reacted to the book (expression), or it argues that the main character is a horrible person (persuasion). Your paper might fail because it does not achieve the general purpose your teacher assigned—to inform.

BUT WHAT HAPPENS IF...?

"I still cannot determine what my general purpose should be." Your best approach might be to ask the teacher. You will want to avoid putting it this way, though: "What do you want in this paper?" That is too general and may suggest that you just want a formula. Ask a specific question: for instance, "Is the general purpose to express myself, to provide information, or to support a claim?"

"But asking the teacher isn't practical, and I really, really don't know what the general purpose is!" You might consult someone else in the class, but if all else fails, we suggest you assume that the general purpose is to persuade. Persuasion is one of the most common types of writing in college.

"The assignment allows me to write almost anything I want." Again, be sure to confirm this interpretation, preferably by trying out a sample approach with the teacher to see if there are restrictions. Even if there are none, do not assume that your paper can wander from one purpose to another. Having a wide-open assignment does not give you license to say everything; it gives you the added responsibility of determining a clear purpose.

Determine Your Specific Purpose

The second part of determining your purpose is deciding what you will do with the assigned subject in order to express yourself, inform readers, or persuade readers. Taking the general purpose and adding your own narrowed topic leads to your *specific purpose*. This specific purpose will eventually be the basis for your thesis sentence—a clear statement of the point of your paper. (We'll say more about the term *thesis sentence* on page 429.)

What is a *specific purpose*?   Take a look at the following chart, which will help you see the difference between an assignment's general purpose and a writer's specific purpose. Each writer has narrowed the topic of *holiday* or *celebration* to the particular one he or she will express feelings about, inform readers about, or persuade readers about in a brief paper.

Lesson 41

plan

IF YOUR GENERAL PURPOSE IS...	YOUR SPECIFIC PURPOSE MIGHT BE...
To express your feelings about a holiday or celebration	To show readers how special it was for your family to go to Mardi Gras in Mobile, Alabama
	To express your discomfort with school-sponsored celebrations of Halloween
To inform others about a holiday or celebration	To explain the history of Mardi Gras in Mobile
	To inform others about the ancient origins of Halloween
To make an argument about a holiday or celebration	To persuade readers that the Mardi Gras celebration in Mobile is better than the one in New Orleans
	To argue that Halloween should not be celebrated in public schools

Understand Your Audience

When you are narrowing your subject and purpose, you should consider your audience. Are you writing for just your teacher, a larger public, or a specific group? Once you make this determination, there are many additional questions to ask. We suggest you start with two: (1) What do readers already *know* about the subject? and (2) What *attitudes* might they already have about it?

Ask Questions about Your Audience.   These questions will help you to consider your audience's knowledge of and attitudes about your subject.

- What should I assume readers already know about the subject?

- What information would readers consider new, necessary, and insightful?

- Will they care about the subject and have strong opinions about it?

- Will they resist any of my ideas?

Lesson 41

plan

Suppose your nursing instructor asks you to present a proposal for improving response time in a hospital emergency room and tells you that your audience is a group of local hospital administrators. Your *general purpose* will be to persuade your readers, and your *specific purpose* will be to argue for your idea about how to solve the problem. In planning, you would keep in mind that administrators often think of the hospital's bottom-line financial situation first, so solutions that require an increase in staff without an increase in revenue will meet with resistance. If, on the other hand, your audience is fellow nurses committed to quality care, you may have to work harder to propose that ER staff spend less time with each patient. What's certain is that your proposal will be strengthened by careful consideration of your audience's point of view.

> **COMMONSENSE TIP:** It can be frustrating to worry about second-guessing an audience, especially if it is one you find intimidating. However, at least consider an audience's general level of expertise and attitude about your subject. If it is distracting to try to define your audience exactly, wait until later. But don't dismiss having at least a *basic* idea of how your audience might react to what you have to say.

Connecting Purpose and Audience

To understand how these abstract suggestions can be turned into something concrete, consider another student's planning choices. Stephanie's teacher assigned a paper during the first week of a writing class. Stephanie understood that, in essence, she had to explain why she chose to go to college.

Her initial impulse was to list several general reasons explaining why she and most people go to college; however, Stephanie decided to consider her writing situation more carefully. First, she took out the assignment sheet (often called a *prompt*) and highlighted the words that indicated the purpose of the paper (general or specific purpose) and the audience.

> Write an **explanation** of **why** you decided to attend college. This **information** will help **me understand** you better as both a **person** and a **writer**. Keep your response to one paragraph of 250 to 300 words, and bring it to our next class meeting.

Obviously, the teacher would be the audience for this paper (the word *me* emphasized this fact). The words *explanation, information,* and *understand* made it clear to Stephanie that the general purpose of this short paper would be to inform—to tell this teacher something new and useful. Stephanie's specific purpose seemed merely to explain why she went to college. As straightforward as this prompt seemed, the more Stephanie thought about it,

Lesson 41

plan

the more she questioned her plan of listing several reasons why most people attend college. She thought about two planning issues more carefully: her specific purpose and how her audience might react to various options.

In devoting more time to planning, Stephanie correctly assumed her teacher would not be really informed if all Stephanie did was briefly cover a number of reasons why most people go to college. First, this teacher had probably heard the same general reasons already, and it is difficult to inform someone in such a position by providing only basic, commonplace explanations. In addition, Stephanie saw that the prompt indicated that the teacher wanted to know the students better as *individuals*, so Stephanie had to think about reasons why *she* in particular went to college—not why people in general go.

Thus, Stephanie's first major decision during the planning stage was to approach her explanation in a way that would not be generic or ordinary, for she indeed had her own special experiences that influenced her choice of attending college. After reflecting on these experiences, she developed a more specific purpose that she eventually turned into the first sentence of her paragraph. Below is a draft, with this "purpose sentence" underlined.

> *Like many people, I decided to go to college because I want job opportunities, but I am also here because I want to avoid the problems my brothers now face. In some ways, I am like other students you have encountered. I am in college because a college degree will give me the skills employers want. What I hope you will understand about me, however, is that I am also in college because I have seen people close to me jump into major responsibilities right after high school, and I have seen how college can often take a backseat to other things. My two brothers, Carl and Tom, had all sorts of plans about what they would do with a college degree, but they postponed these so they could marry and have full-time jobs. I know people are able to go back to college in situations such as theirs, but Carl and Tom are now so caught up with their jobs and families that they do not know when, if ever, they will return to college. Are they happy? I think so. Will a college degree guarantee happiness? I know it does not. However, I decided to go to college before taking on major responsibilities and to make sure I have the opportunity to find out if college is for me. It is still early to tell, but I am glad I can take time to determine what I want to do in life.*

Everything in this paragraph goes back to a unique specific purpose that arose when Stephanie gave time to making plans based around both purpose and audience. Later, we will discuss in detail why writers revise drafts, but it isn't too early to stress that writers must consider how to alter their plans. Stephanie worried that her teacher might find the paragraph *too* personal or might assume Stephanie was making massive generalizations

Lesson 41

plan

about the chances of older adults going to college. Stephanie decided she would stay with her true feelings since these did indeed account for why she chose college, but she chose to delete the last sentence of her draft and add the following:

> *Perhaps my brothers can find out one day if college would make them happier, for I see many older, married students at this college. However, I decided to find out now if college is for me, rather than waiting for "one day" that might never happen.*

In sum, this student started to do what many writers do when first given an assignment: write about the first ideas that come to mind, and cover each idea very quickly. Only after considering a purpose that her audience might appreciate more, did this particular student begin writing a paragraph that avoids these common problems.

Explore Your Subject and Develop Support

For your paper to be effective, you must narrow your topic to something you can manage within the boundaries of the assignment. For example, a three- to five-page essay would hardly cover the broad subject of *nutrition*. But if you spend some time exploring aspects of the topic that most interest you and are appropriate to your purpose and your audience, you might come up with a narrower, more manageable subject like *the importance of folic acid in a pregnant woman's diet*. Here are three prewriting strategies to help you narrow your subject and decide what you might use as supporting information.

ESL

If English is not your first language, you may find it easier to freewrite, cluster, or ask questions in your native language. The idea behind these prewriting strategies is to narrow a topic and explore ideas without the burden of correct spelling or grammar at this early stage.

Freewriting.   This technique is helpful for people whose thinking is often spontaneous and creative (which would include most of us some of the time). Here are some guidelines:

- **Start writing** on the assigned subject or task without worrying about where you are headed. Just do a "mind spill," spontaneously writing whatever comes to mind about the subject and/or your purpose.

- **Write quickly** and legibly, but avoid thinking too long about what you should say next. Just keep pen or fingers moving. Do not worry about spelling, grammar, wording, or anything that slows your thinking. You are writing to generate ideas for yourself, not for others.

Lesson 41

plan

- **Keep writing** whatever comes to mind. There is no magic time limit, but write long enough so that new ideas develop and the words come more easily.

- **Ask questions** if you are running into "writer's block." Don't talk yourself into believing you have nothing to say. If all else fails, explain why you think you have nothing to say, or answer one of these questions: "How has this subject affected me personally?" or "Why has it never mattered?"

- **Reflect** on what you have written after you are done. Reread your freewriting and look for something that interests you or your readers. Circle these parts.

Clustering.   Instead of sentences, use words and brief phrases to explore a subject. Clustering has a visual aspect that appeals to many writers. Here are the basic steps:

- **Write down your subject** in the middle of a blank page. Circle it.

- **Start branching** off this central idea. That is, write down related words that come to mind. Circle each new idea. Draw lines to connect related ideas.

- **Continue branching** as related ideas cross your mind. Don't expect that every idea will have the same number of branches. Your point is to explore ideas, not to draw a tidy diagram.

- **Develop several layers** for at least a couple of topics. If you don't have many layers, you could wind up with ordinary, rather superficial ideas.

- **Reflect** on what you have written after you are done. Then examine the connections you have made and continue to draw lines between groups of ideas. Doing so allows you to consider how ideas support one another.

The next page shows a cluster based around an assignment that asks students to describe ways to enhance safety. One writer, as part of his planning, decided that he needed to narrow the broad topic of "safety" to something more focused and manageable. Notice that this writer developed some ideas more than others.

Think about what clustering does. You not only come up with a more specific subject, you come up with major ideas to bring in to your writing. If this writer decided to write on "road rage," the cluster diagram offers supporting ideas, such as "ways to control temper" and "relaxation techniques."

Lesson 41

plan

COMMONSENSE TIP: Use these planning techniques whenever you need to develop ideas. In this section, we focus on clustering and other techniques to help you narrow your subject and come up with major ideas, but you can use these techniques earlier in the process to choose a subject and determine your audience and purpose. These techniques also help you to find and group supporting ideas.

Questioning. With this technique, you respond to the kinds of questions your audience might ask about your subject and purpose. This technique resembles freewriting, but it is more structured.

- **Write down** your general purpose, specific purpose, and possible audience.

- **Answer the set of questions** that best relates to your general purpose:

IF YOUR ASSIGNMENT IS...	ANSWER THESE QUESTIONS...
Expressive	• What could you say about your own experiences with this subject that would also matter to your readers?
	• What would interest them because they have had *similar* experiences they could relate to mine?
	• What experiences are so unusual that readers would be intrigued?
Informative	• What questions might the audience have about this subject?
	• What do they *need* to know in order to be fully informed?
	• If readers are somehow going to use this information in their lives, what should they know?
Persuasive	• What controversies arise from your subject or claim?
	• How would you defend your position against specific objections raised by readers?
	• What additional information or evidence could you provide that would change their minds?
	• What could you probably never change their minds about?

Using Questions.   This third technique might be the most complex, so consider how one student, Brandon, used questioning when asked to write a persuasive paragraph dealing with computer technology. After freewriting about what he knows most about computers, he chose to write about a computer game. Specifically, he decided on the following:

General Purpose: Persuade

Specific Purpose: The computer game Empire Lord has several problems that keep it from being worth buying.

Audience: People who play computer games regularly.

Brandon had a good idea of what his purpose and audience would be, but he was not sure what to include in just a paragraph. He used questioning to help himself decide not only what to say but what support was most important. Before writing a draft, he chose a question to help him.

How would I defend my position against specific objections raised by my readers?

This game has obvious problems, so I'm not sure why people would object, unless they haven't played it. I guess I need to make it clear I'm writing for people who've only <u>heard</u> about the game, not played it. These readers might think I'm being too harsh because people like different things about games. They might say I'm just basing my opinion on what I personally prefer.

This questioning technique helped Brandon realize that he needed to change his audience slightly (to people who play computer games regularly but have not played Empire Lord). He also discovered a problem that any evaluation can have: how to keep it from being based just on the personal preferences of the writer. The questioning allowed him to discover a potential problem but not what to do about it. Thus, Brandon came up with his own question to help him plan further.

So how can I keep my evaluation from seeming like I'm basing it just on what I want in a game?

Well, I know my personal preferences about games can be unique. For instance, I prefer computer games that aren't connected with this one company that wouldn't answer my e-mail about that other game I bought last year. So I guess I'll stay away from those sorts of preferences. But I know that a lot of people expect a game such as Empire Lord to let you easily play against other people on the Internet and let you play on most standard computers. Those are reasonable expectations, not just "personal preferences." It seems fair for my evaluation to be based on things that would bother most people, not just me.

Through such questioning, Brandon realized how to change his initial plans and how to use reasons that many people, not just Brandon, would consider fair. After some work, here is the end result of this planning.

Lesson 41

plan

If you like "role playing" computer games, you should avoid Empire Lord. In this game, the player picks a character who has to complete a number of missions. When I first played the game, for instance, I chose to be a "warrior" who had to find four missing jewels, and each was guarded by several monsters. This is a common approach in role-playing games, so there is not much new in Empire Lord. However, two major problems keep this game from being worth the current price of about $60. First, most games nowadays allow you to play on-line with other people, but Empire Lord does not allow this option. Once you find the jewels, the game has nothing left for you to do. Playing on-line would allow you to team up with other players or compete against them, meaning you can play the game as long as you can find someone on-line. Without this option, Empire Lord does not allow much diversity. In addition, it has hefty requirements in terms of what kind of computer you can use. I tried it on three new, high-powered computers. On all three, Empire Lord required too much computer memory, and the movements of my characters were sluggish. It is difficult to compete against the monsters in the game when your character moves slowly. If the price drops considerably, the game might be worth a look, but I do not encourage you to run out and pay full price for this flawed game.

Note that Brandon's draft does not actually use sentences from his responses to the two questions. Instead, he used questioning as a way to discover potential problems and then to provide the sort of support that would deal with these problems.

Write a Thesis Sentence

Once you have explored possible topics and purposes, you should write an initial thesis sentence. This sentence expresses the point you want to make in your paper. It may change as you think more about your assignment, but it helps to have a *working thesis* at this point. In most college writing, a thesis sentence has these characteristics:

- It states the writer's single main point.
- It is clear and specific.
- It is placed in the opening paragraph (generally, it is the first or last sentence).
- It prepares readers for the rest of the paper.

Here are some sample thesis sentences based on the general and specific purposes described on page 421.

Lesson 41

plan

THESIS SENTENCES FOR EXPRESSIVE WRITING

When I was young, I never fully appreciated why going to Mardi Gras parades was so important to my family, but now I do.

Halloween might seem a casual, fun-loving holiday for some, but for me Halloween was offensive and uncomfortable when I felt forced to celebrate it in school.

THESIS SENTENCES FOR INFORMATIVE WRITING

The Mardi Gras celebration in Mobile, Alabama, has a colorful history covering some three hundred years.

If you think Halloween is just a "kids' night," you might be surprised to know that this holiday has ancient religious origins.

THESIS SENTENCES FOR PERSUASIVE WRITING

For the public benefit, authorities in Mobile should strictly enforce the no-alcohol policy at this year's Mardi Gras celebration.

Halloween should not be celebrated in public schools.

> COMMONSENSE TIP: See pages 436–37 for a list of different types of topic sentences that indicate the purpose of a single paragraph. Read through these categories to get an idea of the various ways to create a thesis sentence.

ESL

In some cultures, writers avoid making points directly. In English, however, readers appreciate writing that has a clear, direct point. Start by drafting a thesis sentence. You can revise it to make it more straightforward later.

Plan Your Paper's Organization

Once you have some idea about what you want to say, consider how to organize, or arrange, these ideas. Sometimes, deciding how to arrange ideas helps writers come up with a better purpose or better support, so be willing to make changes.

Think of your paper as needing these distinct parts:

1. an **introduction:** a way to announce your subject, draw your reader's attention and interest, and indicate your specific purpose and main point
2. a **body:** the section in which you provide major ideas and supporting ideas to achieve your purpose
3. a **conclusion:** the place where your readers feel a sense of completion

The first step of planning your paper's organization is to remind yourself of your purpose.

COMMONSENSE TIP: If you are still not sure how to word your thesis sentence, try to phrase it in the most direct way possible: "In this paper, my primary purpose is to . . . ." Later, you can revise this sentence to be less formulaic.

The next step is to answer this question: *Does the teacher expect a particular type of organization?* You must determine how much flexibility you have in organizing your paper. Look at the assignment's wording, ask classmates, ask your teacher, or reread any material covered in class about organization. Teachers often expect writers to use a particular organizing structure. Sometimes, they are direct about this expectation by using certain "tip off" words:

"TIP OFF" WORDS FOR A PREFERRED ORGANIZATION

arrange	method of development	pattern
develop	mode	scheme
form	order	shape
format	organize	structure

Your writing instructor may name the type of writing you are to do (such as a business letter, a lab report, or a book review) and expect you to use the organization associated with this type of writing. Most common assignments, however, require you to organize your writing in whatever way best suits your purpose, audience, and subject. In a personal narrative, you might present events in chronological (time) order. In an informative essay, you might, for example, explain a process by proceeding through the steps in the process. Finally, you might develop a persuasive essay by presenting your ideas in order of importance, from strong to strongest. No matter what the assignment, you can think further about your organization by writing an informal outline.

Write an Informal Outline.   Think of an outline as a *tentative plan* for arranging your ideas. Some students remember being told to write an outline with so many formal *dos* and *don'ts*, they have forgotten its real purpose. We suggest you develop an outline that is more than rough notes, but not so formal that it distracts you from your writing process. That is, develop an outline that would be clear to someone else (especially if you want feedback), but avoid becoming frustrated by questions such as "Do I indent three or five spaces?" or "Do I use a Roman numeral or not here?" Even if you are

Lesson 41

plan

given formal rules to follow, it is more manageable to start with an informal outline that focuses on ideas, not technical details. You can revise it later.

Write an informal outline that indicates the following:

- your thesis statement (the point of your paper)
- your major support
- some minor ideas that support the major ones

An outline should also reflect the type of organization that readers expect or the type you have selected.

Here is an outline of one writer's effort to persuade her company's benefits manager to endorse a tuition reimbursement program for employees. The assignment did not specify a type of organization, so the writer decided to give background information, anticipate any opposition, and then base the major body paragraphs on the reasons supporting her thesis.

> *Thesis: As part of the general employee benefits package, the Company should provide tuition reimbursement.*
>
> *Introduction*
>
> > *—Discuss the Company's history of high turnover and poor employee retention.*
> >
> > *—Discuss recent news about the value of adult education.*
> >
> > *—State thesis.*
>
> *Body*
>
> *(Anticipate possible opposition) A tuition reimbursement program is unnecessary.*
>
> > *—Tuition reimbursement is too expensive.*
> >
> > *—The Company's training department sufficiently meets the needs of the company.*
>
> *(Major support point) A tuition reimbursement fund is not wasted money.*
>
> > *—Tuition reimbursement offsets the costs of advertising for, recruiting, and training new employees.*
> >
> > *—Tuition reimbursement as part of a comprehensive benefits package attracts quality job candidates and retains good employees.*
>
> *(Major support point) Tuition reimbursement builds employee confidence and job satisfaction.*

Lesson 41

plan

—*This kind of program helps employees to build job-relevant skills.*

—*Increased job satisfaction means a decrease in employee turnover.*

(Major support point) Tuition reimbursement programs enhance a company's internal training function.

—*Employee education is strengthened by a team approach; company trainers still assess employees' needs and then inform employees about local schools and programs that meet those needs.*

—*The Company's internal training staff is free from repeated new-employee training; staff can focus on developing more customized programs.*

Conclusion

—*Summarize benefits of thesis.*

—*Emphasize that a tuition reimbursement program can help the Company fulfill its mission: to develop quality products and honor quality employees.*

COMMONSENSE TIP: Use question marks, bullets, indentation, or numbered lists to remind you where you have questions or to indicate which ideas are more important than others. The appearance of an outline can help you see how ideas connect. Don't obsess over making your outline look neat and orderly, though.

BUT WHAT HAPPENS IF . . . ?

"I don't know how many paragraphs I should have—especially in the middle part of my paper." There is no magic number of paragraphs a paper needs, but you should consider any number indicated in the assignment, the length requirements of the paper, and how much you need to say to achieve your specific purpose. Unless the assignment calls for a very short paper, you need more than one paragraph in the body. At the same time, be careful not to have too many. For example, more than ten paragraphs in a three-page paper may mean that your paragraphs are too short to be clear, convincing, or interesting.

"I can sketch out major ideas, but I don't know what to put under them." You may find it helpful to do more freewriting, clustering, or questioning (see pages 424–29). Then you could add more to your outline.

Lesson 41

plan

LESSON 42
Drafting

As you begin to draft, you should have a clear plan for your paper based on the following checklist.

_____ I have determined the assignment's *general purpose:* expressive, informative, or persuasive.

_____ I have determined my *specific purpose:* what I specifically want to express, inform readers about, or persuade them to believe (my narrowed topic).

_____ I have considered my *audience* and have an idea of who will (or should) read my paper, their background in the subject, and their attitude toward it.

_____ I have written a working *thesis sentence:* a clear and specific statement of the point of my paper.

_____ I have developed major *support* for my specific purpose: the main explanations, information, evidence, or events that will help me make my overall point.

_____ I have written an *organizational plan:* the way I will arrange at least the major ideas.

(If there is an item on this list that you have not considered, you may want to do some more planning.)

Now you should write a draft, modifying your plan or discarding it if necessary. The key to successful drafting is *flexibility.* We suggest you start with a basic introduction that includes your specific purpose and thesis statement, and prepares your reader for the rest of your paper, and then proceed by drafting according to your informal outline.

COMMONSENSE TIP: Don't spend a huge amount of time on the introduction while you are drafting. If drafting the paper causes you to modify your specific purpose and thesis, you'll need to revise the introduction anyway.

Lesson 42

draft

Pay most attention to presenting the point of your paper (purpose), to developing your ideas (support), and to connecting these ideas to each other (organization). Pay less attention to stylistic and mechanical matters covered in the first part of this book. You can address these matters in the revision stage.

Write Topic Sentences and Paragraphs

Let's start by drafting paragraphs. Keep in mind that each paragraph should include just one main topic. If your paragraph "rambles," or covers too many topics, you run the risk of confusing your readers.

One way writers help readers is by using topic sentences. A topic sentence is usually a one-sentence statement that indicates the purpose, subject, or point of a paragraph. It might help you to think of the topic sentence as the controlling idea for a paragraph. Just as a thesis sentence presents the controlling idea for a paper, a topic sentence presents the controlling idea for each paragraph in the body of your paper. Sometimes, in fact, you might be assigned to write just a paragraph, not an entire essay. In this case, your topic sentence becomes your contract with your readers. (See page 438 for guidelines on completing the single-paragraph assignment.)

There is no law requiring that the topic sentence should be the first sentence of a paragraph, but for two reasons we suggest you start each paragraph in the body of your paper with a topic sentence.

- An introductory topic sentence gives you something to refer to while developing the paragraph, reminding you of the point. You can always alter your use of topic sentences later.

- Topic sentences help readers identify your major ideas.

> COMMONSENSE TIP: One exception to the important role of topic sentences is narration, telling a story (often called a "personal narrative"). When relating an experience, you might not use topic sentences often, though you would still divide the story into paragraphs. Instead of using topic sentences, you would rely on chronological order, telling events as they happened, and careful transitions.

Topic sentences vary in how they convey the main idea of a paragraph. Try various approaches. If you use a question for every topic sentence in a paper (or worse, in all your papers), for example, your readers could find your paper predictable and boring.

Lesson 42

draft

COMMON TYPES OF TOPIC SENTENCES

The Direct Approach explicitly announces the purpose of the paragraph.

> *In this paragraph, I want to explain why the school would lose money with a football team.*
>
> *Now, I want to argue that women are also not treated fairly in terms of health benefits.*
>
> *The purpose of this paragraph is to define a few important terms.*

The Question indicates the paragraph's purpose by posing a question it will answer.

> *Why should we debate this issue anyway?*
>
> *Where does lava come from?*
>
> *What effects did this experience have on me?*
>
> *What is the history of this problem?*

The Nutshell states the major idea — not the purpose — of the paragraph, usually in just one sentence. (This is probably the most common type of topic sentence in college writing.)

> *A second reason for impeaching the governor is that she received illegal contributions.*
>
> *Before long, I realized my aunt was sick.*
>
> *A second difference between astronomy and astrology involves the notion of scientific proof.*
>
> *The island was full of many strange objects.*

Addressing the Reader anticipates what readers might be wondering about or doubting. The paragraph provides a response.

> *You might be wondering why it is necessary to build a new stadium.*
>
> *My opponents would reasonably question my statistics, but the figures are accurate.*
>
> *A response to my solution is that it costs too much; however, money is not a problem.*
>
> *If I were you, I would wonder why the bull didn't attack me.*

Connecting to the Previous Paragraph makes a clear link with the preceding ideas.

> *In contrast, however, the African swallow flies at a much faster rate.*

After you complete the third step, proceed to the next: applying the varnish.

Let me offer one example of this concept.

Nonetheless, I disagree with the aforementioned article.

Before making this argument, though, I want to provide a few definitions.

The Alert calls special attention to a point the paragraph will cover. Readers should understand the importance of the paragraph.

It would be a mistake to assume that students do not care about racism.

If our leaders do not change this law, there will be a terrible price to pay.

Nothing will ever make me forget what I felt when I heard about Juan's death.

Do not forget this next piece of information.

But the most important reason for seeing the movie is that it will never be released on video.

With a topic sentence to guide you as well as your readers, you can now provide the details needed to clarify, support, or expand the paragraph's point.

COMMONSENSE TIP: Be careful about being too direct when you write a topic sentence. Although useful for complex or highly formal papers, it often strikes readers as dull and contrived. However, the direct approach can be useful in a draft to clarify what you should focus on. You could revise it later into something less direct.

Strategies for Writing a Single-Paragraph Assignment

Suppose your assignment is to write not a complete essay but a single paragraph. For example, you may have to write a paragraph-length response to an exam question, or your writing instructor might begin the semester with a paragraph assignment. Fortunately, almost everything covered in this writing guide applies to writing paragraphs. When planning, drafting, and revising a paragraph, you still have to consider basic standards for effective writing (like those outlined on page 408). Here is a checklist for completing the single-paragraph assignment.

Lesson 42

draft

Checklist: Writing a Paragraph

_____ Determine your purpose. See page 418.
  • Determine the general purpose of the assignment (to express, to inform, or to persuade).
  • Determine your specific purpose.

_____ Consider your audience. See page 421.
  • Ask yourself questions about your readers' knowledge of and attitudes about your subject.

_____ Use a prewriting strategy (freewriting, clustering, questioning) to narrow your subject. See page 424.

_____ Write a topic sentence that states the main point of your paragraph. See page 429.

_____ Based on what you considered while prewriting, choose the details, examples, and evidence that best support your topic sentence. See page 430.

_____ Consider how you will organize these supporting ideas so that they clearly build on one another. See pages 430–33.
  • Arrange these ideas in a brief informal outline of your paragraph.
  • Plan a paragraph that is clearly structured. See page 435. In college writing, a paragraph often has the following parts:

    a *topic sentence* that states the main point of your paragraph
    a *body* made up of several sentences that support, explain, or prove your topic sentence
    a *concluding sentence* that takes readers back to the main idea of the paragraph

_____ Write a draft of your paragraph based on your planning. See page 439.

_____ Revise your paragraph. Consider what steps you might take to improve it. See page 445.
  • Ask your teacher and other students for their feedback.
  • Ask yourself revision questions based on your purpose.
  • Ask yourself revision questions based on the five basic standards.

_____ Edit your paragraph by eliminating errors in grammar, punctuation, mechanics, and word use. Follow specific guidelines given in Units 1 through 11 of this book.

Lesson 42

draft

Consider how the following paragraph, written as part of an economics exam, reflects some of the steps in the checklist on page 438.

EXAMPLE ASSIGNMENT: **Explain the difference between a country's gross domestic product (GDP) and its gross national product (GNP).**

EXAMPLE PARAGRAPH RESPONSE:

> *Though they are both important indicators of a country's economic well-being, GNP and GDP are not the same. The GNP is the total market value of all goods and services produced by a country's labor force and capital anywhere in the world. For example, the market value of clothing produced and sold by The Gap, regardless of store and factory location, would figure into the United States' GNP. The GNP would include profits earned from Canadian and European stores, as well as from stores in places like Boston, Atlanta, and Los Angeles. The GDP, on the other hand, is the total market value of goods and services produced by a country's labor force and capital within a country's borders. Profits earned by The Gap in places other than the United States would not count toward the country's GDP. Each of these figures is a separate but equally valuable way to measure a country's economic health.*

As the topic sentence indicates, the paragraph will focus on differences between GNP and GDP, and every sentence afterward explains at least one of these two concepts. Because this is a complex paragraph with technical information, the paragraph ends by reminding us of the overall point.

Put More Support into Paragraphs

Drafting involves arranging and developing the major ideas you sketched out in your outline. You should present each major idea in a paragraph. Then, within each paragraph, you have to provide additional details and support for the major idea. Avoid simply rewording your topic sentence; support it by adding new information, evidence, or ideas in each paragraph. To do this, ask yourself questions based on your purpose and audience.

QUESTIONS TO ASK WHEN DRAFTING PARAGRAPHS

General purpose: *to express*

* If my subject involves an experience, what details can I include to bring this experience to life? How do I make clear to my audience how this experience affected me?

* If I am writing about a more abstract subject (such as something I read or a feeling I have about an idea), what details should I include to describe this subject and, more important, my personal reaction to it?

Lesson 42

draft

General purpose: *to inform*

- Considering limits on the paper's length, what should I tell my audience about the subject? What details, examples, or explanations will they need?

- Have I defined important terms, especially those that have a special meaning?

- To help readers understand the subject, can I compare it to something more familiar? Have I fully described the parts or functions of my subject?

- What information could I add that would be new to readers?

General purpose: *to persuade*

- What are the major reasons why readers should accept the claim I am making?

- To prove my point, can I draw on what other writers have said?

- Can I give real or hypothetical examples to support my argument?

- If readers have doubts about my facts, can I convince them that my information is accurate?

- Have I carefully considered any objections or criticisms my readers might raise?

> **COMMONSENSE TIP:** If your paragraph becomes too long, divide it into two or more paragraphs. You should avoid having more than one purpose or point in a single paragraph, but you certainly can have two or more paragraphs that deal with a similar idea in different ways.

Read a Sample Personal Narrative

Let's consider a sample assignment, one student's writing process, and his draft. The assignment is a personal narrative, one of the most common assignments in composition classes. It is generally a story about yourself, usually focused on an experience that is especially important to you.

Daryl is a twenty-eight-year-old returning student, and his assignment was worded as follows:

> *Write about an experience that made you realize how important your family or friends are to your life.*

Lesson 42

draft

As you go through Daryl's steps, notice how he adjusted his original plan as he drafted and discovered new ideas. He also adapted the process described above to suit his needs; he didn't follow a formula.

Step 1: Determine the general purpose of this assignment. The assignment doesn't seem to call for a persuasive essay because there is no controversy. The general purpose could be informative, since Daryl has to describe an event. But notice that the focus the assignment gives to the writer is the writer's experience, life, friends, family, and the way in which all of this is important to the writer. So Daryl assumes that the general purpose is expressive, though he will need to inform his readers as he writes.

Therefore, Daryl decides that he . . .

will focus on something personally important

does not have to argue a point

should focus more on his life than on "hard facts" or abstractions

Step 2: Consider how the audience might affect the paper. Because the assignment does not specify anything about an audience, Daryl assumes that this paper should be written for his writing teacher, but he also wants other readers to be interested in his life and relate to his experience. He's not altogether comfortable with this decision about who his readers are, however.

Therefore, Daryl decides that he . . .

can be informal

will reconsider his audience at a later stage

Step 3: Narrow the topic to determine a specific purpose. Daryl uses freewriting to explore a more specific purpose and topic. He writes for five minutes about various experiences, but he is most moved when he writes about his son, Russell, who had breathing problems when he was born a year ago. He decides he wants to explore the significance of this event further.

Therefore, Daryl decides that he . . .

will describe the first few days of his son's life

Step 4: Develop support and write an informal outline. Daryl writes a direct thesis sentence he will revise later; for now, he only wants to clarify his specific purpose to himself. In writing other papers, Daryl sometimes had to think quite a bit about what he wanted to say before he outlined a draft. However, with this personal narrative, Daryl already knows in general what he wants to say—the story. He makes a list of specific details that support his thesis. Then he proceeds to outlining, and while doing so, he also decides on the sequence of events he will describe and the organization of his paper.

Daryl writes an informal outline:

Lesson 42

draft

Thesis statement: In this paper, I will describe how the anxiety and excitement of Russell's birth made me realize how important my family is to me.

<u>Introduction:</u> The birth
    -- Russell arrived three weeks early
    -- I was thrilled when I held him

<u>Body:</u>
The scare
    -- Russell started breathing quickly
    -- Gina and I felt so helpless
    -- The doctors put Russell in a special crib for monitoring
The waiting
    -- My mom made an important comment
    -- Our long nights of worrying seemed to last forever
    -- I watched Russell through the glass
The recovery
    -- He started to get better
    -- Pretty soon he was healthy enough to come home

<u>Conclusion:</u> I still have dreams about what could have happened, but this experience made me realize how important my family is to me.

Step 5: Write a draft.   As Daryl works on his draft, he remembers one of the most important aspects of a personal narrative—it must have personal significance. As he writes, the significance of his experience becomes clearer to Daryl himself. He understands why this incident was special: it made him appreciate his family more, and it still causes him to worry over their well-being, even though it has always been difficult for him to say so.

    Therefore, Daryl decides to . . .

    draft his personal narrative with an emphasis on his personal feelings about his son's birth and how those feelings continue to affect him

Before you read Daryl's draft, consider the following guidelines. We tailored the Basic Standards from page 407 to fit a personal narrative.

GUIDELINES FOR PERSONAL NARRATIVES

Purpose.   The essay should be focused on narrating a specific event, one that has a point that is important to the writer and with which the reader can relate.

Support.   The writer should include enough details to describe the people, places, things, and events that are important to the story's point.

Lesson 42

draft

Organization.   Normally, a personal narrative is told in chronological order (the order in which events occurred). It can start and end with general comments about the event (such as background information or an explanation of the point of the story).

Style.   A personal narrative uses precise words when describing events. The style is relatively informal, reflecting the author's personal way of communicating.

Mechanics.   A personal narrative generally follows the same conventions as other college papers do: error-free is best.

Here is Daryl's first draft. How well does it reflect the guidelines listed above? Remember that at this point in the process, Daryl still has time to revise based on feedback from readers and other writers. (Daryl's revision is not included here. You will have the opportunity to revise his draft in the next lesson.)

DARYL'S ROUGH DRAFT

Russell's Birth

Russell arrived three weeks early. He was going by his own schedule and not ours and the doctor's. After a mad rush to the hospital and seven hours of labor, a nurse wrapped my newborn baby in a blanket and weighed him. She put him in my wife Gina's arms and then in mine. When I held Russell, it was love at first sight. I wasn't at all prepared for what happened next, though. Sometimes, I have a hard time telling my family how I feel about them, but the excitement and anxiety of Russell's birth made me realize how important family is to me.

Shortly after Russell was born, something started to go wrong. He started breathing quickly, and his heart started beating faster. The doctor didn't know exactly what was wrong, but she assured Gina and me that the condition was probably temporary. That didn't make us feel much better. Russell was taken away to the neo-natal intensive care room for monitoring and observation. He was put into a special crib that looked like a big glass box, and he was surrounded with all kinds of equipment so the doctors could see how hard his heart was beating. All the while my heart was breaking. He looked sad in the glass box, all by himself.

My mom arrived at the hospital about an hour after Russell was born. As she sat with Gina and me, she didn't say much, and I was wondering what she was thinking. She finally mumbled quietly, "Nothing could ever happen to such a beautiful baby boy." Her voice started to shake, and she started to cry. We did too.

After a couple of days, I had to go home to take care of our three-year-old daughter, but I kept thinking about what my mom said. "Could

Lesson 42

draft

anything happen to my beautiful baby boy?" I wondered. Could something happen to him before he learned to go for walks with me, play with his sister, or throw a baseball? I was filled with new-dad anxiety all over again, but this time, it was more intense. We never imagined our newborn would be sick.

I went to see Baby Russell in his glass crib the next day. His condition was still the same. We talked and talked with the doctors, who were working hard to clear up Russell's infection. Late one night, I looked at him through the glass. I said what my mom said, "Nothing could ever happen to this beautiful baby boy!" Nobody heard me — except Russell, I think. Nobody except me saw what he did. He looked directly at me through all the wires that the doctors put on him. He seemed to say, so softly only I could hear him, "Hiiiiiiiiiiii. . . ." I knew right then what Russell was trying to tell me. He had turned a corner. He closed his eyes and went to sleep, but this time with what looked like a little smile on his face. I smiled too. I think my heart skipped a beat.

That brave little heart started getting better. Gina and I counted our blessings. Russell was soon out of the glass box and back in our arms. We even let his big sister Chandra hold him. Boy, was she proud! In a few days, nobody could even tell that Russell had been so sick.

Sometimes, even a year later, I still wake up at night because I dream of the worst. I peek upstairs to make sure my little girl and boy are safe and sound. When I know they're okay, I can get back to sleep peacefully. I love them very much — even though I don't always tell them how much they mean to me.

Lesson 42

draft

LESSON 43
Revising

If your deadline allows, put your draft aside for a while and return later to the task of revising it. You might make small changes here and there as you draft, but don't consider your writing complete simply because you have put your ideas onto paper. Now it is time to consider how your draft can be improved. You will get the most out of this stage of writing if you understand one of the most often-overlooked principles of writing.

> **COMMONSENSE TIP:** Revision is *more* than looking for problems with individual words and sentences. It means looking for ways to improve your overall purpose, support, and organization. You revise your paper to make it clearer and stronger.

Too often, writers look only at individual sentences and words when they revise. These are important, of course; that is why we wrote this book. However, a grammatically correct paper can be useless if it lacks ideas or is unorganized. This lesson will help you revise your paper.

Ask Questions as You Revise

Many writers are confused about what to revise. As one student put it, "If I knew what had to be revised, I would have done it when I drafted the paper!" But even experienced writers cannot keep track of all the questions they could ask themselves as they write that would improve their paper. Revising, therefore, means looking for opportunities for improvement that perhaps did not occur to you in the midst of putting ideas into words, sentences, and paragraphs.

In college, you are usually writing not just for yourself but for others, so it is useful to obtain feedback from at least one other person. It might be helpful to write down specific questions for this person to consider. Developing a habit of asking yourself such questions will also help you understand what to revise when feedback isn't practical. Here are two sets of questions to ask of your draft:

Questions based on your *general purpose*.

Questions based on *basic standards* that apply to most college writing.

These overlap, but each set of questions presents a different way of thinking about revision. Tailor these to fit your own specific purpose and situation.

Ask Questions about *General Purpose.*   We began this writing guide by telling you to start your writing process by determining your purpose. You should also make a habit of rethinking your purpose at the revision stage. Here are some more questions to ask yourself as you revise.

GENERAL PURPOSE: *TO EXPRESS*

- What is the point of my story? Is that point clear?
- Does this paper give an account of how I really feel?
- What details could I add to help show how I feel or think about my subject?
- Have I brought my subject to life for my readers?
- Are the events in my narrative arranged in an order that makes sense for my purpose and audience?

GENERAL PURPOSE: *TO INFORM*

- What is the point of my paper? Is that point clear?
- What information have I left out? Would readers expect me to cover this material?
- Have I told my readers something that is new or not widely known? Have I provided enough examples or explanations?
- Have I gone beyond the "basic idea" and given my readers a deeper understanding of the subject?
- Can I add more facts, details, or examples, perhaps based on research?
- Are my details and examples arranged in an order that makes sense for my purpose and audience?

GENERAL PURPOSE: *TO PERSUADE*

- What is the point of my paper? Is that point clear?
- Is my claim really arguable? Did I mistakenly word it in a way that nobody could disagree with?
- Where is my strongest support? How can I make it stronger? Where is my weakest support? Should I keep it? If I keep it, how can I strengthen it?
- What criticisms will I face from readers with an opposing viewpoint? What can I do to gain their support?

Lesson 43

rev

- Do my supporting ideas follow each other in an order that makes the most sense for my purpose and audience?

Some of these questions are similar to those you asked when you developed paragraphs and topic sentences (pages 429, 435). It is not unusual for writers to ask themselves similar questions from the beginning to the end of the writing process. After all, if you had to ask completely new questions, you might end up writing a new paper.

Ask Questions Based on *Basic Standards.*

Another way to approach revision is to think about how readers evaluate writing. Practically everything we have discussed so far goes back to the basic standards for good writing that we presented in the Overview: purpose, support, organization, style, and mechanics (see page 407). If readers indeed use these criteria to evaluate writing, then one way to revise is to ask yourself questions about these criteria. Consider how these questions might be tailored to suit both your general and your specific purposes.

BASIC STANDARD: *PURPOSE*

- Is my specific purpose clear?

- Does my thesis control the paper? Do my topic sentences help my paragraphs show, explain, or prove my thesis?

- Have I delivered on my thesis? That is, did I do everything it indicated I would do? If not, should I continue to narrow my specific purpose?

- Or, if my paper does not deliver on my thesis, should I add more to my paper so that it does everything I indicated I would do?

COMMONSENSE TIP: While you were planning and drafting, your thesis sentence was something to start you off, but at this stage, think of it as a contract. In one sense you are promising readers that your paper will achieve whatever purpose you have indicated in your thesis sentence. Make sure the wording is exactly what it should be to match your paper.

BASIC STANDARD: *SUPPORT*

- Where can I add more details, examples, or facts so readers will understand my point?
  On the other hand, should I delete some specifics because they do not clearly support my point?

- Do I give the most support to the paragraphs that are most important for my purpose?

Lesson 43

rev

- In each paragraph, what would my readers possibly disagree with? What could I delete, add, or change to make my argument more convincing?

- Is my support too general or vague as a whole or within paragraphs? What can I do to be more specific?

- Are my details, examples, and evidence too common or obvious?

BASIC STANDARD: *ORGANIZATION*

- Do I have an introduction that alerts readers to my specific purpose and my thesis?

- Does each paragraph revolve around one point?

- Do my paragraphs build on each other? Does each have a clear connection to the one before and after it? If not, can I rearrange paragraphs, add words or sentences to clarify connections, or delete paragraphs that do not fit?

- Within paragraphs, does each sentence relate to the one before and after it?

- Does the conclusion merely summarize? If so, what else could I do to give a sense of closure?

COMMONSENSE TIP: To help you clarify the connections between sentences, consider using transitional words and phrases like these:

also	for example	in fact
as a matter of fact	for instance	in short
as a result	furthermore	indeed
as I said earlier	however	nevertheless
consequently	in addition	next
finally	in brief	therefore
first	in comparison	to sum up

Be careful not to overuse these terms; use them only when they express a true relationship. (See Lesson 4 for guidance in punctuating transitional words.)

BASIC STANDARD: *STYLE*

- Considering my audience and my purpose, is my paper too formal? Too informal? Do I use too much slang? Too many stuffy words? Do I seem too "chummy" or relaxed with readers? Too impersonal?

- Can I combine sentences for more variety? What sentences seem too choppy or too awkward?

- What clearer or more precise words could I use?

BASIC STANDARD: *MECHANICS*

- Have I followed the guidelines in the first part of this book?

You must decide how to answer these questions. We wish we could give the answers as easily as we pose the questions, but your own opinions and writing situation will determine how you will respond. Here is an example of one student's revision process.

Using Questions

Consider how one student, Maria, asked a few questions to help revise a short paper. Here is the assignment:

Write a paragraph (about 250 words) that explains your position about a controversy in a town or city you know well. This is a brief argument, so focus on important reasons.

After freewriting, Maria chose a problem involving her hometown of Marshall, Texas: whether to have a curfew for minors. Maria realized that she needed to take a stance and decided she was against the proposed curfew. Thus, she developed a thesis sentence that would serve as a topic sentence for her paragraph: *"Marshall should not have a curfew for minors."* Using clustering, she considered several reasons supporting her position. (These prewriting and drafting techniques are discussed in the previous two lessons.) Maria then wrote the following draft.

> *Marshall should not have a curfew for minors. First, it's not fair to have a curfew for just minors. Second, how can it be enforced? There are not enough police officers working at night to help with real crimes. Third, a curfew punishes all teenagers just because a few have caused trouble lately after midnight. Finally, the real troublemakers are going to cause trouble no matter what the curfew is. How would a curfew cut down, for instance, on teenagers who sell illegal drugs? This proposed curfew is completely illogical and will not accomplish anything.*

This paragraph was far shorter than what the teacher required. Maria was not sure how to revise the paragraph to make it longer, for the paragraph seemed to express her feelings on the topic. To help her not only with

Lesson 43

rev

the length but also with detecting other problems, Maria looked at the questions dealing with her general purpose.

She considered the assignment again and noticed several important terms from the prompt: "your position," "controversy," "argument," and "important reasons." She realized that her general purpose was not just to express her opinion but to *convince* readers to accept her position. This perspective led Maria to consider one set of questions especially important for persuasive writing:

> *Where is my strongest support, and how can I make it even stronger?*
>
> *Where is my weakest support, and should I keep it? If so, how can I make it strong?*

Maria's first draft was, unfortunately, a "shotgun" approach. She tossed in as many reasons as she could without concentrating on any of them, hoping that at least one reason would work. She also did not make her reasons strong from a reader's perspective. Maria realized she had merely given a list of reasons without really trying to convince people. To improve this draft as well as make it meet the word requirement, she decided to focus on what she thought to be the two most convincing reasons: the first and third reasons from the draft.

Maria was not sure how to make these reasons stronger, so she next considered questions dealing with basic standards. Rather than answering all these questions, she focused on the ones dealing with support, since these are designed to help writers add and improve reasons that strengthen their claims. She thought two in particular would help her add useful support:

> *Where can I add more details, examples, or facts so readers will understand my point?*
>
> *What would my readers disagree with?*

After considering these questions, Maria realized she did not have a single specific example (or any sort of specifics at all) in her draft. Nor had she considered why people might disagree with any of her reasons. The two questions above helped her realize she would be clearer and more convincing if her paragraph would (1) give concrete, realistic details and (2) explain why her reasons are valid despite potential criticism from some readers.

She used her hometown newspaper to provide her with specifics. To deal with potential criticisms, she talked with a friend who supported the idea of a curfew. Her revised paragraph focused on doing a good job with two reasons, rather than superficially covering four vague reasons.

> *Marshall should not have a curfew for minors. First, it is not fair to have a curfew for just minors. I examined the Marshall newspaper for the last three days. There were sixteen crimes described in the paper, and the reporters gave ages for suspects in twelve of the crimes. Only four of the twelve suspects were minors, and only two of these crimes occurred late at night. If the curfew is designed to cut down on crime, should it not be applied to the people who actually commit the most crimes? I do not believe there is enough evidence to prove that minors commit the majority of crimes, so they should not be singled out. In addition, a curfew punishes all teenagers just because a few have caused trouble after midnight. Some people might say that a curfew is not a real punishment at all. They say that minors could stay at home for entertainment, go to a friend's home, or be accompanied by an adult after the curfew. However, keeping people from enjoying themselves in public is a punishment. Some movies, for example, end after the curfew, and many people like to enjoy a late-night meal at a restaurant after seeing a show or dancing. Furthermore, not all parents are willing or able to hang out with their children at night. Forbidding people to enjoy a harmless but enjoyable activity is a punishment, and it is an unfair punishment because teenagers who do not break the law should not suffer simply because a few teenagers are guilty.*

The more Maria thought about specific information and how people might respond to her reasons, the more she realized she could add to even this much longer paragraph. Thus, she added two final sentences not only to give a sense of closure to the paragraph but also to let people know that even more could be said.

> *The idea of a curfew is complex and controversial. I have covered only two reasons, but many issues need to be considered before Marshall adopts a curfew.*

BUT WHAT HAPPENS IF . . . ?

"I now see a need to revise but am not sure how." Suppose you see a problem with your logic in one paragraph. We suggest you go back to the prewriting techniques suggested earlier (see page 424) — or to whatever critical thinking strategies you use to come up with ideas or solve a problem. Don't underestimate the value of using the *basic standards* on page 407 as your own personal revision checklist, though.

"I'm not sure if my revision made the paper any better." We have to be truthful: there are times when revisions hurt rather than help. If you are unsure, it is time to have someone read your draft and give you an honest reaction. Try to get feedback from at least two people.

Lesson 43

rev

COMMONSENSE TIP: When you ask for help, avoid explaining the reason behind a revision, or at least wait until your reader has finished reading and responding. Otherwise, you are basically saying, "Here's why I did this. Tell me I'm right."

"My paper is a total mess. I'm not sure where to start revising." Don't overlook this option: maybe your draft has done the job of helping you explore ideas. Now put it away and start over. This is undoubtedly the hardest thing a writer can do, admit that a draft isn't working. Many people, in fact, cannot bring themselves to start over. But consider it as an option.

COMMONSENSE TIP: One last time before you're ready to turn in the assignment, look back at the wording the teacher used in giving the assignment. Too many students get so caught up in their writing process, they overlook specific requirements.

The bottom line? Writing is a process that is never 100 percent complete. There is no such thing as a perfect draft. If you go about your writing believing that the goal is perfection, you might get discouraged. Instead, think of it this way: the goal is to produce writing that is *as effective as you can make it,* given your deadline.

Lesson 43.

rev

Brief Documentation Guide

In college, it is particularly important that student writers indicate when they are using words or ideas taken from somebody else. Students must let readers know which words or ideas were borrowed and where they originally appeared. This process is known as documentation—properly and clearly indicating the use of other people's words and ideas that are not the writer's own. Improper or incomplete documentation is plagiarism, a serious offense normally considered a form of cheating or fraud.

When writers document sources, they must follow very specific rules for citing the research materials they use. This brief guide provides the basic rules of what is called the MLA system of documentation, which is the most common system for composition courses. This guide is not intended to cover all possible types of sources you might use, just the most common ones. For more information on correctly using other people's ideas, see Lesson 25 (Quotation Marks with Direct Quotations and Paraphrases), or go to Research and Documentation Online at **dianahacker.com/resdoc**.

MLA Format for In-Text Citations

You should provide an in-text citation every time you quote from, paraphrase, or summarize an outside source. Your citation, which usually includes both source and page number, should appear next to the sentences in your paper that refer to the source information. Follow the models below for correct examples of in-text citations.

ONE AUTHOR

"Every day, around thirty-four new food products alone are introduced. The dizzying array of new items reflects a microsplitting of problems to create more 'must-have' new solutions" (Hammerslough 14).

Hammerslough points out that "Every day, around thirty-four new food products alone are introduced. The dizzying array of new items reflects a microsplitting of problems to create more 'must-have' new solutions" (14).

TWO OR THREE AUTHORS

More than 90 percent of the hazardous waste produced in the United States comes from seven major industries, all energy-intensive (Romm and Curtis 70).

FOUR OR MORE AUTHORS

Boys tend to get called on in the classroom more often than girls (Oesterling et al. 243).

CORPORATE AUTHOR OR GOVERNMENT PUBLICATION

Physical activity has been shown to protect against certain forms of cancer "either by balancing caloric intake with energy expenditure or by other mechanisms" (American Cancer Society 43).

UNKNOWN AUTHOR

According to a recent study, drivers are 42 percent more likely to get into an accident if they are using a wireless phone while driving ("Driving Dangerously" 32).

BIBLE

Consider the words of Solomon: "If your enemies are hungry, give them bread to eat; and if they are thirsty, give them water to drink" (*New Revised Standard Bible,* Prov. 25.21).

SOURCE WITHOUT PAGE NUMBERS

"There is no definitive correlation between benign breast tumors and breast cancer" (Pratt).

INDIRECT SOURCES

In discussing the baby mania trend, *Time* claimed that "Career women are opting for pregnancy and they are doing it in style" (qtd. in Faludi 106).

MLA Format for a List of Works Cited

At the end of your paper, you must provide a list of the sources from which you quoted, paraphrased, or summarized. Put the entire list in alphabetical order using the author's last name first and the title as it appears on the title page of the source. If your source has no author, alphabetize it by the first main word of the title. Double-space your works cited page. Begin each entry at the left margin and indent the subsequent lines five spaces.

Books

ONE AUTHOR

Hammerslough, Jane. *Dematerializing: Taming the Power of Possessions.* Cambridge, MA: Perseus, 2001.

TWO OR THREE AUTHORS

Trevor, Sylvia, Joan Hapgood, and William Leumi. *Women Writers of the 1920s.* New York: Columbia UP, 1998.

FOUR OR MORE AUTHORS

Roark, James L., et al. *The American Promise.* Boston: Bedford, 1998.

UNKNOWN AUTHOR

National Geographic Atlas of the World. 7th ed. Washington, DC: National Geographic, 1999.

EDITOR OR COMPILER

Hardy, Henry, ed. *The Proper Study of Mankind.* New York: Farrar, 1998.

EDITOR AND AUTHOR

Ellison, Ralph. *Living with Music: Ralph Ellison's Jazz Writings.* Ed. Robert G. O'Meally. New York: Modern Library, 2002.

EDITION NUMBERS

Garraty, John A., and Mark C. Carnes, eds. *A Short History of the American Nation.* 8th ed. New York: Longman, 2001.

ANTHOLOGY

Dawidoff, Nicholas, ed. *Baseball: A Literary Anthology.* New York: Library of America, 2002.

A WORK IN AN ANTHOLOGY

Lévy, Pierre. "The Art and Architecture of Cyberspace." *Multimedia: From Wagner to Virtual Reality.* Ed. Randall Packer and Ken Jordan. New York: Norton, 2001. 335–44.

SIGNED ARTICLE IN A REFERENCE BOOK

Cheney, Ralph Holt. "Coffee." *Collier's Encyclopedia.* 2001 ed.

UNSIGNED ARTICLE IN A REFERENCE BOOK

"Sonata." *The American Heritage Dictionary of the English Language.* 4th ed. 2000.

Periodicals

ARTICLE IN A MONTHLY MAGAZINE

Commoner, Barry. "Unraveling the DNA Myth." *Harper's* Feb. 2002:
39–47.

ARTICLE IN A WEEKLY MAGAZINE

Corliss, Richard. "Should We All Be Vegetarians?" *Time* 15 July 2002:
48–56.

ARTICLE IN A NEWSPAPER

Haughney, Christine. "Taking Phones out of Drivers' Hands."
Washington Post 5 Nov. 2000: A8.

UNKNOWN AUTHOR

"Consumer Confidence Suffers Sharper Fall than Expected."
Associated Press. *New York Times* 31 July 2002: C6.

EDITORIAL

"Medical Marijuana in Court." Editorial. *New York Times* 25 May
2002: A26.

LETTER TO THE EDITOR

Levy, Ronald. "Distorted View of Israel." Letter. *Boston Globe* 1 Aug.
2002: A18.

ARTICLE IN A JOURNAL

Ryan, Katy. "Revolutionary Suicide in Toni Morrison's Fiction."
African American Review 34 (2000): 389–412.

Electronic Sources

PROFESSIONAL WEB SITE

EPA Laws and Regulations Page. 17 July 2002. United States Environmental Protection Agency. 29 July 2002 <http://www.epa.gov/
epahome/rules.html>.

PERSONAL WEB SITE

Kilbourne, Jean. Home page. 12 June 2002. 1 Aug. 2002 <http://
www.jeankilbourne.com>.

ELECTRONIC MAIL OR ONLINE POSTING

Balbert, Peter. "Re: The Hemingway Hero." E-mail to the author.
15 Mar. 2002.

Carbone, Nick. "Re: E Text Readers." Online posting. 30 Oct. 2001. TechRhet list. 8 Nov. 2001 <http://groups.yahoo.com/group/ TechRhet/message/5122>.

CD-ROM OR DISKETTE MATERIAL WITHOUT A PRINT VERSION

Generations Family Tree 6.0 Deluxe Edition. CD-ROM. Bellevue: SierraHome, 1999.

CD-ROM OR DISKETTE MATERIAL WITH A PRINT VERSION

Singer, Armand, and Michael Lastinger. "Themes and Sources of *Star Wars*: John Carter and Flash Gordon Enlist in the First Crusade." *Popular Culture Review* 9.2 (1998): 65–77. *MLA International Bibliography, 1991–2000/06.* CD-ROM. SilverPlatter. May 2000.

Other Sources

ADVERTISEMENT

Nike. Advertisement. *Vogue* Nov. 2001: 94–95.

INTERVIEW

Tarantino, Quentin. Interview. *The Charlie Rose Show.* PBS. WGBH, Boston. 26 Dec. 1997.

PAMPHLET

Commonwealth of Massachusetts. Dept. of Jury Commissioner. *A Few Facts about Jury Duty.* Boston: Commonwealth of Massachusetts, 1997.

FILM OR VIDEO

Black Hawk Down. Dir. Ridley Scott. Perf. Josh Hartnett, Ewan McGregor, Tom Sizemore, and Sam Shepard. DVD. Columbia, 2001.

SOUND RECORDING

Gershwin, George. *Gershwin: Works for Piano and Orchestra.* Perf. Susan Slaughter and John Korman. St. Louis Symphony Orch. Cond. Leonard Slatkin. Vox, 1992.

TELEVISION OR RADIO PROGRAM

New York: A Documentary Film. The American Experience. PBS. WGBH, Boston. 20 Dec. 1999.

PUBLISHED INTERVIEW

Gould, Stephen Jay. "Life's Work: Questions for Stephen Jay Gould." *New York Times Magazine* 2 June 2002: 18.

APPENDIX A
Grammar without Tears

This brief overview of grammar basics is designed to give you the concepts needed to understand what a sentence is and how it is built. There are two requirements for sentences to be sentences. The first requirement deals with how sentences are built. Sentences must contain both a **subject** (the topic of the sentence) and a **predicate** (what the subject does). Here are some examples of minimal sentences with just single-word subjects and predicates:

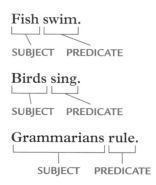

Now we will look at subjects and predicates in more detail.

Subjects

The subjects of sentences are typically **nouns** (names of people, places, things, and ideas) or **pronouns**. The most common pronouns used as subjects are the **personal pronouns** (*I, you, he, she, it, we,* and *they*). Here are some sentences that use personal pronouns (underlined) as subjects:

<u>I</u> know the answer.

<u>You</u> are completely wrong.

<u>We</u> went out for dinner.

In all the examples we have looked at so far, the subject has consisted of a single word. If all sentences were that simple, finding the subject would not be much of a challenge. Most of the time, however, the subject, especially when it is a noun, is used along with other words that modify the subject. The subject word together with all its modifiers is called the **complete subject**. In the following examples, the complete subject is highlighted:

The little boy with the old pole caught the biggest fish.

> └──────────────┬──────────────┘
> COMPLETE SUBJECT

The woman answering the phone gave me directions.

> └──────────────┬──────────────┘
> COMPLETE SUBJECT

A sudden wind from the north chilled us to the bone.

> └──────────────┬──────────────┘
> COMPLETE SUBJECT

The cars in the left lane began to slow down.

> └──────────┬──────────┘
> COMPLETE SUBJECT

A very important part of knowing when a sentence is a sentence is being able to identify the subject part of the sentence and tell it apart from the rest of the sentence (the predicate). Fortunately, there is a simple and completely reliable way to do just that.

> **PRONOUN REPLACEMENT TIP:** The subject of a sentence—whether it is a single-word noun or a long, complicated complete subject—can always be identified by replacing it with one of these subject pronouns: *he, she, it,* or *they.*

Here is the Pronoun Replacement Tip applied to the four example sentences used above:

   He
The little boy with the old pole caught the biggest fish.

   She
The woman answering the phone gave me directions.

   It
A sudden wind from the north chilled us to the bone.

   They
The cars in the left lane began to slow down.

Grammar test 1: Identifying subjects. Underline the complete subjects in the sentences below. Confirm your answer by applying the Pronoun Replacement Tip.

EXAMPLE: All the computers in the lab use Windows.

ANSWER: <u>All the computers in the lab</u> use Windows.

They
TIP APPLIED: <u>All the computers in the lab</u> use Windows.

1.   The early spring weather was completely unpredictable.

2.   The new lamp in the den doesn't give me enough light.

3.   The guys in the back of the bus were hogging all the seats.

4.   The waitress behind the counter finally came out to get our orders.

5.   The telephone and the doorbell both began ringing at the same time.

Predicates

The predicate consists of a **verb** together with its **complement**—whatever the verb requires to make a grammatical sentence. The complement may, in turn, be followed by one or more optional **adverbs** that modify the verb. This is the fundamental pattern of all English sentences:

Subject + Verb + Complement + (Optional adverb)

PREDICATE

Here are three examples of different verbs with different types of complements:

EXAMPLE 1:   **Harry calls Sally every afternoon.**

SUBJECT   VERB   COMPLEMENT   ADVERB

In Example 1, the verb *calls* requires a noun as its complement. In other words, when we *call*, we must call SOMEONE. The adverb *every afternoon* is optional. We would still have a grammatical sentence if we deleted it.

EXAMPLE 2:   **Olive Oyl gave Popeye a present yesterday.**

SUBJECT   VERB   COMPLEMENT   COMPLEMENT   ADVERB

In Example 2, the verb *gave* requires two nouns as its complement. In other words, when we give, we must give SOMEONE SOMETHING.

EXAMPLE 3:   **Thelma told Louise to be quiet.**

SUBJECT   VERB   COMPLEMENT   COMPLEMENT

In Example 3, the verb *told* also requires two complements, but this time the second complement (*to be quiet*) is a completely different kind of structure—an **infinitive** phrase.

There are at least fifty different types of complements. A big part of learning any language is learning which verbs require which type of complement.

Identifying Verbs

The verb is the controlling element of the predicate. In order to identify predicates, then, we must be able to identify verbs. Fortunately, verbs have a distinctive grammatical feature that makes them easy to identify—**tense**. Verbs are unique in that only verbs have past tense, present tense, and future tense forms. A good test for verbs is to see if you can make the word into a future tense by putting *will* in front of it.

> **"WILL" TIP:** Put *will* in front of the word you want to test. If the result makes sense, then the word is a verb.

Compare the following two sentences that both use the word *chain*, but in different ways:

The chain is heavy.

The janitors chain the gate.

In the first sentence, *chain* is not a verb; we can tell this by applying the *Will* Tip:

✗ The **will** chain is heavy.

However, chain is a verb in the second sentence; we can tell this by applying the *Will* Tip:

The janitors **will** chain the gate.

Grammar test 2.   Below are pairs of related words. Use the *Will* Tip to identify which is the verb.

EXAMPLE: **realize/realization**

TIP APPLIED: *will realize* is grammatical, but ✗ *will realization* is not. Therefore, *realize* is a verb, and *realization* is not.

1. large/enlarge

2. sale/sell

3. authority/authorize

4. choose/choice

5. publish/publication

Sentences and Clauses

For sentences to be sentences, they must meet two requirements. We have already seen the first of these requirements: sentences must have **subjects** and **predicates**. The second requirement is <u>that a sentence must be able to stand alone as a complete thought</u>. The reason for this second requirement is that there are other structures besides sentences that have subjects and predicates.

Clauses

We must now introduce a new term: **clause**. **Clause** is a broader term than **sentence**. The term **clause** includes ALL groups of words that have subjects and predicates, not just sentences. Sentences are just one type of clause; though, of course, sentences are by far the most important type of clause.

    Sentences are **independent** clauses. To be independent, clauses must be able to stand alone (make sense by themselves) without being dependent on some other sentence. Clauses that fail to stand alone are called **dependent clauses**. To see the difference between independent clauses (sentences) and dependent clauses, compare the following clauses.

INDEPENDENT CLAUSE (SENTENCE):   He gets upset.

DEPENDENT CLAUSE: Whenever he gets upset

    The independent clause *He gets upset* stands by itself as a complete idea. The dependent clause *whenever he gets upset* cannot stand by itself as a complete idea. It needs to be attached to an independent clause, for example:

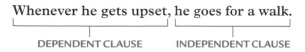

Whenever he gets upset, he goes for a walk.

          DEPENDENT CLAUSE   INDEPENDENT CLAUSE

or

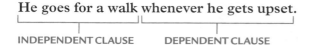

He goes for a walk whenever he gets upset.

INDEPENDENT CLAUSE   DEPENDENT CLAUSE

Distinguishing between Independent and Dependent Clauses

In Unit One, we give the *I Realize* Tip for recognizing independent clauses. We can also use this tip for distinguishing between independent and dependent clauses. Here is the *I Realize* Tip, slightly rewritten to use the terminology of clauses:

> **"I REALIZE" TIP:** You can put *I realize* in front of independent clauses (sentences). However, when you put *I realize* in front of dependent clauses, the result will not make sense.

Here is the *I Realize* Tip applied to the two example clauses given above:

INDEPENDENT CLAUSE: *I realize* he gets upset.

DEPENDENT CLAUSE: ✗ *I realize* whenever he gets upset.

As you can see, when we add *I realize* to an independent clause, the result is a grammatical sentence. However, when we add *I realize* to a dependent clause, the result is ungrammatical.

Grammar test 3.   Label the following clauses as independent or dependent. Confirm your answer by the *I Realize* Tip.

EXAMPLE: Because he feels like it.

ANSWER: Dependent clause

CONFIRMATION: ✗ *I realize* because he feels like it.

1. When I was your age.

2. After it started to rain.

3. Whatever you want.

4. The punishment fits the crime.

5. Which is exactly right.

Summary

The sentence is a fundamental building block of language. Sentences are the way we combine individual words to express ideas and relationships. For a group of words to be a sentence, it must meet two requirements.

- The first requirement deals with how the sentence is built. A sentence must contain both a **subject** and a **predicate**.

The subject is the topic of the sentence. The subject can be as simple as a single-word noun or pronoun, or it can be a **complete subject**, a long string of words consisting of the subject noun along with its modifiers. The subject can always be identified by the following Pronoun Replacement Tip:

> PRONOUN REPLACEMENT TIP: The subject of a sentence—whether it is a single-word noun or a long, complicated complete subject—can always be identified by replacing it with one of these subject pronouns: *he, she, it*, or *they*.

The predicate consists of the **verb** and its **complement**. The complement is whatever is required by the verb to make a complete sentence. The complement may be followed by optional **adverbs** that modify the verb. In order to identify predicates, then, we must be able to identify verbs. A good test for verbs is to see if you can make the word into a future tense by putting *will* in front of it.

> "WILL" TIP: Put *will* in front of the word you want to test. If the result makes sense, then the word is a verb.

- The second requirement for a sentence deals with the meaning of the sentence. Not all structures that have a subject and a complement are sentences. The term **clause** is used for any structure that has a subject and a predicate. Sentences are clauses that can stand alone. These kind of clauses are also called **independent clauses**. Clauses that cannot stand alone are called **dependent clauses**. Below is a test that will help you distinguish between independent and dependent clauses:

> "I REALIZE" TIP: You can put *I realize* in front of independent clauses (sentences). However, when you put *I realize* in front of dependent clauses, the result will not make sense.

APPENDIX B
Commonly Confused Words

Writers sometimes confuse certain words because some words sound alike but are spelled differently. Even a computer spell-checker will not catch these problem words because they are not misspelled; they are simply misused. For example, *breaks* in the following sentence is incorrect:

✗ My car's **breaks** are squealing.

But a spell-check program would not suggest the correct usage

My car's **brakes** are squealing.

because it doesn't "see" the error in meaning.

Below is a list of words that are often confused with one another. (Some of these words have several meanings, but we give only the most common usage.) Use this list of easily confused words to help you edit your writing. If you are unsure about a word that doesn't appear here, consult a dictionary.

WORD	DEFINITION	EXAMPLE
accept	to approve	I **accept** your offer.
except	excluding	I kept all the receipts **except** that one.
advice	a suggestion	Can you give me investment **advice**?
advise	to recommend	I **advise** you not to go there.
affect	to influence or alter	The medication didn't **affect** Lydia at all.
effect	a result	One **effect** of this drug is drowsiness.
aisle	the space between rows	The groom fell down in the **aisle**.
isle	an island	Gilligan was bored with the **isle**.
already	previously	I have **already** eaten lunch.
all ready	completely prepared	Jan is **all ready** for the test, but I'm not.
altogether	thoroughly or generally	She was not **altogether** ready for college.
all together	in a group	The holiday brought us **all together**.
brake	a device for stopping or to stop	The **brakes** in this car are awful.
break	to destroy or divide into pieces	If you **break** the window, you'll have to pay to replace it.
breath	an inhalation or exhalation	Take a deep **breath** before diving.
breathe	to inhale or exhale	I can't **breathe** in a sauna.
capital	a city recognized as the home of a government	The **capital** of Texas is Austin.
capitol	the building where lawmakers meet	The **capitol** building is huge.

WORD	DEFINITION	EXAMPLE
choose	to select	Our group will **choose** topics tomorrow.
chose	past tense of *choose*	She **chose** to make up the test.
complement	to go well with	This wine **complements** the chicken.
compliment	to praise	He **complimented** my leadership skills.
dessert	a tasty sweet	For **dessert**, we had key lime pie.
desert	a dry area	You'll need water to cross that **desert**.
device	a mechanism	This **device** will help you start a car.
devise	to arrange	Ira **devised** this meeting between us.
its	possessive form of *it*	My hamster ate all **its** food.
it's	contraction for *it is*	**It's** going to rain today, so be prepared.
later	subsequently	We ate too much. **Later**, we felt sick.
latter	the last thing mentioned	I see turkey and ham in the refrigerator. I prefer the **latter**.
lead	a metallic element	They used **lead** paint on these windows.
led	past tense of *lead*	The guide **led** us through the canyon.
loose	not snug	Your pants are **loose** in the rear.
lose	to misplace; to fail to win	Did you **lose** the race?
maybe	perhaps	**Maybe** I'll get a raise next month.
may be	might possibly be	The project **may be** ready next week.
passed	past tense of *pass*	I **passed** her on the way to school.
past	previous time	In the **past**, I owned an IBM typewriter.
personal	private	A lot of my e-mail is **personal**.
personnel	staff	All store **personnel** should wear name tags.
principal	head of a school	Report to the **principal's** office.
principle	a basic truth	What **principles** would you fight for?
quiet	little or no sound	It was **quiet** in the library.
quite	very	Marc looked **quite** handsome in that suit.
set	to put	**Set** the glasses on the table, please.
sit	to be seated	The teacher wants us to **sit** in groups.
than	as compared to	My dog is smarter **than** my cat.
then	next	Fix this car. **Then** fix that car.
their	possessive of *they*	The players lost **their** final game.
there	adverb indicating place	Put the printer **there** for now.
they're	a contraction for *they are*	**They're** meeting us after work.
to	a preposition	Russell went **to** his algebra class.
too	very or also	He was **too** tired to work, **too**.
two	the number 2	Shannon wrote **two** papers this week.
weak	not strong	Tomás felt **weak** after the game.
week	seven days	I need a **week** off from work.
weather	the state of the atmosphere	Today's **weather** will be stormy.
whether	if	**Whether** you go or not is your decision.
whose	possessive of *who*	**Whose** turn is it now?
who's	contraction for *who is*	**Who's** ready to leave?
your	possessive of *you*	**Your** car is a mess.
you're	contraction for *you are*	If **you're** hungry, let's get lunch.

APPENDIX C
Glossary of Common Phrasal Verbs

The following is an alphabetical list of one hundred common phrasal verbs.

Each of the verbs on this list is a *separable* phrasal verb (verb + adverb construction). Remember that if the sentence includes an object *noun*, the adverb can be placed either before or after the noun. In other words, the noun can separate the two parts of the verb. Both of these examples are correct:

Carly **turned down** the offer.

Carly **turned** the offer **down**.

However, when the object following the adverb is a *pronoun*, the adverb must be placed after the pronoun. In this case, the pronoun must separate the two parts of the verb.

✗ Carly **turned down** it.

Carly **turned** it **down**.

To learn more about how to identify and correct problems with phrasal verbs, see Lesson 37. You may also want to consult the *Longman Dictionary of Phrasal Verbs* (ed. Rosemary Courtney, 1998), the most complete listing of phrasal verbs and their meanings.

PHRASAL VERB	MEANING	EXAMPLE
ask out	ask for a date	He wanted to **ask** her **out**.
ask over	invite to one's home	We **asked** them **over** for coffee.
back up	support	They **backed** our proposal **up**.
beat out	defeat, overcome	Our plan **beat out** theirs.
blow up	destroy	The bomb **blew** the building **up**.
break down	disassemble, analyze	This chart **breaks** the costs **down**.
break in	train, start	They **broke in** the new staff.
break off	discontinue, stop	We **broke off** the discussions.
bring around	convince	We'll **bring** the others **around** in time.
bring back	return	She **brought** the books **back**.
bring off	succeed in doing	They **brought** the party **off**.
bring up	mention, propose	I'll **bring** the issue **up** to my boss.
brush off	ignore, dismiss	He **brushed** their complaints **off**.
buy out	purchase	We want to **buy** the company **out**.
call off	cancel	They **called off** the meeting.
call up	telephone	Her boss **called** her **up**.
carry away	overcome objections	His idea **carried** them **away**.
carry out	do, follow	Be sure to **carry** the orders **out**.

PHRASAL VERB	MEANING	EXAMPLE
check out	investigate	We plan to **check** the offers **out**.
check over	test for accuracy	They **checked** the bills **over**.
cost out	price	They **cost out** the bid.
cover up	hide	They **covered up** the crime.
crack up	make someone laugh	His stories **crack** me **up**.
do in	kill, destroy	His mistakes finally **did** him **in**.
do over	repeat	I have to **do** my paper **over** again.
drag out	make longer	The boss will **drag** the meeting **out**.
dream up	create, imagine	They **dreamed** the whole thing **up**.
drop off	deliver, leave	I **dropped** the kids **off** at school.
figure out	discover	It's easy to **figure** the answer **out**.
fill in	explain something	Let's go **fill** the newcomers **in**.
fit in	schedule	I'll **fit** you **in** at one o'clock.
fix up	repair, decorate	They **fixed** the office **up** nicely.
follow up	oversee, pursue	I **followed** the plans **up**.
freeze out	exclude, keep out	We'll **freeze** the competition **out**.
get across	explain successfully	At least they **got** their ideas **across**.
give up	quit using	He **gave** junk food **up**.
hand in	submit	It is time to **hand** my paper **in**.
hang up	cause a delay	The problem really **hung** them **up**.
help out	assist	The tutor really **helped** them **out**.
hold up	restrain, delay	The accident **held** them **up**.
lay off	fire	The firm **laid** the employees **off**.
lay out	present, arrange	She wanted to **lay** the options **out**.
lead on	encourage falsely	The ads **lead** the customers **on**.
leave off	omit	I **left** my name **off** the list.
let down	disappoint	Our failure **let** them **down**.
look up	find information	We **looked** their address **up**.
make up	lie about	They **made** the whole story **up**.
mix up	confuse	Our directions **mixed** them **up**.
pass out	distribute	We **passed** the books **out**.
pass up	decline	I couldn't **pass up** chocolate cake.
pay back	repay a debt	We **paid** our loan **back**.
pay off	bribe	They **paid** the police **off**.
phase out	terminate gradually	We will **phase** the product **out** by 2005.
pick up	make happy	The news really **picked** them **up**.
point out	identify	We **pointed** the changes **out**.
polish off	finish	We **polished** the last job **off**.
pull off	succeed in doing	I **pulled** a big surprise **off**.
put back	return	She **put** the book **back** on the shelf.
put off	delay, discourage	We **put off** the decision until later.

PHRASAL VERB	MEANING	EXAMPLE
put on	deceive, tease	You are **putting** me **on**.
rip off	cheat	The salesman **ripped** us **off**.
run down	criticize	They **ran** the opposition **down**.
scale back	reduce	We needed to **scale back** our plan.
seek out	search for	I **sought** the best deal **out**.
sell out	betray	He **sold** his partner **out**.
set back	delay	The rain **set** the job **back**.
set off	trigger, activate	The noise **set** the alarm **off**.
shake up	scare	The accident **shook** me **up**.
shoot down	reject	My lab group **shot** my ideas **down**.
show off	display boastingly	He **showed** his new car **off**.
shut off	stop	They **shut** the radio **off**.
shut up	silence someone	Sam **shut** his partner **up**.
smooth over	fix temporarily	He will **smooth** the situation **over**.
sound out	test one's opinion	We **sounded** them **out**.
spell out	give all details	She **spelled out** the proposal carefully.
stand up	fail to meet someone	My date **stood** me **up** twice!
straighten out	correct someone	The boss **straightened** us **out**.
string along	deceive	He was **stringing** them **along**.
sum up	summarize	My job is to **sum** the proposal **up**.
take in	deceive, trick	Their scheme really **took** us **in**.
talk over	discuss	I'd like to **talk** the plan **over**.
tear down	destroy, demolish	They **tore** the old house **down**.
tell apart	distinguish	I can't **tell** them **apart**.
think up	invent	We **thought up** a new plan.
throw away	discard	I **threw** the old papers **away**.
throw off	confuse, delay	The announcement **threw** them **off**.
track down	find	We **tracked** the book **down**.
trip up	cause a mistake	Our carelessness **tripped** us **up**.
try out	test, explore	I should **try** the new computer **out**.
tune out	ignore	I can't **tune** the distractions **out**.
turn around	change for the better	They **turned** the company **around**.
turn down	reject	She **turned** our offer **down**.
turn in	submit	I **turned** my assignment **in**.
turn off	cause to lose interest	The bad smell **turned** me **off**.
use up	use until gone	I **used** all my money **up**.
wear down	weaken gradually	Some kids **wear** their parents **down**.
wear out	exhaust	The noise **wore** me **out**.
wipe out	destroy completely	The floods **wiped** the city **out**.
work up	prepare	I **worked** the new draft **up**.
write off	cancel, dismiss	They **wrote** the investment **off**.

Answer Key

OVERVIEW: Can you detect problems with sentence basics? *page 15*

One of the highest honors that can be given in the movie industry is the Academy Award**, which** is more commonly known as an Oscar. Winning just one Oscar is a notable feat. A few movies, however, are exceptional: they have won several Oscars. There are four major Oscar awards: **best** actress, best actor, best director, and best picture. Only a few movies have won even three of these four awards. In 1982, *Gandhi* received Oscars for best actor, best director, and best picture. **It** did not win best actress. Two years later, *Amadeus* won the same three awards. **The** best actress Oscar went to Sally Field for her role in *Places in the Heart.* In 1988, *Rain Man* captured three Oscars, **again** failing to capture the best actress award**, which** went to Jodie Foster for her role in *The Accused.*

Some movies have done even better: two movies have won all four major awards. In 1975, *One Flew over the Cuckoo's Nest* won all four of these Oscars. The first movie to win all four was *It Happened One Night,* **which** won way back in 1934.

LESSON 1

Diagnostic Exercise, *page 18*

My roommate has an annoying habit**, not putting** anything away. He never picks up his dirty clothes **until** he has to do his laundry. In the kitchen, there are always dirty dishes on the table. I've asked him to at least put them in the sink **where** they are out of the way. It is always such a mess**; cups** half-full of coffee, cereal bowls with milk in them, and cruddy silverware. The refrigerator is just as bad. Opening the door is like taking a trip to the jungle. We really need to do something about it **because** it is really embarrassing when someone visits.

Sentence Practice 1, *page 20*

1. Jeff ran into the house **carrying** three bags of groceries.
2. He fell down **because** he was careless.
3. My history teacher gave us our final exam**, which** I think I managed to pass.
4. OK
5. They flew over 15,233 sorties **between** 1943 and 1945.

Sentence Practice 2, *page 21*

1. A capital offense is a crime punishable by death**, a** penalty for only the most serious of crimes.
2. This magazine article is about the Valley of Ten Thousand Smokes**, which** is a valley in Alaska having a number of volcanic fissures.
3. I vividly recall January 12, 2002**, the** day my parents made a surprise visit while I was in the middle of holding a wild party.
4. Our astronomy class took a field trip to Mount Palomar, California**, where** one of the world's largest telescopes is located.
5. OK

Editing Practice 1, *page 22*

Ten percent of Americans suffer from *allergic rhinitis,* **which** is the medical term for hay fever**, the** most common allergy. Hay fever is triggered by exposure to pollen**, especially** grass and weed pollens. Flower pollen rarely causes allergic reactions **because** it is too heavy to float very high or far.

During the allergy season, many hay fever sufferers take a drug called an *antihistamine*, **hoping** to combat sneezing, runny nose, and itchy eyes. However, there are other ways to control allergy symptoms, **such** as limiting outside work when the pollen count is high, running the air conditioner in your house and car, and avoiding dust and smoke.

Editing Practice 2, *page 23*

Several players have now broken Babe Ruth's long-standing records, **most** home runs in a season and most career home runs. However, Babe may well be the most famous baseball player of all time, **largely** because . . .

Babe's personality frequently made news **even** when his character got him into trouble. In 1922, his behavior resulted in five suspensions, and in 1925 his drinking and quarreling with management resulted in a $5,000 fine, **a** huge amount at the time for even well-paid players. He gained even more fame, though, when he turned himself around, **hitting** a record sixty home runs in 1927. He had a comeback again in the World Series of 1932. After a September attack of what was thought to be appendicitis, he fought back and played all games in the World Series, **in** which he batted .333. . . .

LESSON 2

Diagnostic Exercise, *page 27*

My friend Miranda is a junior majoring in criminal justice. **She** plans to go to law school. Most law schools accept applicants from all majors, **but** she thinks that majoring in criminal justice would help her prepare for law. All law schools do require good grades and a high score on the LSAT. Her grades are high; she has about a 3.8 GPA currently. She works very hard, **and** she studies more than any person I know. She plans to take the LSAT this fall, **and** she will be studying for it on top of everything else. I admire her energy; I'm sure . . .

Sentence Practice 1, *page 29*

1. Colleen called me today. **She** wants to know if I can help her with her homework.
2. London was the first city to have a population of over one million. **It** reached that milestone in 1811.
3. My son wants to buy a snake, **but** his mother is not happy about the idea.
4. The mascot for Yale is now a bulldog; its mascot over a hundred years ago was a cat.
5. Columbia was once considered part of South America, **but** its government decided in 1903 to proclaim Columbia was part of North America.

Sentence Practice 2, *page 29*

1. OK
2. The first home TV set was demonstrated in 1928; **it** measured only three inches by four inches.
3. The street lights in the city of Hershey look strange **because** they resemble Hershey's chocolate kisses.
4. OK
5. The book was originally titled *Naked Lust*, **but** the name changed because a friend could not read Burroughs's handwriting.

Editing Practice 1, *page 31*

Sausage is a popular food around the globe; it has been around for centuries. Nobody knows for sure who first thought of stuffing ground meat into a casing to form what we now call "sausage." Over 3,500 years ago, the Babylonians made sausage, **and** the ancient poet Homer referred to sausage in his classic work *The Odyssey*. Romans were particularly fond of sausages; they made them from ground pork and pine nuts. In fact, the word *sausage* comes from the Latin word *salsus*; it is . . . One Roman ruler thought sausages were divine, **so** he would not permit . . .

Editing Practice 2, *page 31*

My cousin has never been the overly romantic type, **but** recently he put on quite a presentation when he proposed to his girlfriend. He did so on her birthday; he put the ring inside a toy packet that he placed in a Cap'n Crunch box. It took a bit of effort to get her to open the cereal box and wade through the cereal to the "toy surprise" inside. He carefully timed the proceedings. **He** wanted to be sure that she found the ring during halftime of the Dallas Cowboys game on TV, **when** he was...

When she found the ring, he gallantly hit the mute button for the TV **and** said that he would like for her to be his wife. The ring, by the way, was not a real wedding ring; it was a plastic ring with a tiny boot jingling from it. She took it all in stride **because** she knew he was just trying to make the event memorable by adding some humor. I suppose she appreciated his humor, **but** she...

Unit Two

OVERVIEW: Can you detect problems with multiple-clause sentences? *page 37*

Linguists have long noted that children learn their native language at about the same age and in quite similar ways. Although linguists do not fully understand the reason, they do know that children go through distinct stages. The early laughing and babbling stages seem like imitations of adult language, yet they are largely innate. Because even profoundly deaf children laugh and babble just like hearing children, researchers conclude that the early language stages are at least partially genetic.

When children are around eighteen months, they produce their first truly meaningful words. Around two years, many children combine pairs of words to form what are called "two-word" sentences. Although the grammar of "two-word" sentences differs substantially from adult grammar, the grammar of children's "two-word" sentences is quite stable and regular. Some children stay at the "two-word" stage for months, and are able to express quite complex ideas; however, there is no such thing as a "three-word" or "four-word" grammar stage. When children break out of the "two-word" stage, they jump directly to a simplified form of the adult language.

LESSON 3

Diagnostic Exercise, *page 40*

When he reached the Americas, Christopher Columbus believed he had reached the East Indies, so he called the people that he found *Indians*. That term is still used, but many indigenous people prefer the term *Native Americans*. We tend to think of Native Americans as a group, yet that is really a mistake because there are vast differences in their cultures and languages. We tend to think of the tribes from the plains as being typical Native Americans, for those are the tribes we see represented in movies and on TV. The plains tribes hunted buffalo and lived in tepees, but northwest coastal tribes never saw a buffalo or a tepee in their lives. **These tribes** hunted whales **and** lived in wooden houses.

Sentence Practice 1, *page 41*

1. Pig iron is refined in a blast furnace/ and contains iron along with small amounts of manganese and other minerals.
2. OK
3. Tom decided he would walk to class/ but changed his mind when it started raining.
4. OK
5. John Glenn was the first American astronaut to orbit the planet, and Scott Carpenter was the second.

Sentence Practice 2, *page 42*

1. OK
2. OK
3. My father bought an old sword in England, but he paid too much.
4. OK
5. Tony is dropping by my place to deliver a message, and I suppose I should clean up a bit.

Editing Practice 1, *page 43*

Writing is a form of visible language, but there is a form of writing that is not meant to be seen. Braille is written as a series of dots or bumps, so visually impaired people can "read" it with their fingers. It is written as a series of cells, and each cell contains dots that can be variously arranged. Each particular arrangement of dots has its own meaning, but what the dots represent depends on the style of Braille. There are two forms of Braille: Grade 1/ and Grade 2. Grade 1 Braille is a system in which the dots represent letters/ and some very short words. Grade 2 Braille is not a completely different system, but it is a shorthand version of Grade 1 that is much harder to read.

Editing Practice 2, *page 44*

Humans appear to be the only animals to use language naturally, but there is much about language we may never know. People have come up with various theories. There is no way to prove or disprove these theories, so they are more a curiosity than a scientific hypothesis/ and have acquired nicknames befitting their status. According to the "bow-wow" theory, speech began as imitation of animal sounds/ or cries. All languages have sounds that imitate animal sounds, yet these words are so isolated from the rest of vocabulary that it is hard to attach much significance to them. The "pooh-pooh" theory is the name for the theory that speech arose from instinctive noises resulting from pain/ or fear. For instance, a gasp or cry of fear may have been the primitive beginnings of words used to express those emotions, but again these words are too marginal to be the basis of our language system.

LESSON 4

Diagnostic Exercise, *page 48*

Many places around the globe have universal appeal. They are, **however,** not necessarily accessible to the general public. An international committee has designated some sites as World Heritage Sites that have international value and responsibility. In the United States, **for example,** the committee chose Yosemite Park and the Statue of Liberty. Both of these sites are part of our national parks system. We tend to take our parks system for granted; **however,** it is really unusual. Very few developed countries have extensive public land. **Consequently,** their important public sites are little more than individual buildings. The vast size of some national parks in the American West make them unique; **therefore,** they have attracted visitors from every country.

Sentence Practice 1, *page 51*

1. Bill said he might be late. Indeed, he was four hours late.
2. Little is known about the Pilgrims' *Mayflower*; we do know, however, that it weighed about 180 tons.
3. English is the predominate language in the United States. Nevertheless, over 300 languages are spoken within its borders.
4. none
5. A serious accident has caused major delays. In fact, some commuters have decided to stay home.

Sentence Practice 2, *page 52*

1. Sean Connery is remembered most for his James Bond movies. <u>However,</u> he won an Oscar for a different role in *The Untouchables*.
2. Scott Joplin wrote over sixty musical compositions. He wrote, <u>for instance,</u> an opera entitled *Treemonisha*.
3. none
4. The top position in the British army is field marshal. The top position in its navy, <u>in contrast,</u> is admiral of the fleet.
5. The singer Prince has gone by more than one name. <u>For example,</u> his birth name is Prince Rogers Nelson.

Editing Practice 1, *page 53*

My friend Collette is moving to Oakland, California. **Consequently,** she wants to fix up her house and sell it. My wife said that we should help her because we owed her a favor. Her realtor advised her to repaint the living room**; moreover,** we needed to have the carpets cleaned professionally. She also said that the kitchen was the room that made the biggest impression on potential buyers**; therefore,** we need to spend most of our time making it more attractive.

The biggest task was working on the cabinets**; therefore,** we began by taking them apart. The shelves were in good shape**; however,** they needed to be stripped and cleaned. We replaced all the cabinet knobs with ceramic ones**; then,** we had to get matching handles for the drawers. The biggest job was cleaning the appliances**; for example,** we had to completely disassemble the range and clean every single part. We really got tired of the whole project**; nevertheless,** we knew that all our hard work...

Editing Practice 2, *page 54*

Americans are proud of their political history**; nonetheless,** there are some unpleasant episodes. One particularly troubling aspect is the many attempts to kill presidents**; for example,** we all know about the assassinations of Presidents Lincoln and Kennedy. These are the only two assassinations that most Americans know about**; in fact,** there were two other assassinations of sitting presidents: Presidents Garfield in 1881 and McKinley in 1901. More recently, two men tried to shoot their way into a house where President Truman was staying**; however,** their plot failed when one was killed by a guard.

One might think that assassinations of political leaders are political acts**; in fact,** most assassinations of American presidents were apparently individually motivated. Lee Harvey Oswald, who assassinated President Kennedy, was deeply disturbed**; likewise,** John Hinckley, who attempted to assassinate President Reagan, was mentally ill. The most extreme example is John Schrank, who attempted to assassinate President Theodore Roosevelt. Schrank appeared to be delusional**; moreover,** he said that...

LESSON 5

Diagnostic Exercise, *page 58*

After everybody was asleep Monday night**,** there was a fire in the dorm next door. Fortunately, a smoke-detector went off/ when smoke got into the staircase. While the fire department was fighting the fire, six rooms were totally destroyed. A friend of mine in another part of the building lost all her clothing/ because of the smoke and water damage. If school officials close down the dorm, she will have to find a new place to live. I heard they will make a decision tomorrow as soon as they get a report...

Sentence Practice 1, *page 60*

1. <u>When I visit my parents in New Mexico</u>, I always bring them something from my part of the country.
2. I will go with you/ after I finish eating.

3. <u>After Omar competed in the third basketball tournament of the season,</u> he was not eager to travel again.

4. <u>Because the test included over a hundred questions,</u> I could not finish it in just fifteen minutes.

5. Stephanie wants to leave/ <u>because she smelled a strange odor in the room.</u>

Sentence Practice 2, *page 61*

1. <u>While we were watching some children playing in the park,</u> Bill and I talked about our own childhood.

2. <u>Although sharks are normally found in salt water,</u> some freshwater sharks exist in Nicaragua.

3. We need to stop at the next gas station, <u>even though we stopped at one just an hour ago.</u>

4. <u>Because I tend to work forty hours each week,</u> I have to spend most of my weekends studying.

5. <u>Whenever you are ready to leave,</u> I will be happy to go.

Editing Practice 1, *page 62*

Since I wanted to get into shape, I decided to buy a weight machine that I could use in my basement. I picked the machine I wanted after I had looked at about a dozen different kinds. Surprisingly, it had many features the other machines didn't have, even though it was one of the cheaper ones.

Unfortunately, I forgot to compare two things: the height of the weight machine and the height of my basement. When I finally assembled the metal monster, I discovered that it was four inches higher than my basement ceiling. I was furious at myself because I had made such a dumb mistake. As the thing was such a hassle to move, I didn't want to haul it back to the store. As a last resort, I punched a hole through the sheet-rock ceiling. Whenever I go into the basement now, I see this really ugly hole in my ceiling. Next time, I'll need to plan ahead.

Editing Practice 2, *page 63*

Although many people may not be aware of it, Pearl Buck was the first American woman to win a Nobel Prize in literature. After they had spent years as missionaries in China, her parents returned to the United States for a short time in the early 1890's, during which time Pearl was born. When she was just three months old, Pearl returned to China with her parents. She grew up speaking Chinese because her family lived among the Chinese rather than in a Western compound.

While they were living in China, there were many protests against the Western governments that had controlled China's economy for years. Since she had lived among ordinary people, Pearl was very aware of their daily struggles for bare survival. Because she had such a depth of personal experience in China, her most famous novel, *The Good Earth,* reflected her compassion for the Chinese and their culture. When Pearl Buck died, President Nixon said that she served as a "human bridge between the civilizations of the East and West."

Unit Three

OVERVIEW: Can you detect problems with subject-verb agreement? *page 71*

When I was in high school, my family enjoyed camping, so nearly every school vacation, we would go camping. We soon realized that there **are** two completely different kinds of campers. We called them the "nature lovers" and the "homeboys." The people whom we called "nature lovers" enjoy setting up camp in small, isolated sites where there **are** often no toilet facilities. Of course, the food and water **are** a constant concern, especially when all supplies have to be carried in. "Nature lovers" always try to have a minimal impact on the area that they have camped in. For example, their trash and garbage **are** always taken out.

The "homeboys," on the other hand, are people who want to go to the mountains, beach, or desert without ever actually leaving home. They buy a mobile home—an entire apartment complete with living room, kitchen, and bathroom—that **has** been mounted on wheels. There **are** some mobile homes that even come equipped with satellite dishes so that the "homeboys" will not miss any TV programs while they are in the wilderness.

LESSON 6

Diagnostic Exercise, *page 73*

The beginning of the first public schools in the United States **dates** from the early 1800's. The pressure to create public schools open to children of working-class parents **was** a direct result of the union movements in large cities. In response, state legislatures gave communities the legal right to levy local property taxes to pay for free schools open to the public. By the middle of the nineteenth century, control of school policies and curriculum **was** in the hands of the state government. As school populations outgrew one-room schoolhouses, the design of school buildings on the East Coast **was** completely changed to accommodate separate rooms for children of different ages. Before this time, all children in a schoolhouse, regardless of age, **were** taught together. . . .

Sentence Practice 1, *page 75*

1. The newest <u>schedule</u> for fall classes **is** ready.
2. The federal government's <u>proposal</u> for the pricing of prescription drugs **was** just published in the Federal Register.
3. The <u>problems</u> with his idea about the contest **are** what we would have expected.
4. In the first place, <u>access</u> to the computers in all campus buildings **requires** a student ID.
5. I understand that the <u>problems</u> with the heating system **have** been fixed.

Sentence Practice 2, *page 76*

1. The <u>characteristics</u> of the early hominid found in Java **are** still in debate.
2. <u>OK</u>
3. As a <u>result</u> of the election, the public awareness of the issues **has** been heightened.
4. Senator Blather's <u>motion</u> to adjourn until after the holidays **is or was** rejected.
5. The <u>painting</u>, a Dutch still life in the manner of Rembrandt, **was** sold at auction after the war.

Editing Practice 1, *page 77*

The house cat is one of the oldest domesticated animals. Researchers who study the history of the cat **believe** that the ancestor of all of today's domestic cats **was** a species of small wildcats found in Africa and Europe. The first group of people to bring cats into human habitations **was** in Africa.

However, the first actual domestication of cats as residents with humans was carried out by the Egyptians, who tamed cats to hunt rats and mice in grain storehouses. The pet cats of an important official or government officer **were** sacred. When one of these sacred cats **was** killed by a servant, even accidentally, the servant would be severely punished, possibly even put to death.

Editing Practice 2, *page 78*

One of the largest families of vertebrate animals **is** the family of reptiles. Reptiles include alligators, crocodiles, lizards, snakes, and turtles. They share the feature of being cold-blooded. Reptiles are among the oldest families of animals on earth. Reptiles played a key role in bringing animal life out of the oceans and onto land through the evolution of eggs. Reptiles evolved from amphibians, the first creatures to come onto land. The great evolutionary advantage of reptiles **was** their eggs. Reptile eggs, with their leathery membrane or hard shell, **have** a great advantage: the embryo is encased in its own self-contained sack of fluid. The ability of reptiles to reproduce away from bodies of water **gives** reptiles an enormous advantage over amphibians and **explains** why reptiles were...

LESSON 7

Diagnostic Exercise, *page 81*

Each year there **are** many new movies coming out of Hollywood. Each is designed for a certain segment of the moviegoing audience. There **are** car-crash films aimed at males under thirty. There **are** heart-warming romantic comedies for women over twenty. There **are** even the dreadful "slasher" movies for an audience that it is better not to think about.

Sentence Practice 1, *page 83*

1. There **were** still dozens of presents to wrap.
2. Recently, there **have** been complaints about the noise in the dorms.
3. In the past, there **were** many more independently operated grocery stores.
4. There **are** still five shopping days until Christmas.
5. I didn't like the ending because there **were** too many loose ends that were not tied up.

Sentence Practice 2, *page 84*

1. OK
2. Since it had snowed all night, there **were** only some trucks and buses on the road.
3. There **are** some cookies and pastries to go with the coffee.
4. Fortunately, there **were** a flashlight and some candles in the closet.
5. There **are** lots of things for the kids to do there.

Editing Practice 1, *page 85*

There **are** two countries in the Iberian Peninsula: Spain and Portugal. Portugal occupies most of the western coast, while Spain covers the rest of the peninsula. There **are** three...

Although the coastal plains account for only a tiny portion of the land mass of the peninsula, there is a high percentage of the population in that region. Along the coast, there **are** both a mild climate and fertile soil. In addition, there **are** many rivers that flow into the plains from the mountains in the interior of the country. These rivers provide irrigation water for the fields and orchards in the coastal plains. Especially along the southern coast, there **are** thousands...

Editing Practice 2, *page 85*

The largest distinctive geographical feature in the United States and Canada is the Rocky Mountains. In the lower forty-eight states, there **are** eight states that contain a portion of the Rockies: Idaho, Montana, Wyoming, Nevada, Utah, Colorado, New Mexico, and Arizona. There **are** even branches of the mountains that extend north through two Canadian provinces and into Alaska. There **are** rich veins of minerals, especially gold, silver, copper, lead, and zinc, in the region. Nowadays, however, there **are** greater riches in liquid mining...

The great natural beauty of the Rocky Mountains has made them very popular. There **are** many National Parks throughout the region; two of the best known are Yellowstone and Glacier National Parks. There **are** many winter sports...

LESSON 8

Diagnostic Exercise, *page 88*

I work in a busy law office. Even though we now have voice mail, answering the phone and writing down messages **take** up a lot of my time. I am also responsible for maintaining the law library, although most of the time I do nothing more glamorous than shelving. The law books and reference material **are** always left scattered around the library, and some of the lawyers even leave their dirty coffee cups on the tables. I used to have a relatively comfortable working area, but the new computer terminal and modem **have** now taken up most of my personal space; that's progress, I guess. Despite all the stress, meeting the needs of clients and keeping track of all the information required in a modern law office **make** it...

Sentence Practice 1, *page 90*

1. The <u>milk</u> and the <u>eggs</u> **were/are** still in the car.
2. The <u>causes</u> and <u>treatments</u> of chronic disease **are** becoming much better understood.
3. You don't have to be a health nut to believe that <u>vegetables</u> and <u>fruit</u> **are** the basis of a good diet.
4. <u>Weekends</u> and <u>holidays</u> **last** forever when you're not busy.
5. The <u>advantages</u> and <u>disadvantages</u> always **seem** to balance out somehow.

Sentence Practice 2, *page 91*

1. A <u>rifle</u> and a <u>shotgun</u> **are** used for very different kinds of hunting.
2. <u>French</u>, <u>Latin</u>, and <u>German</u> **are** the main source of English vocabulary.
3. The <u>heat</u> and <u>humidity</u> **make** it very uncomfortable in the summer.
4. A <u>cup</u> of coffee and a <u>cigarette</u> **don't** make a complete meal.
5. <u>What we see</u> and <u>what we get</u> **are** not always the same thing.

Editing Practice 1, *page 92*

In Mozart's opera, *Don Giovanni,* comedy and melodrama **are** mixed together in an unusual way. For example, the character and personality of Don Giovanni **are** surprisingly complex. His charm and bravery **make** him almost a hero at times. Yet at other times, his aristocratic arrogance and deliberate cruelty to women **make** him a complete villain. The seduction of a willing woman and a rape **are** the same to him.

The role and character of his servant Leporello **are** also unusual. At first, his constant complaining and caustic asides to the audience **make** Leporello seem to be just a conventional comic sidekick. Yet in some ways, his observations and reactions to his master's behavior **become** the center of attention. Leporello's admiration for the Don's charm and his repulsion at the Don's treatment of women **reflect** the...

Editing Practice 2, *page 93*

Barbara Kingsolver is the author of six books and a number of short stories. Her books and stories **have** attracted a wide following. One of her most recent novels is *Animal Dreams.* Codi, her sister, and their father **are** the focus of our attention. The story deals with Codi's reluctant return home to a small town in Arizona to take care of her father, who is dying. The events that take place in the story are seen either from Codi's perspective or from her father's point of view. The past and the present constantly **run** together in their minds. One of the main themes in the book is Codi's discovery of how deeply her present life and actions **have** been affected...

Unit Four

OVERVIEW: Can you detect problems with verbs? *page 100*

My wife and I really disagree about old movies. I always **love** to watch them, but my wife is bored by them. She would just as soon watch paint dry as sit through an old film. Last night, for example, we **watched** Hitchcock's 1938 mystery *The Lady Vanishes.* She fell asleep in the middle of it. After the movie **had** finished, I woke her up and started talking about what a great movie it **is**. She was not impressed. To her, the poor quality of the print **made** watching it a chore rather than a pleasure. Whenever I watch an old movie, I **notice** the quality problems for the first few minutes, but they never seem to **bother** me after that.

LESSON 9

Diagnostic Exercise, *page 102*

Last summer we took a trip to Provence, a region in the southeast corner of France, which **borders** on Italy. The name *Provence* **refers** to the fact that it was the first province created by the ancient Romans outside the Italian peninsula. Today, Provence still **contains** an amazing number of well-preserved Roman ruins. While there **are** a few big towns on the coast, Provence **is** famous for its wild country and beautiful scenery. Provence **is** especially known for its abundance of wildflowers in the spring. These flowers **are** used . . .

Sentence Practice 1, *page 104*

1. Key West **is** the southernmost point in the continental United States.
2. Whenever the weather changes, my joints **start** to ache.
3. We visited one ancient monument after another until they all **ran** together.
4. Shakespeare **was** idolized in the nineteenth century.
5. I-405 **goes** around downtown Seattle.

Sentence Practice 2, *page 105*

1. Telephone marketers always call when we **are** eating.
2. According to the style sheet, scientific papers **are** rarely written in the first person.
3. I always try to return messages before I **leave** the office.
4. She broke her ankle skiing down the trail that **leads** to the ranger cabin.
5. When it rains, it **pours**.

Editing Practice 1, *page 106*

Last night I **discovered** how to use the Internet to keep track of my 401k plan. I visited the financial company's Web site, which **includes** a range of resources to help even the most intimidated investor. The first thing I had to do **was** establish a personal identification number (or PIN), just like I did when I **got** a new bank card last year. When I gained access to my account, I **was** able to check my balance, see how much I contribute each month, and shift my money into different funds. The best feature **is** that I can use these resources twenty-four hours a day. This beats trying to reach the customer service staff between 9:00 A.M. and 5:00 P.M., especially since I **work** until 5:30.

Editing Practice 2, *page 106*

Although William Shakespeare died in 1616, performances of his plays **are** alive and well today. A number of theaters and summer festivals **are** devoted to performing his plays. In England, the Royal Shakespeare Company **performs** in London and Stratford-upon-Avon (the small town where Shakespeare was born). In Canada, there **is** a highly successful Shakespeare festival every summer in Stratford, Ontario. In the United States, there **are** theatrical organizations . . .

Ashland's Shakespeare Festival **began** almost by accident as an outgrowth of the old Chautauqua circuit that **provided** entertainment to rural America before the days of radio and movies. After the collapse of Chautauqua, Ashland **found** itself with a good-sized summer theater facility, and faculty from the college **decided** to . . .

LESSON 10

Diagnostic Exercise, *page 111*

Unfortunately, most people **have been** involved in an automobile accident at some time. I **have been** involved in several, but my luckiest accident was one that never happened. Just after I **had gotten** my driver's license, I borrowed the family car to go to a party. Although it **had been** a very tame party, I left feeling a little hyper and silly. It was night, and there were no street lights nearby. I **had parked** a little distance from the house, so my car was by itself. I got into the car and decided to show off a little bit by throwing the car into reverse and flooring it. I **had gone** about 20 yards backward before I thought to myself that I was doing something pretty dangerous. I slammed on the brakes in a panic. I got out of the car and found that my back bumper was about 4 inches from a parked car that I **had never seen**. Whenever . . .

Sentence Practice 1, *page 113*

1. We **have had** a test every week this semester.
2. It **rained** last week during the parade.
3. When we returned from vacation, we found that our house **had been** broken into.
4. I **have been** interested in Egyptology for years.
5. After Holmes **had solved** a case, Watson wrote it up for posterity.

Sentence Practice 2, *page 113*

1. He **wrecked** his knee making a tackle on the first play of the game.
2. I **had already noticed** the problem before you told me about it.
3. He **has worked** overtime for the past six months.
4. We had to forfeit the game after we **had used** an ineligible player.
5. It **has snowed** every day since Christmas.

Editing Practice 1, *page 115*

America **has had** a love affair with the automobile ever since its invention. However, our attitudes about automobile safety **have** always **been** ambivalent, even contradictory. Over the years, we **have been** willing to pay a lot of money for automobiles that go faster and faster, but we **have** always **seemed** to be unwilling to deal with the safety consequences of this increased speed. An interesting case in point is the recent decision by the federal government to eliminate the 55-mile-per-hour speed limit on interstate highways. We **have had** . . .

Editing Practice 2, *page 115*

My friend Dale **had been** living on his parents' farm his whole life when he made himself unwelcome at home. Just before Dale got his license, his father **had bought** a new car that was his pride and joy. One day, after Dale and his best friend **had been** out someplace fooling around, Dale got home late for one of his chores: rounding up the cows for milking. Dale drove his dad's new car into the pasture to get the cows, something his father **had** expressly **prohibited**. When he was out in the pasture, the horn got stuck, so Dale pulled out various wires until the horn stopped. That night, after his father **had gone** to bed, Dale . . .

Unit Five

OVERVIEW: Can you detect pronoun problems? *page 122*

My friend Richard told me that Clyde, the guy **who** sits next to him in his English class, decided to quit school because he'd rather be a rock singer. Richard and **I** both laughed at **this plan** at first, but maybe it is a smart decision. Clyde has changed his major at least four times this year**, according to Richard.** Although **people** might change their major a few times, changing it too often indicates a good deal of uncertainty and can put **them** back several years.

Clyde usually managed to bring up rock music in discussions with Richard, our classmates, and **me**. Often, Clyde's comments would seem completely irrelevant, but **his classmates** bit their tongues and let him go on and on about Radiohead, System of a Down, or another rock group **whom** somehow Clyde managed to fit into the discussion. Of course, **students have** a right to speak up . . .

LESSON 11

Diagnostic Exercise, *page 125*

Soldiers commit a war crime when they violate the norms of acceptable behavior in times of war. Few people want war, but most want their rights and those of others to be respected as much as possible when war occurs. For instance, almost everybody agrees that **prisoners** should have their physical needs attended to and should not be physically or mentally tortured. An officer who orders **his or her** troops...

Sentence Practice 1, *page 126*

1. **Doctors** must have insurance covering them against malpractice.
2. Everyone must bring **his or her** part of the report tomorrow.
3. **College students have** to pick a field that interests them, but they also have to keep an eye on the job market.
4. OK
5. Anybody who hasn't turned in **his or her** test should do so now.

Sentence Practice 2, *page 127*

1. Someone parked **a** car in a place where it will surely be towed.
2. OK
3. OK
4. Did somebody take my book instead of **his or hers?**
5. OK ["Nobody" does not rename "people."]

Editing Practice 1, *page 128*

No other European country has ever spread **its** people and culture around the globe more than England. Each country, of course, has had **its effect** on the world. However, by the end of the nineteenth century, England had its culture firmly planted around the world in such diverse places as Canada, the Caribbean, India, Australia, and South Africa.

Not everyone in England approved of **its** attempt to colonize the world, but most Britons supported colonization because of the economic benefits of commerce with the colonies. British **citizens** had...

Editing Practice 2, *page 129*

Almost everybody who has taken an English class has written a book report about something **he or she has** read for the class. For one assignment, my English instructor, Ms. Kaplan, asked **us** to read two books that **we** wanted to read. In high school, almost **all my English teachers** made...

Ms. Kaplan, though, said that she didn't want to "test" us about the books we read or make us feel that we had to scrutinize each page for **its** "hidden" meaning. She simply asked us to announce the books we read and then be ready to recommend or not recommend them to the rest of the class. Almost everybody seemed to have read **his or her** first selection and truly enjoyed it. One classmate was so enthusiastic about *The Catcher in the Rye,* the novel **she** [or **he**] read...

LESSON 12

Diagnostic Exercise, *page 133*

"Star Wars" was the name of a military program as well as a movie. **The program** was a large research-and-development program calling for military defense in outer space. This **plan** was initiated by President Reagan in the 1980's, and it had the official title of "Strategic Defense Initiative." The public never embraced that **name** as much as...

Star Wars, George Lucas's 1977 film about a space-age military battle, was fresh in the minds of the American people. **Star Wars** was what people could visualize when President Reagan introduced his new program. **The change in name** illustrates the point that many people want to connect new information with something they already know. **Making a connection** helps us to understand and make sense of new things.

Sentence Practice 1, *page 134*

1. OK; meteorite
2. I knew this **problem** was going to happen!
3. This **number** could change, however.
4. That **development** is a surprise.
5. **Having a new route** is nice.

Sentence Practice 2, *page 135*

1. **Listening to her** took over an hour of my time.
2. We need a new air conditioner at our house, but **replacing this unit** will not happen soon.
3. In the early 1800's, **Cincinnati** was built on the increasingly busy Ohio River.
4. Americans do not know that **fact.**
5. World War I was ended by the Versailles Treaty; this **treaty** also led to the formation of the League of Nations.

Editing Practice 1, *page 137*

Some great books do not become great until long after they are written. This **situation** is particularly evident with a book written by William Bradford. He wrote *Of Plimouth Plantation,* one of the oldest books written by Europeans exploring and colonizing the Western Hemisphere. This **book** was not...

This book, written by the governor of Plymouth Colony, chronicles the story of the Pilgrims until 1646. Bradford's book offers considerable detail on the day-to-day lives of the colonists. It contains the oldest known copy of the Mayflower Compact, which was an agreement among the Pilgrims for a democratic-style government. **The book** disappeared...

Editing Practice 2, *page 137*

Slavery has been a sore spot in the history of the United States. **Slavery** is especially troubling considering the role of African Americans in the founding of the country. In 1774, a group of slaves in the American colonies made a famous appeal to Thomas Gage, who was the royal governor of Massachusetts Colony. **The slaves' appeal** proclaimed that they as slaves had a right to the freedoms that the colonists sought from Britain. This **view** was shared...

When the Revolution began, African Americans were exlcuded from the American army. That **situation** changed, however, when the British encouraged the slaves to join their army. Approximately five thousand African Americans would eventually join the American army. This **development** allowed...

LESSON 13

Diagnostic Exercise, *page 141*

My roommate and **I** visited her friend Jeff, who lives in a cabin he built from scratch. That's a formidable project for **me.** My roommate asked Jeff whether he would mind if **she** and I stayed at his place for a few days in the summer. He said that was fine if we would help him build a new storeroom, and we quickly agreed to help him out. I'm not much of a carpenter, but Jeff said he'd be patient and help me learn. For an inexperienced builder such as **me,** building...

Sentence Practice 1, *page 142*

1. The pharaoh visited the burial tomb intended for just **him.**
2. Janet and **I** are going out Saturday night.
3. OK
4. **She** and her cat were rescued by the firefighters.
5. Mom promised to write, and today I received a card from **her.**

Sentence Practice 2, *page 143*

1. Just between you and **me,** we are having an unannounced quiz on Tuesday.
2. Robert and **I** will be calling you soon.
3. OK
4. If not for **me,** you would not be having a birthday at all today.
5. Jill and **he** left yesterday for Atlanta.

Editing Practice 1, *page 144*

Writing has never been the easiest task for someone like **me** who has not written a great deal in the past; however, I am gaining more experience in my technical writing class. Three other students and I are supposed to work on a group paper. One group member, Suzanne, and **I** are supposed to write a definition section of our paper, which is on ethical behavior in accounting. I have two friends who are accountants; I don't necessarily agree with **them** about . . .

An objective analysis of the issue is supposed to be included in the section that Suzanne and **I** were assigned. The interviews were useful because the two accountants each presented different perspectives. They also admitted that the issue of ethics was confusing for **them** as well as **me.**

Editing Practice 2, *page 145*

My roommate, Rusty, asked me to join a money-making enterprise concocted by **him** and his father. The plan they devised sounds simple: Rusty's dad would purchase fifty compact refrigerators that we would lease out to college students living in the dorms. Rusty's dad would supply the capital, while Rusty and **I** would do the labor. When Rusty told me the plan, I was skeptical. I talked it over with **him** and . . .

Rusty's dad lives in town and owns a place where we could store any refrigerators Rusty and **I** could not lease. We placed ads and notices around town and in the school paper. The week before class began, thirty students came by to do business. It wasn't stressful, but we had to stay around all day waiting on people. Rusty and **I** won't . . .

LESSON 14

Diagnostic Exercise, *page 149*

An experience that we all have had is working for a bad boss. One boss **whom** we have all had is the petty tyrant, a person **who** loves to find fault with every employee **who** works in the building. It seems that the petty tyrant is more interested in finding employees **whom** he or she can belittle than in getting the job done. Even worse than the petty tyrant is a supervisor **who** is inconsistent. An inconsistent boss is a person **whom** the employees can never depend on. A game that this kind of boss loves is playing favorites. One day, this boss is your best buddy; the next day, the boss acts as if he or she doesn't know the name of a person **who** has . . .

Sentence Practice 1, *page 150*

1. The person **who** answered the phone took my order for a cheese pizza.
2. Somebody **who** was here a minute ago left this pen.
3. I called the couple **who** had answered the ad.
4. OK
5. A friend **who** was staying with us this weekend ate your candy.

Sentence Practice 2, *page 151*

1. OK
2. I need to know the name of the mechanic **who** supposedly fixed your car.
3. A guy **whom** I knew in high school sits next to me in my math class.
4. The first person **who** makes fun of my hat is going to be sorry.
5. OK

Editing Practice 1, *page 152*

I have several teachers **who** use some form of group work. My freshman composition class involves group activities, but Ms. Isaacs, **who** teaches...

Ms. Isaacs believes that we need to become accustomed to working in groups even though they are not effective when they comprise people **who** prefer to learn independently. Of course, any group is likely to have at least one person **who** would prefer to work alone, but usually the group can adjust when it's just one or two individuals **who** learn little from group activities. Early in the course, Ms. Isaacs asked us to write a brief essay describing how we have functioned in groups; she then used these essays to help assign us to groups. My group is composed of people with **whom** I can...

Editing Practice 2, *page 153*

Most Americans **who** have a religious affiliation are Christians, but other religions are thriving within the United States. Jews are a relatively small minority in this country, but their religion is one **that** was already established by the time of the American Revolution. Muslims, **who** are a growing presence...

Some religious denominations are much smaller in terms of the number of people **who** subscribe to their beliefs, yet these religions have found a niche in American society. For instance, one small religious group, referred to as Ethical Culture, is composed of some 7,000 members and was founded in 1876 by Felix Adler, a humanist philosopher **who** stressed...

LESSON 15

Diagnostic Exercise, *page 157*

My psychology teacher, Ms. Crystal, had each member of the class complete a questionnaire that would help him **or her** consider an appropriate career. I had already decided on a career, but she said the questionnaire would offer options. I've always wanted to be an electrical engineer because I like to design things; **engineers spend** much of **their** time drawing designs and writing specifications. Ms. Crystal said my survey results indicated I should consider being an accountant. She also told me, however, that the survey was just one resource for choosing a career. I agree. **People have** to consider what **they know** better than anyone else: **their** own interests.

Sentence Practice 1, *page 159*

1. **Leaders have** to be responsible to **their** constituents.
2. OK
3. We must hire a secretary **who is** organized and efficient.
4. OK [as long as this particular writer's accountant is, as it seems, a male]
5. Everyone should vote in the next election.

Sentence Practice 2, *page 159*

1. **Professional wrestlers** usually must practice not only **their** wrestling moves but **their** ability to speak to a crowd.
2. If you ever put your children into day care, meet the person who will watch your children, and see if **he or** she is patient.
3. Has nobody done **the** homework today?
4. A writer must choose words carefully.
5. I've never met anyone who brushes **his or her** teeth as often as you.

Editing Practice 1, *page 160*

College students have many options about what **they** might study. I am torn between geology and teaching. On the one hand, I have long been interested in being a geologist in the private sector, perhaps for an oil company. A geologist spends much time outdoors collecting samples, and I like working outdoors. A geologist also works in **an** office...

On the other hand, my mother is a teacher and has encouraged me to follow in her footsteps. **Most teachers have** a good deal of stress put on **them** by students, parents, and administrators; however, **teachers also have** many rewards, such as knowing that **they have** helped somebody succeed in his **or her**...

Editing Practice 2, *page 161*

At one time or another, almost everybody has wondered what it would be like if he **or she** were born at another time or place. I don't think a person is necessarily unhappy or out of place simply **by having** such thoughts. Perhaps it's a way to explore possibilities in **a person's** present circumstances.

When I was much younger, I wondered what it would be like to be an early colonist in the Americas. The life of a colonist was not easy; he **or she** had to cope with starvation, the wilderness, and financial ruin. When I was a teenager, I dreamed of being an astronaut—again, a person who often puts his **or her** life in danger to explore a new world. Even today I think about such adventures, and perhaps it's all a clue that I would not be happy confined in an office. I'm not saying that being a businessperson is dull, but **people need** to find the sorts of challenges and environments that reflect **their** own...

Unit Six

OVERVIEW: Can you detect incorrectly placed and mispunctuated modifiers? *page 169*

I started college fifteen years ago but dropped out to have children. **Since my children are** able to take care of themselves now, I decided to go back to school. Students wrote papers the old-fashioned way **back then**—they typed them. When I started back to school, I realized I was completely out of date. The students were using computers to write their papers. At first I stuck by my faithful typewriter, an old Royal. However, my writing class, which required multiple drafts, quickly changed my mind. My papers were taking way too much time, **since I was doing multiple revisions on a typewriter.** I broke down and bought an inexpensive computer. It only took me about a week to learn to use it. Now that I've gotten used to it, I cannot imagine...

LESSON 16

Diagnostic Exercise, *page 171*

To change a baby's diaper, follow these simple steps. First, lay the baby on a flat surface. If the surface is off the ground, use safety straps to secure the baby. Unfasten the tapes, and remove the soiled diaper. To clean the diaper area, use a wet cloth or a disposable "baby wipe" product. (To avoid an unexpected spray or puddle, you may want to cover the diaper area immediately.) While gently holding the baby's ankles with one hand, use your other hand to slip the back part of the diaper under him or her. Bring the front part of the diaper between the baby's legs, and fasten it...

Changing a diaper is a fairly mechanical process; **however,** the process...

Sentence Practice 1, *page 173*

1. Although Wally Amos is best known for his brand of cookies, he was also the first African American talent agent for the William Morris Agency.
2. In France, shepherds once carried small sundials as pocket watches.
3. Even though he was best known as an actor, Jimmy Stewart was a brigadier general in the U.S. Air Force Reserve.
4. After eating, our cat likes to nap.
5. Whenever I walk, our dog likes to go with me.

Sentence Practice 2, *page 173*

1. To keep people from sneaking up on him, Wild Bill Hickok placed crumpled newspapers around his bed.
2. Before his career was suddenly ended, Jesse James robbed twelve banks and seven trains.
3. Therefore, he was a successful criminal for a time.
4. Believe it or not, the official state "gem" of Washington is petrified wood.
5. When she was in a high school band, singer Dolly Parton played the snare drum.

Editing Practice 1, *page 175*

When I was much younger, I used to run marathons. Even for my age-group, I was never very fast. I did it for the exercise and for the challenge of it. Beginning with walking just a few miles every day, I gradually worked myself up to running in full-fledged marathon races—26 miles, 385 yards. Fortunately, for slow-pokes like me, the organizers of marathons tolerate very slow runners. In fact, the volunteers who do most of the work at marathons are remarkably supportive of the noncompetitive runners. Waiting until the last stragglers finally limp in to the finish line, the volunteers often have to stay at the course for five or six hours. After the race comes the cleanup. It is utterly amazing what a mess several hundred runners can make. The average runner probably uses a dozen paper cups, all of which . . .

Editing Practice 2, *page 175*

As you might expect, there are heavy physical demands on marathon runners. In addition to the common problem of fatigue, the greatest problem marathon runners have is with their feet. Among all marathon runners, the universal topic of conversation is shoes. Every brand is minutely compared in terms of weight, support, and cost. Since most runners train on asphalt, running shoes wear out amazingly quickly. Replacing an expensive pair of shoes every few months gets to be pretty costly; nevertheless, every runner has learned that running in worn shoes is asking for foot and ankle problems. Despite the fact that running shoes are tremendously expensive, there is no doubt that they are getting better and better. The improved design of modern running shoes has eliminated many of the nagging foot and ankle problems that used to plague runners. For most runners, the main issue in shoes is the trade-off between weight and support—the more . . .

LESSON 17

Diagnostic Exercise, *page 179*

It was strange going back to my tenth-year high school reunion, which was held last summer. Monica, who was my best friend as a senior, didn't even recognize me. I guess she didn't expect to see me bald. I also saw a friend/ whom I've stayed in touch with over the phone but haven't actually seen in years. He told me that he recently moved to California, where he plans to start a new business. Since I now live in Oregon, we agreed to try to get together next summer. After the reunion, I had dinner with him and Monica in a restaurant that we used to go to when we were in high school.

Sentence Practice 1, *page 181*

1. essential
2. nonessential. Bo is reading *The Silmarillion,* which was written by J.R.R. Tolkien.
3. essential
4. nonessential. This neighborhood cafe, which first opened in 1939, is one of my favorite places to drink coffee.
5. nonessential. My parents were married in the Middle East country of Yemen, where a wedding feast can last three weeks.

Sentence Practice 2, *page 182*

1. nonessential. My roommate is from Seattle, which is over 600 miles from here.
2. nonessential. Queen Latifah, who is best known as a rap artist, has also been a television host and an actress.

3. essential
4. essential
5. essential + nonessential. The only river that flows north and south of the equator is the Congo River, which crosses the equator twice.

Editing Practice 1, *page 183*

I went to high school in San Bernardino, which is not far from Los Angeles. It's been ten years since I graduated from high school, and I've rarely been back to my hometown since attending San Diego State University, which is fairly...

For one thing, my favorite teacher, who taught world history, is now the principal, and the principal/ who was there when I attended/ is now the school superintendent. About half the teachers whom I had classes with have left entirely, and several of the ones who are still there are considering retirement. I found the new cafeteria, which...

Editing Practice 2, *page 184*

I am presently rooming with Harold Lee, who is very practical. We couldn't afford to spend much for Christmas gifts this year, so we decided to can some vegetables. First, we made a relish/ that was primarily composed of tomatoes, onions, and cabbage. The tomatoes, which we bought at the local market, had to be completely green. The jars had to be carefully sterilized, and the directions confused us. Luckily, we received expert advice from my mom, whom I called in a panic. Once we understood the process better, we went on to asparagus, which...

LESSON 18

Diagnostic Exercise, *page 187*

Every summer I try to visit my Aunt Margie, a vigorous sixty year old. Aunt Margie lives in a small town in Minnesota, a state in the northern part of the American Midwest. Though I dearly love Aunt Margie, there is one area that we have nearly come to blows over: coffee. Like most midwesterners, she drinks coffee all day long; and, like most midwesterners, her coffee is very, very weak. The trouble is, I am from Seattle, the home of Starbucks. Starbucks, one of the fastest growing companies in the United States, has made espresso into a lifestyle choice. My favorite drink, a double mocha, has the caffeine equivalent of a dozen cups of Aunt Margie's coffee. The first (and only) time I made coffee at Aunt Margie's house, she had a fit because it was so strong. She not only threw out all the coffee I had made, she made me wash the pot. From then on, she made the coffee, the kind you can see through.

Sentence Practice 1, *page 189*

1. Ian Fleming, the creator of 007, named James Bond after the author of a book about birds.
2. Ian Fleming also wrote *Chitty Chitty Bang Bang*, a popular children's book.
3. Tim's mother, a registered nurse, thinks I have a virus.
4. Richard, a guy in my geology class, fell asleep during the lecture.
5. Spanish Fort, a small town in south Alabama, was the site of one of the last battles of the Civil War.

Sentence Practice 2, *page 190*

1. nonessential. My roommate, a political science major, plans to run for public office one day.
2. nonessential. He has a date this Friday with Janet Spain, the woman who sits next to you in History 101.
3. essential. This note is for your friend Natalie.
4. nonessential. Matthew Henson, an African American, codiscovered the North Pole with Robert Peary in 1909.
5. nonessential. I had to take Junior, one of my cats, to get his shots.

Editing Practice 1, *page 191*

Gary, my nephew, called and suggested we throw a surprise birthday party for my mother, who just turned sixty-five. I'm not much for birthday parties, but I agreed to help. We asked my friend Sharon to assist. Sharon, an interior-design major, has an excellent eye for decorating, so she took charge of turning my living room, a very plain room, into a more festive place for the occasion. My mother, who has a notorious sweet tooth, is particularly fond of chocolate, so we ordered an enormous cake made of dark chocolate. Gary asked my oldest sister, Stephanie, to . . .

Editing Practice 2, *page 192*

World War II, one of the best-known wars of all time, was followed a few years later by a conflict that still is not well understood. The Korean War, a conflict between the United Nations and North Korea, was never officially a war. Harry Truman, the U.S. president at the time, never asked . . .

This war caused many problems for the United States, possibly because its status and purpose were not clear. General Douglas MacArthur, the commander of the U.N. forces, was removed from office for insubordination to President Truman, the Commander in Chief. After the landings at Inchon, a major turning point, the North Koreans . . .

LESSON 19

Diagnostic Exercise, *page 196*

Studying for hours, **I felt my eyes grow tired.** I felt I could not read another word. I walked to the snack bar for a cup of coffee. When **I arrived,** the place was closed. **I decided** against walking a mile to another place **and thought** that maybe I should just quit for a while and get some sleep. I returned to my room and tried to decide what to do. **I was torn** between the need to sleep and the need to study. **The** alarm clock went off and made me realize it was time for class. After struggling to stay awake in class, **I decided** to get some sleep and then get back to work.

Sentence Practice 1, *page 197*

1. Realizing that it was time to eat, the cafeteria staff served lunch to the hungry students.
2. Hoping there was plenty of air in the ship's tank, the scuba diver explored the sunken wreck a bit longer.
3. After seeing the wreck, Sharon realized her day was ruined.
4. While reading my e-mail, I heard a knock at the door.
5. Running up the stairs, Colleen fell and broke her nose.

Sentence Practice 2, *page 198*

1. After the business partners read the contract carefully, they decided to wait a few days before both parties would sign.
2. While the tourists were relaxing in the sun, dark clouds suddenly appeared.
3. Enraged by his pitiful score, Ted hurled his tennis rackets across the court.
4. Breaking the pencil in anger, Ted revealed his bad temper again.
5. Feeling hungry because I skipped lunch, I realized that eating supper seemed a really good idea.

Editing Practice 1, *page 199*

Worried that he would be late for class, **Oliver turned his leisurely walk** into a trot. He quickly entered the science building. Whenever **he was** late for class, his chemistry teacher always seemed to notice. **He met an** old friend who wanted to chat, **so** his chances of arriving on time diminished. Oliver didn't want to be rude, so he left as soon as he could. **He thought about** skipping his class altogether, **and** several options went through his mind. He decided he would simply try to walk in without being noticed.

No one seemed to notice him as he opened the classroom door as quietly as possible. But then Dr. Wilson said, "Oh, I hope it wasn't too much trouble for you to join us today, Oliver." **While he attempted** to explain why he was unavoidably detained, his excuses only made him look even more foolish. **While he was walking** to his assigned seat, . . .

Editing Practice 2, *page 200*

Having a horrible time finding a birthday present for her boyfriend Shane, **Rose realized that his few hobbies provided little inspiration.** Remembering that he had once said he liked electronic "toys," **she decided** to go to an electronics store. She would not leave until she found something. **She looked up "electronics stores"** in the yellow pages, **and** a nearby mall seemed to have an ideal store.

While **she was** looking through aisles of merchandise, Rose's curiosity was aroused by a foot-long racing car with antennae. Since there was a demo model available, she took it for a spin down the aisle. **When it ran into a wall,** the car's hood flew off. While **she was** quietly attempting to put the car back together without anyone's noticing, its two front wheels broke off. She decided that this particular model was not quite sturdy enough. Discouraged by her adventures with electronic toys, **she decided that** a new . . .

LESSON 20

Diagnostic Exercise, *page 204*

My brother called **today** and said he would travel to Europe. He plans to go as soon as school is out this summer. A travel agent told him it would cost **only** $400 for a round-trip ticket to London. The agent he spoke with said **enthusiastically** that he should take advantage of this price. My brother asked whether I wanted to go with him, but I have already committed myself to a summer job. He talked for **almost** an hour . . .

Sentence Practice 1, *page 205*

1. OK
2. Hamsters are pregnant for **only** sixteen days.
3. We read **almost** forty short stories in my American literature class.
4. My biology teacher said **yesterday** that there are 138,000 varieties of butterflies and moths.
5. OK

Sentence Practice 2, *page 206*

1. OK [unless "slowly" is referring to the man's pace of reading, in which case "slowly" should be moved before "reading"]
2. **Yesterday,** Iva said she found my keys. OR Iva said she found my keys **yesterday.**
3. He bought that DVD for **only** ten dollars.
4. OK
5. OK

Editing Practice 1, *page 207*

My friend Janet **regularly** tells me what her literature teacher discusses. **Yesterday,** Janet . . .

Take, for instance, the popular character Batman. The character today is violent and even scary to law-abiding citizens. The fact that he lurks in the shadows and **frequently** is a creature of the night is interesting. Perhaps readers envy Batman for being outside the law. Indeed, heroes who border on being lawbreakers are **commonly** best-selling characters in the comics — a trend suggesting that readers seem **barely** satisfied . . .

Editing Practice 2, *page 208*

Generally, a person whose brain is damaged runs the risk of aphasia. Sometimes, this disorder, called *dysphasia,* happens when damage occurs to the part of the brain devoted to language production or comprehension. All people with aphasia have some language ability remaining, but it has been impaired in some way. Strokes account for **almost** 85 percent of aphasia cases. Eating an unhealthy diet, avoiding exercise, or **frequently** smoking...

Unit Seven

OVERVIEW: Can you detect problems with apostrophes? *page 216*

During last **year's** summer break, I spent two weeks traveling in Italy. My big adventure was renting a car and driving in Italian traffic. I had heard **everyone's** jokes about Italian drivers. For example, a **friend's** Italian cousin told him that it was OK to go the wrong way on a one-way street as long as you drove backward. But I found that **Italians'** driving was no worse or better than **Americans'** driving. Nevertheless, there are some real differences. We are used to **Americans'** complaining about the price of gasoline, but we need to count our blessings. Gasoline in Italy costs about $5 a gallon. Roads are surprisingly well maintained; **I'm** sure there are more potholes in New York City than in all of Italy put together. The biggest problem I encountered was parking. The older towns, narrow streets, and lack of open space meant that there often was absolutely no place to park inside the **cities'** walls.

LESSON 21

Diagnostic Exercise, *page 219*

The student government announced today the election results for representation in the student senate. Almost half the students **didn't** vote at all, and there **weren't** many candidates running. **I'm** not sure why, but apathy was widespread. My guess is that many students **don't** think the senators have much real power, or perhaps the candidates' qualifications and goals were unclear. **It's** clear that students **aren't** enthusiastic...

Sentence Practice 1, *page 221*

1. **Let's** get one thing straight. [Let us]
2. It **won't** be a problem, I promise you. [will not]
3. **I'm** afraid that we **weren't** ready for the test. [I am/were not]
4. **They're** ready for you now. [They are]
5. Even if it's raining, we still have to go. [OK, it is]

Sentence Practice 2, *page 221*

1. I think that's OK. [OK, that is]
2. **You're** really in trouble now. [You are]
3. Do you want to come; **we're** going to the early show. [we are]
4. **There's** nothing wrong with my punctuation. [There is]
5. **It's** six of one, and half a dozen of the other. [It is]

Editing Practice 1, *page 222*

People **don't** think often about where their favorite foods come from, but the subject can be interesting. For instance, there **isn't** much...

In France, waffles go back to at least the fifteenth century. Street vendors would sell them in front of churches during religious festivals. **They'd** cook waffles with shapes reflecting religious themes to attract the attention of the celebrators. In modern Mexico, waffles are topped with cinnamon and sugar. In tropical countries, **they'll** often...

Editing Practice 2, *page 223*

Many holidays are celebrated around the globe, but **they're** often celebrated in diverse ways. For example, Christmas is celebrated in many countries, but each culture has **its** own Christmas traditions. In France, for example, the Noël celebration begins right after December 6 (the feast day of St. Nicholas) and **doesn't** end until January 6. Many French have a grand meal that **isn't** served...

In Brazil, Christmas **isn't** simply a product of one culture; it represents a blend of Portuguese, African, and indigenous Indian cultures. On Christmas Eve, for instance, a traditional dinner includes a stuffing **that's** made...

LESSON 22

Diagnostic Exercise, *page 227*

Paul Ortega has been one of my **family's** friends over the years. Although he was born in Mexico, he speaks English like a native because his **father's** employer relocated his family to Arizona when Paul was six. By the time he graduated from high school in Phoenix, **Paul's** English was as good as **anyone's.** Nearly every summer, however, Paul and his **sisters** went back to Mexico City, where they stayed at a **relative's** house. As a result, he is completely at home in either **country's** culture. He and my father have been business **partners** for years. Their **company's** success has been due largely to Paul's ability to conduct business in both Mexico and the United States.

Sentence Practice 1, *page 230*

1. It's **nobody's** business.
2. I really like that **guitar's** sound.
3. The **ladder's** rungs were covered with paint.
4. **Plato's** dialogues are still an important part of philosophy.
5. The team met to discuss the **tumor's** treatment.

Sentence Practice 2, *page 230*

1. The whole community was opposed to the **bridge's** destruction.
2. Some of **Wagner's** operas are the longest ever written.
3. I hastily scribbled my notes on the **envelope's** back.
4. We were met by the **hospital's** administrator.
5. An **Englishman's** home is his castle.

Editing Practice 1, *page 231*

Many years ago, when soccer was not so widely played, I volunteered to be our elementary **school's** soccer coach. Although I enjoyed watching soccer, I had never actually played it myself. My situation was like **everybody's.** Without **parent** participation, there simply would have been no **kids'** soccer then. Fortunately, the American Youth Soccer Organization ran clinics for beginning coaches. They correctly assumed that we didn't know the rules or even the basics of building **players'** soccer skills. In many ways, it was a good time to be involved. We were there strictly for the **kids'** benefit. We didn't keep track of a **team's** win-and-loss record. Each game was played for its own sake. I think the kids got a lot out of it because they knew it was for them. They were not just acting out their **fathers'** and **mothers'** past athletic successes.

Editing Practice 2, *page 232*

Last summer we spent a week at Tanglewood, the Boston **Symphony's** summer home. That week featured contemporary **composers'** works. Contemporary classical music is not **everyone's** favorite music. It is demanding music to listen to because of the **music's** reliance on dissonance rather than harmony. The most interesting concert was by the pianist Ursula Oppens. Several of the pieces she played had been commissioned by her, and several of the other **composers'** pieces had been dedicated to her. Clearly, she was a contemporary **musician's** musician. While I really found the music she played to be very difficult to get into, I couldn't help liking her. She engaged **everybody's** attention, even people like me who are not fans of contemporary classical music. She played some of the most difficult piano music I have ever heard at breathtaking speed. Even though she took the music very seriously, she was also having such a great time playing it that the **audience's** enthusiasm matched hers.

LESSON 23

Diagnostic Exercise, *page 235*

Economists' recommending that we tie Social Security benefits to the stock market has started a fierce debate. In the long run, advocates argue, retired persons would more than get their **money's** worth from **retirees'** putting their money in the stock market. For the last fifty years, the argument goes, the value of stocks has increased an average of 10 percent a year. At that rate of return, money doubles in seven **years'** time. Social **Security's** increasing only 1 or 2 percent a year cannot compare with money invested in the stock market. With just Social Security, retired **persons'** outliving their incomes is a major long-term issue. On the other hand, what retiree wants to stay up nights worrying about whether the stock **market's** going into free fall, as it sometimes has?

Sentence Practice 1, *page 237*

1. Wilbur hated **Orville's** flying all those kites.
2. I didn't get **Sunday's** newspaper.
3. The **restaurant's** being open so late in Spain was a shock.
4. This **week's** lesson is from St. Paul.
5. They are debating this **year's** budget.

Sentence Practice 2, *page 238*

1. The attack of September 11 was this **century's** first major U.S. crisis.
2. I don't know if it was worth two **weeks'** wages.
3. That is **tomorrow's** problem.
4. **Donald's** selling Boardwalk turned out to be a big mistake.
5. I can't do it on a **minute's** notice.

Editing Practice 1, *page 239*

In **today's** political climate, we are discovering that never has so much money been spent on so few voters. We have all been dismayed by **politicians'** spending so much money on campaigns. In just four **years'** time, the amount of money spent on political campaigns has nearly doubled. The entire credibility of the political system is being threatened by **politicians'** endlessly seeking financial support. It demeans politicians, who are forced to devote most of their time to fundraising. Political **parties'** depending on special interest groups erodes our confidence in the fairness of the political system. One symptom of the **public's** disengaging from the political process is the fact that the turn-out in this **year's** election was the lowest in a hundred years.

Editing Practice 2, *page 240*

There was an article about young **people's** eating habits in **today's** paper. According to the article, American children are fat and getting fatter. The article blamed the situation on a number of causes: **children's** eating habits, **teenagers'** eating more and more fast food, and **everybody's** failing to get enough exercise. The article talked about high school **students'** getting over half their daily calories from soft drinks. **Adults'** fussing about their **children's** eating habits is nothing new, but clearly the magnitude of the problem has changed. For example, every week our paper runs an old photograph of local interest. This **week's** photograph was of a high school dance from 1950. There were about two hundred teenagers in the photograph, and every single person was skinny by **today's** standards!

LESSON 24

Diagnostic Exercise, *page 244*

Some old **friends** of mine stopped by my apartment for coffee. My roommate's coffee pot was broken, so I made them some instant coffee. I'm not good at making coffee, but everybody had two **cups** apiece. The coffee was pretty old, yet nobody seemed to care. We talked about our **schedules** for...

Sentence Practice 1, *page 245*

1. I can't wait to turn my **essays** in. [contraction]
2. We bought some maple **bars** at Trudy's Cash-and-Carry. [possessive]
3. The 1930's was one of the darkest **periods** in America's history. [special word and possession]
4. I got two A's and two B's on four grammar **tests.** [two special words]
5. Gary's excuses were the lamest **reasons** I've ever heard. [possession, contraction]

Sentence Practice 2, *page 246*

1. I can't believe that **classes** were canceled today. [contraction]
2. The president's remarks certainly raised some **eyebrows** around the table. [possessive]
3. Now that I have everyone's attention, I'd like to begin. [possessive, contraction]
4. There're four s's in "possession." [contraction, special word]
5. Do you want to ask the **Flores** to give us a ride to Paolo's party this weekend? [possession]

Editing Practice 1, *page 247*

My nephew's birthday was a few **days** ago, and I wasn't sure what to get him. Jimmy just turned four, and he likes all **kinds** of...

The toy **stores** I visited, however, carried the usual stuff: monster toys, superhero dolls, assorted airplanes and cars, and hundreds of computer **games**. I wasn't terribly inspired, so I decided to look at some of my old toys from the late 1970's. They were all broken. However, I went through my mother's attic and found three old military-type action **figures** from the 1960's...

Editing Practice 2, *page 248*

Edith Wharton was one of the best-known **novelists** of the early 1900's, but much of her fame in the late 1990's results from movie **versions** of...

Undoubtedly, her settings and themes were influenced by her parents' lifestyle. Not only were the **Whartons** well-off financially, but their ancestry could also be traced back to prestigious **New Yorkers.** Her childhood was spent among the well-to-do **socialites** of New York City, Rhode Island, and various parts of Europe. Despite her upbringing, Wharton's stories often presented satiric **portraits** of...

Unit Eight

OVERVIEW: Can you detect punctuation and capitalization problems? *page 256*

Because my **history** class ends at 11:30 and my **math** class begins at noon, I have little time to eat lunch. I can still hear my **mother** saying, **"You** need a nutritious lunch," so I try to eat something quick that is still filling and at least remotely healthy, such as / vegetable soup, a whole-wheat roll, and fruit juice. Luckily, several vendors on campus sell ethnic food, which is usually more nutritious than hamburgers and fries. Yesterday, my friend **S**arah asked me where / we could go to get a quick bite to eat. / I told her, "Let's go to the student union for gyros!" She was surprised to learn that they contain / meat, salad, and yogurt. She was also surprised to learn / **how** good they taste.

LESSON 25

Diagnostic Exercise, *page 258*

Until recently, poor picture quality and a high price tag have prevented consumers from purchasing digital cameras. Industry analyst Kevin Kane recently said, **"The** next several years will be key in determining what part digital cameras will play in leisure and business budgets.**"** Kane also reported that / digital cameras are now becoming affordable enough for the average consumer. / Like PC's, fax machines, and cellular phones, digital cameras first attracted the interest of technology enthusiasts. But recreational photographers like Sanjei Rohan of Spokane, Washington, just appreciate the convenience. "As a rock climber, I have seen some amazing landscapes," he says. "I take pictures, download them to my computer, and e-mail them to my cousins in Nebraska, where they have fewer rocks to climb." Industry analysts predict a sharp growth in consumer enthusiasm.

Sentence Practice 1, *page 260*

1. In a letter written in 1801, Beethoven stated: "I want to seize fate by the throat."
   In a letter written in 1801, Beethoven stated that he wanted to grab fate by its throat.
2. Speaking to the Nez Percé tribe, Chief Joseph said, "From where the sun now stands, I will fight no more forever."
   Speaking to the Nez Percé tribe, Chief Joseph said that he would not fight any longer.
3. In a review of another writer's book, Ambrose Bierce wrote, "The covers of this book are too far apart."
   In a review of another writer's book, Ambrose Bierce indicated that its covers were too far apart.
4. In her novel *Frankenstein*, Mary Wollstonecraft Shelley wrote: "I beheld the wretch—the miserable monster whom I had created."
   In her novel *Frankenstein*, one of Mary Wollstonecraft Shelley's characters said that he saw the miserable monster he had created.
5. John Wayne gave this advice on acting: "Talk low, talk slow, and don't say too much."
   John Wayne said that actors should talk low and slowly without saying too much.

Sentence Practice 2, *page 261*

1. In a letter John Hinckley wrote to an actress on the day he shot President Reagan, Hinckley said, "The reason I'm going ahead with this attempt now is because I just cannot wait any longer to impress you."
   In a letter John Hinckley wrote to an actress on the day he shot President Reagan, Hinckley said that he wanted to impress this actress.
2. Cher once said, "The trouble with some women is they get all excited about nothing, and then they marry him."
   Cher once said that some women's trouble is that they become excited about somebody who is not special and then marry him.
3. In 1901, former slave Booker T. Washington wrote: "My life had its beginning in the midst of the most miserable, desolate, and discouraging surroundings."
   In 1901, former slave Booker T. Washington said that he was brought up in the middle of "miserable, desolate, and discouraging surroundings." [This paraphrase maintains significant wording from the original.]
4. As Mae West said in one movie, "When I'm good, I'm very good, but when I'm bad, I'm better."
   In one movie, Mae West said that she could be good but was even better when she was bad.
5. Franklin Roosevelt once said: "I see one-third of a nation ill-housed, ill-clad, ill-nourished."
   Franklin Roosevelt once said that he saw much of the nation suffering from poverty.

Editing Practice 1, *page 262*

Many Americans have spoken or written of the need for the United States to provide fair treatment to women. In 1850, for instance, Sojourner Truth, a former slave, said of the feminist cause, "If the first woman God ever made was strong enough to turn the world upside down all alone, these women together ought to be able to turn it back and get it right side up again!" A few years later, Lucy Stone said, ~~that~~ "From the first years to which my memory stretches, I have been a disappointed woman." She went...

The women's movement became increasingly active after the Civil War. After being arrested for leading the fight for women's right to vote, Susan B. Anthony said, "It was we, the people—not we, the white male citizens, nor we, the male citizens—but we the whole people who formed this Union." She went on to argue that ⸝she and all women should be allowed to vote based on the amendments made to the Constitution as a result of the Civil War.⸝ These amendments . . .

Editing Practice 2, *page 263*

The music of the 1960's often reflected a belief that ⸝change should—and would— occur if people were willing to act and to work together.⸝ Some popular songs of that period became theme songs of the civil rights movement. For example, "We Shall Overcome," which was an African American spiritual song of the nineteenth century, became an anthem of the protest marchers. One key statement is repeated over and over in the song: "We shall overcome." That is . . .

"O Freedom" was another African American spiritual that became a protest song of the 1960's. This song proclaims, "before I'd be a slave, I'd be buried in my grave." As popular hits . . .

LESSON 26

Diagnostic Exercise, *page 267*

Yesterday, my literature teacher asked, "Who can name three poems written by African Americans?" I was able to come up with "Incident," which was written by Countee Cullen. Herman, the guy who sits next to me, named Langston Hughes's "Harlem." I started to bring up "Letter from Birmingham Jail"; however, I quickly recalled that is an *essay* by Martin Luther King, Jr. Then, somebody in the back row mentioned Hughes's "Same in Blues," and somebody else remembered Richard Wright's "Between the World and Me." Our . . .

Sentence Practice 1, *page 268*

1. Grace asked, "When will we get our tests back?"
2. OK
3. OK
4. The title of the first chapter is "Where Do We Go Next?"
5. Charlene responded, "Why are you following me?"

Sentence Practice 2, *page 269*

1. Did she say, "The store opens at noon"?
2. OK
3. OK
4. A panicked man yelled, "Don't push that button!"
5. OK

Editing Practice 1, *page 270*

Have you ever heard the song "Dixie"? Most Americans have heard this song but have not considered its usefulness as a source of information about the Civil War. Other songs of that time, for instance, the spirituals sung by slaves, offer a personal look at the slaves' lives and hardships. In "Go Down, Moses," the lyrics refer to attempts by Moses to free his people from slavery, yet the song is also a poignant cry for the freedom of African Americans. In contrast to this melancholy spiritual is "Dixie." This battle hymn of the Confederacy, with its upbeat tempo, is a celebration of the South. Other songs, such as "The Bonnie Blue Flag," were even more explicit about loyalty to the Confederacy, but the one most remembered today is "Dixie."

Editing Practice 2, *page 271*

Many conflicts have given rise to what might be called "war songs." Each war, it seems, becomes the subject of popular music. World War I, for example, had its protest songs, such as "I Didn't Raise My Boy to Be a Soldier." This song captured many Americans' desire to stay out of the war. Once the United States entered the war, though, many songs served to rally the troops and the general public. One of the most famous is "Over There." All good American parents and "sweethearts," according to this song, should be proud and eager to send their loved ones to fight in the war. George M. Cohan received a Congressional Medal of Honor for composing this immensely popular song. In Irving Berlin's "Oh, How I Hate to Get Up in the Morning," however, . . .

LESSON 27

Diagnostic Exercise, *page 274*

In the early 1900's, "pulp" magazines were extremely popular. These magazines were named for the cheap pulp paper they were printed on. They contained various types of stories: adventures, detective stories, romance tales, and Western stories. One of the most successful pulp publishers was Street and Smith; this firm sold millions of magazines. Most old issues, however, have been destroyed or lost. Higher quality magazines were printed on glossy paper, which gave them the nickname "slicks." The terms "pulp" and "slicks" are still used today to distinguish simple action-oriented fiction from the more sophisticated writing that might appear in more upscale magazines such as the following: *Cosmopolitan, Esquire,* and *Harper's.*

Sentence Practice 1, *page 276*

1. Next week, we will have a major test, one that will be difficult.
2. OK
3. OK
4. Allyson and I went to the same high school, Pine Tree High School.
5. Ken brought several items: napkins, glasses, and forks.

Sentence Practice 2, *page 277*

1. Her truck failed to start because the battery was dead.
2. I read an article about Ralph Bunche, the first African American to win the Nobel Peace Prize.
3. Annie ordered a parfait, a dessert made of ice cream, fruit, and syrup.
4. OK
5. I need to go the store, which is only about one mile away.

Editing Practice 1, *page 278*

Langston Hughes is one of the best-known African American poets, his fame having begun in 1915, when he was thirteen. At that time, he was elected poet of his graduating class, an unusual selection not merely because he was one of only two African American students in his class but because he had never written any poems. Hughes explained that nobody else in the class had written any poetry either. His classmates elected him, however, because . . .

Even though such reasoning had an element of stereotyping, Hughes was inspired, and wrote a graduation poem that the teachers and students enthusiastically received. He went on to publish many types of writing: poems, . . .

Editing Practice 2, *page 279*

Some science projects can take time. Others, however, are relatively easy. A terrarium is a small environment that is built for living plants and animals; it is not terribly difficult to make. It can be built out of containers such as a large glass jug, a plastic container, or even a glass baking pan covered with plastic wrap. A particularly good container, however, is . . .

The bottom of the container must be lined with a shallow layer of pebbles; this layer allows for good drainage. A couple of inches of a sand and soil mixture go on top of the pebbles. The terrarium then needs a small dish of water placed into the soil so that the rim of the dish is level with the top of the soil. Then a variety of plants and minerals can be added, including ͵ ferns, moss, rotting bark, and a few rocks. The terrarium must be covered with glass or plastic ͵ and . . .

LESSON 28

Diagnostic Exercise, *page 283*

My roommate, who is shopping for a new car, looked at several types, including Fords, Nissans, and Mazdas. She knew which features she wanted, like ͵ automatic transmission, cruise control, and leather seats. However, she quickly discovered that such features were not within her budget. To get the best deal for her money, I suggested that she consult sources such as ͵ her mechanic or *Consumer Reports* magazine. She did some research, but she seemed disappointed because there was no clear choice. She finally narrowed her choices to ͵ a Ford Taurus and a Nissan Altima . . .

Sentence Practice 1, *page 284*

1. Many farmers in this area grow cotton, grain, and turnips.
2. Kamilah and Doug saved enough money to travel throughout Denmark, Germany, and Belgium.
3. My college will not offer several courses I need, such as English 100 and Math 201.
4. We will need to buy a textbook, gloves, and a dissecting kit.
5. Some actors who changed their names are Jane Wyman, Raquel Welch, and Rudolph Valentino.

Sentence Practice 2, *page 285*

1. Some famous people had dyslexia, such as Leonardo da Vinci, Winston Churchill, Albert Einstein, and George Patton.
2. OK
3. OK
4. Many languages have contributed to English, especially French, Latin, Persian, and German.
5. New words in English arise from many sources, including gang culture, popular music, and the computer industry.

Editing Practice 1, *page 286*

In the past, my English teachers discussed various types of writing, including ͵ poetry, drama, and short stories. In my present English class, the teacher discussed the writing we'll do this semester. She discussed three other types of writing that my previous teachers had not covered: expressive essays, arguments, and informative papers. She mentioned that there are many ways a writer can develop an essay, such as using ͵ narration, comparison and contrast, and definition. For her class, we are required to write ͵ six long papers, three fairly short papers, and several in-class paragraphs. Some of these assignments will allow us to pick our own topics, but a few will not. She has already mentioned that we will write about the following: educational reform, male-female relationships, and discrimination. The class seems challenging, but I'm looking forward to it. Next semester, I am looking forward to taking ͵ a technical writing class . . .

Editing Practice 2, *page 287*

Many people try to get rid of "tummy" fat so they'll feel better about ͵ their appearance, their self-image, and even their relationships with significant others. However, fat has also been linked to health risks such as ͵ heart disease, high blood pressure, and strokes. The most dangerous type of abdominal fat can't even be seen; it's the fat around vital organs like ͵ the intestines and . . .

Two factors that determine how much fat a person has are ͵ gender and . . .

LESSON 29

Diagnostic Exercise, *page 291*

My sister is attending a **community college** in Kansas City, and we've been comparing our courses. Her **Spanish** class is much different from mine because hers includes discussion of **Hispanic** and **Latino** cultures. Her teacher, **Professor** Gonzales, . . .

Sentence Practice 1, *page 293*

1. My **father** has a job teaching **biology** in eastern Delaware.
2. OK
3. OK
4. Students write in almost every class at this **university,** even **physical education** courses.
5. Tenskwatawa was a **Native American** leader who encouraged his people to give up alcohol along with **European** clothing and tools.

Sentence Practice 2, *page 294*

1. In the 1860's, Montana's present **capital,** Helena, was named Last Chance Gulch.
2. Citizens of Rio de Janeiro are normally called *Cariocas.*
3. Did you say that **Aunt** Iva is arriving today?
4. The **Rhone River** and the **Rhine River** both rise out of the Alps of Switzerland.
5. My **grandmother** believes she can meet with the Pope during our visit to Rome.

Editing Practice 1, *page 295*

Mary, also called **Molly,** Dewson was a pioneer in encouraging women to be active in **politics** and the **federal government**. In the 1928 presidential campaign, she worked for candidate Al Smith and helped mobilize female supporters. Smith never became president, but Dewson did not abandon her **feminist** efforts.

In 1930, Dewson continued to mobilize women to campaign for Franklin Roosevelt's successful bid for governor of New York. Later, she worked for his **presidential** campaigns. Perhaps her greatest accomplishment, though, was becoming **head** of the Democratic **party's** efforts to recruit women for **government** jobs. She also worked with Democrats in training women to serve in election campaigns. Though she died in 1962, her legacy lives on, and millions of men as well as women have been affected positively by her efforts to involve women in the **democratic** process.

Editing Practice 2, *page 296*

Last week, the **university** I'm attending announced that all history majors would be guaranteed that they could receive a degree in **history** in no more than four years. As a **sophomore** planning to be a history major . . .

I spoke with an advisor, **Professor** Hearns, about the guarantee. She said the **college** would do its part in regularly offering courses that are most in demand. In particular, she said that each semester the department would offer several sections of American **History** I and **Cultural History** of Asia.

Unit Nine

OVERVIEW: Can you detect problems with faulty parallelism and the passive voice? *page 303*

I planned a trip recently. While I enjoy traveling, I really hate packing. I must choose what to take, pick the appropriate luggage, and **try** to cram everything in. It's not too bad if I am going to a single place for a single purpose. The problem is when I want to do different things: walk in the country, **dress up** for a nice dinner, and meet business colleagues. **I can take the wrong things,** or I can easily end up with three wardrobes to carry around. The biggest problem for me is shoes because they are heavy and take up so much space in my suitcase. The shoes that **I choose** never seem to be the right ones. What I should do before I pack is close my eyes, take a deep breath, and **take** three pain relievers.

LESSON 30

Diagnostic Exercise, *page 305*

We all go to college for different reasons — to get an education, meet new people, and ~~to gain~~ the skills for a job. The best programs are ones that reach several of these goals at the same time. I like to take courses that interest me and ~~building~~ build skills that will lead to a job. For example, it is great to read about something in a class and then ~~applying~~ apply it in a practical situation. That is why I am doing an internship program. I have the opportunity to get credits, develop professional skills, and ~~to~~ make important...

Sentence Practice 1, *page 306*

1. Before leaving, I have to call my mother, write a report, and ~~to~~ pay my bills.
2. College gives us a chance to be away from home and **gain** independence.
3. This book will teach you ways to write better, make good grades, and ~~to~~ amuse your friends.
4. A standard formula for speeches is ~~beginning~~ to begin with a joke and to conclude with a summary.
5. Student representatives on committees are required to attend all meetings, take notes, and ~~to~~ report to the student government.

Sentence Practice 2, *page 307*

1. OK
2. I have to put the cat out, water the plants, and ~~to~~ leave a house key with a friend.
3. This semester, I started working at home in the mornings and ~~to do~~ doing my school work later in the afternoons.
4. I do not want you to lose the directions and ~~becoming~~ become lost.
5. OK

Editing Practice 1, *page 308*

It used to be that schools just taught students to read, write, and ~~to~~ do arithmetic, and that was it. When students left school, there were plenty of blue-collar jobs, for example, on the automobile assembly line. The assembly line required workers who were willing to be punctual, work at a steady pace, and ~~to~~ follow instructions. These jobs often paid pretty well — well enough for a worker to support a family, to buy a new car, and **to** make the down payment on a house. Because the work was broken down into tiny routines, workers never needed to receive any training more sophisticated than basic first aid or even ~~developing~~ to develop technical knowledge relevant to the industry. The work was designed to be simple, make little demand on the workers, and **ensure** that...

Editing Practice 2, *page 309*

Nowadays, there are far fewer manufacturing jobs around because companies are able to subcontract to the cheapest bidder, get components manufactured overseas, and ~~to do~~ the same work with fewer workers because of automation. These developments leave Americans jobs that require workers to meet extremely short deadlines, **to** produce customized...

These changes in the workplace mean that American workers must become much more sophisticated to function in a high-tech world. For example, they need to learn to read technical manuals, communicate with many different technical specialists, and ~~to~~ be able to upgrade themselves constantly. What companies need are students who are able to read, write, and ~~to~~ engage in...

LESSON 31
Diagnostic Exercise, *page 313*

Matt's apartment manager called him, wanting to know why he played his music so loudly. **The phone call surprised Matt;** he didn't think his music was loud. He apologized, but he said his radio was playing at only a fourth of its potential volume. Apparently, **this response satisfied the manager. She told Matt** that...

Sentence Practice 1, *page 314*

1. Those kids uprooted the plants.
2. Your shouting frightened the children.
3. You broke the television.
4. Your actions hurt me.
5. Eudora Welty wrote the story.

Sentence Practice 2, *page 315*

1. The hungry workers quickly ate the meal.
2. On Monday, a driver who pulled in front of me hit my van.
3. The custodians cleaned all rooms over the weekend.
4. Another dancer violently bumped my dancing partner.
5. The farmers sprayed the pesticide.

Editing Practice 1, *page 316*

My parents greatly influenced me to love reading. Both of them are avid readers, yet **they rarely hassled me** to read...

Almost every type of reading material has an appeal for me, but **I most often read** science-fiction stories. **I consumed them** during my teenage years; often, **I would read** one a week. Now that I'm in college, I have less time to spend on pleasure reading, but **I carved out some time** from my schedule to devote to reading...

Editing Practice 2, *page 317*

I consider parking on this campus to be a real problem. The school is in the middle of a large city, and **students, teachers, and people working in the city search for** available parking places. When **the school needed** more classrooms, the parking lots it once had disappeared. As the city grew, the parking places gave way to more and more stores. All this growth has its advantages, but **the school and city did not carefully consider** parking needs.

Students can buy parking permits, but the better lots are expensive. **The school and city encourage riding** the bus, but...

Unit Ten ESL

OVERVIEW: Articles with Geographic Proper Names, *page 323*

No articles for specific mountains or small bodies of water; use *the* **with** the names of mountain ranges and large bodies of water (such as oceans and seas).

Can you detect problems involving articles? *page 324*

We live in **a** time of ~~the~~ great technological change. The engine that is driving this change is the computer. It is hard to believe how quickly ~~the~~ computers have become **an** absolutely essential part of our personal and professional lives. Many of us first used computers as ~~the~~ greatly improved typewriters. With computers, we were able to edit and revise ~~the~~ essays with a few keyboard commands without going to **the** trouble of having to retype **the** entire document over again. In **the** business world, computers were first used as ~~the~~ greatly...

As ~~the~~ computers have become more common and more powerful, they have begun to redefine what it means to write and to calculate. For example, it used to be that **the** distinction between writing **a** term paper and publishing **a** book was as different as day and night. That is no longer the case. What I write at my computer in my office can be sent out over **the** Internet and be more widely distributed than any published book ever was. It used to be that **the** jobs of **the** bookkeeper and the financial planner were completely different. That is no longer the case. With ~~the~~ financial planning software, I can do **an** analysis of dozens of alternative business choices and decide which one works best, and even throw in **a [the OK]** strategy for minimizing taxes at the same time.

LESSON 32

Diagnostic Exercise, *page 326*

The **modernization** of agriculture has meant a huge increase in just a few crops — **wheat** and **rice** for ~~a~~ human consumption, **corn** for ~~an~~ animal consumption, and **cotton** for industrial **production**. This specialization in a few crops is called ~~a~~ *monoculture*. **A** monoculture has some disadvantages: it reduces ~~a~~ biodiversity and requires huge amounts of **energy** and fertilizer.

Sentence Practice 1, *page 329*

1. We studied the country's system of **transportation**.
2. The company hoped to improve their **productivity**.
3. The desks were made out of **metal**.
4. We helped the campers get their **gear** out of the trucks.
5. The amount of trade directly affects the **prosperity** of nations.

Sentence Practice 2, *page 329*

1. Good **planning** gave us good results.
2. During winter we didn't get ~~a~~ sunlight for days.
3. His idea was ~~a~~ complete nonsense.
4. We were not able to get ~~a~~ good information on those topics.
5. News **reporting** during wartime **is** always confusing and misleading.

Editing Practice 1, *page 330*

Gold has long been one of the most valued of metals. **Jewelry** made of gold has been discovered at an excavation in Iraq that dates from 3500 B.C. The high level of **artistry** in the **workmanship** suggests that the craft of working **gold** had been evolving...

From ancient times to today, gold has been highly prized for a number of reasons. Its soft yellow color makes it intrinsically beautiful; unlike **iron, copper,** and most other metal **[metals,** meaning different kinds of metal, is also **OK],*** ~~a~~ gold does not rust... (*raises error count to 4)

Editing Practice 2, *page 331*

One of the most remarkable Americans who ever lived was Benjamin Franklin. He was born in 1706 in Boston. His **education was** quite limited because his father, who made candles and soap, was unable to send him to school beyond the age of ten. It is amazing that one of the most educated men in the Age of **Reason** was entirely self-taught. Franklin learned to be **a** printer, and by the time he was twenty-four, Franklin was the owner of his own print shop in Philadelphia. He began publishing a highly successful newspaper, writing much of the **material** himself as his own editor. Through the newspaper and other **publishing,** Franklin...

Adding to his already substantial **fame** was his work as an inventor and scientist. Two of his most famous inventions were bifocal eyeglasses and a much more efficient stove, called the Franklin Stove. His research on **electricity** made him world famous.

Franklin's great personal **reputation** and knowledge of civic affairs made him a natural political leader. He had enormous **influence** on the Revolutionary War. For example, he helped draft the Declaration of Independence and was one of its signers. However, his most important **impact** on the war **was** his role in obtaining the diplomatic **support** and eventual military intervention of France on the side of the colonies. After the war, Franklin's **wisdom** and common **sense** played a key role in resolving fundamental conflicts in the **creation** of the Constitution.

LESSON 33

Diagnostic Exercise, *page 335*

Doctors have long known that we need to have iron in our diet. Recently, however, **a** new study has revealed that we may be getting too much iron. The human body keeps all **the** iron it digests. **The** only way we lose stored iron in **the** body is through bleeding. John Murray, **a** researcher at the University of Minnesota, discovered that people who live on **a** very low iron diet may have **a** greatly reduced risk of **a** heart attack. Another study found that diets high in meat have **a** strong correlation with a high risk of heart disease. Apparently, when people have **a** high level of iron, [**the**]* excess iron... (*raises error count to 10)

Sentence Practice 1, *page 337*

1. Reason: Uniqueness
2. Reason: Defined-by-modifiers
3. Reason: Normal expectations
4. Reason: Defined-by-modifiers
5. Reason: Normal expectations

Sentence Practice 2, *page 338*

1. Reason: Normal expectations
2. Reason: Uniqueness
3. Reason: Defined-by-modifiers
4. Reason: Normal expectations
5. Reason: Defined-by-modifiers

Editing Practice 1, *page 339*

All of us have seen movies that were completely forgettable except for **a** single scene. For some reason, this scene has always stuck in our minds. Often, **the** scene is not even a major part of **the** plot. It is usually some little piece of character development that struck us, or it is **a** funny or whimsical episode. For example, a few years ago I saw **a** French film whose title I can no longer even recall. In this otherwise forgettable movie, there was **a** long scene that showed someone fixing dinner and chopping **a** big pile of garlic while carrying on **a** long and animated conversation with the dinner guests. Everything in **the** scene was perfectly normal except that the cook was wearing **a** mask and snorkel while he prepared **the** garlic.

Editing Practice 2, *page 339*

My nomination for the Unforgettable Scenes from Forgettable Movies Award is **a** scene in one of Humphrey Bogart's last movies, *Beat the Devil*. **The** movie is set in rural Italy on the Amalfi Coast. Bogart and Sydney Greenstreet are taking **a** taxi up **a** narrow mountain road. Just below **the** top, **the** taxi stalls, and they have to get out to push it. **The** driver walks alongside **the** driver's seat and steers as Bogart and Sydney Greenstreet push from behind. Bogart and Greenstreet get into **a** terrible argument as they are pushing, and **the** taxi driver is dying to hear what they are talking about. All three men get so involved in **the** argument...

LESSON 34

Diagnostic Exercise, *page 343*

Scientists have long known that ~~the~~ honeybees are somehow able to tell ~~some~~ other bees where to look for ~~some~~ food. In the 1940's, Karl von Frisch of the University of Munich discovered that the type of **the** dance that **the** bees make when they return to their beehive is significant. It seems that **the** honeybees are...

Sentence Practice 1, *page 345*

1. Most countries tax **the** cigarettes and **the** alcohol heavily.
2. During a heavy storm, **the** streams often are blocked by **the** leaves and **the** other trash.
3. Typically, **the** employers look for **the** skilled and trained workers.
4. ~~The~~ researchers have found that **the** American diets contain **the** excess fats.
5. ~~The~~ detergents work by making **the** water super wet.

Sentence Practice 2, *page 345*

1. ~~The~~ substitutions in **the** recipes often lead to **the** disasters.
2. ~~The~~ global warming is becoming a common topic in **the** academic conferences.
3. Increasingly, **the** tourism is an important source for **the** national budgets.
4. ~~The~~ classical painting is normally divided into **the** landscapes, **the** still lifes, and **the** portraits.
5. In America, unlike **the** many countries, you can usually get **the** prescriptions filled at **the** grocery stores.

Editing Practice 1, *page 346*

The history of **the** furniture reflects the history of **the** culture. Relatively little is known about the furniture of **the** ancient societies, simply because furniture is usually made of **the** perishable materials—wood and sometimes fabric—that have not survived. Our limited knowledge of Egyptian, Greek, and Roman furniture is based mostly on **the** paintings and **the** sculptures. The only actual surviving pieces of furniture are from **the** burials. For example, King Tut's tomb in Egypt contained piles of elegantly decorated royal furniture. About the only surviving examples of everyday Roman furniture are from **the** two cities near Naples that were buried under **the** tons of volcanic ash...

Editing Practice 2, *page 347*

The American linguist Deborah Tannen is best known for her books about the differences in the language of **the** men and women. Her books show that **the** men tend to use language in a very competitive way. For example, **the** conversations among a group of men are marked by ~~some~~ competition to be the center of attention.

Women tend to be careful about taking **the** turns in **the** conversations. Even in **the** animated conversations, the interruptions tend...

Unit Eleven ESL

OVERVIEW: Can you detect problems with verbs? *page 356*

Do you know what **the most photographed city in the world is?** It is Venice. Venice is ~~being~~ one of the most unusual cities in the world. This **fascinating** city is built on thousands of small muddy islands in a marshy lagoon. Why **would** anybody choose to live on these swampy, mosquito-infested islands? Nobody sought them **out** for their ocean views. The first settlers in the lagoon were refugees from the Italian mainland, fleeing Attila the Hun after the fall of Rome. What the islands **gave** them was protection from anyone not intimately familiar with the area. The lagoon is filled with mud banks that are invisible in the muddy water even at high tide. Unless you **know** exactly where the channels **are**, it is impossible to navigate through them. The early settlers marked the channels with poles, and when they were threatened by invaders, they simply pulled them **up**. When the invaders' fleets got stuck on the mud banks, the settlers would attack the invaders' stranded boats one at a time and completely wipe them **out**.

LESSON 35

Diagnostic Exercise, *page 359*

Every weekday morning at 6 A.M., my alarm **goes** off. By 6:15, the breakfast dishes are on the table, and the coffee **is brewing.** I always **get** the children up next. It is very hard for them to get going. On Mondays, they **resemble** bears coming out of hibernation. While they **are taking** their showers with their eyes still closed, I get everyone's clothes ready. Since the youngest child still **needs** a lot of help getting dressed, I usually **spend** some extra time with her talking about the day's events. By 7 A.M. we all **are sitting** at the table for breakfast. The children **love** pancakes and waffles, but there just isn't time to make them except on weekends. Breakfast goes by quickly, unless somebody **spills** the milk or juice. I **wish** we had more time in the morning, but every morning I am **amazed** when I **look** back and **realize** that...

Sentence Practice 1, *page 362*

1. Hurry up! The train **is leaving** now.
2. I couldn't come to the phone because we **were eating** dinner when you called.
3. Disco **is** still wildly popular in some places in Europe.
4. The book **belongs** to one of my friends.
5. The book **is being** used by one of my friends at the moment.

Sentence Practice 2, *page 362*

1. By this time next year, I **will be working** in New York.
2. As of now, that **seems** to be the best alternative.
3. My roommate always **hated** to get up in the morning.
4. She **is running** an errand right now, but she will be back in just a minute.
5. Hi! I **am returning** your phone call.

Editing Practice 1, *page 363*

You all **know** the old joke that research **shows** that the amount of sleep that we **need** is always five minutes more. I never **use** the snooze button on my alarm clock because I **hit** it without actually waking up. In fact, I **find** that I must put my clock clear across the room so that I **am forced** to...

I am not a morning person, to put it mildly. I **hate** getting up, and I **am** nauseated by the thought of breakfast. Since I am so dopey in the mornings, I have learned to be methodical. While the water **is warming** up in the shower, I set my clothes out. I fix two pieces of toast while I **am making** the coffee. As I **am leaving** for the office, I grab the morning paper to read on the bus while I **am riding** to work. When I finally do get to work, I almost **resemble** a...

Editing Practice 2, *page 364*

This year, both my husband and I **are going** to school in programs that **require** a lot of writing. We are both pretty good writers and **tend** to get good grades on our papers. However, we **go** about the process of writing in completely different ways. He is compulsive about how he writes his papers. First, he **brainstorms** the topic and **groups** all his thoughts into clusters. From the clusters, he makes a list of topics that he **wants** to include...

I am completely the opposite. I **think** that I would go crazy if I wrote the way my husband does. I **spend** just as much time on my papers as he does, but I write in a completely different way. I **spend** my time thinking about my papers before I ever write a word. I write my papers in my head. When I **feel** that I know what I want to say, I sit down and write a complete draft. I **need** to go over this draft...

LESSON 36

Diagnostic Exercise, *page 368*

The Smithsonian Institution is an **amazing** system of museums and art galleries in Washington, D.C. The Smithsonian is a **required** stop for every **concerned** visitor to

Washington. Recently, I spent a **fascinating** day at the National Museum of Natural History. The only problem is that there is so much to see that the **overwhelmed** visitors find themselves frantically rushing from one **interesting** exhibit to another without taking the time to understand all the information in the exhibits. One solution to this **frustrating** problem is to take a tour...

Sentence Practice 1, *page 370*

1. The speaker ignored the **interrupting** noises.
2. OK
3. The riders struggled to keep their balance on the **rocking** train.
4. He grinned and proudly waved his newly **stamped** passport.
5. Be sure you take just the **prescribed** dose of the medicine.

Sentence Practice 2, *page 370*

1. It was a very **alarming** experience.
2. We walked carefully beside the newly **plowed** fields.
3. OK
4. It was a very **tempting** offer.
5. We began classifying the **cataloged** samples.

Editing Practice 1, *page 372*

I have quite **conflicting** feelings about the National Museum of Natural History. On the one hand, it is in a **depressing** building. Even a casual visitor can't help noticing the **water-stained** walls and **crumbling** plaster in the remote hallways. Clearly, a **penny-pinching** Congress has not adequately provided the museum with the **needed** funds. One recent report said that repairing **storm-damaged** roofs alone would absorb...

On the other hand, the new exhibits are lively and colorful. We can only hope that in these difficult times, Congress can develop a **balanced** plan that maintains the old building and provides for **exciting** new exhibits.

Editing Practice 2, *page 372*

One of the things that strikes visitors to Hawaii is the **amazing** variation in climate. Waikiki Beach, for example, has only about 20 inches of rain a year. Without irrigation, Waikiki would be a dusty plain, as it was shown in photographs from missionary times. However, Manoa Valley, the valley behind the beach, has gradually **increasing** amounts of rainfall until, at the back of the valley, less than 10 miles from Waikiki Beach, there is an **astonishing** 130 inches a year. Another **interesting** fact about the valleys in Hawaii is that, despite the **astonishing** rainfall at the backs of the valleys, there are only a few rivers. The reason for this **surprising** fact is that the volcanic soil is remarkably porous. The rain is absorbed into the ground before it can run off. In most places in the world, such **overwhelming** rain could not be held by the **saturated** soil and would create streams and rivers to carry off the excess water.

LESSON 37

Diagnostic Exercise, *page 376*

It used to be that making a plane reservation was a simple matter. You found a travel agency and **called it up.** Since the agency didn't work for any airlines, it looked for the best fare and **found it out.** There was no direct cost to you, since the airlines paid the commission; they **built it in** to the price of your ticket. After the airlines were deregulated, however, this system began to fall apart. Faced with much greater competition, airlines identified commission costs as an unnecessary expense, and they **cut them down** by reducing the commission they paid agencies. Some airlines, like Southwest, even **cut them out** entirely. As a result, most travel agencies stopped selling tickets to those airlines. If you want to know about their fares you must deal with each of the airlines separately. The catch, of course, is that if you call one of them, they can talk only about their fares, and you have no way to **check it out** to see if you have the best bargain.

Sentence Practice 1, *page 379*

1. She emphasized the point to **get it across**.
2. OK
3. I promised to **pay them back.**
4. The news **cheered them up** enormously.
5. We promised to **bring them back** as soon as we could.

Sentence Practice 2, *page 380*

1. Jason really liked her, so he **asked her out.**
2. I don't believe what he said. I think he just **dreamed it up.**
3. They are afraid that they **let us down.**
4. The project didn't get full funding, so we had to **scale it back.**
5. He was **punished for it.**

Editing Practice 1, *page 381*

Nineteen ninety-eight was the year of cable TV. It was the first year in which more American TV viewers **tuned it in** than watched the three major networks—ABC, CBS, and NBC. In the old days before cable, the three networks had a captive audience that had to **turn them on.** In those days, the networks competed for prime-time viewers by trying to get viewers to **keep them on** during the whole evening. They believed that if they could get viewers to watch a hit show, then the viewers would tend to **tune them in** for the rest of the evening. For this strategy to work, the networks had to first come up with a highly popular "anchor" program for each evening, and then they had to turn programs out that were compatible with it. A classic example of this strategy is ABC's *Monday Night Football. Monday Night Football* pulls in a large percentage of male viewers. To keep this audience from changing channels, ABC always **follows it up** with programs aimed at male viewers. The other two networks . . .

Editing Practice 2, *page 382*

We all should try to eat healthy foods, but it is hard to **balance them out.** I know I don't eat as well as I should. There is probably way too much fat in my meals and snacks, but I try to fix **them up** with salads and fresh fruit. I don't eat enough vegetables because it is so hard to fit **them into** my hectic schedule, though I suspect that the real reason is that it is so easy to leave **them off** my shopping list. Since so many of us have to eat on the run, I wish it were easier to get healthier fast food. A cheeseburger and an order of fries is over 2,000 calories. You would have to exercise all day to burn **it off.** Usually the only alternative is a generic salad bar with head lettuce and sad-looking carrot sticks. You see people getting a plate and then loading **it up** with lettuce, which they then drench with salad dressing that probably has more calories than a steak dinner. I suppose the only real alternative is to fix a good lunch at home, pack **it up**, and take it with you.

LESSON 38

Diagnostic Exercise, *page 386*

ANNA: When does your flight leave?
MARIA: At 6:15. Why **are** you so worried? We're not going to be late, are we?
ANNA: I don't think so, but how long **does** it **take** to get to the airport?
MARIA: It depends on the traffic. If the roads are crowded, it will take an hour.
ANNA: How soon **will** you be ready to leave?
MARIA: Don't get upset. I'm nearly done packing now. Have you seen my alarm clock?
ANNA: I don't know where it is. When **did** you **use** it last?
MARIA: For my interview, two days ago. Here it is in the dresser drawer.
ANNA: Where **did I leave** the car keys?
MARIA: Come on! Now you're the one who is going to make us late. Why **didn't** we get started sooner?

Sentence Practice 1, *page 389*

1. Who **did** you **talk** to?
2. Where **did** Sara **find** the books?
3. When **do/did** we plan to leave?
4. Why **didn't** they bring their lunches?
5. How soon **can** you be ready?

Sentence Practice 2, *page 390*

1. Why **did** the library **close** early last Saturday?
2. Who **should** we thank for the party?
3. Where **did** you **park** the car?
4. Why **didn't** you ask?
5. OK

Editing Practice 1, *page 391*

ANNA: Which terminal **should we go to?**
MARIA: I think we go to Terminal C. Most international flights leave from there.
ANNA: Where **did** we **park** last time?
MARIA: In the short-term lot outside Terminal C. How long **can** you park there?
ANNA: As long as you want, but you must pay by the hour. Sometimes it is full, though.
MARIA: Why **don't** you just drop me off at the curb?
ANNA: Don't be silly. You've got too many bags. Which parking space **did** that car leave from?
MARIA: Over there on the left. How much money **does** the meter take?
ANNA: Don't worry, I have a lot of change. What gate **does** your flight leave from?

Editing Practice 2, *page 391*

ANNA: What airline **are you taking?**
MARIA: United. Where **is** its counter?
ANNA: I see it. Let's get in line.
MARIA: How long **will** we have to wait? I wanted to go to the duty-free shop.
ANNA: I told you we should have left earlier. When **does** the next flight **leave?**
MARIA: Don't get so upset. There is plenty of time. Why **are** you in such a big rush? Are you going somewhere tonight?
ANNA: Don't be silly. Where **would** I go on a Monday night?
MARIA: I don't know. Who **did** you **talk** to on the phone just before we left?
ANNA: Never mind. Let's talk about something else.

LESSON 39

Diagnostic Exercise, *page 396*

Sometimes non-Americans ask why **the American court system is so cumbersome.** To understand that, you need to know something about where ~~did~~ it **came** from and how ~~did~~ it **evolved**. Until the Revolutionary War, the American legal system was exactly what the British legal system **was**. Despite the many advantages of the British legal system, colonial Americans felt that the British had used the powers of the government to override the rights of individual citizens. This deep distrust of the ability of the government to abuse its power explains why the American system **is** so heavily weighted in favor of the defendant. Often court cases in the United States are fought on the ground of what admissible government evidence **is.**

Sentence Practice 1, *page 398*

1. I realized **what I needed to do.**
2. We couldn't agree on **which movie we wanted to see.**
3. They asked us **when the plane left.**
4. **Why that is a wrong answer** seemed obvious to the whole class.
5. **How you dress** tells a lot about you.

Sentence Practice 2, *page 398*

1. It depends on **how you felt about it**.
2. OK
3. You can leave **what you don't like**.
4. We were surprised at **how late it was**.
5. **What they did** was very important to all of us.

Editing Practice 1, *page 400*

In my Film as Literature class, we have had many discussions about **what the difference is** between a book and the filmed version of it. What ~~do~~ I like about the class is that we all have such different ideas. Some students don't really care about what the movie **is** like. They feel that no movie can be as good as the book it came from. What **they** don't like is the movie's simplification of the book. I don't think what they **are** saying is fair. We need to remember how much shorter a movie **is** than a book. Can you imagine sitting through a movie that lasts as long as it would take to read the book? Who wants to have a movie take as long to see as it takes to read the book? I believe what ~~do~~ movies show us is the director's interpretation of the book. Sometimes that interpretation is more interesting than the book it came from.

Editing Practice 2, *page 400*

How students are taught writing has changed greatly in the past decade. Back in the dark ages, when I went to school, writing wasn't really taught as a topic in its own right. Professors almost never explained why your writing **was** good or bad. It seemed completely subjective—either they liked what ~~did~~ you **wrote** or they didn't. There didn't seem to be anything else to say. One of the big changes has been to look at writing as a process that can be studied. How ~~do~~ good writers write is substantially different from how ~~do~~ bad writers write. The biggest single mistake that poor writers make is to try to do too much at one time. They try to figure out what they **are** trying to say at the same time as they are trying to write a finished paper. Usually when they do this, they end up writing the first sentence over and over, thinking that if they just could find the "right" first sentence, their paper would flow effortlessly. Good writers first explore the topic, working out what ~~do~~ they want to say before they ever try to actually write a finished product.

Index

(If English is not your first language, you may find the ESL index helpful. The ESL index follows this main index.)

ESL Index

If English is not your first language, you may have noticed the icon (⚚) as you flipped through this book for the first time. This index offers an alphabetical listing of topics that may be especially challenging for non-native speakers of English.

Correction Symbols

Many instructors use correction symbols to point out grammar, usage, and writing problems. This chart lists common symbols and directs you to the help that you need to revise and edit your writing. The numbers below refer you to specific lessons in this book.

art	article	32, 33, 34
cap	capitalization	29
coord	coordination	3
cs	comma splice (run-on)	2
dm	dangling modifier	19
frag	sentence fragment	1
fs	fused sentence (run-on)	2
mm	misplaced modifier	20
no ˅	unnecessary apostrophe	24
pass	passive voice	31
plan	further planning needed	41
pron agr	pronoun agreement	11
pron case	pronoun case	13, 14
pron ref	pronoun reference	12
revise	further revision needed	43
run-on	run-on	2
sexist pron	sexist pronoun	15
shift	verb tense shift	9
s-v agr	subject-verb agreement	6, 7, 8
trans	transition	4, 43
ts	topic sentence/thesis statement	41, 42
usage	wrong word	Appendix B
vf	verb form	36, 37
vt	verb tense	9, 10, 35
˄	comma	4, 5, 16, 17, 18
//	faulty parallelism	30
:	colon	28
;	semicolon	27
˅	apostrophe	21, 22, 23
" "	quotation marks	25, 26
¶	new paragraph	41, 42
˄	insert	
⎯ or ⎯	delete	
⌒	close up space	
∾	reverse words or letters	